PHILOSOPHIZING

About

For Paul. —*Laurie*

For Barbara and to the memory of Dot and Stew. —*Scott*

PHILOSOPHIZING

About

SEX

LAURIE J. SHRAGE
and
ROBERT SCOTT STEWART

broadview press

Library and Archives Canada Cataloguing in Publication

Shrage, Laurie, 1953–, author
    Philosophizing about sex / Laurie J. Shrage and Robert Scott Stewart.

Includes bibliographical references and index.
ISBN 978-1-55481-009-3 (pbk.)

    1. Sex—Philosophy. I. Stewart, Robert Scott, author II. Title.

HQ23.S57 2015   306.701   C2015-900048-3

Broadview Press is an independent, international publishing house, incorporated in 1985.

We welcome comments and suggestions regarding any aspect of our publications—please feel free to contact us at the addresses below or at broadview@broadviewpress.com.

North America
PO Box 1243
Peterborough, Ontario
K9J 7H5, Canada
555 Riverwalk Parkway
Tonawanda, NY 14150
USA
Tel: (705) 743-8990
Fax: (705) 743-8353
email: customerservice@
broadviewpress.com

UK, Europe, Central Asia,
Middle East, Africa, India, and
Southeast Asia
Eurospan Group
3 Henrietta St.
London WC2E 8LU
United Kingdom
Tel: 44 (0) 1767 604972
Fax: 44 (0) 1767 601640
email: eurospan@
turpin-distribution.com

Australia and New Zealand
Footprint Books
1/6a Prosperity Parade
Warriewood, NSW 2102
Australia
Tel: +61 2 9997 3973
Fax: +61 2 9997 3185
email: info@footprint.com.au

www.broadviewpress.com

Edited by Martin R. Boyne
Cover design by Michel Vrana
Cover image: *In Bed: The Kiss*, Henri De Toulouse-Lautrec (1892)
Interior typesetting by Jennifer Blais
Typeset in Minion Pro

Broadview Press acknowledges the financial support of the Government of Canada through the Canada Book Fund for our publishing activities.

PRINTED IN CANADA

Contents

Preface

The philosophy of sexuality is a subfield with a growing body of work and a surge of new research. The topics and questions in this field fall into most areas of traditional philosophy, including ethics, political theory, epistemology, metaphysics, history of philosophy, philosophy of science, philosophy of mind, personal identity theory, philosophical anthropology, and so on. Existing textbooks in this area generally cover work in ethics and political philosophy but leave out work in the other areas. Moreover, while there are a number of books designed to introduce students and scholars to this subfield, the large majority of them are anthologies or readers. Anthologies have many benefits, but they tend to lack a unifying framework that a true textbook can provide, as well as the background information and concepts that students typically need.

In addition, many of the topics addressed in existing anthologies in the philosophy of sexuality have become dated. For example, in the 1970s and 1980s, philosophers contributed to public debates about the morality of homosexuality or whether much pornography should be banned. Since then these questions have mostly been decided in a number of countries, as we can see in various changes to our laws. For example, in most liberal democracies, sodomy laws have either been repealed or struck down by the courts, and the anti-pornography ordinances once proposed and defended by feminist scholars and activists either have failed to win approval or have been declared unconstitutional. In the meantime, many new issues have come into focus, such as how to regulate virtual pornography, cybersex, and "sexting," and who should have access to civil marriage.

Philosophizing About Sex provides a critical guide to current philosophical debates and scholarship about human sexuality. Each chapter takes a general issue (e.g., freedom, privacy, education, objectification, violence, responsibility, etc.,) and shows how recent and ongoing public debates about sexuality can be illuminated by a philosophical investigation into these larger issues. For example, debates over sexual assault, sexual expression, sex education, sex work, and so on involve larger questions about the foundations of morality, law, science, and politics.

Ancient Greek philosophers, medieval theologians, Enlightenment thinkers, and contemporary humanists have all reflected and commented upon various aspects of sexuality, including its purpose, permissibility, normalcy, and dangers, as well as appropriate restrictions on sexual behavior. Each chapter in this book draws on both historical and contemporary philosophical perspectives to analyze current controversies about our sexual doctrines and policies. By asking deceptively simple questions about sex (for example, what counts as a sexual activity?), this book demonstrates how complex the answers can be.

Philosophizing About Sex can be used in various courses, such as the Philosophy of Sex and Love, Social Philosophy, and Introduction to Philosophy. It can also serve as an extensive literature review for scholars in related areas. It is suitable for undergraduates in all fields, and will introduce both non-majors to philosophy and philosophy majors to the history of philosophical writing about sex. Each chapter includes discussion questions and a list of further readings.

Although writing is often a solitary activity, even for jointly written books, many people are actually involved in the process at some point and in some way. Both of us have benefitted from discussions with colleagues, friends, students, and family regarding the issues dealt with here. Additionally, some of the material in this book was presented at various conferences over the past few years, and we take this opportunity to thank audience members who offered helpful comments as well as our institutions—Florida International University and Cape Breton University—for funding our travel. Finally, we would like to thank Broadview Press, and in particular Stephen Latta, Martin Boyne, Tara Lowes, and Broadview's anonymous reviewer, for all their work in helping to see this manuscript through to publication.

Chapter 1

Defining Sex

In this book, we will employ the tools of philosophy to examine the grounds and limits of our knowledge about sex, and which forms are valuable or impermissible. Philosophers often raise deceptively simple questions, such as "what is sex?", and then show how difficult it is to provide good answers to many seemingly obvious questions. In the course of formulating and refining our answers, we gain an appreciation for how complex and difficult it is to produce new knowledge and understandings, even of familiar topics. Each time we engage in philosophical inquiry, we acquire intellectual tools and strategies for investigating other subjects and questions.

In each chapter, we will identify a general issue or concept that philosophers write about (e.g., freedom, privacy, responsibility, knowledge) and then relate this concept to public debates about sex. For this chapter, the general philosophical issue is whether speakers genuinely understand the meanings of the terms that they commonly use to describe the world and communicate with others. For example, what makes something good or bad, true or false, or sexual or nonsexual? In what follows, we will investigate the meaning of 'sex.' By the end of this chapter, you will see that delimiting the category of acts that count as sexual is quite challenging. You will also become more familiar with the general philosophical project of investigating the meanings of abstract and fundamental concepts.

There are discussion questions and suggestions for further reading at the end of each chapter. Our goal is to prepare you to discuss intelligently the issues raised by the discussion questions. Because each chapter can provide you with only an overview of philosophical writings on a given issue, we supply you with a list of additional resources for further exploring the chapter topics.

What Is a Sexual Act?

On January 26, 1998, U.S. president Bill Clinton uttered his now-famous statement on a nationally televised broadcast: "I did not have sexual relations with that woman, Miss Lewinsky."[1] Because Clinton had uttered nearly the same words ten days earlier in a deposition in a sexual-harassment lawsuit brought against him, a lively debate ensued about whether the president's denial amounted to perjury. In defense of the president, his legal advisors asserted that the relevant legal definition of 'sex' did not extend to the behavior of the passive partner in an act of oral sex. The judge in charge of the case had provided the relevant definition by stipulating, for the purpose of the deposition, that a person engages in sex only when one "knowingly...causes...contact with the genitalia, anus, groin, breast, inner thigh, or buttocks of any person with an intent to arouse or gratify the sexual desire of any person."[2] Assuming that Lewinsky initiated contact with the president's "private parts" with the intention of arousing his sexual desire, then she apparently had sexual relations with Clinton, but not the other way around, if we adhere to the judge's definition.

Given the evidence in this affair—the semen-stained dress and Lewinsky's confessions—Clinton's formal testimony about the nature of his relationship with his intern was perplexing, then and now.[3] Yet is there some interesting, non-technical account of sex by which Clinton's denial is nevertheless true? Or did the judge simply supply an overly narrow and imprecise definition of 'sex' that allowed the president to mislead and avoid committing perjury? For instance, in an intimate bodily encounter between two persons, does it sometimes make sense to conclude that only one party engaged in sex? If Clinton did not knowingly cause contact with Lewinsky's genitalia (a questionable assumption after the circulation of the Starr report[4]) in order to excite or satisfy her sexual desire, but only permitted Lewinsky to act upon his body, did he, or only she, commit a sexual act? The ancient Greeks appeared to view sex, in some contexts, as an act undertaken by one person who merely uses the body of another in order to seek

---

1   "Bill Clinton on Monica Lewinsky: I did not have sexual relations... or wait, maybe I did," YouTube, http://www.youtube.com/watch?v=otBFsw3O8VA; Jake Miller, "15 Years Ago: Bill Clinton's historic denial," CBS News, January 26, 2013, http://www.cbsnews.com/news/15-years-ago-bill-clintons-historic-denial/.

2   "The Starr Report, Special Report," *Washington Post*, 1998, http://www.washingtonpost.com/wp-srv/politics/special/clinton/icreport/7groundsi.htm.

3   For many outside the U.S., and some inside too, the intense interest in President Clinton's relationship with Lewinsky was completely bewildering. In Ch. 12 we consider the differences among various countries regarding their views on the sex lives of their politicians.

4   "The Starr Report, Special Report," *Washington Post*, 1998, http://www.washingtonpost.com/wp-srv/politics/special/clinton/icreport/icreport.htm.

and obtain sexual pleasure. They tolerated pederasty, a practice in which adult men engaged in sexual acts with adolescent boys.[5] Because the younger man allegedly remained a passive, erotically detached participant, his role might be described as someone who attended to the sexual needs of another man.

Some contemporary sex workers describe their work in similar terms. They see themselves as simulating or facilitating sexual acts for their customers. Much like an actress in a movie sex scene, the sex worker gives a performance of sex without actually having it. Her customer, who primarily seeks his own arousal and gratification, may imagine that he has aroused the woman he has hired and this may enhance his pleasure. Nevertheless, a sex worker typically remains emotionally and erotically detached while performing her job and manipulating her client's body, using at times sexual parts of her own body. For her, this is a simulation of sex and not the real thing. Although some may find this account of a prostitute's work as misleading as Clinton's initial denials, consider the fact that there are numerous instances of intimate bodily exchanges that involve asymmetrical meanings for the participants. A nurse who coaxes a patient to take a meal is not sharing the experience of eating, even if she swallows some food to entice her patient to eat. A doctor can examine a patient without either of them attaching any sexual meaning to the instances of bodily contact involved. Should one of them attach sexual meaning to the encounter, this does not change the nature of the act for the other. The documentary film *Straight for the Money*[6] explores the asymmetrical experiences that are common in the context of sex work by featuring lesbian sex workers whose clients are predominantly men. The women in the film engage in intimate bodily acts with men, as part of their profession, and yet they identify as lesbians rather than bisexuals. Genuine sex is something they have with their girlfriends, not their clients. The movie shows how a sex worker can indulge her clients' straight fantasies "for the money," while investing such encounters with little emotional or erotic significance. By contrast, her clients are paying for and getting sex. Nevertheless, the meaning that the client attaches to the experience need not define the nature of the activity for the sex worker.

Consider another example before we come back to Clinton. Sexual assault survivors are often stigmatized for their alleged loss of sexual purity and integrity (and sometimes virginity). However, we should question whether the victim (or even the assailant), in an act of rape, is engaging in sex. By deploying more subtle and nuanced notions of 'sex,' we might better analyze what has taken place when an assailant "knowingly causes contact with the genitalia ..." of another through an act that is violent and nonconsensual. Although the victim suffers an attack

---

5   Brent Pickett, "Homosexuality," *Stanford Encyclopedia of Philosophy* (2011), http://plato. stanford.edu/entries/homosexuality/.

6   "Straight For the Money: Interviews with Queer Sex Workers" (1994), *New York Times*, http://movies.nytimes.com/movie/434909/Straight-For-the-Money-Interviews-with-Queer-Sex-Workers/overview.

that involves some contact with her sexual body parts, it may make little sense to describe the victim as having engaged in sex. Some feminist activists describe 'rape' as violent acts that aim to humiliate, intimidate, or terrorize another, where assailants use their own or their victim's sex organs to execute a physical attack.[7] Although such assaults have the potential to cause severe psychological harm, as well as unwanted pregnancies, it does not follow that the victim was emotionally or erotically connected to the encounter in ways that are characteristic of, or requisite for, sexual acts. Moreover, the meaning that assailants assign to their acts need not define the meaning of the experiences for their victims.

Because not all instances of contact with the sexual body parts of another amount to having sex, we can ask whether there is a coherent and interesting sense in which Clinton really did not have sex with Lewinsky. Let us presume that he consented to Lewinsky's act of initiating contact with his genitals, and that he comprehended her intention to arouse and gratify his sexual desire. Let us also presume that he communicated his consent, so that she acted with the knowledge of his intention to submit to her action and his concomitant expectation of arousal and so forth. If these presumptions are not too wild, then Clinton's behavior differs from the sex worker, rape survivor, and the ancient Greek boy lover, because he intended to participate in an erotic exchange and be sexually aroused and gratified, even if somewhat passively. If the purpose of, or intention behind, an action is important for defining that action, and not just the physical parts and motions involved, then Clinton's intimate acts with Lewinsky rise to the level of ordinary, recreational sex.

While the judge's stipulated definition of sex during Clinton's trial may have been overly narrow, just how broad should an adequate definition of 'sex' be? Do cybersex or masturbation fit our ordinary notions, or fit the theories of the relevant experts? Must sex involve our bodies in some way, and must it involve more than one person to be genuine sex? And when it involves our bodies, must it involve some amount of skin-to-skin contact, or contact with particular body parts? Which body parts are typically involved in a sexual act, and is some kind of penetration necessary for sex to occur? If we say that skin-to-skin contact or penetration is not necessary, and only arousal and stimulation, then a lap dancer and her fully-clothed client could be having sex, which in some jurisdictions would violate laws against public sex and prostitution. As is perhaps evident, we need adequate working definitions of 'sex' in order to formulate policies and laws aimed at protecting our safety, health, and well-being, and not merely for making moral judgments about our political leaders or fellow citizens. Moreover, we need adequate definitions of 'sex' in order to be able to study sexual behavior and its consequences.

---

7   See, for example, Patricia L.N. Donat and John D'Emilio, "A Feminist Redefinition of Rape and Sexual Assault: Historical Foundations and Change," *Journal of Social Issues* 48, no. 1 (1992): 9–22.

How might we go about investigating the nature of sex so that we can, at a minimum, supply a general, working definition? Our investigation so far leads us to conclude that Clinton did have sexual relations with Lewinsky—at least in one non-legal, ordinary sense of this term. Yet we are far from developing a general theory or definition of sex. Philosophers are well known for generating many more questions than answers, and some students may find this frustrating or pointless. However, you will probably agree that it is better to have no answers than to have wrong or simplistic ones, and developing reliable and complex answers unfortunately requires patient, systematic inquiry. Philosophy's main contribution to human knowledge may be its tendency to promote robust skepticism toward commonly accepted beliefs, which then provokes us to retrace our logical steps or leaps and to look for more plausible alternatives.

In a philosophical inquiry, we typically refine or reformulate the questions we ask so that they can be productively debated. For example, in asking "what is sex?" we could be raising any of the following issues: How is 'sex' understood in a particular cultural and historical context? How should 'sex' be defined for a particular legislative or judicial purpose? Or what does 'sex' mean in the context of scientifically studying human and nonhuman animal behaviors? Once we figure out which issue is most relevant, we can adapt and refine our investigative approach. For example, to pursue the first question, we will probably want to access artifacts from the relevant historical context, or we may need to interview cultural insiders and informants. To answer the second, we will need to analyze the purpose of a law or policy. To answer the third question, we will need to consult current biological and psychological approaches to explaining human and animal behavior.

Once we have answers to one or more of these related questions, we may be in a position to formulate a more general account of the nature of sex. Alternatively, we may decide that a general definition is not possible, and therefore the only fruitful way to approach the topic is to offer partial definitions for different purposes (e.g., for improving our sexual-assault policies, for studying the history of sexual norms, and so on). The second outcome does not necessarily represent theoretical failure, but rather the understanding that we are dealing with a complex and somewhat vague concept whose meaning is tied to its context of use. Throughout this book, we will raise many abstract and general questions about sex, as philosophers often do, and you, the reader, should try to decide if the questions we have formulated can be profitably debated or whether there are better ways to ask some questions in order to expose the most interesting or pressing issues.

How Many People Does It Take to Have Sex?

In his well-known essay "Sexual Perversion," [8] Thomas Nagel attempts to capture what is distinctive about human sexuality. He argues that human sexuality is

8   Thomas Nagel, "Sexual Perversion," *The Journal of Philosophy* 66 (1969): 5–17.

defined, in part, by a dynamic that involves the communication of desire and the effect of such communication on desire. Nagel develops his analysis by describing what happens in a paradigm case of sexual interaction. In the paradigm case, there are two people who find each other sexually attractive and who become increasingly aroused by paying attention to each other's bodily presentation and communicative acts. When these imply some level of sexual interest, they each take notice of how the other's expression of sexual interest increases in response to their own flirtatious gestures. There is a complex psychological dynamic in this exchange, involving escalating levels of reciprocal desire, accompanied by the participants' awareness of the effect that their communication of sexual attraction and desire has on the other. In Nagel's paradigm case, each agent recognizes and respects the other as a subject with intentions and desires, while simultaneously desiring and enjoying physical intimacy with the other's body. Sex, as described by Nagel, is a thoroughly social act, involving two subjects and their nonverbal communication through bodily movement, gestures, and contact. Neither subject, through this interaction, necessarily becomes a mere object for the other, devoid of intentions and psychological complexity.

By contrast, some philosophers have held that our sexual appetites reduce the people we desire to sex objects. What is characteristic of sexual interaction is that one person desires the body of another and ignores (perhaps temporarily) that other's subjectivity. Jean-Paul Sartre claimed that when I recognize the other as a subject, I experience myself as an object within the field of the other's consciousness. To avoid my own objectification, I objectify the other who becomes a thing upon which I act and exert my will.[9] Immanuel Kant claimed that our sexual appetites cause us to desire specific body parts of the other (e.g., breasts, genitals), just as we might desire a piece of fruit. Kant finds our sexual desires to be uniquely problematic because their fulfillment necessitates treating the persons to whom the desired body parts belong as a mere means to the gratification of our own bodies' appetites, and not as ends in themselves. In nonsexual interpersonal relationships, exploiting another's abilities or talents may provide a means to my goals; but ordinarily, in Kant's view, I continue to recognize my nonsexual friends and acquaintances as human subjects with goals of their own. In contrast, sexual acts inherently involve reducing another, even if only momentarily, to a non-conscious, dehumanized thing, because I must use this person's sexual body parts—and unavoidably the person who inhabits them—as an object to satisfy my desire.[10] For Sartre and Kant, then, sexual acts are essentially acts of masturbation that involve two people, where both participants borrow the body of the other to indulge their own appetites, as if the other were a banana or sex toy.

---

9   For a good introduction to Sartre's philosophy, see Thomas Flynn, "Jean-Paul Sartre," *Stanford Encyclopedia of Philosophy* (2011), http://plato.stanford.edu/entries/sartre/.

10   Immanuel Kant, *Lectures on Ethics*, trans. Louis Infield (New York: Harper and Row Publishers, 1963). See also Evangelia (Lina) Papadaki, "Feminist Perspectives on Objectification," *Stanford Encyclopedia of Philosophy* (2014), http://plato.stanford.edu/entries/feminism-objectification/.

For Nagel, human sexual acts can sometimes lack an intersubjective dynamic of mutual desire and recognition, and when they do they are incomplete or truncated, and perverted or unnatural. Nagel tries to minimize the negative assessment that these terms normally imply by arguing that perverted sex is not necessarily bad or immoral sex; it just falls short of the distinctive, rich psychological and emotional experience that human beings are capable of having. On Sartre's and Kant's accounts, sex is never intersubjective, because, even if we aim for this, we will ultimately fail. This is due to the nature of consciousness for Sartre, and due to the nature of the sexual appetite for Kant. For these philosophers, sex is ultimately a solitary experience, whether one indulges one's sexual appetites with the body of another human being, an animal, or a non-conscious thing. Nagel's conception of sex is certainly more romantic, and the one that we see represented in many movies and much popular culture. Yet Sartre's and Kant's accounts may be truer to the actual experiences of many people.

When two people's bodies are locked in a sexual embrace, are their thoughts lost in their own fantasies and physical sensations, or are they focusing on the effects of their nonverbal sexual communication on each other? If both kinds of sexual encounters are common, is it possible to say which is distinctively human, or which is better as an emotional or pleasurable experience? Is the psychologically complex interaction Nagel describes complete if it lacks intense physical pleasure for one or both participants? And which components of sex are more important, the bodily or the mental ones? Perhaps the best sexual experiences involve a hybrid of Nagel's and Sartre's paradigms, where there are moments of escalating intersubjective awareness precipitated by reciprocal expressions of desire and arousal, alternating with intense bodily sensations that permit us to focus only on our own body and its physical contact with the body of our partner. People who can attend only to their own sensations and gratification during a sexual encounter are usually regarded as selfish and, therefore, morally flawed or antisocial. Indeed, it would be somewhat tragic if Sartre and Kant were right, and humans are incapable of treating their sexual partners as full subjects with desires of their own, and thereby being considerate and kind in this sphere of life. Perhaps Nagel, Sartre, and Kant are all wrong and there is no paradigmatic sexual encounter, but instead a range of sexual pursuits from the romantic and social to the nonromantic and solitary (a topic we discuss further in Ch. 5). In some sexual interactions, people exploit each other for their own purposes within agreed-upon limits (e.g., paid sex), or use their own bodies for sexual pleasure (solitary sex), and in other cases people use sex to emotionally enrich an ongoing social relationship. In the next section, we will explore sex that does not involve direct contact with the body of another.

Is Cybersex Genuine Sex?

The movie *Sleeper* (1973) by Woody Allen features an "orgasmatron"—a machine that enables those who enter it to experience relatively quick and frequent orgasms. While *Sleeper* offers few clues about how such futuristic technology might work, another film, *Barbarella* (1968), depicts machine sex with a less mysterious though probably equally strange device. In *Barbarella*, Jane Fonda becomes trapped in a piano-like mechanism that surrounds her body and strikes her various internal chords. In the film *Demolition Man* (1993), Sylvester Stallone and Sandra Bullock each place on their head a device that looks like a bike helmet with headphones. These helmets apparently stimulate parts of their brains in order to simulate the experience of arousal and orgasm.[11]

The *Barbarella* machine is akin to a personal vibrator, which causes orgasm by direct stimulation to a person's genitals (though the movie appliance is somewhat larger than the standard variety). By contrast, the device in *Demolition Man* appears to work on a person's mind or brain. The helmets cause the wearers to have the subjective sensations of sex with each other, without the objective activities of partner sex taking place. These films raise questions about which parts of oneself are engaged when one is sexually aroused to the point of climax—one's brain, one's genitals, one's entire body, one's mind, or some combination of mental and physical components? Can we simulate the experience of sex with our minds and with minimal use of our bodies? Can our bodies enjoy sex without our minds fantasizing about the experience? While *Barbarella* suggests a future in which sex machines or robots replace sexual partners,[12] *Demolition Man* suggests a future in which we sexually engage with real human beings, but through advanced communication technologies rather than directly with our bodies.

Questions about the bodily and mental components of sex raise a larger issue that philosophers call "the mind/body problem." Do we have both a mind and body, or is the body only a projection of the mind (or vice versa)? If we have both a mind and a body, how do they communicate, or how are our mental and material sensations coordinated? Those philosophers who grant greater metaphysical or ontological status to the mind and its ideas view bodies as entities that the mind constructs from the flow of sensations and other mental contents. For such philosophical "idealists," a physical body is simply a complex mental representation that could be caused either by an entity with properties resembling the body or by another more powerful mind. In an idealist conceptual framework, it is coherent to imagine a person existing without a body or with a different body, as the body is merely a contingent, nonessential aspect of a person. In contemporary terms, the body is similar to an avatar—a 3D digital persona that one assumes or creates. The primary difference between my avatar and my ordinary body is that the latter is somehow always present in my experience,

---

11 "Sleeper—The Orgasmatron," YouTube, http://www.youtube.com/watch?v=lsrd7E5nzIQ; "Barbarella in the Excessive Machine," VideoSift, http://www.videosift.com/video/Barbarella-in-the-Excessive-Machine; "Demolition Man sex scene," YouTube, http://www.youtube.com/watch?v=k80UQWWUIYs.

12 David Levy, *Love and Sex with Robots* (New York: Harper Perennial, 2007); Leah Reich, "Sexbot Slaves," *Aeon Magazine*, June 6, 2014, http://aeon.co/magazine/altered-states/how-will-sexbots-change-human-relationships/.

and I am unaware of how my mind constructs this idea from the flow of mental representations. By contrast, agents have greater control over the visual appearance and properties of their avatars, which they can design to outwardly represent various inner personas.

Some philosophers believe that bodies are more real than nonphysical entities. These are the philosophical "realists," who hold that our mental representations correspond to objects that exist outside of, and independently of, our minds, and which cause our ideas. There are materialists who believe that only bodies exist, and that minds are simply the effects of physical matter and processes. A materialist typically holds that we are identical with our material bodies, and therefore the avatars we create would stand in a very different relation to the self than our physical human body. The avatars that inhabit various virtual worlds, according to a materialist, are simply virtual costumes or disguises. There are also dualists who hold that both mental and material substances exist. Dualists see the human body as having a privileged relationship with the mind, in that they are interdependent. But dualists face the most difficulty explaining how physical and mental stuff interact. There are many different varieties of idealism, realism, and materialism, and students of philosophy will eventually explore the intricacies of these metaphysical accounts. For our purposes, we will employ these distinctions to analyze machine-assisted and mediated sex.[13]

Sexual acts regularly involve a variety of mechanical and non-mechanical technologies, including contraceptive devices, performance-enhancing drugs, dildos and other sex toys, creams and gels, mirrors, and so on. If we include beds and intimate body apparel along with these technologies, then there are few forms of sex that take place without some sort of technology, however simple. Films such as *Sleeper, Barbarella,* and *Demolition Man* may give us a glimpse at the future of sexual technology. Arguably, the most advanced technologies developed so far, and not just for the movies, are called "teledildonics" or "cyberdildonics."[14] These technologies typically involve body suits or strap-on devices with electrical moveable parts that another person (or programmed machine) controls remotely using a computer or cell phone. The moveable parts in the body suit, when controlled by another, simulate the sensation of being touched by another. This form of cybersex may be accompanied by one-way or two-way webcams, so that the cyberlovers see and hear each other in real time while they have long-distance sex via computer-controlled sex toys.

---

13 For helpful and critical summaries of current research about idealism, realism, and materialism, search the table of contents of the online Stanford Encyclopedia of Philosophy (http://plato.stanford.edu) and the Internet Encyclopedia of Philosophy (http://www.iep.utm.edu).

14 Burke Denning, "Technologasm?! The Rise of Teledildonics and Adult Haptic Devices," *Kinsey Confidential*, May 15, 2012, http://kinseyconfidential.org/technologasm-rise-teledildonics-adult-haptic-devices/. For an interesting history of mechanical sexual aids, see Rachel Maines, *The Technology of Orgasm: "Hysteria," the Vibrator, and Women's Sexual Satisfaction* (Baltimore: Johns Hopkins University Press, 2001).

Is cybersex, with such sophisticated technology, real sex or only a simulation of sex? Teledildonic sex, accompanied by visual and voice communication via two-way webcams, comes quite close to paradigmatic sex. The only thing missing is skin-to-skin contact and the exchange of body fluids, and perhaps some sensory inputs such as smell and taste. How essential are these to sex, and can they be simulated too?[15] The Sylvester Stallone character in *Demolition Man* seems to think that all "natural" sensory inputs are essential, but then he may simply be a socially backward person—a country bumpkin with limited comprehension of sexual practices in the modern world. Some Catholic theologians regard sexual activities that are incapable of causing pregnancy (oral sex, sex with effective contraception, or same-sex coupling) as a perversion of nature. But the laws of most secular democracies today do not treat non-procreative sexual activities as perverse or immoral, even though the reproductive dimension that some think is integral to sex is absent. Is teledildonic sex a perversion of nature because physical contact between two people is absent or facilitated with technology?

For the idealist who equates the real with mental phenomena, what matters most are the subjective properties of a sexual experience and not what we speculate to have objectively caused a sexual experience. If the experience of cybersex (in its teledildonic or other forms) is qualitatively similar in all essential respects to ordinary sex, then cybersex should be granted the same metaphysical status as ordinary sex. Even dualists and materialists may come to see some cybersex sex as having enough of the essential components of ordinary sex to qualify as real sex. For example, teledildonic cybersex may enable two people to control each other's bodily sensations and states in ways that are not essentially different from ordinary sex. Whether sexual stimulation is achieved through skin-to-skin contact or mouse-computer-Internet-dildo-skin contact may eventually be viewed as an arbitrary variation in our legal, cultural, and scientific definitions of sex, as cybersex becomes more familiar.

Remote but simultaneous, sexually arousing interactions involving teledildonic equipment and two-way webcams with sound may include the essential components of ordinary sex, but are all of these components essential to sex? If the two-way webcams were eliminated, but the partners communicated by texting images and words, would this count? If the teledildonic equipment was eliminated, but the partners instructed each other over two-way live webcams how and where to touch themselves, would this count? If the teledildonic equipment and webcams were eliminated, but the partners communicated instructions using texting or voice via cell phones regarding how and where to touch themselves (and what sex toys to use), would this count? If one partner was replaced by an automated avatar, who provided sex-talk and instructions on how and where to touch oneself (and with what body part or device), would

---

15 For a defense of the importance of direct sensory inputs in sexual and other human encounters, see Richard Kearney, "Losing Our Touch," *New York Times*, August 30, 2014, http://nyti.ms/1B4IbkY.

this count? The metaphysical idealist is more likely to count the activities further down this list as *real* sex, as long as they produce the flow of sensations and perceptions that are characteristic of sexual experiences. Whether this is a good reason to take idealism seriously as a metaphysical theory is a question that we'll leave for other philosophers and students of philosophy to decide.

There are a number of further philosophical issues that could be explored in relation to cybersex. Will automated avatars ever be as intelligent as real persons, so that sex with an avatar would be indistinguishable from remote sex with a real person? (Philosophers interested in artificial intelligence call this "the Turing test," which is named after the philosopher who developed it.) In online-only sexual activities, does it matter if one's partners misrepresent their age or gender, since there is no skin-to-skin contact with that person's body? Because cybersex frees one from many of the embarrassing physical limitations of one's body, might it potentially lead to better sex than ordinary sex? Is cybersex a useful tool for sex education? Are there any forms of cybersex that should be illegal, such as paid cybersex or forced cybersex? Can one's avatar be raped and, if so, what type of injury results and how serious is it? We will take up some of these questions in future chapters.

Does Sex Have a Purpose?

Sex has many purposes. It can be pursued for pure physical pleasure and sensual entertainment, emotional bonding, reproduction, and relaxation and health. The question "does sex have *a* purpose?" generally means: does sex serve a natural or divine purpose that outweighs its other uses? In "Plain Sex," Alan Goldman provides a negative answer to this question. He argues both that sex serves no higher (or cosmic) purpose, and that we should not try to understand sex in terms of some end or use to which it can or should be put. As an alternative, Goldman provides a non-teleological and allegedly simple account of sex: "sexual desire is desire for contact with another person's body and for the pleasure which such contact produces; sexual activity is activity which tends to fulfill such desire of the agent."[16] Goldman contends that he is offering the "minimal criterion," or the necessary and sufficient conditions, of "normal sexual desire." He criticizes Nagel's account that reciprocal personal attention, which escalates toward psychological and physical intimacy, is paradigmatic of sexual desire, because this account exceeds what minimally counts as sex. Similarly, he opposes other teleological accounts of sex because they impose ends and goals that may be part of some encounters (e.g., reproduction, communication of love, etc.), but are not necessary for normal sex.

Goldman's account avoids adding romantic varnish to an act that, like Kant, he sees as belonging to our animalistic tendencies. Unlike Kant, though, Goldman does not believe the desire for another person's body must morally

---

16   Alan Goldman, "Plain Sex," *Philosophy and Public Affairs* 6 (1977): 268.

degrade the desired other to the status of an inhuman thing. This is because he regards our animal-like inclinations as an aspect of human nature and not as something antithetical to our humanity. For this reason, Goldman formulates a definition that will include sexual activities aimed at satisfying our "lower" as well as "higher" impulses and desires, without morally judging the former as inferior or perverted. Moreover, unlike Kant, sexual desire extends to the whole body and not just the genitals, and so it includes a greater range of intimate bodily contact. This avoids Kant's reductionist approach to sex, in which persons are basically reduced to their sexed body parts.

However, persons are somewhat objectified on Goldman's account because physical contact with their bodies is necessary for fulfilling another's sexual desire. Moreover, although Goldman's sexualization of the entire body avoids classifying many sexual acts as abnormal or perverse (e.g., those involving feet, any bodily orifice, and so on), his account does exclude some activities from normal sex, such as masturbation, and phone sex or cybersex.

By trying to define 'sex' in a way that frees it of ordinary romantic and moral norms, Goldman reflects another kind of romantic thinking: the romance of the nonhuman natural world. In essence, Goldman has only replaced one romantic conception of sex with another. In order to detach sex from its usual cultural and moral baggage, Goldman imagines sex to originate in and belong to a natural world purified of human conventions, but populated with bodies and their simple pleasures. Like Demolition Man's desire for simple pleasures, Goldman's "plain sex" depends on a romantic picture of some uncorrupted natural domain that serves as a primary source of beauty and goodness. While the nonhuman universe is certainly sublime, there is probably no need to strip sex of more complex desires in order to understand or appreciate it.

Rather than trying to free sex of human and divine goals, we might simply recognize the multiplicity of goals that sex serves. The problem with the question "does sex have a purpose" is that it implies that the various aims of sex can be narrowed down to a single, principal goal. Even Goldman's plain-sex definition attributes a basic purpose to sex, which is to fulfill our "lower" (bodily) rather than "higher" (psychological) human desires or appetites. While trying to avoid a teleological account, Goldman manages to narrow the aims of normal sex so that he rules out sexual activities where the desire for bodily contact with another is not central. Masturbation and cybersex can only be mere substitutes for sex, rather than alternative forms of erotic experience not requiring or aiming at bodily contact with another.

Similarly, Goldman's definition of 'sex' marginalizes the sexual desires and tastes of people who practice "BDSM" (bondage, discipline, domination, submission, and sadomasochism). Sexual desire in a BDSM encounter involves desires to dominate or submit to another, which can be accomplished with language, or other forms of play involving ropes, paddles, whips, boots, and so on. Although bodies are involved in acts of sexual domination and submission, BDSM activities do not necessarily involve or aim at contact with the body of another.

BDSM practices typically encompass the psychological complexity of Nagel's paradigm case, in which dominants and submissives recognize and respond to complex intentions in ways that escalate reciprocally.[17]

By exploring different definitions of sex, we may not be able to say which is right or the best one. However, each definition teaches us something about the assumptions with which we approach sex. Those who participate only in "vanilla" (non-kinky) sex may overlook those aspects of sex that are heightened in a BDSM encounter. For example, the very act of undressing before another, or undressing another, involves exercising or submitting to another's control. Non-kinky sex is often organized around power-roles and scripts attached to the gender of the persons in an encounter, rather than negotiated. Yet non-kinky sexual partners often ignore the power dynamic in their relationship and instead focus their attention on other aspects, such as each other's bodily appearance, in order to add sexual charge and energy to their interaction. For the BDSM community, sexual desire may be more responsive to recognizing and entering particular power roles than to the potential for contact with a certain kind of body.

BDSM practices suggest, *contra* Goldman, that sex may involve more than the so-called simple pleasures of the flesh. Although Goldman eschews definitions that burden sex with higher aims, such as reproduction, his account burdens sex with the achievement of lower aims, similar to the desire to relieve an itch. There are sexual activities in which the "lower" aims of the body are paramount, as Goldman suggests, but also those in which the "higher" aims of our psyches take precedence. In short, sex appears to have various and multiple aims, and a complete account of sexual desire should leave room for diverse and incommensurable practices.

---

17 For recent studies of BDSM, see Margot Weiss, *Techniques of Pleasure: BDSM and the Circuits of Sexuality* (Durham, NC: Duke University Press, 2011), and Staci Newmahr, *Playing on the Edge: Sadomasochism, Risk, and Intimacy* (Bloomington: Indiana University Press, 2011).

Discussion Questions

1. What makes any activity sexual (e.g., kissing, touching, etc.)?
2. Have "sexual assaults" been misdescribed as sexual acts?
3. Do animals have sex or do they merely mate?[18]
4. How is the desire for sex similar to, and different from, other desires?
5. In what ways are sex acts often technologically assisted? Is there a more "primitive" way to have sex and, if so, how does it compare to technologically enhanced forms?
6. Must we be sexual? Is life-long celibacy problematic?

Further Reading

Adeney, Douglas. "Evaluating the Pleasures of Cybersex." *Australian Journal of Professional and Applied Ethics* 1 (1999): 69–79.

Collins, Louise. "Emotional Adultery: Cybersex and Commitment." *Social Theory and Practice: An International and Interdisciplinary Journal of Social Philosophy* 25 (1999): 243–70.

Diprose, Rosalyn. "Generosity: Between Love and Desire." *Hypatia: A Journal of Feminist Philosophy* 13 (1998): 1–20.

La Caze, Marguerite. "Existentialism, Feminism, and Sexuality," in *The Continuum Companion to Existentialism*, edited by F. Joseph, J. Reynolds, and A. Woodward, 155–74. London: Continuum International Publishing Group, 2011.

Morgan, Seiriol. "Cybersatisfaction or Dildonic Dangers? What Are the Implications of Virtual Sex?" *Philosophical Writings* 3 (1996): 29–37.

Solomon, Robert C. "Sexual Paradigms." *Journal of Philosophy* 71 (1974): 336–45.

---

18 For an interesting new study of the "sex" lives of animals, see Menno Schilthuizen, "Here's What the Sex Lives of Animals Can Tell Us About Our Own," *Huffington Post*, May 1, 2014, http://www.huffingtonpost.com/menno-schilthuizen/animal-sex-book_b_5235014.html.

Chapter 2

Sexual Attraction

Is sexual attraction a function of how we are designed by nature, or is it highly susceptible to social and cultural forces? When we choose our intimate partners, are we acting freely or in accordance with forces that we don't really understand? In this chapter, we will explore different strategies for explaining how sexual attraction and desire work, and the implications of each approach for human freedom and happiness. Philosophers are interested in the general questions of whether we have free will and what the prerequisites are for a fulfilling life. Understanding the basis of sexual passion and how it impacts both our behavior and well being is an important part of these larger projects.

Do Opposites Attract?

Why do we find some people sexually attractive and others not at all? Sometimes we find people sexually attractive who, in other ways, are not appealing to us. How is sexual attractiveness related to other traits people possess, such as moral decency, intelligence, physical beauty, gender, ethnicity, or age? In 1859, Arthur Schopenhauer advanced the theory that we are constituted by nature to find sexually attractive those individuals with whom we can produce beautiful children.[1]

---

1   Arthur Schopenhauer, "The Metaphysics of the Love of the Sexes," in *The World as Will and Idea*, Vol. III, Supplements to the Fourth Book, Chapter XLIV, trans. R.B. Haldane and J. Kemp, 6th ed. (London: Kegan Paul, Trench, Trübner & Co., 1909), *(continued)*

A beautiful child, he alleged, is one that conforms to the natural human form or archetype. Schopenhauer wrote, "the delight we take in the other sex, however objective it may seem to be, is nevertheless merely instinct disguised, in other words, the sense of the species striving to preserve its type."[2] To preserve the human type, nature equips us with a desire for those, and only those, individuals whose physical and other features will correct features of our own that deviate from the true type. He writes,

> every one in the first place will infinitely prefer and ardently desire those who are most beautiful—in other words, those in whom the character of the species is most purely defined; and in the second, every one will desire in the other individual those perfections which he himself lacks, and he will consider imperfections, which are the reverse of his own, beautiful. This is why little men prefer big women, and fair people like dark, and so on.

Schopenhauer also claims that men are naturally disposed to prefer women of child-bearing age, in good health, free of bodily deformities, and with sufficient plumpness suitable for sustaining fetal life. Given the alleged procreative aims of the sexual drive, such preferences seem predictable (or perhaps explicable).

Schopenhauer relies on his theory to account for tastes that appear bound by culture and time:

> A small mouth ... is very essential, as it is the specific characteristic of the human face as distinguished from the muzzle of the brutes. A receding, as it were, a cut-away chin is particularly repellent, because *mentum prominulum* [i.e, a protruding chin] is a characteristic belonging exclusively to our species.

He goes on to specify in greater detail the preferred shape of the nose, forehead, eyes, and other body parts. Schopenhauer also discusses the qualities of intellect and personality that each sex will prefer in the other:

> a woman universally is attracted by the qualities of a man's heart or character, both of which are inherited from the father. It is mainly firmness of will, determination and courage, and

---

http://www.gutenberg.org/files/40868/40868-pdf.pdf. The original German edition was published in 1859; for more information about Schopenhauer's works and philosophy, see http://plato.stanford.edu/entries/schopenhauer/.

2 "Metaphysics of Love," *Essays of Schopenhauer*, http://ebooks.adelaide.edu.au/s/schopenhauer/arthur/essays/chapter10.html. All subsequent quotations from Schopenhauer will be from this source.

maybe honesty and goodness of heart too, that win a woman over; while intellectual qualifications exercise no direct or instinctive power over her, for the simple reason that these are not inherited from the father. A lack of intelligence carries no weight with her; in fact, a superabundance of mental power or even genius, as abnormities, might have an unfavourable effect. And so we frequently find a woman preferring a stupid, ugly, and ill-mannered man to one who is well-educated, intellectual, and agreeable.... When a woman says that she has fallen in love with a man's mind, it is either a vain and ridiculous pretence on her part or the exaggeration of a degenerate being.... Let it be understood that here we are simply speaking of that attraction which is absolutely direct and instinctive, and from which springs real love. That an intelligent and educated woman esteems intelligence and brains in a man, and that a man after deliberate reasoning criticises and considers the character of his *fiancée*, are matters which do not concern our present subject. Such things influence a rational selection in marriage, but they do not control passionate love, which is our matter.

In this passage, Schopenhauer acknowledges that we do not always choose the partners whom nature has selected for us. Sometimes our instincts are restrained by rational deliberation and selfish goals, such as marital peace. For Schopenhauer, passionate or "real" love is unlikely to guarantee a happy marriage, because instinct will pull individuals together for the quality of their offspring and not social compatibility. Yet counter-instinctive pairings will likely result in ugly children, or perhaps no children at all. For example, Schopenhauer speculates: "if a big woman choose[s] a big husband, in order, perhaps, to present a better appearance in society, the children, as a rule, suffer for her folly."

Given that sexual attraction is based on unconscious reproductive goals that are hard wired, it is inevitably heterosexual for Schopenhauer. However, the chance for a happy or stable pairing of complementary opposites is very slight. Most such pairs or marriages are doomed to fail because our individual interests (e.g., in finding a soul mate) will be sacrificed to nature's reproductive quality controls. This bleak scenario is due, in part, to Schopenhauer's somewhat strange sex-linked rules of inheritance that dispose women to seek stupid men, and men to overlook a woman's character. Moreover, because opposites must normalize each other's deformities, the weak will be paired with the strong, the meek with the courageous, the neat with the messy, the masculine with the feminine, and so on—i.e., Martians and Venusians, in contemporary parlance. This system is not designed for mutual understanding or social compatibility.

To capture the dynamics of attraction between those who are complementary opposites, Schopenhauer invokes the now-familiar idea of sexual chemistry. But his description is not particularly romantic. He writes,

> Before a truly passionate feeling can exist, something is
> necessary that is perhaps best expressed by a metaphor in
> chemistry—namely, the two persons must neutralise each other,
> like acid and alkali to a neutral salt.... The particular degree
> of *his* manhood must exactly correspond to the particular
> degree of *her* womanhood in order to exactly balance the one-
> sidedness of each. Hence the most manly man will desire the
> most womanly woman, and *vice versa*, and so each will want
> the individual that exactly corresponds to him in degree of sex.

Will masculine women desire feminine men, then (and vice versa), to "balance the one-sidedness" of their gender traits? If so, then Schopenhauer's account should also predict the behavior of gender-variant individuals.

For those who are familiar with the theory of evolution, as it is currently understood,[3] what may seem odd about Schopenhauer's nineteenth-century version is the notion that survival of the fittest means, in part, survival of the most beautiful. For Schopenhauer, nature's tendency to preserve a species' beauty involves each generation's return to some original form. If his account of sexual attraction were correct, species would change less and probably be less "fit" or adaptable. Schopenhauer's forms or archetypes may presuppose the will of a powerful creator who aims to preserve an original design. To preserve this design, however, the will of the creator (and species) produces couples that cannot fulfill each member's so-called higher (i.e., emotional, intellectual, spiritual) needs. Schopenhauer attempts to capture this aspect of the human condition by offering an image of two lovers "pathetically" discussing the harmony of their souls, while remaining oblivious to the impersonal reproductive demands that have brought them together. Once the lovers have consummated their "love" and fulfilled their instinctual, species-oriented needs, Schopenhauer speculates that mutual discontent, if not "violent discord," will follow.

If Schopenhauer is right about sexual love, then we cannot change the cosmic forces that drive us to love. Nevertheless, without the tragicomic dimensions of sexual love there would be much less material for great plays, novels, music, opera, poetry, and film. Schopenhauer's theory anticipates the familiar plot and setting. At first, our attraction to another takes us by surprise, overwhelms us, preoccupies and distracts us, and renders us incapable of observing any character faults or defects. In this incapacitated state we are quickly led to folly. While beguiled by the other's charms, we remain completely ignorant that our condition is the effect of the will of the species, which is stronger than our individual will. Schopenhauer demystifies the power of love by equating it with the expression of a natural instinct to bring into being an individual who does not yet exist, but must exist for the species to continue. Our feelings of love have

---

3   Darwin's *On the Origin of Species* was published in 1859, around the same time as Schopenhauer's essay.

little to do with our personal preferences and interests, or the qualities of our mates on which we consciously focus. Having now revealed the true aims and purpose of love, Schopenhauer shows how sexual attraction inevitably leads to broken hearts and disappointed dreams, but, fortunately, lovely children.

Schopenhauer's basic narrative of love may ring true to our experiences and observations, in some respects. For example it's not uncommon for people to focus on the appearance of a potential intimate partner and try to imagine what their offspring would look like. And sometimes we cannot explain to ourselves, or others, why we find some people sexually alluring and others not, as if there were mysterious and unconscious forces at work. However, although the idea that "opposites attract" still persists, few today probably imagine it to involve a natural eugenics program, as Schopenhauer did. Rather than view sexual attraction as the expression of some impersonal forces related to the survival of our species, today we are more likely to attribute it to each individual's idiosyncratic disposition and desires.

Schopenhauer makes some interesting comments about race and attraction that seem oddly prescient and countercultural. He writes:

> Blonde people fancy either absolutely dark complexions or brown; but it is rarely the case *vice versa*. The reason for it is this: that fair hair and blue eyes are a deviation from the type and almost constitute an abnormity, analogous to white mice, or at any rate white horses. They are not indigenous to any other part of the world but Europe,—not even to the polar regions,—and are obviously of Scandinavian origin. *En passant*, it is my conviction that a white skin is not natural to man, and that by nature he has either a black or brown skin like our forefathers, the Hindoos, and that the white man was never originally created by nature; and that, therefore, there is no *race* of white people, much as it is talked about, but every white man is a bleached one. Driven up into the north, where he was a stranger, and where he existed only like an exotic plant, in need of a hothouse in winter, man in the course of centuries became white.... In love, therefore, nature strives to return to dark hair and brown eyes, because they are the original type....

Schopenhauer's claim that "there is no *race* of white people" turns out to be correct, given current scientific understandings of race.[4] Yet he appears to ignore how the forces of European racism shape behavior and ideas about beauty in many societies. He therefore overlooks the cultural value attached to the rare and "abnormal" bleached-out northerner and to the associated racial status of "white."

---

4 "Race: Are We So Different?" *A Project of the American Anthropological Association*, http://www. understandingrace.org/home.html.

But his account challenges racist assumptions that sexual attraction across "races" is abnormal or perverse. Interestingly, Schopenhauer sees racial differences in human physiology as relatively insignificant variations in human form, which is consonant with current biological and anthropological accounts. Twentieth- and twenty-first-century scientists have discredited the idea that there are distinct human races—white or black—in the sense of genetically distinct human groups.

Schopenhauer is well known for his pessimistic view of the human condition, but we should not reject his theories simply because of their negative implications. His theory of attraction does have the virtue of accounting for phenomena that otherwise seem inexplicable: for instance, why two people whose consciously expressed desires and tastes should lead them to repel each other instead find each other irresistible. Schopenhauer's account also explains why such relationships rarely last (with or without the "social glue" of marriage), and why relationships with the potential for greater stability (e.g., with our "soul mates") often lack passion. Nevertheless, the idea that sexual love is entirely the expression of teleological procreative forces, and that there is a true human form and sex-linked paths for character or intelligence inheritance, is implausible given current accounts of biological and psychological evolution. Moreover, Schopenhauer's account cannot explain passionate love between two people of the same sex, or two short people, or between people over fifty who are beyond the life stage of reproduction. There are a few empirical studies that support the existence of universal standards of beauty, but it does not follow from this alone that we select objectively beautiful mates to serve subconscious reproductive aims.

Is there an alternative theory that better explains the mystery and magic of sexual attraction? In looking for another account, we should probably look beyond evolutionary biological accounts of sexual attraction and explore the impact of social and cultural upbringing on sexual attraction. Biological accounts tend to reduce sexual attraction to the mating instinct and then attempt to explain the latter. But is sexual attraction primarily about a subconscious mating drive? Sexual liberation movements from the 1960s onward have promoted the idea that the aim of sex is not only reproduction and, in fact, reproduction is seldom the aim of sexual acts (even at a subconscious level). We spend a short part of our lives procreating, while we spend many more years as sexually active agents. Often we seek sexual partners with whom we can't procreate or with whom we have no desire to procreate. So when we look for sexual partners, what else might we be looking for, other than their suitability for procreating with us?

How Are a Person's Sex, Gender, and Sexual Orientation Related?

Imagine that you wake up one morning and, upon inspecting yourself, you discover that your body has been transformed. You now have a body opposite in sex to your former body, or so it appears. You look in the mirror and see a man where once there was a woman, or vice versa, a woman where once there was a man.

Nevertheless, your sex identity has not changed; only your body has changed. You still feel like the person you've been all your life—a man or woman (boy or girl)—and so this new body feels very alien to you. You look at your breasts, your hips, your groin, your face, and are utterly shocked to see body parts that you would have previously expected to find on the other sex. While the image reflected back to you in the mirror is decidedly of the other sex, you nevertheless do not feel that you belong to that sex. It suddenly dawns on you that you have a choice: you can either begin to live and represent yourself to others as the sex opposite to which you have identified until now, or you can continue to live and present yourself as the sex with which you have always identified. What should you do?[5]

Would a person really have a choice in the situation described above? If we think that our sex is simply a function of our bodily anatomy, then a change in bodily anatomy would automatically involve a change in sex. If one is a biological determinist about sex identity, then the sex of the person in the thought experiment has somehow changed, and the only choice that person has is how to cope with the change. In the first part of Jeffrey Eugenides's 2002 novel *Middlesex*,[6] the main character, Calliope, is a girl. Calliope has an intersex condition that causes her external genitalia to appear female at birth. But at puberty her gonads begin flooding her body with "male" growth chemicals (hormones), and Calliope's body becomes "virilized." At a visit with her physician, she and her family discover that she is chromosomally XY. Eventually Calliope becomes Cal and identifies as a boy.[7] Calliope's/Cal's condition poses dilemmas similar to our "thought experiment," and shows that such situations are not merely hypothetical. Did Calliope have a choice about whether to identify as a boy? Was he a boy from birth, who was mistakenly assigned the sex status "female"? This issue is complicated by the fact that some intersex kids with Calliope's condition continue to identify and live as girls.

Treating sex as if it were simply a matter of anatomy is problematic. In Cal's case, his external genitalia do not align with his gonads and sex chromosomes. Because genitals are more accessible to visible inspection than chromosomes or gonads, these often trump other parts of our sex anatomy when we are assigned to a sex category. In his groundbreaking book *Making Sex: Body and Gender from the Greeks to Freud*,[8] the historian Thomas Laqueur recounts how the

---

5   Example originally published in L. Shrage, "Anatomy Is Not Destiny: Sexual Orientation and Gender Variance," *Review Journal of Political Philosophy* 10 (2012): 41–58.

6   Jeffrey Eugenides, *Middlesex* (New York: Farrar, Straus & Giroux, 2002).

7   For more information about the intersex condition of the character in this novel, see Intersex Society of North America, "*Middlesex*," http://www.isna.org/books/middlesex; Genetics Home Reference, "5-alpha reductase deficiency," http://ghr.nlm.nih.gov/condition/5-alpha-reductase-deficiency; and Stephanie Hsu, "Ethnicity and the Biopolitics of Intersex in Jeffrey Eugenides's *Middlesex*," *MELUS* 36, no. 3 (fall 2011): 87–110, http://muse.jhu.edu/login?auth=0&type=summary&url=/journals/melus/v036/36.3.hsu.pdf.

8   Thomas Laqueur, *Making Sex: Body and Gender from the Greeks to Freud* (Cambridge, MA: Harvard University Press, 1992).

criteria for sexing bodies changed from century to century, with new develop-ments in science and changing conceptions of gender differences. One reviewer of a more recent work (*Sex Itself: The Search for Male and Female in the Human Genome*, by Sarah Richardson) traces these changes:

> What really determines sex? A look back in history reveals that scientific advances keep changing the answer. In the 16th century, scientists believed that differences in blood were the cause. The pelvis was the culprit in the 18th century. By the 19th century, scientists shifted focus to the skull, then to the brain and, in the 20th century, to hormones. Now, scientists believe that sex differences lie in the human genome.[9]

Although scientists in the twenty-first century rely more on genetics to explain the human body, Richardson questions whether the x and y chromosomes can really account for sex differences. She contends that scientists have exaggerated the role they play in the development of our reproductive anatomy.[10]

Sexing bodies has become more complicated as we've gained new knowledge about human anatomical development. The biologist Anne Fausto-Sterling, for example, has questioned whether only two sex categories can capture the ana-tomical diversity of our species. In her early work, Fausto-Sterling identified five sexes, and she later suggested that a scale from male to female would be better for sorting the variety of human bodies we encounter.[11] Her sex-sorting systems recognize that "mixed" bodies occur with regularity and comprise one (or more) per cent of the human population.[12] Bodies do not divide neatly into two categories at the level of chromosomes (i.e., there are more patterns than xx and xy, such as xo, xxy, and xxyy). Bodies can also be "mixed" at the level of gonads, in that some have one ovary and one testis, and there are gonads with a combination of ovarian and testicular tissue. In addition, bodies are ambiguous at the level of genitalia (i.e., with parts regarded as too large to be a clitoris but too small to be a penis). Finally, there are bodies with "mixed" parts (e.g., a penis and ovaries, or xy chromosomes and a vagina). Rather than view these bodies as abnormal or defective, Fausto-Sterling sees our sex categories as too deficient to

---

9   Susan Fisk, "Sex and the Human Genome: Are Scientists Repeating Their Mistakes from the Past?", *Gender News*, Clayman Institute for Gender Research, Stanford University, June 12, 2012, http://gender.stanford.edu/news/2012/sex-and-human-genome.

10 Susannah Locke, "What Your Science Teacher Told You about Sex Chromosomes Is Wrong" (interview with Sarah Richardson), *Vox*, http://www.vox.com/2014/6/3/5776396/why-theyre-not-really-sex-chromosomes.

11 Anne Fausto-Sterling, "The Five Sexes: Why Male and Female Are Not Enough," *The Sciences* (March/April 1993): 20–24, http://capone.mtsu.edu/phollowa/5sexes.html; see also Anne Fausto-Sterling, "Two Sexes Are Not Enough," *Nova*, October 30, 2001, http://www.pbs.org/wgbh/nova/body/fausto-sterling.html.

12 Anne Fausto-Sterling, *Sexing the Body* (New York: Basic Books, 2000).

capture the diversity of naturally occurring bodies. Fausto-Sterling's work challenges the idea that intersex bodies are freakish and require medical correction. In the past few decades, many patient advocates who have intersex conditions (or bodies that don't fit our limited sex categories) have begun speaking out against the disfiguring surgeries and treatments that were imposed on them as children. Rather than force their bodies to conform to a set of cultural expectations about biological sex, Fausto-Sterling and others are proposing that we change our categories to better fit a diverse range of bodies.[13]

Fausto-Sterling is part of a generation of theorists who hold that sorting bodies into sex categories involves historically and culturally shaped notions about how many sexes and genders exist and about which features of our bodies determine our sex identities. Sex, like race, is "socially constructed" because, although both identities are based on anatomical features of our bodies, there is no scientific justification for choosing particular body parts to be paradigmatic of a person's race or sex (e.g., skin color rather than hair texture or facial features, or chromosomes rather than gonads). Moreover, the categories themselves are crude proxies that we use, often incorrectly, to make inferences about other aspects of a person (e.g., national origin, gender identity, etc.). Both race and sex are social constructions that involve sorting the people we encounter according to the concepts we have acquired from our cultures, and especially from the languages that we speak.[14]

Sex involves classifying someone as male or female (or neither or both), while gender involves recognizing certain personal qualities and behaviors that traditionally have been associated with a particular sex.[15] A person may identify as female but be predominantly masculine in terms of gender expression, which shows that sex does not always predict gender expression, or vice versa. The link between sex and gender expression is less rigid or natural than may have once been thought. According to Jack (Judith) Halberstam, we should recognize that masculinity is not something that only male-bodied people do.[16] Conversely, femininity is not something that only female-bodied people do.

Judith Butler argues that gender expression is a form of imitation and performance that becomes part of our daily repertoire from an early age, so that we come to view a certain kind of gender expression as natural to people of

---

13 See, for example, Joy L. Johnson and Robin Repta, "Sex and Gender: Beyond the Binaries," in *Designing and Conducting Gender, Sex, and Health Research*, ed. J. Oliffe and L. Greaves (London: Sage, 2012), http://www.sagepub.com/upm-data/40428_Chapter2.pdf.

14 Jason Antrosio, "Anthropology, Sex, Gender, Sexuality: Gender Is a Social Construction," *Living Anthropologically*, May 16, 2012, http://www.livinganthropologically.com/2012/05/16/anthropology-sex-gender-sexuality-social-constructions/.

15 For an interesting hermeneutical account of 'sex' and 'gender,' see Georgia Warnke, *After Identity: Rethinking Race, Sex, and Gender* (Cambridge: Cambridge University Press, 2008).

16 Judith Halberstam, *Female Masculinity* (Durham, NC: Duke University Press, 1998).

each sex.[17] In other words, gender is merely a set of aesthetic and behavioral styles achieved through repetition and practice, and therefore being a woman or man simply amounts to being able to give an authentic-looking performance, so that one can "pass" as a woman or man. We constantly assess others and ourselves in terms of how well we each impersonate and interpret our gender. Performing as a woman or as a man is so ingrained in our behavior that most people cannot switch from one gender to another. Moreover, in many societies, when people encounter someone whose gender expression is thought appropriate to the other sex, they may find this surprising and disturbing, and attempt to explain it with theories about the person's mental health or sexual disposition. By contrast, in societies that recognize multiple genders or gender intermediaries, people who are gender-variant (relative to the norm) are more integrated into their communities.[18]

Judith Butler's work reflects the influences of the philosopher Michel Foucault, who showed how "the homosexual" was an invention of nineteenth-century medicine and social science.[19] The introduction of the category of 'homosexuality' reflected changes in the understanding of sexuality, from a set of sinful acts that anyone might be tempted to commit to a set of psychological dispositions that differentiate people. People who are psychologically disposed to be sexually attracted to people of their own sex are now presumed to be fundamentally different from those who are attracted to someone of a different sex. We talk of homosexuals and heterosexuals as if they denote natural varieties of people. Butler extends the Foucauldian analysis of homosexuality to gender: a person who is thought to be psychologically disposed toward one of the two basic kinds of gender performance is recognized as a woman or a man. But these kinds or varieties of people are in some sense cultural fictions or simplifications that can be deployed to serve certain social ends. For Foucault, stigmatized identity categories (e.g., homosexual, woman) can serve to perpetuate various forms of social control. Butler, like Foucault, explores whether the social solidarities that we form based on these identities (e.g., as women) are genuinely liberating.[20]

---

17 Judith Butler, *Gender Trouble: Feminism and the Subversion of Identity* (New York: Routledge, 1990).

18 For example, the film *Two Spirits* explores understandings of gender among indigenous Americans. See http://www.pbs.org/independentlens/two-spirits/film.html. See also the documentary "Two Spirit People," *Frameline*, 2012, http://www.frameline.org/now-showing/frameline-voices/two-spirit-people; "Fa'afafine: Samoan Boys Brought Up as Girls," *ABC/Cinemedia*, 2005, http://www.abc.net.au/ra/pacific/people/hazy.htm; and "Third Gender," *TransUnity*, http://transunity.com/third-gender.

19 Michel Foucault, *The History of Sexuality: An Introduction*, trans. Robert Hurley (New York: Vintage Books, 1990). See also, David Halperin, *One Hundred Years of Homosexuality: And Other Essays on Greek Love* (New York: Routledge, 1990).

20 For example, should we organize together on the basis of our assigned sex, or on the basis of experiences of discrimination due to our gender identity or expression? The latter group would include most but perhaps not all women, as well as transwomen, transmen, and many lesbians and gay men.

Scientists and social movements are continually introducing new categories of people. For example, the term "intersex" is now giving way to "disorders of sex development" (DSD).[21] Intersex individuals are now classified as individuals with some type of DSD. Unfortunately, labeling intersex conditions as a "disorder" contributes to stigmatizing people with rare—but healthy—body types. Yet it does enable people with a DSD to get access to medical treatment, should they need or want it. Similarly, people who are gender-variant, or transgender, have been classified as having "gender identity disorder" (GID) and, more recently, "gender dysphoria."[22] Again, while this new terminology may suggest that such people have a mental health problem, it does allow people who have gender dysphoria to get access to medical treatment, if the condition itself, or the discrimination they face because of it, causes them distress.

Most educated people now know that there are no significant biological or genetic differences among the groups that historically were understood to represent distinct "human races."[23] Yet, while racial categories are socially constructed, these identities reflect social experiences and solidarities that are meaningful and real. Many countries now allow people to self-identify their race, although at one time race represented a legal status that was assigned by others and that was part of a system of unequal rights and privileges. Some theorists have proposed that we resist the practice of classifying people by race, especially because we tend to use fairly crude methods, and because the practice may promote misunderstandings about the nature and origins of the racial distinctions we make. But other theorists argue that these categories still serve political and socially useful purposes. Before we make race invisible, we need to address ongoing social inequities based on race, and this requires continuing to count people by race.

Today, individuals can opt out of hegemonic systems of racial classification to some degree, by refusing to formally identify according to one of the available racial categories, or by inventing new categories of mixed race. However, should people be able to opt out of both formal and informal systems for classifying people by sex? In most societies, a person is assigned a sex at birth, and this sex is recorded on one or more official documents, such as a birth certificate. Generally, it can be very difficult for a person to correct a sex designation on official documents, including identification documents such as passports, health and educational records, and driver's licenses. However, recently Denmark approved a law that allows people to control the sex listed on their official documents

---

21 "Disorders of Sex Development (DSD) Resources," *University of Michigan Health System*, November 2012, http://www.med.umich.edu/yourchild/topics/dsd.htm.

22 "Gender Dysphoria," *PubMed Health*, http://www.ncbi.nlm.nih.gov/pubmedhealth/PMH0002495/.

23 For some useful articles on the current science of race, see "Ten Things Everyone Should Know About Race," *Race—The Power of an Illusion*, 2003, http://www.pbs.org/race/000_About/002_04-background-01-x.htm; and Alan Goodman, "Two Questions about Race," *Is Race "Real"?* June 7, 2006, http://raceandgenomics.ssrc.org/Goodman/.

without first obtaining a medical diagnosis, or enduring "sex-reassignment" surgery.[24] Should the approach taken by Denmark be a model for other countries, and for all official records? Or should sex simply be left off of official papers, and not included for anyone, as is becoming more common with race? Do government officials or others need to know a person's sex?[25] Because sex does not always predict a person's gender expression, perhaps official documents need to list both, or neither?

The existence of people with third sex or gender identities complicates our categories of sexual orientation. The sociologist Aaron (Holly) Devor asks, "when we speak of same-sex sexuality, do we mean the same thing as when we speak of same-gender sexuality? And what exactly is same-sex sexuality for people who live in intermediately-sexed bodies or who live between genders?"[26] Devor is pointing out that our categories of homosexual, lesbian, gay, bisexual, heterosexual, etc., rely on essentialist and binary understandings of sex. Indeed, most lesbians, gay men, bisexuals, and heterosexuals identify as such based on their own and others' presumed uncomplicated sex identities. Furthermore, many lesbians and gay men rule out as partners those who share their gender identity but are not perceived to be of the same sex. To answer one of Devor's questions, then, same-sex sexuality is not the same as same-gender sexuality. Same-gender sexuality could include a "born woman" and a transwoman, for example. But Devor also raises the issue of how to describe the sexual orientations of people who are neither male nor female, or neither men nor women. Is the general category of 'queer' adequate for this?

Just as our categories of sex and gender have expanded, it is likely that our categories of sexual orientation will expand as well, in part to accommodate new understandings of sex and gender. For example, there are now recognized sexual orientations that are not focused around a potential partner's sex, or that reject sex and gender binaries, such as pansexual, omnisexual, and polysexual. If we take "same-sex sexuality" to define what it means to be queer, we might exclude those with complex sex identities, or whose sexual orientations do not revolve around a partner's sex, but yet who identify as queer. Some activists use the phrase "gender queer" to capture the non-normative subject positions of people who are transgender, but this term refers to one's gender identity, not sexual orientation.

There is a growing consensus that sex, gender, and sexuality involve related but independently formed identities, in the sense that neither one of these identities is prior to, or causes, the others. At one time, some psychologists believed

---

24 "World Must Follow Denmark's Example after Landmark Transgender Law," *Amnesty International*, June 12, 2014, http://www.amnesty.org/en/en/news/denmark-transgender-law-2014-06-12.

25 For an exploration of this question, see L. Shrage, "Does the Government Need to Know Your Sex?" *Journal of Political Philosophy* 20 (2012): 225–47.

26 Holly Devor, "Who Are 'We'? Where Sexual Orientation Meets Gender Identity," *Journal of Gay & Lesbian Psychotherapy* 6 (2002): 7, http://web.uvic.ca/~ahdevor/WhoAreWe.pdf.

that transgender identities represented an unhealthy psychic strategy for coping with homosexual desire.[27] But this theory assumes that sex, gender, and sexuality are causally interconnected in two typical ways (male/masculine/attracted to women, and female/feminine/attracted to men), so that when atypical patterns of expression or desire occur, subjects will try to force their identities back into one of the two "normal" alignments. But few psychologists hold today that there are only two healthy and normal patterns of alignment in regard to a person's sex, gender, and sexuality. Instead, questions about how these identities get formed, and how their connections are understood both by subjects and theorists, are very much open to debate.

Stevi Jackson offers one plausible but still controversial hypothesis that "gender is temporally prior to sexuality since we acquire a sense of ourselves as gendered long before we become reflexively aware of ourselves as sexual."[28] To evaluate this claim, we need to parse out what it means to be aware of ourselves as gendered or sexual beings. From birth, children are addressed and described in language that marks their gender ("hey little girl!" "what a big boy!"). Children typically learn the behavioral rules that attach to these identities when they are quite young, and these rules may include who is a permissible romantic and sexual partner for each gender. However, if our sexual dispositions supervene upon the sex and gender traits of ourselves and others, then the latter would have to be established earlier. Alternatively, if our sexual interests and attractions can be formed independently of a sense of ourselves and others as gendered beings, then temporal priority may not be necessary.

Are We Born Gay or Straight?

We began this chapter by asking whether sexual behaviors exhibit a capacity to make free and conscious choices, and how these choices might contribute to human happiness or misery. Philosophers and social scientists are divided on the question of how fixed or fluid our sexual orientations or dispositions are. Some believe that these dispositions are relatively stable and rigid; others believe that they are somewhat malleable and can shift with changes in one's social environment or experiences. For example, in the 1970s, feminist activists introduced the idea of the "political lesbian": a woman who chooses, based on her political solidarities, to form intimate relationships only with women. As the "gay rights" movement took off in that decade, many activists questioned whether a person could have this kind of control over their sexual desires and interests. These activists challenged the idea that their sexual dispositions represented mere preferences that they could change at whim. Some gay and lesbian activists began to

---

27 For a summary and critique of this theory, see M.H. Wyndzen, "Autogynephilia and Ray Blanchard's Mis-Directed Sex-Drive Model of Transsexuality," *All Mixed Up* (2003), http://www.genderpsychology.org/autogynephilia/ray_blanchard/.

28 Stevi Jackson, *Heterosexuality in Question* (London: Sage, 1999), 175.

promote the idea that sexual orientations are fixed at birth or that some people are just born gay. They argued that no one would choose to be gay in an intensely homophobic world, because to choose to be gay is to choose to be an object of scorn and social exclusion. Therefore, being gay must be a condition that one has little control over, and is just a fact that some discover about themselves and eventually reveal to others by "coming out."

Scientists, physicians, and philosophers have attempted to understand the origins of homosexuality for centuries. Currently there are two basic approaches to the origins of homosexuality. Because there is evidence of same-sex sexual relationships in most societies throughout history and around the world, and in many species of animals, some theorists hold that homosexual desires and behaviors are biologically based. These theorists are often referred to as "essentialists" (or "biological essentialists," "sociobiologists") because they believe that recurrent and universal social phenomena have biological causes, and therefore explanations.[29] By contrast, social constructionists (whom we discussed above) argue that, when we apply the category 'homosexual' to people in ancient or radically different societies, we wrongly project aspects of the present onto the past, or aspects of one's culture onto another.[30] They point out that modern understandings of "homosexuality" do not fit, for example, the pederastic practices of Ancient Greece (see Ch. 1), or the same-sex intimate acts that take place in contemporary but geographically remote societies. In general, social constructionists argue that we illuminate human behavior by identifying the historically and culturally specific beliefs that shape them.

Biologists have attempted to explain same-sex sexual behaviors in two basic ways: either as a genetic trait that is, in some way, adaptive and therefore can be explained by natural selection, or as an acquired trait that is produced as a fetus (or the human brain) develops and is exposed to unusual hormone levels or proteins.[31] The first approach must be able to explain how homosexual behaviors and related traits can lead to 'reproductive success' (passing on one's DNA), which at first may seem counterintuitive. The second approach must find evidence of neurological differences between gay and straight people. At present, there are many competing biological theories and little consensus around any one of them. Because heterosexual behaviors are required to some degree for reproductive success and are considered part of "normal" human behavior, they appear to need no special biological explanation. However, heterosexuals engage in many sexual practices

---

29 Pickett, "Homosexuality." See also Edward Stein, *The Mismeasure of Desire: The Science, Theory, and Ethics of Sexual Orientation* (New York: Oxford University Press, 2001).

30 Historians and anthropologists describe these intellectual mistakes as varieties of presentism, anachronism, or ethnocentrism.

31 William Kremer, "The Evolutionary Puzzle of Homosexuality," *BBC News Magazine*, February 17, 2014, http://www.bbc.com/news/magazine-26089486. See also R.C. Kirkpatrick, "The Evolution of Human Homosexual Behavior," *Current Anthropology* 41, no.3 (2000): 385–413, http://www.fed.cuhk.edu.hk/~lchang/material/Evolutionary/evo%20homosexual%20 review.pdf .

that are non-procreative (e.g., oral sex) and that do not always lead to acts that are potentially procreative. So we might question why homosexuality receives so much attention from scientists, and whether this is due to cultural factors, such as the belief that homosexual behaviors are strange, uncommon, or abnormal.

Social constructionist accounts of human sexuality attempt to access and articulate the perspectives of those who participate in a seemingly abnormal sexual practice or custom in order to explain them. In other words, they attempt to illuminate uncommon or unfamiliar practices by explaining how those who engage in them understand what they are doing. This approach involves both historical and ethnographic investigation. It can also involve studying the history of medicine and law in order to learn how sexual practices have been altered through medical and legal regulation. Theorists who see sexual identities and practices as social constructs often examine how they vary across social and cultural contexts. In particular, some theorists investigate how sexual identities "intersect" with other identities, such as class and ethnic identities. Intersectional analyses emphasize the diversity that exists within any social group, and seek out the perspectives of those who are the least privileged and often least visible.[32] For example, in studying levels of wealth and income among gay people, it is important to consider lesbians of color and not only white gay men.

Whether we are born with our sexual orientations basically intact or whether our sexual choices are shaped by cultural influences is still up for debate. Even if we find that our sexual identities and desires are socially ingrained, it would not follow that we have much control over them. It could be that our sexual dispositions are formed over many years, starting from early childhood, and therefore they may be relatively stable for most people. Yet if our sexual identities and desires turn out to be more malleable than previously thought, should we, or our society, seek to change some of them? It may be more important to evaluate sexual behaviors less in terms of their origins, and more in terms of whether they are harmful to ourselves and others. No one has yet demonstrated that same-sex sexual relationships or practices are harmful, and so there seems to be little reason to try to discourage them.

At the beginning of this chapter we explored Schopenhauer's evolutionary account of sexual attraction, in which our sexual desires serve our species goal of bringing a new and true-to-type generation into being. To fulfill this species goal, sexual love is destined to lead us to misery, since we must pair with someone who is opposite us in terms of physiognomy, character, and so on. There is now some empirical evidence that, at least in contemporary industrialized societies, people seek partners who resemble, rather than complement, themselves. Using massive amounts of data from dating websites, some researchers have

---

32 For a good introduction to the concept of "intersectionality," see "A Primer on Intersectionality," *African American Policy Forum*, http://aapf.org/wp-content/uploads/2013/01/59819079-Intersectionality-Primer.pdf and http://www.whiteprivilegeconference.com/pdf/intersectionality_primer.pdf.

been able to test the theory that opposites attract, and find it to be false.[33] People tend to find attractive those who are like themselves in terms of their socio-economic class, religious upbringing, and levels of education. There is also some evidence that people, including gay men, find attractive people who physically resemble themselves.[34] Of course, Schopenhauer could respond that these studies merely show that when cultural environments or narcissistic tastes influence our sexual choices, they blunt our instincts—to the peril of our species.[35] In fact, it is difficult to determine whether the patterns that researchers are now finding in the empirical data reflect only transitory trends or timeless patterns. However, they do make us question whether the drive to reproduce is what fundamentally structures sexual attraction among humans, or even nonhumans.[36]

33 Emma Pierson, "In the End, People May Really Just Want to Date Themselves," *FiveThirtyEight Life*, April 9, 2014, http://fivethirtyeight.com/features/in-the-end-people-may-really-just-want-to-date-themselves/; Tia Ghose, "Attracted to Your Opposite: Brain Chemicals May Tell," *Live Science*, October 8, 2013, http://www.livescience.com/40254-brain-chemicals-guide-attraction.html.

34 Jeffrey Bloomer, "The 'Boyfriend Twin' and Our Tendency to Date People Who Look Like Us," *Slate*, April 10, 2014, http://www.slate.com/blogs/outward/2014/04/10/boyfriend_twin_photos_do_gay_men_date_people_who_look_similar_to_them.html.

35 A more recent version of Schopenhauer's theory is that we instinctively seek people who are physically opposite to ourselves in order to diversify the human gene pool and avoid inbreeding. See Eliana Dockterman, "Dating Narcissism: Why We Look for Ourselves in a Partner," *Time*, April 11, 2014, http://time.com/59476/dating-narcissism-why-we-look-for-ourselves-in-a-partner/. For a philosophical critique of current theories of mate selection offered by evolutionary psychologists, see Neil McArthur, "Stone Age Sex," *Aeon Magazine*, June 18, 2014, http://aeon.co/magazine/being-human/is-human-sexuality-determined-by-evolution/.

36 See Mary Bates, "Sexual Healing: Bonobos Use Sex to De-Stress," *Wired*, March 18, 2014, http://www.wired.com/2014/04/sexual-healing-bonobos-use-sex-to-de-stress/.

Discussion Questions

1. What patterns have you noticed in how your friends or family members select their sexual partners? Do these patterns support or challenge Schopenhauer's account of sexual attraction?
2. Is Schopenhauer right that sexual attraction is not a good basis for finding a long-term domestic partner?
3. Can we change our sex or only our sex assignment?
4. Should we add more categories of sex and gender on official forms, or should we just allow people to check more than one of the two available boxes (F and/or M)?
5. Should sex and gender identities be voluntarily assumed, or should some governmental or medical authority control these statuses?
6. Is it important to know whether we are born gay or straight, or not? Explain.

Further Reading

Alcoff, Linda Martin. *Visible Identities: Race, Gender, and the Self.* New York: Oxford University Press, 2005.

Blackburn, Simon. *Lust: The Seven Deadly Sins.* New York: Oxford University Press, 2004.

Cuomo, Chris. "Dignity and the Right to Be Lesbian or Gay." *Philosophical Studies: An International Journal for Philosophy in the Analytic Tradition* 132 (2007): 75–85.

Garry, Ann. "Intersectionality, Metaphors, and the Multiplicity of Gender." *Hypatia* 26 (2011): 826–50.

Hacking, Ian. "How Natural Are Kinds of Sexual Orientation?" *Law and Philosophy: An International Journal for Jurisprudence and Legal Philosophy* 21 (2002): 95–107.

Hale, Jacob. "Are Lesbians Women?" *Hypatia* 11 (1996): 94–121.

Haslanger, Sally. *Resisting Reality: Social Construction and Social Critique.* New York: Oxford University Press, 2012.

Scruton, Roger. *Sexual Desire: A Moral Philosophy of the Erotic.* New York: Free Press, 1986.

Stein, Edward. *The Mismeasure of Desire: The Science, Theory, and Ethics of Sexual Orientation.* New York: Oxford University Press, 2001.

Warnke, Georgia. *After Identity: Rethinking Race, Sex, and Gender.* Cambridge: Cambridge University Press, 2008.

Zack, Naomi. *Inclusive Feminism: A Third Wave Theory of Women's Commonality.* Lanham, MD: Rowman and Littlefield, 2005.

Chapter 3

Sexual Objectification and Autonomy

What does it mean to sexually objectify a person, and is this always wrong? If people consent to sex acts that are potentially harmful or degrading to them, are these acts then acceptable? When do limits on our sexual choices infringe upon our sexual autonomy? Philosophers are interested in questions about the basic requirements of morality and the basic conditions for living a free and dignified life. In this chapter we will investigate particular sexual practices that may not meet these requirements and conditions.

Is It Wrong to Sexually Objectify Someone?

The eighteenth-century German philosopher Immanuel Kant held that the fulfillment of sexual desire was not possible without acting immorally toward another human being or oneself, in most cases. This is because it is almost impossible to satisfy our sexual urges without treating another person or oneself as a mere thing.[1] When I treat someone instrumentally in order to satisfy non-sexual desires, such as a desire for a haircut, I can use someone as a means to my end while simultaneously recognizing her as a subject. That is, I can simultaneously

---

1   Kant, *Lectures on Ethics*. See also Papadaki, "Feminist Perspectives on Objectification."

recognize my hair stylist as something of intrinsic value—an end in itself—and not something with only extrinsic value—a means to my end. The hands that cut and reshape my hair belong to a person with whom I interact and negotiate in the process of obtaining a haircut. Sometimes, of course, people do use others non-sexually as mere means, such as when someone fails to pay or tip a person for a haircut, or in other ways fails to acknowledge the humanity of and autonomy of a service provider.

But sex is different. Martha Nussbaum explicates Kant's view as follows:

> The idea seems to be that sexual desire and pleasure cause very acute forms of sensation in a person's own body; that these sensations drive out, for a time, all other thoughts, including the thoughts of respect for humanity that are characteristic of the moral attitude to persons. Apparently he [Kant] also thinks that they drive out every endlike consideration of the pleasure or experience of the sex partner, and cause attention to be riveted on one's own bodily states. In that condition of mind, one cannot manage to see the other person as anything but a tool of one's own interests, a set of bodily parts that are useful tools for one's pleasure.... At the same time, the keen interest both parties have in sexual satisfaction will lead them to permit themselves to be treated in this thinglike way by one another....[2]

Nussbaum points out that there are seven ways to treat a person as a thing, most of which are incorporated into Kant's image of a sexual act. A person is objectified when she or he is treated as (1) a tool, is denied (2) self-determination or (3) agency, is viewed as (4) interchangeable with other objects or (5) lacking boundaries, or is regarded as (6) something that can be owned and sold, or as (7) something that lacks feelings or inner states. For Kant, sexual partners cannot avoid treating each other as mere interchangeable instruments, lacking autonomy, agency, boundaries, or feelings. The very act of sex itself involves violating another's physical boundaries, and interacting with the person's body as if it were an inanimate object, like a piece of food that one tastes to derive pleasure. Such violation may result in the loss of bodily and mental integrity (e.g., transmitting an STD, causing an unwanted pregnancy, or psychological trauma) to oneself and another. To mitigate the wrongs of sexual objectification, Kant contends that sex is permissible only within marriage. Marriage entitles people to reciprocal rights of sexual use for life, so that sexual partners cannot treat each other as fungible objects. Marriage transforms two people into a single social and legal unit so that, when they sexually exploit each other, in a sense they exploit themselves.

In many societies, women are taught not to permit a man to sexually use and exploit them without a commitment of marriage. Women are considered

---

2   Martha Nussbaum, *Sex and Social Justice* (New York: Oxford University Press, 1998), 224.

highly vulnerable to sexual degradation because they are typically viewed as sexually passive creatures who only control to some degree who has sexual access to their bodies. To mitigate their sexual corruption and ruination, smart women are supposed to secure marriage before yielding to sex. Men presumably avoid sexual objectification and exploitation because they use others sexually and are not themselves used. For Kant, though, men are equally vulnerable to sexual objectification when their humanity is subordinated to their own and another's sexual desires. Because marriage is an institution that obliges each spouse to respect the humanity of the other, it thus offers social and moral safeguards to sexual partners regardless of their gender.

Leaving aside the question whether marriage actually does guarantee respectful treatment between marriage partners, are there ways to protect oneself and one's partner from the harms of sexual objectification and exploitation without resorting to marriage? Some of the harms of sex would be avoidable if sexual desire did not cause us to ignore or deny the humanity, autonomy, agency, integrity, irreplaceability, and subjectivity of our sexual partners. Does sexual desire represent a more powerful force than other human appetites, so that we are unable to behave morally toward others when we seek to fulfill such desires? Are urges for sex more powerful than, say, urges for fortune, fame, influence, love, or companionship? Why does Kant assume that sexual desires are more powerful, and therefore more morally problematic, than desires for other goods? Is there any empirical evidence to back up this assumption, or only religious texts depicting humans as sinful and depraved creatures?

If we start with the premise that sexual desires are powerful but nevertheless permit us to attend to the humanity of our sexual partners, then it is possible to conceive of sexual relationships that can avoid morally degrading one's partners and oneself. Of course, many actual sexual relationships will be morally problematic and involve egregious exploitation, but our premise assumes that an urge for sex is not necessarily incompatible with maintaining a moral attitude toward a potential sex partner. Patricia Marino has argued that respect for a partner's sexual autonomy is sufficient for moral sexual relationships, and it is not necessary that sex take place in the context of enduring, equal, and reciprocal relationships.[3] For Marino, casual sex and paid sex can respect a person's sexual autonomy if the transaction acknowledges and attempts to fulfill each participant's ends, which they continually communicate to each other.[4] In the next section we will explore whether obtaining another's consent to participate in a sexual act is sufficient to show respect for that person's ends and autonomy.

---

3   Nussbaum suggests that sex in the context of an ongoing, reciprocal, and respectful relationship can avoid morally impermissible forms of objectification, even when it occasionally meets one or more of her conditions 1–7 above.

4   Patricia Marino, "The Ethics of Sexual Objectification: Autonomy and Consent," *Inquiry* 51 (2008): 345–64.

Is Consent a Sufficient Condition for Moral Sex?

To meet the minimum requirements of moral decency, sexual acts should be consensual and non-coercive. This means that personal boundaries should not be crossed without the *genuine consent* of both participants. Genuine consent occurs when a person who is mentally competent freely or voluntarily agrees to something. To be mentally competent, in this context, one must have reached an age of maturity sufficient to understand the nature and potential consequences of the sexual activities in which one agrees to participate. Moreover, at the time of consent, one's judgment should be unimpaired (e.g., by alcohol, sleep, etc.). To give consent freely, one must have both the physical ability and social authority to withhold consent. An employee, child, patient, or a person who feels physically threatened will typically not be in a position to deny or give consent freely. The legal scholar Catharine MacKinnon contends that, in male-dominated societies, women often lack sufficient social power to withhold consent from their husbands, boyfriends, and male bosses, and therefore ordinary heterosexual sex in such contexts is frequently nonconsensual.[5] If this is true, then we need to dismantle the structures of male domination in all areas of society, in part to enable women to gain equal control over the terms of sexual intimacy. Empowering women in both the private and public sphere will involve redesigning social institutions so that they deter coercive sex between family members or co-workers (e.g., by having policies on sexual harassment, and on spousal and acquaintance rape). MacKinnon and other feminist activists have led efforts in the past few decades to accomplish this, with some success (see Ch. 4 for a discussion of sexual harassment and rape).

If someone genuinely consents to be sexually subordinated within the context of a relationship or particular sexual activity, and agrees to have her own desires, inner states, and personal boundaries ignored, is this acceptable? For example, a sex worker may agree to put a price on her availability for sexual intimacy, and then engage in sexual acts in which her client uses her body as a tool for his sexual pleasure. She may consent to sexual activities that put her at risk for an STD or psychological harm (such as sex without a condom, or sex with men she finds physically repulsive or who treat her disrespectfully). Is this all right, if she understands the nature and potential consequences of her paid sexual activities, and freely agrees to them in return for a sum of money or equivalent gift? In the next section, we will consider whether consensual adult sex work is morally permissible. Meanwhile, let us return to the issue of consent more broadly.

Seiriol Morgan argues that the consent of both parties is not sufficient to render a sexual act moral, and that we need to consider the motivations of the actors involved. Morgan considers literary and real-life "Don Juan" characters who seduce respectable married women only to prove their own sexual prowess and to

---

5   Catharine MacKinnon, *Toward a Feminist Theory of the State* (Cambridge, MA: Harvard University Press, 1989).

compete with other men. These acts typically have devastating consequences for the women who are duped and seduced, in terms of their social standing, reputations, and economic security. Some women may fully understand the social risks of their actions, and yet they may choose to cooperate with their seducer because of the exhilaration and passion that his sexual attention elicits. Morgan claims that the seducer acts immorally, even if he has his lover's consent, because he obtains consent by exploiting her emotional vulnerability and because he is indifferent to, or possibly takes some pleasure in, her social downfall.[6] Indeed, for some men, the greater the seductive challenge, due to a particular woman's social circumstances or character, the sweeter its success. Morgan argues that such acts of sexual conquest, even when both parties participate voluntarily, are morally objectionable because they stem from problematic intentions on the part of the seducer, and because they can cause serious emotional and social damage to the woman seduced.

Morgan's examples and analysis suggest that genuine consent is a necessary, but not sufficient, condition for moral sex. If he is right, then consensual sex acts and practices that present a high risk of foreseeable harm to one or more participants, and in which one party acts with intent to harm or indifference to the risks, are *prima facie* morally wrong. For this reason, contemporary practitioners of BDSM (Bondage/Discipline, Domination/Submission, Sadomasochism) draw a distinction between *hurt* and *harm* in order to defend consensual but extreme sex practices (e.g., physical restraint, whipping, gagging, piercing, pinching, and so on). Sometimes activities that hurt or cause pain, such as having surgery or a dental procedure, cause little or no harm and, instead, promote health and well-being. Those who practice BDSM claim that extreme sex practices can help people develop trust and self-discipline, relieve stress, and have emotionally rewarding experiences, similar to dangerous sports. Moreover, morally responsible BDSM practitioners take considerable care to minimize the risks of lasting harm or injuries, while inflicting or enduring momentary pain and discomfort.

Because extreme sex practices can be dangerous, despite the precautions taken, we should ask what level of foreseeable risk is acceptable for the activity to be morally permissible.[7] This is a little like asking what level of risk is acceptable for activities such as football, space travel, or fertility treatments. In all these cases the participants aim to avoid causing harm, while recognizing that their activities place them at elevated levels of risk. By contrast, the Don Juan seducer typically has malicious intentions in that he aims to, and takes pleasure in, destroying a woman's reputation and social standing, or does this to humiliate a male competitor to whom she may be related. Given his egotistical aims, such seducers rarely attempt to minimize the harm to their lovers by keeping

---

6   Seiriol Morgan, "Dark Desires," *Ethical Theory and Moral Practice* 6, no. 4 (2003): 377–410.

7   For an interesting discussion of BDSM and consent, see Morten Ebbe Juul Nielsen, "Safe, Sane, and Consensual: Consent and the Ethics of BDSM," *International Journal of Applied Philosophy* 24, no. 2 (2010): 265–88.

their conquests secret. Thus, even when a woman consents, knowing the risks involved, the seducer's "dark desires" render the sexual act evil. Thus, it seems that genuine consent and reasonably good (or the lack of bad) intentions are both necessary for a sexual act to pass the test of minimal moral decency.

Is It Wrong to Pay, or Be Paid, for Sex?

If moral sex requires more than genuine consent, then consensual paid sex too must meet this higher standard. So the primary question in this section is whether the harms associated with consensual paid sex can be sufficiently minimized, and whether the actors involved typically act with negligence or malicious intent. What are the potential harms of a practice in which one person buys and another person sells sexual services? Not long ago, many believed that sex outside of marriage was morally wrong. But many societies today are significantly more tolerant of premarital sex and adultery. Is "prostitution" a stigmatized practice that, with greater understanding and acceptance, could enrich the lives of many people? Or do markets in sexual services represent egregious forms of labor, sexual, and gender exploitation?

Some feminists and moral theorists believe that, just as it's not acceptable for a person to consent to be enslaved, it should not be permissible for a person to agree to be someone else's sexual servant or subordinate. These theorists claim that prostitutes become sexual subordinates when they allow their bodies to be sexually used by another, even if temporarily and even if they receive some compensation. Carole Pateman argues that sexual capacities, like children or bodily organs, are intimately connected to both who we are and our well-being, and thus they should not be exchangeable, like commodities in a market.[8] Similarly, Scott Anderson argues that sexual autonomy is a critical and important form of autonomy, which no contract or practice should override. In other words, sexual freedom is inalienable. Because sex workers enter into agreements in which the performance of various sexual acts is obligatory, sexual labor takes away the worker's sexual freedom. For this reason, Anderson argues, sexual encounters with others should not be facilitated or coerced by market mechanisms or legally enforceable contracts.[9]

Martha Nussbaum responds to critics of consensual adult prostitution by pointing out that our intellectual and artistic capacities are intimately connected to who we are. Yet few object to permitting people to enter contracts to write books or give lectures, or give dance or .music recitals—that is, to exchange these capacities like goods in a market. Lawyers and other professionals routinely allow their intellectual skills to be used to further the ends of others.

---

8   Carole Pateman, *The Sexual Contract* (Stanford, CA: Stanford University Press, 1988).

9   Scott Anderson, "Prostitution and Sexual Autonomy: Making Sense of the Prohibition of Prostitution," in *Prostitution and Pornography: Philosophical Debate About the Sex Industry*, ed. J. Spector, 358–93 (Stanford, CA: Stanford University Press, 2006).

Nussbaum questions why sexual capacities should be protected more than intellectual and artistic capacities. Furthermore, many forms of paid work involve the use of even intimate parts of our bodies, such as the work of someone who is a food tester, or agrees to have her body used to test new drugs or medical instruments.[10] Nussbaum suggests that the prevalence of myths about sexually promiscuous women, and the social stigmas that attach to the latter group, may explain why societies aim to protect women's sexual capacities more than other capacities. If this is the case, then prohibitions on consensual sex work that aim to protect women or public morals may be overly paternalistic.[11]

Debra Satz argues that markets in which women, primarily, sell sexual services to men perpetuate pernicious stereotypes of women that can exacerbate existing gender inequalities.[12] Such markets reinforce stigmatizing, but culturally prevalent, images of women as the sexual servants of men. Moreover, they also reinforce the erroneous idea that men as a group have limitless sexual needs that can be met only if they are entitled to purchase sexual services from others. Such notions about men and women serve to justify and maintain gender inequalities in many spheres of life. Therefore, even if people enter sex markets freely and without coercion, the effects of such markets on gender equality should be disturbing to feminists and others who support women's equality. For these reasons, some feminists do not support legitimizing sex work, even though some women would genuinely consent to perform it.

The question then is whether the sale of sex inevitably promotes the subordination of women, and whether sex workers have less autonomy than other workers, or have less ability to resist exploitative working conditions and avoid forced labor. Some feminists view prostitution as a form of institutionalized male violence against women and children, and not only as an institution that subordinates women. Accordingly, some countries have introduced criminal restrictions that reconfigure the prostitute as a victim and her customer as a sexual predator.[13] Because women and children, on average, have less social power and economic resources than men, men who offer money for sex are thought to be exercising male privilege by coercing sex from vulnerable, and possibly destitute, women and children.

Feminists have mobilized for several decades to end male sexual violence and "take back the night," and their social agenda includes eliminating

---

10 Martha Nussbaum, "'Whether from Reason or Prejudice': Taking Money for Bodily Sexual Services," in *Sex and Social Justice*, 276–98 (New York: Oxford University Press, 1998).

11 While Nussbaum appears to hold that the prostitute's work can be carried out with dignity and moral respect, she is less convinced that the work of women in conventional pornography meets these criteria.

12 Debra Satz, "Markets in Women's Sexual Labor," *Ethics* 106 (1995): 63–85. See also Laurie Shrage, "Should Feminists Oppose Prostitution?" *Ethics* 99 (1989): 347–61.

13 See especially the Swedish laws: "100 Countries and Their Prostitution Policies," *ProCon.org*, http://prostitution.procon.org/view.resource.php?resourceID=000772. See also "Historical Timeline," *ProCon.org*, http://prostitution.procon.org/view.timeline.php?timelineID=000028.

prostitution and violent pornography, along with rape, and domestic violence. But during the same decades, a feminist-oriented international sex workers' rights movement has also mobilized to advocate for decriminalizing all adult, consensual sex work. Sex-worker activists see themselves not as victims but as adult businesswomen who aim to provide services that are valued by their customers in a respectful and mutually advantageous exchange.[14] Their efforts to build public support and respect for their work have been thwarted, however, by feminists and some conservative allies who see the sex industry as a form of social breakdown and moral corruption.

In the contemporary world, there are forms of sex work (as well as agricultural, manufacturing, and service work) that involve gross violations of basic human rights and are unquestionably harmful and degrading. These practices of "trafficking in persons" may involve forced labor and nonconsensual sex, child labor and the sexual abuse of children, wage theft, unsafe working conditions, fraud, deception, abduction, indentured servitude, or slave labor. Women and children comprise the majority of people trafficked, and therefore preventing trafficking can address serious forms of male violence against women and children. But there are also practices of sex work in which adults work voluntarily, form collectives to defend their rights and improve their working conditions, and take precautions to protect themselves against violent customers, STDs, and other risks of their trade. A UN Commission in 2012 released a report that states, "Some governments deploy anti-human trafficking laws so broadly that they conflate voluntary and consensual exchanges of sex for money with the exploitative, coerced, often violent trafficking of people (primarily women and girls) for the purposes of sex."[15] The report alleges that bad laws, and overly broad uses of good laws, impede effective efforts to prevent the spread of HIV and other STDs, and do little to protect women and children.

The failure to distinguish voluntary adult sex work, which can have relatively decent working conditions, from various forms of trafficking in persons, which can involve forced labor and sexual violence against women and children, can lead to misguided policies. These policies often undermine the ability of adult sex workers to secure safe working conditions. Several years ago a judge in Ontario, Canada, Justice Susan Himel, issued a ruling asserting that existing criminal laws "force prostitutes to choose between their liberty interest and their security of the person as protected under the Charter of Rights and Freedoms."[16] Justice Himel's ruling was recently upheld in a unanimous ruling

---

14 See "The Sex Workers Project," http://sexworkersproject.org/, and "Sex Workers Rights Organizations and Projects Around the World," http://www.bayswan.org/orgs.html.

15 Amanda Swysgood, "U.N. Commission Calls for Legalizing Prostitution Worldwide," *CNSnews. com*, July 23, 2012, http://cnsnews.com/news/article/un-commission-calls-legalizing-prostitution-worldwide.

16 Licia Corbella, "Allowing Brothels Will Make Things Worse for Prostitutes," *Real Women of Canada*, June 8, 2013, http://www.realwomenofcanada.ca/allowing-brothels-will-make-things-worse-for-prostitutes/.

by the Supreme Court of Canada, when it "struck down all three prostitution-related prohibitions—against keeping a brothel, living on the avails of prostitution and street soliciting—as violations of the constitutional guarantee to life, liberty and security of the person."[17] The court gave the government of Canada one year in which to reshape public policy and laws regarding prostitution to make them consistent with Canada's Charter of Rights and Freedom. In response, the government is proposing a new set of laws that are harsher than the earlier ones, in that they "criminalize the purchase of sexual services, and target those who benefit from prostitution ... [and] also make illegal the sale of sex through print media or the Internet."[18] These laws appear to focus on punishing the business owners and customers "who benefit from prostitution," but they will force prostitutes to work unsafely in order to protect their clients and associates.

In the Netherlands, where adult sex work has been legal and regulated for over a decade, sex workers have made progress in improving the safety of their work but have made fewer gains in improving the image of their profession.[19] Still, many feminists and human-rights activists believe that sex businesses cannot be made safe enough, and legal brothels only provide sexual predators easier access to women, who are drawn into dangerous and demeaning work.[20] So the question remains whether sex work is significantly different from other jobs that are often dangerous and demeaning. Can the workers' rights and safety best be protected by criminal restrictions, or do these regulations make sex work less safe and more degrading?[21]

What Does It Mean to Have Sexual Autonomy?

In the 2009 film *Up in the Air*, Ryan Bingham (George Clooney) lives a life that is ungrounded or unmoored in many senses of the term. First, his job entails spending many hours on airplanes, flying around the country to different cities. He does not spend much time in any one place and, instead, he seeks the comforts of home in airport lounges and hotel rooms when he is not on a plane.

---

17 Mike Blanchfield, "Supreme Court Strikes Down Canada's Anti-prostitution Laws as Charter Breach," *Global News*, December 20, 2013, http://globalnews.ca/news/1042861/supreme-court-strikes-down-canadas-anti-prostitution-laws/.

18 Will Campbell, "Sex Workers Take to Canada's Streets to Protest Prostitution Legislation," *Globe and Mail*, June 15, 2014, http://www.theglobeandmail.com/news/politics/sex-workers-take-to-canadas-streets-to-protest-prostitution-legislation/article19177042/. See also Jake Flanagin, "What It Takes to Legalize Sex Work," *International New York Times*, June 25, 2014, http://nyti.ms/1lpGU27.

19 Joshua Cruz and Swaan van Iterson, "The Audacity of Tolerance: A Critical Analysis of Legalized Prostitution in Amsterdam's Red Light District," *Humanity in Action*, http://www.humanityinaction.org/knowledgebase/312-the-audacity-of-tolerance-a-critical-analysis-of-legalized-prostitution-in-amsterdam-s-red-light-district.

20 Corbella, "Allowing Brothels Will Make Things Worse for Prostitutes."

21 Laurie Shrage, "Feminist Perspectives on Sex Markets," *Stanford Encyclopedia of Philosophy* (2012), http://plato.stanford.edu/entries/feminist-sex-markets/.

Second, Ryan appears to have no strong attachments to family members or friends. He ruminates on whether to go to a niece's wedding, given that he has not been very involved in her or his sister's life. He explores casual sex with women when their flight paths cross. Third, Ryan moonlights as a motivational speaker, instructing others about how to free themselves from relationships and jobs that keep them stuck in one place. His approach to life helps him rationalize his main job, in which he acts on behalf of corporate downsizers by assisting in firing their hardworking, faithful employees. He believes he is lessening the burdens of the people he helps to fire, by freeing them from pointless commitments. Of course, to really free themselves, those fired must also detach themselves from all the commitments their employment allowed them to take on, including the support of spouses and children. But some of the newly fired, unable to face being set free, pursue the ultimate freedom from life's burdens: death. Ryan understands the dark side of his work, and at moments we see he is "up in the air" or indecisive about the principles that have given meaning to his life. By the end of the movie, his actions show that he no longer holds to these principles.

Although Ryan is a mature man, he has managed to avoid acquiring much "baggage" in his life, including romantic relationship entanglements that could periodically ground him. Then he meets Alex and begins what seems to be another casual affair. "Think of me as you with a vagina," Alex tells Ryan and, at this point in the film, Alex does appear to be his ideal match. But another woman enters Ryan's life in the form of a younger coworker, Natalie. Natalie is an efficiency expert who proposes to cut out Ryan's and his coworkers' travel and have them fire their victims across a computer screen, via videoconferencing, rather than in person. Ryan opposes Natalie's plan because it would make their already brutal work seem more uncaring and impersonal. Of course, her plan would also completely change his lifestyle and rob him of his status as an elite airline passenger with all the accompanying perks and privileges. To prove to Natalie the error of her ways, he drags her with him on one of his excursions so he can show her the right, but less efficient, way to dismiss someone.

While traveling as the odd couple, Ryan and Natalie exchange their philosophies about life. Although Natalie promotes efficiency over kindness in the workplace, she shows she is more generous and considerate toward those in her private life. She questions Ryan's unwillingness to make commitments to people, which she believes define and give meaning to a person's life. Although Natalie appears immature and inexperienced, she has a mature take on adult responsibility and regards caring for others as an opportunity for emotional growth and an enriched life. Then her fiancé breaks up with her, awkwardly but efficiently, via a text message. This amusing incident shows that Natalie is not necessarily wrong about how to live meaningfully in the familial realm, but that she is wrong about her efficiency plan for the company, as her plan would enable corporations to dismiss their employees in ways nearly equivalent to a text message. Ryan thus succeeds, somewhat unexpectedly, in convincing Natalie of the need for the personal touch when giving an employee the ax. But Natalie's good sense about the familial side of life, and Ryan's growing feelings for Alex, unsettle his views on personal and family attachments.

The characters in *Up in the Air* offer two models of sexual autonomy. Ryan exemplifies "negative freedom": the freedom from ties or commitments to others that can limit one's movements, opportunities, and choices. Natalie exemplifies "positive freedom": the freedom to make choices that limit future choices, but that sustain and deepen our relationships with others and promote emotional and intellectual growth.[22] Alex, meanwhile, exemplifies someone who tries to have both: a "real life" defined by earlier choices and commitments, and an occasional escape from normal life where she allows herself to pursue opportunities that impose no constraints.[23] Part of what makes *Up in the Air* an interesting film is that it depicts the lives defined by these characters' choices in both attractive and unattractive ways. When Ryan finally achieves his goal of racking up enough frequent flyer miles to keep him up in the air indefinitely, as a well-cared-for corporate customer, we see the emptiness of this achievement. Yet, at his niece's wedding, we witness young people hitching up and tying themselves down because of community expectations and the lack of opportunity for worldly adventures. We don't know if this marriage will produce bitter, lonely, and unfulfilled people (as the bride's divorced mother—Ryan's sister—reminds us can happen) or will enable emotionally rich and meaningful lives. Alex's double life requires her duplicity with each partner, which keeps her from being emotionally close to either one. The character who shows the most promise for living meaningfully, but without being too tied down, is the socially awkward and childish Natalie. At the end of the film, she quits her heartless job and reestablishes herself in a more promising one in San Francisco. What Natalie perhaps represents is the courage both to make choices that will tie her down and also to uproot herself and remake her choices when life requires that.

Up in the Air lays out well the dilemmas of modern life with respect to fidelity in private and public life. Should individuals detach themselves from communities and families so that they can be free to chase opportunities for good sex, work, and parties? Or is a life without commitments devoid of worthwhile forms of relationships and security? When we make commitments to others (e.g., lovers, employees, etc.), must they trap us in life-long situations that ultimately thwart our happiness? Or should our commitments be understood as conditional promises, and, if so, will these provide us with the feelings of love and security that we need to flourish?

Sexual autonomy is a concept that we will discuss throughout this book. For example, as we saw in the last section, sex work raises a number of issues about

---

22 Ian Carter, "Positive and Negative Liberty," *Stanford Encyclopedia of Philosophy* (2012), http://plato.stanford.edu/entries/liberty-positive-negative/.

23 For a film clip in which Alex explains how she sees her relationship with Ryan, see "Up in the Air (9/9) Movie CLIP - You Are a Parenthesis (2009)," http://www.youtube.com/watch?v=Wje5oR4NqYI.

the commodification of women's sexuality and the objectification of women. Scott Anderson questions whether women (or men) who perform sex work have genuine sexual autonomy, given that they contract to participate in sexual encounters defined by their clients' interests and expectations. Feminists have questioned whether women in heterosexual relationships have genuine sexual autonomy given that their sexual expression and activities are often controlled or directed by their male partners. If autonomy involves having a right to or capacity for self-determination, will tolerance for markets in sexual services, or double standards of sexual conduct for men and women, diminish people's sexual autonomy? Is a commitment to restrict our sexual activities to one person less threatening to our sexual autonomy than a contract to provide sexual services for one hour? In Ch. 12, we will consider whether the choice to be a sexual submissive in a BDSM encounter or relationship diminishes one's autonomy, or whether the choice to cede control over oneself is compatible with having the right and capacity for self-determination.

What Is the Connection between "Exoticizing" and "Eroticizing" Someone?

When we exoticize someone, we view that person as having traits that are culturally unfamiliar and even mysterious. Sometimes that which is culturally strange is regarded with fear or disgust, but often we confront foreign people or things with an interest in, and an openness to, new experiences. Interactions with people who appear culturally different and exotic may induce alternating perceptions of danger and excitement. Accordingly, the expression "vive la différence" encourages us to move away from the familiar and predictable and to seek variety.

We often travel to foreign places in order to experience things and people who are different. In the film *Heading South*, North American women travel to the Caribbean in order to enjoy sex with men who are considered racially and culturally exotic. Typically, these relationships are understood as vacation romances and affairs and involve a flow of money or gifts from the women to the men. Scholars have documented many forms of "romance tourism" or "sex tourism" in our contemporary world, often involving people from wealthy "first world" countries who seek sexual experiences with people from poorer "third world" nations.[24] For example, European and American men often travel to Thailand to pursue sex with local women, from whom they expect culturally distinct forms of eroticism. These relationships often involve explicit exchanges of sex for money, and are considered a form of prostitution.

---

24 See Kamala Kempadoo (ed.), *Sun, Sex, and Gold: Tourism and Sex Work in the Caribbean* (Lanham, MD: Rowman and Littlefield, 1999); Jeremy Seabrook, *Travels in the Skin Trade: Tourism and the Sex Industry*, 2nd ed. (London: Pluto Press, 2001); Michael C. Hall and Chris Ryan, *Sex Tourism: Marginal People and Liminalities* (New York: Routledge, 2001).

Do sexual relationships that are sought because of the exotic appeal that one partner has for the other (sometimes mutual and sometimes one-directional) involve objectionable forms of objectification or exploitation? This theme is explored in Spike Lee's film *Jungle Fever* (1991), and in David Henry Hwang's play *M. Butterfly* (1988). In both works, the failure of the protagonists to understand the pernicious cultural stereotypes that shape how they view each other leads to tragic results. But can people in these situations correct their distorted images, and, if they do, will the allure of the other remain? Both works are likely to lead viewers to somewhat negative and cynical conclusions.

Today, on interracial dating websites, people advertise for someone who is racially other by using metaphors, such as "coffee looking for cream" or "looking for my ebony queen." The AfroRomance dating site, whose motto is "where love is more than skin deep,"[25] claims to "specialize in bringing together singles who want to date different races." Can anything more than "skin deep" love come out of such pursuits? Surely it is a good thing to be open to romance across racial, national, and other cultural boundaries.[26] But are interracial dating sites promoting something akin to romance tourism, where difference is eroticized and becomes the primary basis of attraction?

Alternatively, should people look for romance and sexual relationships only within their own racial/ethnic group in order to ensure that cultural stereotyping will not be the source of attraction, or the source of eventual disgust? Of course, partners in apparently monocultural relationships can exoticize one another as well, by deploying stereotypes about gender, age, or birthplace, or bodily differences such as hair color (e.g., blondes, redheads, etc.). Do people generally avoid the familiar and known, and seek mysterious others for sexual relationships? If, as Kant suggests, we must exploit our lovers for our own selfish pleasures, we might find this easier to do with lovers whose inner states we perceive as different from our own.

Because sexual relationships involve crossing ordinary social boundaries to enter parts of each other's lives not normally visible to others, the challenge and excitement of violating these boundaries may be heightened when the boundaries are wider and seemingly impenetrable. People who seek greater comfort or security with intimate partners may avoid pursuing exotic others for this reason. The philosopher Roger Scruton alleges that same-sex relationships are perverted because lesbians and gay men seek partners with bodies and gender identities that are the same as their own. He argues that those who seek such relationships are narcissistic, because they love only those who resemble their own reflection.[27] If one takes this principle to its logical extreme,

---

25 http://www.afroromance.com.
26 This may be more important for people from dominant social groups, as a way of showing that they are not racist or ethnocentric. People from oppressed groups may want to show social solidarity by primarily dating members of their own group.
27 Roger Scruton, *Sexual Desire: A Philosophical Investigation* (New York: Continuum, 2006).

however, anyone who loves someone of the same race, ethnicity, religion, nationality, etc., is similarly narcissistic. Why do social conservatives apply the principle of "vive la différence" only to gender, and not to other varieties of individual difference?

Does the pursuit of sex and romance across ethnic or racial divides reflect a lack of social solidarity with the members of one's own group, or a form of internalized self-hatred? This is a difficult question for members of oppressed groups, especially when the object of their affection is a member of the oppressor group. When Jews are attracted to German gentiles, or persons of color to Scandinavian blondes, should they feel ashamed? When feminist women are attracted to macho men (or men in general), should they question the depth of their feminist commitments? When people with brown eyes fetishize blue-eyed people, do they reflect a lack of awareness of the racial meanings of their aesthetic preferences? If we think sexual desires are irrational and that we have little control over them, then we can't hold people accountable for the types of people they find erotically attractive. And if we can't hold people accountable for their sexual tastes, then of course there is no point in morally or politically critiquing them.

But are our sexual preferences or orientations a matter of subconscious and mysterious tastes, or do they reflect social values and beliefs to which we consciously subscribe? The saying "it's just as easy to fall in love with a rich man as a poor one" suggests the latter, though such advice is often offered with a sense of irony. Nevertheless, while it may be unwise to choose lovers in order to enhance our social position, the lovers we do choose often seem to reflect these kinds of aims. In this era, where both women and men have many different options for meeting prospective lovers and partners (e.g., social and family networks, workplace, online dating, social media, membership in a faith community, etc.), the strategy we choose will often determine whether we cross ethnic and class divides in our search. Moreover, within any of these strategies are sub-strategies that reflect our values and beliefs. For example, those who take the online approach will have to choose among websites that promote in-group matching ("JDate," "All Black Dating," "AsiaFuns,") or interracial coupling (as mentioned earlier), or those that are less transparent about the social identities of the site's members. Whichever route we take, our choices will reflect exogamous and endogamous rules,[28] to borrow the terminology of anthropologists, whether we are aware of these rules or not.

The problem of exoticizing others is similar to the problem of objectification in that both involve treating others as lacking individuality, or unique inner states, perspectives, and feelings. When we exoticize or objectify others, we project onto them our own desires, assumptions, and stereotypes about who they

---

28 Exogamy is a practice in which one chooses a mate from outside one's social group (defined in terms of race, religion, class, nationality, etc.), whereas endogamy is the practice of choosing a mate from within one's social group.

are and what they are like. Ann Cahill has argued that we should focus not on the problem of objectification—i.e., the problem of treating people as objects or mere bodies—but on the problem of sexually constructing others in ways that are derivative of our own sexualities. Women, in particular, are often treated as projections of men's fantasies about women, and similarly, ethnic minorities are often treated as projections of the dominant ethnic group's fantasies and anxieties about the minority group. She argues that we need an ethics of sexuality that does not devalue bodies and treat the sexualities of others derivative of our own, but that involves the mutual recognition of one another as a unique complex of bodily and mental attributes.[29]

Kant holds that it is wrong to reduce persons to their body, because the body is a mere passive thing, unlike the person who inhabits it. But Cahill challenges us to move beyond mind/body dualisms that see the body as lower in value. If bodies are regarded as equally important and inseparable parts of ourselves, then focusing on a person's body does not necessarily involve ignoring their humanity or agency. While human bodies are spatio-temporal objects, they are alive and sensitive, and not mere inanimate, passive matter. So perhaps the problem of objectification needs to be recast so that we understand there is nothing degrading about being identified with one's body (as we often do with people who are different), but rather it is degrading to have one's body treated as an inanimate, passive, fungible object.

---

29 Ann Cahill, *Overcoming Objectification: A Carnal Ethics* (New York: Routledge, 2011).

Discussion Questions

1. Is it possible for two people who have vastly different amounts of social power (due to their socioeconomic status, age, citizenship status, occupation, etc.) to have genuinely consensual sex?
2. Are there morally relevant differences between paying someone for sex and paying someone for other kinds of service?
3. Give examples of sexual seduction that fail the test of basic moral decency due to the intentions of one or more of the participants.
4. How valuable is sexual autonomy relative to other forms of autonomy?
5. Do the requirements of genuine consent and respect for another's autonomy rule out spontaneous sex between strangers (e.g., people who have just met and know very little about each other)?
6. In a racist society, can sex partners of different races avoid exoticizing each other?

Further Reading

Anderson, Scott. "On Sexual Obligation and Sexual Autonomy." *Hypatia: A Journal of Feminist Philosophy* 28 (2013): 122–41.

Bogle, Kathleen. *Hooking Up: Sex, Dating, and Relationships on Campus.* New York: NYU Press, 2008.

Cahill, Ann. *Overcoming Objectification: A Carnal Ethics.* New York: Routledge, 2011.

Coetzee, J.M. *Disgrace.* London: Vintage, 2000.

Elliston, Frederick. "In Defense of Promiscuity." In *Philosophy and Sex*, edited by Robert Baker and Frederick Elliston, 222–46. Buffalo, NY: Prometheus, 1975.

Halwani, Raja Fouad. "Are One Night Stands Morally Problematic?" *International Journal of Applied Philosophy* 10 (1995): 61–67.

Marino, Patricia. "The Ethics of Sexual Objectification: Autonomy and Consent." *Inquiry: An Interdisciplinary Journal of Philosophy* 51 (2008): 345–64.

Varden, Helga. "A Kantian Conception of Rightful Sexual Relations: Sex, (Gay) Marriage, and Prostitution." *Social Philosophy Today: Science, Technology, and Social Justice* 22 (2007): 199–218.

Chapter 4

Sex and Violence

How is sexual violence different from other forms of violence? Are the laws pertaining to sex offenses based on sound principles and informed judgments, or do they reflect society's fears and prejudices? In this chapter we will explore whether the policies we have for addressing rape, sexual harassment, and child sexual abuse are adequate, and what the consequences are of overzealous responses to, or social neglect toward, sexual assault and aggression. Philosophers are interested in defining the general contours of a just society, and this involves examining instances of social injustice and understanding the origins of unjust practices. Violent and coercive sexual acts, and our laws and practices for responding to them, provide much material for exploring the requirements of justice.

Are Laws Prohibiting Sexual Offenses Effective and Just?

According to a 2009 editorial in *The Economist*,

> America's sex-offender laws are the strictest of any rich
> democracy. Convicted rapists and child-molesters are given
> long prison sentences. When released, they are put on sex-
> offender registries. In most states this means that their names,
> photographs and addresses are published online, so that
> fearful parents can check whether a child-molester lives nearby.
> Under the Adam Walsh Act of 2006, another law named after

a murdered child, all states will soon be obliged to make their
sex-offender registries public.[1]

In the U.S., many sex-offender laws were approved in the wake of highly pub-
licized and horrific crimes involving the rape and murder of young children.
Fortunately, the crimes that have triggered many sex offender laws are relatively
rare.[2] Yet sexual assault and child sexual abuse are serious social problems in
need of well-designed social policies that can address less gruesome cases. The
latter are typically underreported by victims and the media.

One problem with current sex-offender laws is that they also apply to many
victimless and non-violent sexual offenses. As *The Economist* authors report:

> In all, 674,000 Americans are on sex-offender registries—more
> than the population of Vermont, North Dakota or Wyoming.…
> According to Human Rights Watch, at least five states require
> registration for people who visit prostitutes, 29 require it for
> consensual sex between young teenagers and 32 require it for
> indecent exposure. Some prosecutors are now stretching the
> definition of "distributing child pornography" to include teens
> who text half-naked photos of themselves to their friends.[3]

Sex-offender laws typically include statutory offenses, such as sex between a
young adult (18 or older) and a minor teenager whose consent, by law, does not
count as consent.

Given that the category of "sex offender" is considerably broad, the punishments imposed often do not fit the crimes. Some U.S. states prohibit former sex
offenders who have completed their prison sentences from living near places
where children potentially congregate, such as schools, parks, and bus stops.
Many states now publish their sex-offender registries online, with the photos and
addresses of former sex offenders, which essentially makes anyone on these lists
a social pariah, subject to social ostracism and isolation. People prosecuted for
sex offenses, including nonviolent and statutory crimes, often suffer severe and
lasting consequences, such as the loss of jobs, homes, friends, and the ability to
live anywhere within the boundaries of some cities.[4] These consequences affect
not only the offender but also his family (the vast majority of offenders are men).

---

1   "Illiberal Politics: America's Unjust Sex Laws," *The Economist*, August 6, 2009, http://
    www.economist.com/node/14165460.

2   J.S. Levenson and D.A. D'Amora, "Social Policies Designed to Prevent Sexual Violence: The
    Emperor's New Clothes?" *Criminal Justice Policy Review* 18 (2007): 168–99, http://minnesota.
    publicradio.org/features/2007/06/18_sexoffenders/emperorsclothes.pdf .

3   "Illiberal Politics." To view the lists of offenses requiring registration as a sex offender in each
    state, see Federal Bureau of Investigation, "Sex Offender Registry Websites," http://www.fbi.
    gov/scams-safety/registry/registry.

4   "Illiberal Politics"; Levenson and D'Amora, "Social Policies."

In addition to generating harsh punishments, these laws interfere with the monitoring and medical treatment of potentially dangerous sex offenders, thus failing to protect the public.[5] Because the laws apply to non-violent offenders, public resources are wasted trying to track and monitor a large population, and law-enforcement efforts are less effective at tracking potentially dangerous offenders.[6] Moreover, because the laws render it virtually impossible for past sex offenders to find places to live and work, these laws prevent the reintegration of former sex offenders into their communities, which hampers efforts to rehabilitate them and lower recidivism rates.[7]

Unfortunately, how the public responds to sex crimes depends on who the victims and perpetrators are. The long social neglect of the problem of prison rape shows that sex crimes are often overlooked when there is little public sympathy for the victims.[8] Although recently there has been increased attention to the problem of sexual assault on college campuses, the record shows that college administrations have generally failed to respond seriously to many complaints.[9] Historically, laws have ignored sexual assault when the victims were men, when the perpetrator and victim were of the same sex, or when the victim was a sex worker or any woman whose behavior was judged by others as "loose." Moreover, because many of the harms of sexual assault are psychological, they often go unacknowledged, even when they are highly debilitating to the victims. Many sexual crimes go unreported because the victims are young or frightened, suffer shame and depression, or lack knowledge of their rights and how to exercise them.[10] Moreover, many sex crimes are committed by family members and acquaintances, and this also inhibits reporting and pressing charges. The laws of most societies are especially ineffective in protecting women and children from family members and acquaintances who sexually abuse and victimize them. Unfortunately, current laws that mandate public registries and notification, and residence restrictions, do not protect vulnerable persons (typically women and children) from sexual assaults and coersion committed by relatives and friends

---

5   Levenson and D'Amora, "Social Policies."

6   For a helpful discussion of the overuse of the criminal-law system to tackle social problems, see Douglass Husak, *Overcriminalization: The Limits of the Criminal Law*, (New York: Oxford University Press, 2008).

7   Kelly K. Bonnar-Kidd, "Sex Offender Laws and Prevention of Sexual Violence or Recidivism," *American Journal of Public Health* 100 (2010): 412–19, http://www.ncbi.nlm.nih.gov/pmc/articles/PMC2820068/.

8   Dan Harris, "Prison Rape Widely Ignored by Authorities," *ABC News*, April 14, 2014, http://abcnews.go.com/WNT/story?id=131113&page=1.

9   Jennifer Steinhauer and David Joachim, "55 Colleges Named in Federal Inquiry into Handling of Sexual Assault Cases," *New York Times*, May 1, 2014, http://nyti.ms/1hhHVnh. For an overview of sexual assault statistics on college campuses, see "One in Four," http://www.oneinfourusa.org/statistics.php.

10 Often, victims do not report sex crimes to the proper authorities, such as when they report them to school or church officials rather than law-enforcement officials, or they do not report them quickly enough to allow for the collection of physical evidence.

when the former are isolated in homes where a potentially dangerous sex offender may reside.

While the laws against sexual offenses are typically ineffective in protecting vulnerable persons, they can be deployed in ways that subject nonviolent and relatively innocent persons to unjust prosecution and persecution. Under current laws, an adult but socially and sexually immature teenager who inappropriately shares a nude photo of his minor girlfriend with his friends can be (i) branded as a sex offender, (ii) serve a sentence that should be reserved for violent and dangerous criminals, and (iii) be subject to post-sentence residence and monitoring restrictions that can destroy his life.[11] Similarly, a person who patronizes a prostitute, has consensual sex with a 17-year-old when he is a young adult, exposes himself in public while drunk, or downloads free child pornography once or twice can face harsh penalties. Yet a serial rapist who is a student on a college campus often receives a fairly light punishment.[12] Do our sexual-offense laws target people who are viewed as "perverts" or pedophiles, while ignoring sexual predators who are viewed as more "normal," e.g., a college student who repeatedly "seduces" barely-legal teenagers (i.e., over 18) with drinks and then physically overpowers them?

Some U.S. jurisdictions have now passed "Romeo and Juliet laws" that reduce the penalities for statutory crimes, for example, consensual sex between teenagers.[13] However, there is still a need, in most jurisdictions, to cull substantially the list of nonviolent offenses that require registration, public notification, and residency restrictions. In general, the list should include only those kinds of offenses that led to the creation of public sex-offender registries and housing restrictions, such as child rape or aggravated sexual assaults. Registered sex offenders should be periodically reevaluated and removed from registries when they no longer pose a significant public threat.

Another needed reform is to redirect public resources toward the vigilant enforcement of court-imposed restraining orders against family members (e.g., spouses, domestic partners, parents, etc.) where there is a documented history of domestic violence and child abuse. Too often women and children are repeatedly victimized by adult family members because of the reluctance of society to intervene. Wives, girlfriends, and children are often forced to retreat to domestic-violence shelters, where they live in fear of being discovered by their abusers, while existing restraining orders remain ignored or unenforced

---

11 Deborah Feyerick and Sheila Steffen, "'Sexting' lands teen on sex offender list," CNN, April 8, 2009, http://www.cnn.com/2009/CRIME/04/07/sexting.busts/index.html. We deal with sexting more fully in Ch. 9.

12 Dave Gustafson, "Serial Rapists Commit 9 of 10 Campus Sexual Assaults, Research Finds," *AlJazeera America*, October 28, 2013, http://america.aljazeera.com/watch/shows/america-tonight/america-tonight-blog/2013/10/28/serial-rapists-commit9of10campussexualassaultsresearchfinds.html.

13 "Romeo and Juliet Law and Legal Definitions," *USLegal*, http://definitions.uslegal.com/r/romeo-and-juliet-law/.

and the abusers are free to stalk and threaten them. Similarly, rape victims on college campuses often leave school to avoid their attackers, while school administrators are reluctant to remove or punish the perpetrators.[14] And rape victims who are inmates in federal and state prisons often have little ability to avoid their abusers, while prison rapists go unpunished.[15]

Philosophers who are interested in general issues of social and political justice should ask why, especially when sex offenses are involved, our policies are so unjust. Is it because laws are often passed when there is a social disturbance, such as a horrific crime, and then politicians offer bad laws to prove they are tough on crime? Or do sex-offender laws in particular reflect a lack of social sympathy toward prisoners and women, but abundant overprotective instincts toward children, including teenagers, when it comes to sex? Do sex-offender laws reflect general social biases that favor more privileged and "respectable" citizens, such as husbands, parents, prison guards, and religious leaders, or men in general? Perhaps sex-offender laws reflect excessive public fear about crimes committed by strangers, and too little fear about those committed by acquaintances? Do sex-offender laws target people thought to be sexually and socially deviant rather than violent? Have sex crimes, historically, been handled differently from other kinds of crimes? For example, have they been regarded as crimes against a family's or woman's honor, rather than ordinary physical assaults, and therefore avenged only when sexual honor or innocence was at stake? If sex-offender laws are based on outdated notions, ignorance, or pernicious social prejudices, and if they treat people unequally for morally irrelevant reasons, then they are unjust. It will take both general philosophical inquiry into the possibly deeper sources of unjust laws, as well as empirical studies to test any given theory, in order to develop proposals for making broad changes to sex-offender policies.

Why Do Some Governments Take Steps to Eradicate Sexual Harassment?

What interests do governments protect when they adopt policies aimed at minimizing sexual harassment? Harassment of any sort, whether it is based on

---

14 Some speculate that many school officials have acted to protect the reputation of their institution at the expense of sexual assault victims. In addition to speaking out and exposing colleges that have failed to address the problem, survivors of sexual assault on college campuses are calling for a new criterion for evaluating acquaintance rape cases. The campaign, called "yes means yes," requires an alleged assailant to provide evidence of consent, rather than placing the burden of proof on the victim to show that there was a lack of consent ("no means no"). See Jessica Valenti, "Beyond 'No Means No': The Future of Campus Rape Prevention Is 'Yes Means Yes,'" Guardian, September 2, 2014, http://www.theguardian.com/commentisfree/2014/sep/02/-sp-campus-rape-prevention-yes-means-yes.

15 Over a decade ago, the Prison Rape Elimination Act (PREA), a U.S. federal law, was approved, but implementing it has proved difficult. Laura Sullivan, "Enforcing Prison Rape Elimination Standards Proves Tricky," NPR, April 2, 2014, http://www.npr.org/2014/04/02/298332579/enforcing-prison-rape-elimination-standards-proves-tricky.

another's sex, race, ethnicity, age, sexual orientation, gender expression, religion, or any arbitrary trait, is morally noxious and potentially harmful. Nevertheless, sexual harassment has come under greater scrutiny than most other forms of harassing behaviors, and employees and students today are regularly subject to sexual-harassment codes of conduct and given training so they can identify and prevent sexual harassment. So why has sexual harassment been singled out for special attention and intervention?

Sexual harassment typically involves unwelcome sexual attention, speech, and conduct in a workplace or educational setting. Theorists and policy makers who support sexual harassment policies do not all agree on why we need them. Some argue that the primary problem with sexual harassment is that it perpetuates discrimination against women. Others argue that sexual harassment is problematic because those subject to it are often robbed of their dignity and autonomy.[16] There may be other reasons for being concerned with sexual harassment, such as the inappropriateness of sexual behavior and expression in the workplace (unless, of course, the workplace is a sex-toy shop, strip club, or even the restaurant chain Hooters). Yet employers who are concerned about merely inappropriate sexual behavior in the work setting can probably find ways to satisfactorily address the problem. So in what follows, we will focus on the first two reasons offered, in order to explain how sexual harassment can rise to the level of wrongdoing that requires societal and governmental intervention.

Courts in the United States and Canada[17] treat sexual harassment as a form of sex discrimination and recognize two types: "*quid pro quo*" and "hostile environment." *Quid pro quo* harassment typically involves a person of higher authority or status in a work setting offering a job benefit in exchange for some act of sexual intimacy. Hostile environment sexual harassment generally occurs when a person is subject to a work setting that undermines that employee's or student's performance due to the prevalence of offensive or demeaning sexual speech or expressive materials. While men can be victims of both types of sexual harassment, the majority of complainants are women. Because sexual harassment can lead to the loss of jobs, promotions, and pay, and jeopardize a person's economic security, sexual harassment imposes unjustified burdens on its victims. When women constitute the large majority of the victims, then sexual harassment will perpetuate systemic and ongoing discrimination against

---

16 Elizabeth Anderson, "Rethinking Sexual Harassment: A Review Essay," *Philosophy and Public Affairs* 34, no. 3 (2006): 284–311.

17 For the situation in the U.S., see "Sexual Harassment Claims of Abusive Work Environments Under Title VII," *Harvard Law Review* 97 (1984): 1149–1469. For Canada, see Deborah Ann Campbell, "The Evolution of Sexual Harassment Case Law in Canada," Queen's University Industrial Relations Centre (1992), http://irc.queensu.ca/articles/evolution-sexual-harassment-case-law-canada.

a protected class of citizens who, historically, have been subject to social oppression and inequality.[18]

Sexual harassment can constitute a form of sexual coercion when those who perpetrate it occupy positions of power relative to their victims and engage in *quid pro quo* sexual harassment. Sexual coercion violates a person's right to liberty and self-determination, and those who endure it can suffer a loss of self-esteem. For this reason, sexual harassment robs individuals of autonomy and dignity. Hostile environment sexual harassment can also rob victims of self-respect when they are subject to public humiliation through offensive sexual behavior and expression.[19] Again, when the victims of this kind of sexual harassment are predominantly women, sexual harassment contributes to the ongoing social subordination of women.

Sexual harassment is a difficult concept to define. The concept seems to conflate two ideas: hostile or offensive behavior toward someone because of that person's *sex*, and hostile or unwelcome *sexual* behavior toward another. Some theorists have argued that workplace policies should focus on the former conception (i.e., the harassment of coworkers and subordinates, or even supervisors, because of the person's sex or gender, or gender expression). This definition of sexual harassment, some argue, better highlights the problem of overt sexism (and heterosexism) in the workplace and does not problematize all sexual expression or relationships in the workplace.[20] But this narrowing of the definition of sexual harassment ignores how sexual behaviors and relationships in the workplace can involve abuses of power and conflicts of interest that often harm the party lower in the institution's hierarchy. For this reason, sexual-harassment policies typically aim both at minimizing the degrading or offensive treatment of a coworker due to that person's sex, and at discouraging sexual relationships among parties when there is a significant conflict of interest, such as between a supervisor and subordinate.

Some critics of sexual-harassment laws argue that they are unnecessary, and that they violate ordinary due-process protections that are important to any system of justice. They go on to say that workers who have suffered some form of sexual harassment can sue their employers or coworkers under other laws. In the U.S., for example, workers can sue for breach of contract or the intentional infliction of emotional distress.[21] Other critics worry about the government's

18 Margaret Crouch, "The 'Social Etymology' of 'Sexual Harassment,'" *Journal of Social Philosophy* 29, no.3 (1998): 19–40.

19 Anderson, "Rethinking Sexual Harassment."

20 Vicki Schultz, "Reconceptualizing Sexual Harassment," *Yale Law Journal* 107 (1998), http://ssrn.com/abstract=61992. For criticism of the view that sexual harassment is a residue of patriarchal social structures, see Iddo Landau, "On the Definition of Sexual Harassment," *Australasian Journal of Philosophy* 77 (1999): 216–23.

21 Mane Hajdin, *The Law of Sexual Harassment: A Critique* (Selinsgrove, PA: Susquehanna University Press, 2002). See also Iddo Landau's review of this book in *Business Ethics Quarterly* 15 (2005): 531–36.

over-regulation of private industry and argue that sexual harassment can be addressed through voluntary self-regulation on the part of employers. These critics point out that employers have an interest in minimizing all forms of hostile and degrading behavior between employees. Therefore, the government need not impose negative sanctions on employers who fail to institute intrusive and restrictive sexual-harassment policies, according to some opponents. Instead, the government could provide employers with positive incentives to strengthen meritocratic decision-making, insure that subordinates have appropriate avenues through which to grieve workplace actions, and require managers to show just cause in regard to dismissals, demotions, or pay decisions. The adoption of such practices by employers, some argue, would go further toward eliminating the sexist treatment of women in the workplace than the practice of policing sexual behavior and expression.

Mane Hajdin argues that sexual-harassment laws permit the unjust treatment of individuals as part of a misguided attempt to rectify a social injustice. In order to limit their liability in sexual-harassment lawsuits, employers often set up quasi-judicial processes that supposedly show zero tolerance for sexual harassment. These processes sometimes give greater rights to complainants than defendants in terms of access to professional advice and appealing decisions.[22] Moreover, complainants are rarely held accountable for "frivolous" uses of the law, that is, complaints that have no basis in fact but that can be costly to the defendant in terms of time, money, and reputation. In sum, critics assert that because these policies often fail to incorporate ordinary due-process rules that protect the innocent, disgruntled employees or students can easily abuse them.

Of course, some criticisms of sexual-harassment law can be addressed by revising sexual-harassment codes so that they conform to the ordinary principles of due process. Perhaps when employers face sexual-harassment lawsuits from defendants who can successfully show that their constitutional rights have been violated, such revisions will be made. As to the redundancy of such codes, it's not clear that doing away with them is practical. While there are other avenues of redress for sexual-harassment victims, such as initiating a lawsuit, litigation is a costly way to deal with the problem, both for society and for the individuals involved. So having quasi-judicial but fair practices to mediate disputes can save time and money. Moreover, while employers have an interest in minimizing hostile and degrading behavior in the workplace, some would likely be negligent or unreasonably slow in setting up effective mechanisms for this, if doing so were completely voluntary. And lastly, critics set up a false choice between creating negative and positive incentives to eradicate sex discrimination in the workplace, as the government can do both.

Margaret Crouch points out that sexual harassment takes place on streets and buses, and in other public places, and yet sexual-harassment policies focus only on places of work (including schools). Crouch claims that lewd remarks,

---

22 Hajdin, *The Law of Sexual Harassment.*

catcalls, and other sexually explicit gestures toward women in public spaces similarly serve to perpetuate women's social subordination because they violate the normal rules of interaction between strangers. The normal rules of civil and polite behavior among strangers entail not being intrusive or not making another an object of attention, unless a special circumstance provides an opening. When women are repeatedly treated as appropriate objects for visual inspection and public commentary, women may feel exposed, uncomfortable, and possibly intimidated when out in public. Such "girl watching" behaviors by men, in groups or alone, define public spaces as male, and they send a message to women that they must tread carefully.[23]

Crouch admits that there is no clear remedy for sexual harassment in public spaces. She mentions that the EU and UN have followed the example of the U.S. in treating only workplace sexual harassment as a form of legally actionable discrimination. Where countries do have laws prohibiting harassing women in public, typically the stated purpose is to protect respectable women from insults to their supposed sexual modesty. Alternatively, some countries have established women-only buses and train cars so that women can avoid being groped in crowded spaces. Such policies do not necessarily reflect a commitment to equality and liberty for women but instead suggest a concern about protecting chaste women, who are commonly viewed as weak and vulnerable citizens.

Crouch mentions that some feminist groups have staged protests to raise public awareness about the social and political consequences of unwanted sexual attention. For example, some activists have tried turning the tables by taking pictures of sexual harassers and posting them on the Internet. Sexually harassing behaviors constitute a form of speech or expression, and generally they fall short of the criteria necessary for censoring speech, such as the likelihood of inciting violence, creating a threat to public safety, or materially damaging someone's reputation by knowingly spreading falsehoods. And, generally, sexually harassing behaviors fall short of the criteria for assaultive or stalking acts. Given this, the best response to harassing street speech may be more speech and expression, such as organizing a public protest.

In cases of workplace harassment, the employer can be held accountable for maintaining an atmosphere free of sex discrimination. But who can be held accountable for maintaining such environments on public streets, buses, or trains? In a workplace, typically the harassment must be persistent and egregious to be actionable, which means that the harasser must repeatedly engage in clearly unacceptable behavior toward the same person. But street harassment is not like this; typically one man engages in not particularly egregious behavior toward a lot of women. So even if class-action lawsuits were possible against the appropriate municipal agencies or bus companies, we might want to question whether this is the best response to rude or hostile sexist speech directed at strangers in

---

23 Margaret Crouch, "Sexual Harassment in Public Places," *Social Philosophy Today* 25 (2009): 137–48.

public places. Do we want our courts deciding what is permissible or impermissible speech directed toward a woman in a public venue, or what forms of attention a "reasonable woman" (to borrow a standard from sexual-assault cases) would welcome when she is sitting on a bus?

Crouch considers cases where it is acceptable to deviate from the normal rule of not staring at strangers. If someone is out in public in a costume, accompanied by a pet, or is engaging in attention-grabbing behavior, such as hopping, then staring at, or initiating conversation with, that person is often tolerated. But given this, some might argue that going out in public in five-inch heels and a mini-skirt is similar to wearing a costume or engaging in attention-grabbing behavior. Whereas it is virtually certain that a reasonable woman does not want to be denied a promotion or get raped, it is less certain that she does not want men to notice and comment upon the figure she cuts as she moves through the streets, even when the speech is crude and ineloquent. So it remains an open question whether prohibiting vulgar sexual attention in public would empower women, or whether it would simply empower governments to limit public speech and expression in undemocratic ways.

In 2003, the British government passed the *Antisocial Behaviour Act*, which "allows police and community support officers to issue dispersal orders to any group of two or more people, within a designated area, whose behaviour they believe is likely to cause harassment, alarm or distress to members of the public. Refusing to leave or returning to the area constitutes a criminal offence."[24] While preventing sexual harassment in public places may not have been the primary aim of this Act, conceivably such laws could be used for such purposes. Activists and scholars who are interested in finding adequate ways to address sexual harassment in public places should study the efficacy of new laws as they are put into practice, as well as whether the loss of liberty they involve is a serious problem.

Today, efforts to minimize public sexual harassment need to consider digital communication and the Internet as sites for public sexual harassment. Individuals may now find that they are subject to unwanted sexual attention when someone tags them in a group photo on a social media website. Sometimes these forms of sexual harassment escalate to online stalking, hazing, bullying, and violations of privacy that are legally actionable. For example, consensual "sexting" can turn into malicious harassment and violations of privacy when a former partner circulates the photos to third parties or on a "revenge porn" website[25] (see also Ch. 9). Because of culturally prevalent ideas about women and sexual modesty, such public and online voyeurism tends to target women and tends

---

24 "Antisocial Behaviour Act 2003," *Guardian*, January 19, 2009, http://www.theguardian.com/commentisfree/libertycentral/2008/dec/16/antisocial-behaviour-act.

25 Erica Goode, "Victims Push Laws to End Online Revenge Posts," *New York Times*, September 23, 2013, http://www.nytimes.com/2013/09/24/us/victims-push-laws-to-end-online-revenge-posts.html?smid=pl-share.

to have more devastating effects when the victims are women. Yet it is also often aimed at both men and women because of their sexual orientation or gender expression.[26] The serious and harmful consequences of hazing, bullying, stalking, threatening, or privacy-violating speech are evident, and therefore it's easier to justify restricting these, but the difficult question is when offensive sexual speech crosses the boundary and constitutes a form of bullying, stalking, and so on.

Are Sexual Assaults More Injurious than Other Kinds of Assaults?

In some societies, when a woman is raped, she may be pressured by family members to marry her rapist.[27] Although this practice seems absurd, cruel, and horribly unjust to women, is there a conception of sexual harm that helps make sense of it? Presumably the forced marriage is intended to restore both the rape victim's honor and that of her family. But how does this do so? Is this the ultimate case of blaming the victim? Why does an act of rape dishonor the victim and her family, rather than the rapist? One way to make sense of this practice is to assume that the victim's honor is equated with her virginity, which when lost (even through rape) robs her of her honor and good standing and renders her unmarriageable (to men other than the rapist). She is now socially "ruined," and therefore the rapist can now mitigate the symbolic and social harm done to her and her family by marrying his victim. However, through marriage, the rapist gains legitimate sexual access to his victim, and the victim enters a potentially lifelong arrangement with the man who has raped her and to whom she is now expected to submit sexually.

By the standards of a society that values individual happiness and autonomy, the above system for addressing sexual assault does not properly punish perpetrators, and it further victimizes victims by sentencing them to a life of forced sexual servitude. But for a society that values family honor, female chastity, and marital status more than individual happiness and freedom (and where the idea of women's sexual autonomy may seem absurd), the forced marriage of a rapist and his victim is at least intelligible, if highly problematic.

When women's fundamental and equal rights to sexual autonomy, bodily integrity, and personal happiness are recognized, then sexual assault is a wrong committed against individual women. David Archard argues that rape is

---

26 For example, see "Tyler Clementi," *New York Times*, http://topics.nytimes.com/top/reference/timestopics/people/c/tyler_clementi/index.html.

27 Delia Lloyd, "Marrying Your Rapist: A New Low in Women's Rights in Morocco," *Washington Post*, March 21, 2012, http://www.washingtonpost.com/blogs/she-the-people/post/marrying-your-rapist-a-new-low-in-womens-rights-in-morocco/2012/03/19/gIQAEC27RS_blog.html. See also Morgan McDaniel, "From Morocco to Denmark: Rape Survivors around the World Are Forced to Marry Attackers," *Women's Media Center*, May 2, 2013, http://www.womenundersiegeproject.org/blog/entry/from-morocco-to-denmark-rape-survivors-around-the-world-are-forced-to-marry; Kalpana Sharma, "Should a Woman Marry Her Rapist?" *The Times of India*, October 28, 2010, http://timesofindia.indiatimes.com/life-style/relationships/man-woman/Should-a-woman-marry-her-rapist/articleshow/6558340.cms.

"seriously wrongful, in as much as rape is an indefensible harming of a legitimate interest in safeguarding what is central to our personhood."[28] According to Archard, "our interests in our sexual bodily integrity and in our sexual self-determination are at the heart of our being. Sex and sexuality are central to who we are. … To put things all too bluntly and simply, … rape is very wrongful for violating what we are."[29] Archard's view explains why rape is a serious offense—even in a society in which a woman's honor is not dependent on maintaining her virginity. In any society, sexual assaults are acts that can redefine who we are, given how important "sexual bodily integrity" is to our understanding of ourselves. Archard argues that the loss of sexual bodily integrity and autonomy occurs whenever sex is nonconsensual, whether or not the assault was experienced as painful, and whether or not it was accompanied by physical force or other forms of battery. If sex is nonconsensual, the victim suffers a loss of control over her body, sexuality, and freedom, which can be experienced as terrifying, humiliating, or not much at all if the victim is not fully conscious or too young to understand what is being done to her.

Archard's account of the wrongfulness of rape focuses less on how the victim experienced the act or whether she attempted to ward off her attacker, and focuses more on the perpetrator's failure to obtain consent. If courts were to adopt this understanding of rape, then the only relevant evidence needed to prove a rape would be evidence about whether the sexual act was performed with or without consent.[30] The use of physical force by an assailant, or evidence of physical injuries on the victim, would only be relevant to proving aggravated rape, not rape itself. Archard's account recognizes that not all acts of rape are the same: some acts involve physical force and some involve only verbal threats; some are more brutal in terms of the physical injuries inflicted, the degree of force used, and the subsequent trauma to the victims; some victims are conscious and some are unconscious during a rape; some rapes are committed by strangers, and some by acquaintances, spouses, or other relatives. All of these factors may be relevant to deciding what additional charges to bring against the accused, and what forms of punishment to impose, if the defendant is found guilty. But the basic wrong of rape involves violating another's right to sexual bodily integrity and autonomy through nonconsensual sex, however it is accomplished.

If we define rape as nonconsensual sexual acts, then we need to provide some criteria for judging when a sexual act is nonconsensual. Courts today usually

---

28 David Archard, "The Wrong of Rape," *The Philosophical Quarterly* 57 (2007): 390.

29 Ibid.

30 In many U.S. jurisdictions now, sexual assault is legally defined as the penetration of a bodily orifice of another person with one's body part or other object without consent. See, for example, Federal Bureau of Investigation, "Frequently Asked Questions about the Change in the UCR Definition of Rape," May 20, 2013, http://www.fbi.gov/about-us/cjis/ucr/recent-program-updates/new-rape-definition-frequently-asked-questions. In some jurisdictions, rape is still conceptualized as an act involving physical force.

judge that the victim did not give consent in the following kinds of situations: if the victim was in an incompetent state (due to intoxication, mental disability, or age); if the victim was threatened with a weapon or potential physical injury; if the victim conveyed in words or body language a denial of consent; and if a victim's withholding of consent was ignored or overcome by the use of physical force. A more unclear case of nonconsensual sex might involve a victim who is threatened, not with immediate physical injury, but with a future harm to herself or her loved ones, or with a nonphysical form of injury, such as the loss of a job or some form of public humiliation. While such a threat is coercive, it may not rise to the level of coercion that counts as a sexual assault, if the victim appears to have had the ability to flee.[31] In the past, some courts have considered a victim's sexual history, her clothing, her location, or whether she was in a romantic or sexual relationship with the accused to determine whether a sexual act was consensual. Feminist activists have long fought for legal reform in order to change practices that blamed the victims of sexual assaults.[32]

As with many kinds of crimes, the motive and mindset of the accused are also considered by courts in order to judge what kind of act took place and the degree of guilt. Was the accused in an incompetent state (due to intoxication, mental disability, or age)? Did the accused intend to sexually assault his victim, was it a premeditated assault, or did the accused act only with negligence or recklessness toward the complainant? Moreover, did the sexual assault occur in the midst of another crime, such as a kidnapping or robbery? A less clear case may be when an accused wrongly but sincerely believes his victim's resistance or denial of consent does not express her true desires, but merely disguises her true and opposite desires, for which she may be ashamed. Many feminists have argued that this should not be a permissible legal defense.[33]

---

31 For an interesting discussion of this question, and of how sexual harassment and sexual assault both involve abuses of social power, see Michal Buchhandler-Raphael, "The Failure of Consent: Re-conceptualizing Rape as Sexual Abuse of Power," *Michigan Journal of Gender and Law* 18 (2011): 147–228, http://repository.law.umich.edu/cgi/viewcontent. cgi?article=1014&context=mjgl. Recent revelations about sexual assault in the U.S. military suggest that sexual harassment and sexual assault are closely connected, and that "sexual assault, whether in the military or in civilian life, is solely about the abuse of power, about control and domination." Michael F. Matthews, "The Untold Story of Military Sexual Assault," *New York Times*, November 24, 2013, http://www.nytimes.com/2013/11/25/opinion/the-untold-story-of-military-sexual-assault.html?smid=pl-share.

32 Rebecca Whisnant, "Feminist Perspectives on Rape," *Stanford Encyclopedia of Philosophy* (2013), http://plato.stanford.edu/entries/feminism-rape/.

33 Ibid. See especially the work of Lois Pineau. Camille Paglia has criticized "'No' means no" feminist anti-rape campaigns: "It's ridiculous to think that saying no always means no. We all know how it goes in the heat of the moment; it's 'no' now, it's 'maybe' later, and it changes again." *Sex, Art, and American Culture: Essays* (New York: Vintage, 1992), 58. For responses to Paglia, see Jaclyn Friedman and Jessica Valenti, *Yes Means Yes: Visions of Female Sexual Power and a World without Rape* (Berkeley, CA: Seal Press, 2008); and Charlene Muehlenhard, "Examining Stereotypes about Token Resistance to Sex," *Psychology of Woman Quarterly* 35 (2011): 676–83.

As with many crimes, there are often no third-party witnesses. And even when there is physical evidence that sex between two people occurred, through the collection of semen and a DNA test, there might be little tangible evidence regarding whether the act involved threats of physical force and harm that prevented the victim from fleeing. How should courts weigh a victim's testimony that she believed she would be harmed if she did not cooperate? If the accused is a complete stranger to the complainant, and the complainant is a credible witness, should physical evidence of sex be enough to win a conviction? When acts of rape are prosecuted under criminal law, the standards of proof are typically quite high. For this reason, it is often quite difficult to get a conviction for a rape in court, and many rapes go unreported because of this. Moreover, many are unreported due to the shame and fear of retaliation that victims often experience when reporting a rape. Yet there need to be safeguards in place to protect the innocent against false allegations, which is why the standards of proof need to remain high. In the U.S., many black men have been wrongly accused of rape by white women and then convicted due to racist prejudices and fears on the part of juries and judges.

While boys and men can be raped, the vast majority of rape victims are girls and women. Because the majority of victims are female, the prevalence of rape in a community has indirect effects, such as making the majority of women and girls feel insecure about their physical safety. These feelings of insecurity are often exacerbated by the prevalence of sexually harassing behaviors that fall short of physical violence. In some cities around the world, women have organized "Take Back the Night" marches in order to draw attention to and protest societal toleration for rape, often shown by the failure to respect the right of women and girls to personal security. In societies that tolerate rape, women lack safe access to public spaces and cannot participate fully in public life. In the U.S., these protest marches are often organized annually on college campuses and have done much to raise awareness about the problems of date and acquaintance rape.

Is Cyber-rape a Form of Sexual Assault, Sexual Harassment, or Offensive Speech?

Writing in *The Village Voice* in 1993, Julian Dibbell described a virtual rape that occurred at LambdaMOO, "an object-oriented MUD."[34] A MUD is a multi-user dungeon in which participants invent online personas (avatars) and role-play in real time, often through text messages. The cyber-rape occurred when one avatar was able to make several other avatars perform somewhat perverse sexual acts against their will that were viewable to the other participants. While sex among avatars is common in cyberspace, cyber-rape involves virtual sex without consent.

---

34 Julian Dibbell, "A Rape in Cyberspace," *Village Voice*, December 23, 1993, http://www.juliandibbell.com/texts/bungle_vv.html.

Surprisingly (or perhaps not), the virtual victims and their RL (real life) authors in the LambdaMOO attack reported that they experienced genuine (not merely virtual) emotional trauma from the breach of civility involved. In the weeks following the attack, according to Dibbell, the members of LambdaMOO held meetings to discuss the incident. They ultimately succeeded in getting the perpetrator banished from this online community, or at least until he managed to return in the form of another avatar.

Dibbell chronicles the community's struggle to define the crime committed by one of its members and to develop an appropriate sanction. One issue is whether nonconsensual virtual sex counts as a form of rape. Does it trivialize the crime of rape to describe nonconsensual cybersex as cyber-rape? Is anybody really forced to do anything, since the RL "victims" can simply sign off? What seemed to make the LambdaMOO incident humiliating to its RL victims is that other players could observe these virtual assaults on their avatars. Moreover, unlike other online communities and games where cyber-violence and aggression are tolerated and expected, LambdaMOO is a non-violent utopian community with rules of civility that reflect the norms of conduct in real life. If nonconsensual cybersex represents a serious breach of civility and the established norms of this community, then is the punishment of preventing the offending avatar from participating in the community appropriate and fair? Was the punishment too harsh, or did it not go far enough?

Role-playing via avatars is one way to explore one's sexual fantasies, including fantasies that involve antisocial, violent, and dangerous behaviors that would not be tolerated in real life. Indeed, one could argue that it is healthy to explore such fantasies in a safe environment, that is, a context in which pursuing one's fantasies will cause little, if any, harm. Did the enacted fantasy of the LambdaMOO assailant harm anyone? It did cause emotional distress to some of the other MUD users, and, in real life, the intentional infliction of emotional distress is recognized as a crime in some jurisdictions. Nevertheless, the incident here would probably not meet the standards of proof required in most legal contexts, due to the difficulty of ascertaining the accused's intent and to the amorphous nature of the harm here. Would a reasonable person be distressed by an offense committed against her online persona, to which she is only anonymously connected? Perhaps this depends on the relationship between an individual and her avatar. How meaningful and important is this relationship, even if the avatar is a work of the imagination? Dibbell writes, "Since rape can occur without any physical pain or damage, I found myself reasoning, then it must be classed as a crime against the mind." [35] The implication is that cyber-rape is similarly a crime against the mind: against the mind of the person whose avatar is attacked.

Consider a case of an author who uses a so-called "pen name" and publishes a book. Suppose another writer publishes a lewd and vulgar review of the book, in which he conjures up an image of someone defecating on the book.

---

35 Ibid.

Further, suppose the book author finds reading the review to be emotionally distressful. A book is a work of the mind or imagination that is closely identified with its author. Has this author been harmed in a way that requires punishing the person who perpetrated the harm? Because the reviewer's act involved only throwing around a bunch of words, imposing a punishment in this kind of case would probably violate the book reviewer's right to freedom of speech. In a democracy, we tolerate many forms of speech, including offensive speech, and we limit speech only when there is a proven link between a speech act and a material harm (i.e., where there is "a clear and present danger," such as inciting an act of violence).[36] A lewd book review and the virtual sexual assault of an avatar do not rise to the level of harm that typically justifies restricting speech, though this does not rule out lesser sanctions, such as the social ostracism that followed the LambdaMOO incident.

But perhaps social ostracism and community banishment are still too harsh. Dibbell reports a meeting in which the perpetrator showed up and was interrogated by other online community members about his motives. He was apparently unable to make them coherent or to engage the sympathy of the others present, and some afterwards viewed him as a psychopath or sociopath. Would a better community have tried to rehabilitate this individual? Perhaps most efforts at rehabilitation would exhaust the resources or patience of an online community. Moreover, any efforts to reintegrate the guilty could make their victims feel as if their well-being and dignity were not being respected.

Dibbell points out that some of the women who participate in online role-playing have experienced real rape in real life, and cyber-rape could extend the trauma of RL experiences. Because most women feel threatened by the possibility of rape, given that the vast majority of the victims are female, role-playing that involves violent and explicit sexual *content* without the consent of other participants may have a different impact on women players. For instance, the failure to punish or prevent nonconsensual cybersex could discourage women from participating in online games and communities. If women and girls were to participate in lower numbers in MUDs, MOOs, and so on, this could have RL consequences, such as discouraging women and girls from considering careers in computer and informational technology fields. Given this, should the sponsors of online communities be required to take steps to prevent cyber-rape, because such conduct involves *de facto* gender discrimination and exclusion?

Alternatively, should we just expect women and girls to put up with the rough play of men and boys if they expect to fully participate in public life? Should women fight cyber-rape with creative and bold virtual actions, rather than pursuing regulation in the form of community rules that banish cyber-rapists (or company rules that instruct webmasters to terminate the accounts of violators)? Perhaps potential victims could develop virtual weapons that would

---

36 "The 'Clear and Present Danger' Test," *Exploring Constitutional Conflicts*, http://law2.umkc.edu/faculty/projects/ftrials/conlaw/clear&pdanger.htm.

allow them to virtually imprison or torture their assailants. On the frontier of the Internet, maybe we should expect only frontier justice.

One could argue, however, that cyber-rape is a more serious act than other virtual attacks, or writing a lewd book review, in that, to recall Archard, it violates who or what we are. It is not just a crime against the mind, but also a crime against the self. Maintaining control over our bodies and their sexual expression, including our avatar bodies, is critical for maintaining a healthy self-image and self-respect. This is different from maintaining control over the products of our bodies and minds, such as a book.[37] Our real and avatar bodies might survive a shooting, a beating, or a rape, but there is more long-lasting and serious damage to the self when an act of violence involves rape. If the damage and suffering to a RL self, which is attached to a particular avatar, is significant and enduring when someone else takes control over that person's avatar and forces it to perform a sexual act, then cyber-rape may need to be treated more seriously than other forms of violent role-playing. So the termination of the offender's account by a powerful webmaster, as happened eventually in the LambdaMOO case, is perhaps justified.

Cyber-rape can, of course, become more serious in two types of cases: when the RL players behind the avatars are known to each other, and when the interaction moves offline into real life. The perpetrator of the LambdaMOO incident was evidently a university student. Suppose he happened to know the RL identity of the players attached to the avatars that his avatar assaulted. Moreover, suppose those players were also students at his university. In this situation, the perpetrator's actions could be a form of sexual harassment. What may differ here from ordinary cases of sexual harassment is that the victim can more easily remove herself from the hostile situation without giving up her job or access to

---

37 Before the age of the Internet, there was another controversy over a public virtual rape. *The Nation* published a book review by Carlin Romano in which he imagines himself (and also a fantasy character) raping the author of the book he is reviewing: Catharine MacKinnon. Romano's aim was to illustrate the distinction between real acts of rape and representations of rape, and thereby to show the absurdity of MacKinnon's views about pornography, in which she often conflates the real and the imaginary. Perhaps not surprisingly, MacKinnon alleged that Romano's words constituted a form of public rape. In fairness, both Romano and MacKinnon seem to be overlooking some aspects of Romano's speech act. Romano's public and facetious rape fantasy about a real (and not fictional) person could, in another context, amount to a form of sexual harassment. MacKinnon, who successfully led efforts to make sexual harassment legally actionable, should have more accurately described Romano's speech as a potential case of sexually harassing conduct in a public forum, for which there was then (and still now) no proper legal redress. While readers of *The Nation* would surely recognize Romano's expressed rape fantasy as an attempt to make a serious intellectual point, in a different context Romano's speech could reasonably be understood as a threat and thereby discourage its target from fully participating in public life. Yet, by calling Romano's speech act "rape," MacKinnon suggests that, even in its appropriate context, such speech should be censored and writers like Romano presumably criminally prosecuted, which is absurd. David Streitfeld, "Does Rape in Words Equal Rape in Deed?: Media: a critic's blunt reply to author Catharine MacKinnon's assertion that 'to say it is to do it' ignites a furor over fact and fantasy," *Los Angeles Times*, January 5, 1994, http://articles.latimes.com/1994-01-05/news/vw-8761_1_catharine-mackinnon.

an education. But why should the victim have to remove herself from an activity she finds worthwhile simply because another participant is engaging in wrongful behavior? Shouldn't the person engaging in the wrongful behavior be made to cease or desist? It seems reasonable for university codes of conduct to prohibit nonconsensual cybersex in such cases, and to impose sanctions.

In cases where an online player intends to take the interaction with another player offline, then any form of deception or coercion can become more serious. Some writers use the term "cyber-rape" for a form of stalking that begins online and eventually ends in a real-life rape. Such assaults are better described as a form of crime in which the perpetrator uses the Internet to identify potential victims. These are not virtual or fantasy assaults but real assaults, and they should be punished as real crimes.

Another form of cyber-rape occurs when players agree to role-play a rape scene in virtual reality. In this case, the rape fantasy is acted out with the consent of all parties, and therefore, technically, it is not nonconsensual virtual sex. Such activities might be classified as a form of BDSM, a practice that will be discussed in Ch. 12. Virtual BDSM, like the RL versions, typically involves *informed* consent and allows participants to stop the action or exit a scene whenever they so choose. In virtual BDSM, exiting a scene should be as easy as signing out. What counts as informed consent is somewhat more difficult, as virtual and RL sexual partners do not always discuss every detail of the acts they will perform. In virtual reality, the standards for informed consent probably do not need to be set very high, given that the role-playing does not involve real bodies or, potentially, real physical injuries, and given that players can exit the action quite easily. In RL BDSM, this is not necessarily the case if, for example, bondage is practiced, or spanking with paddles and whips. In RL BDSM, dominants generally get to know their submissives' desires before inflicting real bodily pain or using restraints. In virtual BDSM, perhaps a general outline of the online actions one would like to explore should be discussed beforehand. One gamer emphasizes that any negotiation should make it clear that it is acceptable to say "no," and no pressure tactics should be used; otherwise it is not genuine consent.[38]

Is Rape a Byproduct or a Weapon of War?

In civil and world wars throughout human history, hundreds of thousands of female civilians have been raped.[39] Are mass rapes a consequence of the social

---

38 Shataina, "The Inevitably-Named 'Rape in RPGs'" *GameGrene*, March 22, 2005, http://www.gamegrene.com/node/447.

39 Robin Schott, "War Rape, Natality and Genocide," *Journal of Genocide Research* 13 (2011): 5–21; Claudia Card, "Rape as a Weapon of War," *Hypatia* 11 (1996): 5–18; Sally Scholz, "Just War Theory, Crimes of War, and War Rape," *International Journal of Applied Philosophy* 20 (2006): 143–57; Debra Bergoffen, "Exploiting the Dignity of the Vulnerable Body: Rape as a Weapon of War," *Philosophical Papers* 38 (2011): 307–25; Liz Philipose, "The Laws of War and Women's Human Rights," *Hypatia* 11 (1996): 46–62.

breakdown and lawlessness that often ensue in contexts of military conflict? Is sexual access to the enemy's women an understood part of the spoils of war? Or is the mass rape of an enemy's female population a calculated strategy and policy in war, aimed at demoralizing, terrorizing, or destroying the society of one's opponents? Recent scholarship on mass rapes during or after armed conflict has explored the latter hypothesis. As a tool or weapon of war, mass rape is a crime committed against a group, as well as violence directed toward specific individuals.

Most political philosophers and ethicists view mass rape as an illegitimate weapon of war, similar to the use of biological weapons or torture. In some cases, mass rape may be part of a project of genocide or ethnic cleansing, by culturally contaminating the reproductive organs of the enemy's women and their offspring, and by severing raped women from their communities. Some theorists see mass rape not only as *similar* to the use of biological weapons or torture, but as an *actual form* of biological warfare and torture. For example, Claudia Card argues that sperm, in the context of genocidal rape, is a biological weapon. Building on the work of Beverly Allen, Card writes,

> the use of sperm as a weapon fits the conception of biological warfare that is found in international documents in that a product of a living organism (the rapist) is used to attack a biological system (the reproductive system) in members of the enemy population. Although this attack need not produce illness, it is designed to produce social chaos. It surely succeeded in Bosnia-Herzegovina. Sperm need not carry the HIV virus or other STDs in order to be toxic. It need not harm the reproductive system, considered from a physiological point of view. But it surely does use the reproductive system against the people. Sperm so used becomes a social and psychological toxin, poisoning the futures of victims and their communities by producing children who, if they survive, will remind whoever raises them of their traumatic origins in torture.[40]

In 2001, the International Criminal Tribunal for the Former Yugoslavia agreed, at least in part, with this analysis and found three Bosnian Serb soldiers guilty of "crimes against humanity" for their role in the mass rapes of Bosnian Muslim women and girls.[41] Crimes against humanity are recognized in international law as especially atrocious acts, often committed against unarmed civilians or prisoners, and typically with government approval or backing. Organizing death or

---

40 Claudia Card, "The Paradox of Genocidal Rape Aimed at Enforced Pregnancy," *The Southern Journal of Philosophy* 46 (2008): 187.

41 Debra Bergoffen, "From Genocide to Justice: Women's Bodies as a Legal Writing Pad," *Feminist Studies* 32 (2006): 11–37.

rape camps, torturing prisoners, intentionally causing mass starvation, the mass slaughter of civilians, and deploying biological weapons and other weapons of mass destruction—all of these count as crimes against humanity.

Robin Schott writes that mass rape is a form of torture "in which sexual difference becomes used as an instrument of torture. In this case, torture involves the sexual violation of women's bodies and the violent use of their reproductive capacities."[42] Mass rape sometimes serves as a tool of political domination and colonization, when invading forces deploy it to subjugate a population and cause social chaos and demoralization. It serves to demoralize the male soldiers of the opposing side, who then feel powerless to protect their wives and children. Moreover, because of the severe trauma that rape and forced pregnancy cause, they can perpetuate psychological and social harms that last for generations.[43] Forced impregnation and childbearing represent the power of an invading group to exploit and colonize the human resources of the conquered group. Impregnated women and their children are often rejected by their communities, and they suffer from feelings of shame and humiliation as well as severe deprivation and bodily harm. Viewing mass rape as a weapon of war, rather than as an unavoidable consequence of war, should inform international governing bodies that are creating international courts and laws, so that these institutions can respond adequately to such mass atrocities.

Is Manipulative Sexual Seduction Fair Play?

Sometimes a person (often a man) will engage in deception in order to get a woman to agree to have sex. For example, suppose a man makes a false promise (a promise he does not intend to keep) to a woman he is dating (e.g., committing to marriage or to a sexually exclusive relationship) in order to get her to agree to have sex. If this man is the woman's employer or teacher, and he promises her a promotion or good evaluation in order to induce her to have sex, this would be *quid pro quo* sexual harassment. But outside of the workplace, when people manipulate others in order to induce them to perform a sexual act, there are few formal sanctions. Making false promises and emotionally manipulating another are, in most situations, not illegal. There may be informal sanctions, such as the loss of friends and reputational damage, but otherwise no laws are broken when a person sexually seduces another by using deception. Even in cases where the manipulative tactics are cruel, there are rarely formal sanctions: for example, when a man feigns interest in an inexperienced or emotionally vulnerable woman in order to get her into bed, when he is only doing so to win a bet with a friend.

The difficult issue in these cases is whether the person seduced has truly consented to sex if she has done so under false pretenses or by emotional manipulation.

---

42 Robin Schott, "Natality and Destruction," in *Birth, Death, and Femininity: Philosophies of Embodiment*, ed. R. Schott, 61 (Bloomington: Indiana University Press, 2010).

43 Ibid.

If she has not truly consented, then the act could be viewed as a form of rape, and some victims certainly feel used and abused in ways similar to survivors of rape. The question here is whether the use of deceit, fraud, emotional manipulation, or nonviolent threats in order to seduce another vitiates the latter's consent. Suppose a person threatens to break up with her partner if he or she does not agree to have sex? Or suppose a person threatens to expose another's secret if he or she does not agree to have sex? Sarah Conly argues that our moral categories are too black and white with regard to sexual wrongs. We need to acknowledge shades of gray, when it comes to sexual wrongdoing, and not classify all sexual wrongs as "rape." Conly suggests that to categorize aggressive seduction as rape can trivialize the wrongs done to victims of actual rape, but to treat aggressive seduction as non-rape, and therefore acceptable, fails to acknowledge some level of wrongdoing.[44]

In cases of manipulative seduction, the victim typically has some choices that are not open to victims of rape. Moreover, we might expect adults not to be easily duped and, therefore, not to believe automatically what they are told, even by lovers and close friends. While adults can be gullible and emotionally dependent, we expect them to be somewhat savvy and able to discern the motives and aims of others.[45] It's at least arguable that, if people agree to sex under false pretenses, they nevertheless have agreed to sex, as long as they have genuine alternative options, such as refusing sex or first investigating their partner's claims and motives. Therefore, policies that aim to protect adult women and men from unscrupulous seducers could legitimately be viewed as paternalistic and overprotective.[46] Nevertheless, as Scott Anderson points out, we should be sensitive to cases where the social power imbalance between women and men is such that a woman's alternatives can be rather dire. For example, in societies where women are economically dependent on men, refusing sex could lead to a loss of support and extreme poverty.[47] Yet some power hierarchies that exist outside work or educational institutions may need to be dealt with by reforming marriage policies and other structural inequalities, and not just policies regarding sex.

There is a concept in the law of "rape by deception," and several years ago there was a controversial case in Israel involving a Jewish woman and a man

44 Sarah Conly, "Seduction, Rape, and Coercion," *Ethics* 115 (2004): 96–121.

45 A "Let the buyer beware" approach to deceptive sexual seduction can be found in Alan Wertheimer's *Consent to Sexual Relations* (Cambridge: Cambridge University Press, 2003). See also Stephen Kershnar's review of Wertheimer, *Notre Dame Philosophical Reviews*, February 3, 2004, http://ndpr.nd.edu/news/23677-consent-to-sexual-relations/.

46 Douglas Husak considers the following case: "A and B are dating. A makes advances. B says, 'I don't want to go further unless you really care about me.' A says that he does, but later tells mutual friends that he was lying. However much we might blame A for his deception, do we really want to say that it renders B's consent invalid? Has A proceeded without B's valid consent? Should A's conduct be criminalized? Few commentators would go this far" (278). D. Husak, "The Complete Guide to Consent to Sex: Alan Wertheimer's *Consent to Sexual Relations*," *Law and Philosophy* 25 (2006): 267–87.

47 Scott Anderson, "Sex under Pressure: Jerks, Boorish Behavior, and Gender Hierarchy," *Res Publica* 11 (2005): 349–69.

who allegedly presented "himself as a Jewish bachelor available for a romantic relationship, whereas in fact he was a Muslim and a married father of two."[48] In Ch. 10, we will consider the forms of transparency between sex partners that should be morally and, perhaps, legally required. The problem with criminalizing sexual acts that involve deception, and calling them "rape," is that we give people the ability to bring criminal charges in cases that fall into morally gray areas, as Conly suggests. Also, we give the courts the power to mete out harsh punishments in ways that can reflect ethnic and other prejudices about who can be appropriate sex partners, as the Israeli case shows. Drawing the line between immoral behavior and criminal wrongdoing is philosophically complex, and not only with respect to sexual conduct. People can manipulate others to take risks with their money or health in ways that cause genuine harms, and yet not violate any laws—for example, by enticing others to get involved with risky investment schemes or take drugs.

Some political and legal theorists are investigating ways to address the gray areas of wrongdoing without criminal prosecution. For example, some have proposed using civil lawsuits in cases of some sexual assaults and malicious, coercive seduction.[49] A preventative (rather than reactive) approach can involve mobilizing public education campaigns aimed at increasing public awareness of the problems caused by coercive sex. In response to government pressure to do a better job handling sexual-assault complaints, colleges and universities are developing more explicit rules about what counts as genuine consent to sex in their institutional codes of conduct, and making students and staff aware of these new standards.[50] Pre-college sex education programs could do more to teach children social skills that would enable them to avoid unwanted sex, as well as the skill of negotiating consensual and mutually desired sex. Another somewhat bold approach involves survivors publicly "outing" date rapists and others who engage in predatory, manipulative seduction, in order to deter and not simply punish potential perpetrators.[51] Such an approach would only work in communities in which women are already somewhat empowered so they need not fear retaliation for exposing the identities of men who engage in immoral and manipulative, but not criminal, sexual practices. Finally, in societies that celebrate and valorize "Don Juan" figures through their expressive culture and social norms, victims of

---

48 Dina Newman, "Unraveling the Israeli Arab 'Rape by Deception' Case," BBC News, September 17, 2010, http://www.bbc.co.uk/news/world-middle-east-11329429.

49 Ellen Bublick, "Civil Tort Actions Filed by Victims of Sexual Assault: Promise and Perils," National Online Resource Center on Violence Against Women (2011), http://www.vawnet.org/applied-research-papers/print-document.php?doc_id=2150.

50 Tovia Smith, "A Campus Dilemma: Sure, 'No' Means 'No,' but Exactly What Means 'Yes'?" NPR, June 13, 2014, http://www.npr.org/2014/06/13/321677110/a-campus-dilemma-sure-no-means-no-but-exactly-what-means-yes.

51 Malia Schilling, "Outing a Rapist," Ms. Blog, April 10, 2013, http://msmagazine.com/blog/2013/04/10/outing-a-rapist/.

such men and their allies will need to create new kinds of expressive works that expose the unattractive and cruel nature of manipulative seduction.

Another gray area, morally and legally, is the sexual seduction of a child by another child. Although sex between children may not meet the legal standards of consent, are there circumstances where sexual intimacy between children meets minimal moral standards of consent?[52] For example, in a case where two children are roughly equal in terms of physical, social, and emotional maturity, and where both children seem interested in sexual exploration with each other, does either engage in moral wrongdoing? If one child takes the lead and initiates some kind of sexual touching, is that child a manipulative seducer, given the inexperience and vulnerability of the other child? Do children have sexual rights, for example, the right to information about sex appropriate to their level of understanding, as well as the right to engage in some level of sexual intimacy with socially equal and willing (though underage) friends, such as kissing and intimate touching? Do parents have absolute authority over what their child can learn or do sexually, or is a parent's authority limited by a child's right to sexual information and bodily control? Some parents might view a sexual act between two sixteen-year-olds differently than one between two seven-year-olds, but specifying what is sexually appropriate or acceptable at each age level, or what is an acceptable age difference among sexually active children, is quite challenging and extremely controversial. Nevertheless, it is important to address such questions so that children are not unfairly punished by adults or prosecuted under the law for statutory crimes in cases of tolerable and relatively harmless sexual behaviors. In Ch. 7, we will explore more issues involving sex and children.

---

52 The sexual seduction of a child by an adult is unacceptably manipulative because of the inequality between the adult and child in terms of social authority, experience, and knowledge. Deciding when a minor should be held to adult standards for an offense raises difficult issues in regard to sex crimes, as well as with other kinds of offenses. We might question, though, whether a harsh and punitive response to sexual activities between children of comparable maturity may be more damaging than the activities themselves.

Discussion Questions

1. Under what circumstances should a person be criminally prosecuted for "sexting"?
2. Are the sex-offender laws in your society overly harsh? Explain why or why not.
3. If a man is sexually harassed at work, is this a form of sex discrimination?
4. How are gender harassment and sexual harassment interconnected, but also separate, problems? Give examples.
5. When does an act of aggressive seduction cross the line and become a sexual assault?
6. Is "cyber-rape" a serious social problem?
7. How is the mass rape of an enemy population similar to, and different from, the use of biological weapons?
8. What is the difference between using strong persuasive tactics to get someone to have sex and manipulative seduction?

Further Reading

Alcoff, Linda Martín. "Then and Now." *Journal of Speculative Philosophy: A Quarterly Journal of History, Criticism, and Imagination* 26, no. 2 (2012): 268–78.

Cahill, Ann J. "Foucault, Rape, and the Construction of the Feminine Body." *Hypatia: A Journal of Feminist Philosophy* 15, no. 1 (2000): 43–63.

Du Toit, Louise. "Sexual Specificity, Rape Law Reform and the Feminist Quest for Justice." *South African Journal of Philosophy* 31, no. 3 (2012): 465–83.

Haddad, Heidi Nichols. "Mobilizing the Will to Prosecute: Crimes of Rape at the Yugoslav and Rwandan Tribunals." *Human Rights Review* 12, no. 1 (2011): 109–32.

Rocha, James. "The Sexual Harassment Coercive Offer." *Journal of Applied Philosophy* 28, no. 2 (2011): 203–16.

Chapter 5

Sexual Perversion and Sodomy Laws

In this chapter, we examine some sexual activities that have been and continue to be thought of as "atypical" and/or "unnatural" in some way. Philosophers are interested in exploring the basis for categorizing particular sexual behaviors as 'deviant' or 'perverse,' and the moral implications and social consequences of these attributions. Are unnatural acts wrong, and should those who commit them be criminally prosecuted or forced to seek psychiatric treatment? Because our judgments about the naturalness or normality of sexual conduct can significantly influence how we treat people, it is important to determine if these judgments are defensible or based on social prejudice.

How Do We Distinguish "Normal," Weird, Unnatural, Perverted, and Harmful Sex?[1]

Notions of sexual perversions have a long history in philosophy, dating back at least to those two pillars of Western thought: Plato (424/23–348/47 BCE) and

---

1   Parts of this section were published previously in R.S. Stewart, "Constructing Perversions: The DSM and the Classification of the Sexual Paraphilias and Disorders," *Electronic Journal of Human Sexuality* 15 (2012), http://www.ejhs.org/volume15/DSM.html, and R.S. Stewart, *(continued)*

Aristotle (384–322 BCE). The position advanced by Aristotle has been particularly influential. Aristotle thought that all events have what he called a "final cause," which he described as the thing or state toward which an action is aimed.[2] For example, my walking to the fridge is aimed at getting a drink to quench my thirst, or my getting in my car is aimed at driving to work. Such a conception of things is called a teleological view, from the Greek root *telos*, which means end or goal or purpose. While it is quite common to think of human action as teleological, as is the case in the two examples above, Aristotle went much further than this and claimed that *all* events had a *telos*. Hence, rain falling or the sun shining must, according to Aristotle, have a *telos* or purpose (e.g., to allow crops to grow). Aristotle also believed that humans themselves had a *telos* or purpose, as did all of our organs. His view was that the *telos* of sex and of our genitals was reproduction: hence, all uses of the sexual organs outside this purpose were thought to be unnatural and were condemned as perverse. This view was adopted in the thirteenth century by St. Thomas Aquinas (1225–74), one of the leading scholars of the Roman Catholic Church, who classified all perversions as *dysteleological*, unnatural, and thereby sinful. This view is still endorsed by the Roman Catholic Church today.

Let's call this the traditional view of sex and of sexual perversion. Note an important feature of this view: namely, it defines what 'normal' sexual desire is and then defines 'perverse' sexual desire as a deviation from the norm.[3] Another important element of this view is its dualistic view of humans. Dualism maintains that humans are a combination of two things: mind (or soul) and body. Yet the two parts are rarely taken to be equal: the mind or soul has historically been considered to be far more important to our essence than the body has. Aristotle defined humans as the rational animal and he believed that our reasoning abilities come from our minds and not our bodies. We are, he thought, really an embodied mind. Christianity has a somewhat similar view but makes a much more radical split between body and the soul. The soul is what we essentially are, and it is the soul, not the body, that lives on after the death of the body. Indeed, Christianity has repeatedly warned that the body must be guarded against, for it is the body that typically leads us astray, and this is something particularly true with respect to our physical sexual desires. Plato held a similar view, which he expressed in an allegory where he compared a person to a charioteer and two horses: the charioteer represents reason and it must, Plato argued, reign in the

---

"Saying How You Feel: Men and Women on Sexual Arousal and Desire," *The International Journal of Interdisciplinary Social Sciences* 6, no. 10 (2012): 203–12.

2   See Aristotle, *Physics*, Bk. II.

3   More would have to be said here, since not all deviations from the norm are taken to be perverse. Thus, the Roman Catholic Church allows for a postmenopausal woman or an impotent man to engage in intercourse with their husband or wife even though they are, strictly speaking, deviating from the norm. The main point still holds, however. Norms are defined first and then perversions are taken to be deviations *of a certain type or kind* from that norm.

two horses representing our base, bodily appetites and our spirit. Failure to do so leads to devastating results.[4]

To a remarkable extent, this traditional view continues to be held and/or to be influential to this day, in likely but sometimes also in unlikely places. It is not surprising, for example, that the Roman Catholic Church continues to believe that we must tightly control our carnal desires and channel them toward the only legitimate sexual activity—procreative intercourse between a married man and woman. Sexual behavior outside of or inconsistent with this norm is considered perverse. But it is rather odd to think of such a modernist thinker as Sigmund Freud (1856–1939), the Austrian psychiatrist and father of psychoanalysis, holding remnants of the traditional view.

Freud radically altered many of our views about sexuality, by contending, for example, that young children are sexual beings and that libido or sexual desire lies behind much human behavior. Yet his views on sex were in some ways quite conservative, from today's perspective at least, and influenced by the traditional view. According to Freud, sexual activity could be perverse either in its object or in its aim. In object perversions, a person fixates on a single object that is inappropriate in some way. The object can be another person (in, for example, homosexuality, incest, and pedophilia) or a non-human object (as happens, for instance, in zoophilia or bestiality, transvestism, and various fetishes). Aim perversions, he maintained, focus instead on an inappropriate end of our sexual desire. Examples here include exhibitionism, voyeurism, sadism, masochism, or any other activity where the pleasure of sexual activity aims at something other than what Freud thought the proper aim of sex: namely, intercourse between a man and woman. Hence he thought that oral and anal sexual fixations were perverse.

In order to understand Freud's view on perversions we need to link it to his theory of "psychosexual development." According to Freud, we are supposed to pass through five stages of such development, beginning when we are very young infants and carrying through puberty, at which time we enter adulthood. These are: (i) the oral, (ii) the anal, (iii) the phallic, (iv) the latent, and (v) the genital. With the exception of stage (iv), which Freud thought of as a period relatively free from sexual desire (approximately between the ages of 5–7 and when puberty starts between 10 and 13), these stages indicate the erogenous zones that are the source of our libido or sexual desire during specific ages. Freud maintained that the last stage of this process represented full adult maturity, where sexual desire is focused on heterosexual penis–vagina intercourse and reproduction. When an adult fixates on oral or anal sex, s/he aims at an area of the body appropriate only for an earlier stage in development. In a sense, then, perversion for Freud is an arrest, fixation, or regression to an earlier stage of psychosexual development and indicates a failure on one's part to move forward to the proper end and

---

4   Plato, *Phaedrus*, 245c–257b, in *The Collected Dialogues of Plato Including the Letters*, edited by Edith Hamilton and Huntington Cairns (Princeton, NJ: Princeton University Press, 1961).

object of sex: heterosexual, genital intercourse. Failure to reach this end stage, he said, is often an indication of a neurosis or mental illness.

As should be clear, this theory, though completely different in its specifics from the earlier theories we mentioned from Aristotle and Aquinas, shares with them a teleological picture of adult sex as at least potentially procreative. As we shall see in Ch. 11, Freud even used his theory to suggest that post-pubescent women who focus on clitorally-generated orgasm are immature and need to focus instead on vaginal orgasm, if they are to be fully mature women.

Like earlier views regarding perversion, contemporary philosophical accounts begin with a notion of 'normal' sexual desire and then define perversions as deviations from the norm. Seiriol Morgan has argued that much of the contemporary philosophical discussion regarding sexual desire (and hence, indirectly, of perversion) can be categorized within two broad camps, which he labels the hedonistic or reductionist view on the one hand, and intentionalist views on the other.[5]

Intentionalist accounts maintain that "understanding the interpersonal intentionality that occurs during sexual intercourse is essential for understanding sexual desire." On this view, human sexual desire is not an appetite, like the desire for food or water, since sexual desire requires that one "appreciate the significance of and respond to the mental states of others."[6] Thomas Nagel's position on sexual desire is a paradigmatic case of such an intentionalist view. Nagel maintained that sexual desire begins as self-conscious desires for another that can only be completed in mutual desire. Simply stated, in experiencing full or complete sexual desire, I must not only be turned on by you, but I must also be turned on by you being turned on by me, *and vice versa*. That is to say, sexual desire must not only involve awareness that another feels sexual desire toward one, but also that this awareness increases one's sexual desire, and vice versa: it is, then, a "multi-level interpersonal awareness" of escalating desire.[7] On this account, sexual perversion is any incomplete version of this complex of mutual desire, thus making all narcissistic practices sexual perversions. For example, as Nagel sees it, the exhibitionist is perverse because he cares only for what turns him on, and not for the person or persons to whom he exposes himself. Indeed, for some exhibitionists, sexual excitement is increased if their "audience" is turned *off* by what they are doing. One can see how this would apply to all sorts of other sexual activities typically thought of as perversions: voyeurism, sadism, masochism, pedophilia, bestiality or zoophilia, and so on.

Robert Solomon presents another version of the intentionalist view. According to Solomon, sex is essentially about the communication of feelings through the medium of the body. Though the message communicated through sex can often be love, it need not be. One can communicate almost

---

5   Seiriol Morgan, "Sex in the Head," *Journal of Applied Philosophy* 20, no. 1 (2003): 1–16.
6   Ibid., 2.
7   Nagel, "Sexual Perversion."

anything, from being pleased at what one's partner is doing, to domination over them. On this view, perversions are failures at communication of a certain kind. Obviously, in ordinary discourse, whether written or oral, we can be misunderstood and hence fail to communicate our message. We wouldn't want to call such a common occurrence a perversion of communication, however. Perversions of communication would have to do something beyond this; for example, we might say that the intention to deceive is a perversion of communication. Hence, by extension, attempting to deceive your sexual partner through your physical gestures and responses—such as indicating that you love them when you don't, or that you enjoy what they are doing when you don't—would be sexual perversions on Solomon's view. So too would be the attempt to communicate with a person or entity incapable of understanding your meaning. This might cover all sorts of perversions, such as having sex with children, animals, or inanimate objects.[8]

The reductionist or hedonistic view of sexual desire maintains that the intentionalist view misses the essential and fundamental aspect of sexual desire by trying to explain sexual desire as a *mere means to something else*, such as interpersonal interaction or communication through body language. As Alan Goldman puts it, while "one may receive pleasure in a sex act from expressing certain feelings, ... sexual desire is essentially the desire for physical contact itself: it is bodily desire for the body of another that dominates our mental life for more or less brief periods."[9] Goldman thus reduces sexual desire to a desire for physical pleasure. This is not to say that sex can't be used as a means to the various ends that intentionalists like Nagel and Solomon say it is; rather, according to reductionists, these are merely incidental to sexual desire and fail to get at its essence. Hence, sexual behaviors that do not aim at communication or mutual interaction are not sexually perverse.

It is actually quite difficult to see what would constitute a perverse sexual desire on this view since, it would seem, *no* sexual activity that is physically pleasurable can be labeled perverse. Indeed, as Rockney Jacobsen argues, the reductionist cannot really explain what makes something perverse, or even that there are sexual perversions at all.[10] And this is odd: surely one wants to say that the desire to eat feces and/or rub it all over one's body (coprophilia) is a perversion of sexual desire, whatever sexual desire turns out to be exactly. Thomas Nagel expands on this point by discrediting those views of sexual desire, including the reductionist view, which sees sexual desire as an appetite.

8   Robert Solomon, "Sexual Paradigms," *Journal of Philosophy* 71, no. 11 (1974). Reprinted in Alan Soble, ed., *The Philosophy of Sex: Contemporary Readings*, 3rd ed. (Lanham, MD: Rowman and Littlefield, 1977).

9   Alan Goldman, "Plain Sex." Reprinted in Soble, ed., *The Philosophy of Sex*, 42.

10 Rockney Jacobsen, "Arousal and the Ends of Desire," *Philosophy and Phenomenological Research* 53, no. 3 (1993): 617–32.

As such it may have various objects, some more common than others perhaps, but none in any sense natural. An appetite is identified as sexual by means of the organs and erogenous zones in which its satisfaction can be to some extent localized, and the special sensory pleasures which form the core of that satisfaction. This enables us to recognize widely divergent goals, activities, and desires as sexual, since it is conceivable in principle that anything should produce sexual pleasure and that a nondeliberate, sexually charged desire for it should arise (as a result of conditioning, if nothing else). We may fail to empathize with some of these desires, and some of them, like sadism, may be objectionable on extraneous grounds, but once we have observed that they meet the criteria for being sexual, there is nothing more to be said on *that* score. Either they are sexual or they are not: sexuality does not admit of imperfection, or perversion, or any other such qualification—it is not that sort of affection.[11]

Against this view, Nagel argues that even if, *contra* his position, we do consider sexual desire an appetite; this does not preclude claiming that some sexual desires are still perverse.

Let us approach the matter by asking whether we can imagine anything that would qualify as a gastronomical perversion. Hunger and eating are importantly like sex in that they serve a biological function and also play a significant role in our inner lives. It is noteworthy that there is little temptation to describe as perverted an appetite for substances that are not nourishing. We should probably not consider someone's appetites as perverted if he liked to eat paper, sand, wood, or cotton. Those are merely rather odd and very unhealthy tastes: they lack the psychological complexity that we expect of perversions. (Coprophilia, being already a sexual perversion, may be disregarded.) If on the other hand someone liked to eat cookbooks, or magazines with pictures of food in them, and preferred these to ordinary food or if when hungry he sought satisfaction by fondling a napkin or ashtray from his favorite restaurant—then the concept of perversion might seem appropriate (in fact it would be natural to describe this as a case of gastronomical fetishism). It would be natural to describe as gastronomically perverted someone who could eat only by having food forced down his throat through a

---

11 Nagel, "Sexual Perversion," 6–7.

funnel, or only if the meal were a living animal. What helps in such cases is the peculiarity of the desire itself, rather than the inappropriateness of its object to the biological function that the desire serves. Even an appetite, it would seem, can have perversions if in addition to its biological function it has a significant psychological structure.[12]

In addition to this, reductionists have a further problem in that their explanation of sexual desire misses much of what is integrally involved in it. Sex, as Robert Nozick has argued, is not simply a matter of friction, i.e., of two bodies rubbing against each other. If that were the case, then it would be difficult to understand the excitement and indeed the tension of sex and its release. Nozick argues that the truly intense and at times frightening thing about engaging in sex is that we let another inside both our physical and psychological boundaries that we normally keep tightly closed. Think, for example, of those people who are "close talkers," who seem to have no sense of personal space and make us uncomfortable by their physical proximity. Yet sex (at least of the physical variety) can happen only when we let people inside that space. Indeed, we literally either enter another's physical body with part of ours or physically surround a part of another's body with a part of ours when we engage in a great many sexual acts. And this clearly has a psychological dimension as well as a physical one.[13] Morgan makes this point by claiming that *who* we are having sex with is often vitally important to the sexual experience, and this makes little sense on the reductionist model. For example, think of the lure of the famous. Having sex with a celebrity might be incredibly exciting only or primarily because they are a celebrity. Or having sex with your rival's partner may be exciting for that reason and not primarily because of the sheer physical pleasure of it. Bluntly stated, though sex is physical, much of its meaning and intensity comes from the mind, not the body. The reductionist thus seems to have an inadequate notion of sexual desire and, as a result, an inadequate notion of sexual perversion as well.

This is not to say that the intentionalist view of sexual desire and perversion is correct either. According to Morgan, the intentionalist makes the opposite error from the reductionist by putting too much emphasis on the mental and intentional aspects of sexual desire, thereby downplaying or missing the physical element of sex. In general, Morgan argues, the reductionist and the intentionalist are both guilty of adhering to an outmoded radical dualism wherein everything is strictly body or mind. We would be much closer to the truth if we thought instead of sexual desire as falling on a continuum, with body on one end and mind on the other. On such a view, though there will be cases where sexual desire in its essence is exclusively (or almost exclusively) either a physical or

---

12 Ibid., 7.
13 Robert Nozick, *The Examined Life: Philosophical Reflections* (New York: Simon and Schuster, 1989).

mental event, in almost all cases sexual desire will be a combination of the two. An adequate conception of sexual perversion, then, will have to take account of this mind–body continuum and avoid both the complete denial of perversion, as the reductionists do, or the inclusion of too many things as perverse, as the intentionalists tend to do.[14] We will examine the dangers of including too much in our definition of perversion by considering the influence that intentionalist views such as Nagel's have had on contemporary psychiatry. In short, we will argue that this has resulted in classifying far too much sexual activity as a medical affliction in need of treatment. That is, intentionalist views of sexual desire and perversion have helped to overmedicalize sexual activity.

As you will recall, Nagel thought that all sexual arousal that failed to achieve "multi-level interpersonal awareness" was perverse. Interestingly, Nagel's view shares much in common with the view of the American Psychiatric Association (APA), which publishes the *Diagnostic and Statistical Manual of Mental Disorders* or DSM, which is used to diagnose and treat all mental disorders in the United States and Canada. The book, whose first edition was published in 1952, is now in its fifth edition (the DSM-5); it lists and describes all mental illnesses and indicates how to treat them. Included are sexual perversions, which the APA refers to as "paraphilias," such as pedophilia, sadism, masochism, exhibitionism, fetishism, and partialism (the exclusive focus on a part of the body). Like Nagel, the APA first defines 'normal' or normophilic sexual desire and then defines sexual perversion as a deviation from that norm. "The paraphilias," according to the APA, "are characterized by arousal in response to sexual objects that are not part of normative arousal-activity patterns and that in varying degrees may interfere with the capacity for *reciprocal, affectionate sexual activity.*"[15]

In defending the APA's description of sexual desire, Robert Spitzer says that just as the function of the heart is to pump blood and that of the eyes is to see, "sexual arousal brings people together to have *interpersonal sex*. Sexual arousal has the function of facilitating pair bonding which is facilitated by *reciprocal affectionate relationships.*"[16] Nagel, Spitzer, and the APA all view normophilic sexual desire as necessarily involving a reciprocal, interpersonal awareness of some sort. Moreover, as Spitzer adds, "There is a normal development of sexual arousal and sometimes it can go wrong."[17] The DSM-5 distinguishes between paraphilic behaviors and disorders. The latter are those that cause a patient distress or are potentially harmful to the patient and others.[18] This new approach to paraphilias

---

14 Morgan, "Sex in the Head."

15 American Psychological Association, *DSM III-R* (1987), 279; emphasis added.

16 Robert Spitzer, "Sex and Gender Identity Disorders: Discussion of Questions for *DSM –V*," *Journal of Psychology and Human Sexuality* 17, no. 3 (2006): 114; emphasis added.

17 Ibid., 114.

18 "A Guide to the DSM-5," *Medscape*, May 21, 2013, http://www.medscape.com/viewarticle/803884_14.

aims to lessen the stigma that attaches to atypical, but non-destructive, sexual behaviors when they are regarded as medical problems or mental disorders. But if the harm of unusual sexual behaviors or tastes is understood to encompass the inability to form reciprocal or affectionate sexual relationships, then the new approach may differ from the old only in the requirement that the harm be actual rather than potential, or that the inability causes distress to the patient.

Note that the claim being made by Spitzer (and Nagel) is *prescriptive* in some way. They do not present interpersonally meaningful and bond-strengthening sex as a mere *description* of how most people behave, but as how *normal* people behave (and therefore how people *should* behave). This was in fact part of Goldman's criticism of the intentionalist view. Nor is there any empirical evidence to suggest that the majority of people behave in such a manner sexually. Indeed, Nagel at least explicitly admits that his view of 'normal' sex is "evaluative in some sense." But, as he goes on to say, the evaluation isn't a moral one, nor does the evaluation even distinguish between "good" and "bad" sex: "It is not clear that unperverted sex is necessarily *preferable* to the perversions. It may be that sex which receives the highest marks for perfection *as sex* is less enjoyable than certain perversions; and if enjoyment is considered very important, that might outweigh considerations of sexual perfection in determining rational preference." [19] So what sort of evaluation is Nagel making regarding non-perverse sex?

In answering this question, special attention must be given to Nagel's reference to sexual "perfection" in the passage just cited. What he, along with Spitzer, is offering us is a notion of sexual desire that is not just intentionalist but also "perfectionist." That is, it offers us an ideal of sexual behavior. Given this, it is completely unwarranted for Nagel to call deviations from the ideal a perversion. Think of an analogy. Let's say we have constructed a description of what constitutes an ideal red wine. Surely if one were to choose a deviation from this ideal— say something less expensive—this shouldn't be thought of as a perverse red wine, or as a perverse desire for red wine. Unfortunately, however, both Nagel and Spitzer fall into this problematic way of thinking about sex. Moser and Kleinplatz criticize the APA for its perfectionist assumptions about sex and argue for the removal of paraphilias in future editions of the DSM: the "judgment of what constitutes reciprocal, affectionate sexual activity is clearly value laden and suggests an underlying, implicit, theoretical orientation. There are no data to suggest that individuals diagnosed with a paraphilia have any more difficulty maintaining relationships than 'normal' heterosexuals, who have staggering divorce rates." [20]

This prescriptive and perfectionist account of normophilic sexual desire is more problematic for the APA than it is for Nagel. This stems from the function of the DSM, namely, to present a description of, and treatments for, various types of mental *illness or disorder*. Hence, by their own criteria, all mental

---

19 Nagel, "Sexual Perversion," 16, 17.

20 Charles Moser and Peggy Kleinplatz, "DSM-IV-TR and the Paraphilias: An Argument for Removal," *Journal of Psychology and Human Sexuality* 17, no. 3 (2005): 102.

disorders must "be associated with present distress ... or disability ... or significantly increased risk of suffering death, pain, disability, or an important loss of freedom." [21] Curiously, however, when we examine the criteria for classifying or diagnosing someone with a paraphilia in *DSM-IV-TR*, we find that such distress or disability is required only for some paraphilias and not for all of them. Specifically, a diagnosis of pedophilia, voyeurism, exhibitionism, and frotteurism (the inappropriate touching, rubbing, or groping of others in crowded public places) requires only that "the person has acted on these urges." [22] While this may be an important issue with respect to determining criminality, it seems an odd criterion for determining mental illness. [23]

This problem gets more acute as we move beyond the rather narrow parameters of sexual paraphilias—even given the catch-all classification "Paraphilia not Otherwise Specified" [24]—to a consideration of all the "sexual disorders" listed in the current *DSM*. Consider sex addiction as an example. Although it is not listed explicitly in the *DSM IV-TR*, that work does include a miscellaneous diagnosis called "Sexual Disorder Not Otherwise Specified" that includes the following two examples, both of which, we would argue, come uncomfortably close to a description of sexual addiction: (i) "distress about a pattern of repeated sexual relationships involving a succession of lovers who are experienced by the individual only as things to be used," and (ii) "compulsive sexuality in a relationship." [25] Interestingly, sexual addiction has been included in the *DSM* before. *DSM III-R*, published in 1987, listed "nonparaphilic sex addiction" within the catch-all category "Sexual Disorders Not Otherwise Classified." The category was deleted because, as Schmidt said in preparing recommendations for the *DSM-IV*, "the results of the review reveal abundant clinical evidence of sexual activity that can be characterized as excessive" but there was "no scientific data to support a concept of sexual behavior that can be considered addictive." [26] In their suggestions for *DSM-5*, however, Manley and Koehler contend that such a diagnosis be returned to the *DSM* through a redesigned nosology that would include "Sexually Excessive Behavior Disorders," encompassing such "sex

21 APA, *DSM-IV-TR* (2000), xxxl. (*TR* stands for *Text Revision*.)

22 Ibid., 566.

23 See, e.g., Moser and Kleinplatz, "DSM-IV-TR and the Paraphilias"; Igor Primoratz, "Sexual Perversion," *American Philosophical Quarterly* 34, no. 2 (1997): 245–58; and Frederick Suppe, "The Diagnostic and Statistical Manual of the American Psychiatric Association: Classifying Sexual Disorders," in *Sexuality and Medicine*, ed. Earl Shelp, vol. 2, 111–35 (Dordrecht: D. Reidel, 1987).

24 APA, *DSM-IV-TR* (2000), 576.

25 Ibid., 582. It should also be noted that "nymphomania" and "satyriasis" continue to be listed in the International Classification of Diseases and Related Health Disorders in its most recent edition as subtypes of hypersexuality (WHO, *ICD-10* [2007]).

26 C.W. Schmidt, "Changes in Terminology for Sexual Disorders in DSM-IV," *The Psychiatric Clinics of North America* 18 (1992): 107–21. Passage cited in G. Manley and J. Koehler, "Sexual Behavior Disorders: Proposed New Classification in the DSM-V," *Sexual Addiction and Compulsivity* 8 (2001): 257.

addictions" as excessive masturbation.[27] As Janice Irvine has argued, though, this leads to a concern that physicians and psychiatrists are coming to have the 'power to regulate and define large areas of human experience, even those ... that [fall] outside of their training and expertise."[28]

This issue really concerns the medicalization of all behavior, including sexual behavior, and we will return to this issue in Ch. 11. To conclude this discussion, however, we present a cautionary tale from Daniel Bergner's *The Other Side of Desire*. One of the characters he describes in the book is a man referred to as Jacob, who has a foot fetish. One "treatment" option for Jacob would have been to tell him that there is nothing inherently wrong with his desire since it harms no one, and that he should be open with his wife about his predilection. Instead, however, faced with Jacob's self-loathing over his paraphilia, he and his therapist agree to a treatment of chemical castration. Such castration is achieved through anti-androgens that work by preventing or inhibiting the biologic effects of androgens, or male sex hormones, typically by blocking the appropriate receptors in the brain and thus obstructing the androgens' pathway. Unfortunately, these drugs are "horribly imprecise," and act like "a club" by "bludgeoning the hormonal foundation of desire rather than addressing specific desire."[29]

Hence, while someone can experience some sexual desire while on a drug such as Lupron, the drug administered to Jacob in the book, such desire will typically be faint, if it exists at all. The hope is that removing the desire for aberrant objects, such as feet, will lead to the onset of more conventional longings for genital sex. Amazingly—perhaps bizarrely—that burgeoning new conventional desire will then be intensified by prescribing a drug such as Viagra, as was the case with Jacob. While one can see readily why such a treatment would be employed for pedophiles, the case is less clear for a foot fetishist. One can imagine, then, a quite different treatment for Jacob that would begin by accepting foot fetishism and then working with him (and his wife) to an accommodation of his desire. But in a world where we overmedicalize behavior and where there is a great deal of financial interest in such overmedicalization and subsequent treatment, we can end up creating a great deal of harm. Not all of it will be as dramatic as it was for Jacob, but all diagnoses of mental disorder bring with them at least some stigmatization. And surely we don't want a definition of sexual desire and perversion that has this damaging result.

We pursue the damaging results that can come from classifying certain non-coercive sexual practices as perverse in the next section by examining sodomy in particular. Historically, sodomy has been considered paradigmatically

---

27 Ginger Manley and Jean Koehler, "Sexual Behavior Disorders," 260.

28 Janice Irving, "Reinventing Perversion: Sex Addiction and Cultural Anxieties," *Journal of the History of Sexuality* 5, no. 3 (1995): 429–50. Also see, Irving K. Zola, "Medicine as an Institution of Social Control," *Sociological Review* 20 (1972): 487–504.

29 Daniel Bergner, *The Other Side of Desire: Four Journeys into the Far Realms of Lust and Longing* (New York: HarperCollins, 2009), 24.

perverse, and it has been the subject of laws throughout history, continuing to the present day. Indeed, there are currently at least nine countries where people can be put to death for being found guilty of committing sodomy.

Should There Be Laws against Sodomy?

Across time and cultures, sodomy has encompassed a number of different behaviors. Webster's Dictionary defines it as: "(1) anal or oral copulation with a member of the same sex, (2) enforced anal or oral copulation with a member of the opposite sex, (3) bestiality." The word itself comes to us from the biblical story of the ancient city of Sodom. Genesis 18–19 tells us that the inhabitants of Sodom, along with its sister city, Gomorrah, were evil, and that God destroyed them for their sins. It is unclear, however, what their sins were, and different interpretations have been offered by the three Abrahamic religions (Judaism, Christianity, and Islam), as well as by different factions within these. According to some, God's wrath was directed at the cities' rampant homosexuality and other "deviant" sexual acts. Others, however, argue in favor of a nonsexual account of the sins of Sodom and Gomorrah, pointing to passages in the Bible (or the Torah or Koran) such as Ezekiel 16:49, which mentions no sexual vice amongst the sins of the Sodomites: "Behold, this was the guilt of your sister Sodom: she and her daughters had arrogance, abundant food and careless ease, but she did not help the poor and needy. Thus they were haughty and committed abominations before Me." Here, the major crimes of the Sodomites were arrogance, profligacy, and a failure to be hospitable and help the poor and needy.

Whatever the correct interpretation of these passages is (if indeed there is one correct interpretation), Sodom has been associated historically with the "sin" of homosexuality and various other sexual acts taken to be 'unnatural' in some way. As such, laws against sodomy have been thought by many to be sanctioned by the holy scriptures of the Abrahamic religions, even if, as we shall see, the laws changed over time and place and outlawed different sexual acts. In some cases, the laws apply specifically to anal sex between gay men, and/or to bestiality. In other cases, the laws also include anal sex between a man and a woman. Sometimes fellatio is also included, particularly when it occurs between two men. Only rarely do sodomy laws incorporate cunnilingus, whether between a man and a woman or between two women. At times, however, sodomy laws have outlawed *all* sexual acts that are not at least potentially procreative. In other words, such laws have made criminal all sexual acts except penile-vaginal sex.

One of the reasons why various laws have defined sodomy differently is that sexual mores or customs change, and so what is thought to be perfectly acceptable behavior at one time or in one place is thought to be unacceptable at other times and in other places. Consider as an example the Ancient Greek practice of pederasty, discussed in Ch. 1. To put it in its most controversial form, pederasty was a practice whereby adult men had sex with adolescent boys. As such, from today's standards, it not only involved homosexuality but also ephebophilia or hebephilia (adult sexual interest in adolescent or pubescent children). Pederasty would thus be considered both immoral and illegal in almost all countries at the present time. We need to be careful here, however, because just as laws and what is considered moral can change over time, so too can the very concepts we use to think about things. 'Homosexuality' is certainly one of these concepts, as is the concept of a 'child' or 'childhood' (which today typically extends to 16 or 17 but which ended much earlier in ancient times). In the contemporary, post-Freudian world, we conceive of homosexuality to include not only certain types of *acts*, but also certain types of *dispositions,* which are thought by many to be unchangeable and central to our very identity. Ancient Greek concepts of pederasty, however, were very different from this, since pederasty was not taken to be a sexual orientation or part of one's identity. According to Greek custom, the older man, who was typically in his mid-20s to mid-30s, was supposed to form a strong bond of friendship with his younger beloved (usually in his mid to late teens) that was to last a lifetime, long after any sexual relationship had ended. The older lover was supposed to act as a mentor to the younger boy and introduce him to society. In all likelihood, the older man would be married and the younger man typically retained a sexual relation with his older male lover only until he too married. The *acts* engaged in by pederasts in Ancient Greece also differentiated them from many of the acts engaged in by contemporary gay men. In Ancient Greece, pederasts typically did not engage in either fellatio or anal sex and restricted themselves instead to intercrural or interfemoral sex, which is a form of non penetrative sex where a man either rubs his penis between the thighs of his partner from behind, or the partners face one another and rub their penises together.[30] Comparing contemporary gay men or pedophiles to Ancient Greek pederasts, then, is rather like comparing apples and potatoes.

Although pederasty was somewhat controversial in Ancient Greece, the practice was considered perfectly acceptable, at least among certain classes. Indeed, some believed the love between two men, or between a man and an adolescent boy, to be the highest and best form of sexual relation. Male love united people who were considered intellectually and socially superior, as opposed to sex with a subordinate, such as a woman or a slave. Though Plato in his old age condemned homosexuality in his last work, *The Laws,* we can find many passages in earlier works that make exactly the opposite point, at least with respect to the practice of pederasty. In *The Symposium,* for example, one of the characters argues that young men who have sex with older men exhibit "daring, fortitude, and masculinity—the very virtues that they recognize and welcome in their lovers—which is proved by the fact that in after years they are the only men who show any real manliness in public life. And so, when they themselves have come to manhood, their love in turn is lavished upon boys. They have no natural

---

30 See, e.g., Kenneth Dover, *Greek Homosexuality* (New York: Vintage Books, 1977); and
     Joan Roughgarden, *Evolution's Rainbow: Diversity, Gender and Sexuality in Nature and People*
     (Los Angeles: University of California Press, 2004).

inclination to marry and beget children. Indeed, they only do so in deference to the usage of society, for they would just as soon renounce marriage altogether and spend their lives with one another." [31]

Sex between members of the same sex became a persecuted practice in the Western world only when Christianity gained ascendancy, which was after the Roman emperor Constantine converted to that religion in the fourth century CE. St. Augustine (354–430 CE) was influential in this change and for turning sex, in general, into a sin. In his seminal work, *The Confessions*, Augustine condemns his early profligate life in favor of a life of celibacy and communion with God. According to Augustine, the best Christians are celibate and devote all of their energy to the worship of God. Sex was allowable only to those who could not achieve a celibate life. For them, the only way to avoid sin was to marry and to limit their sexual activity to procreative sexual activity with their spouse. Following this line of thinking, the Justinian Code in Roman Law of 529 CE made homosexual sex (including sodomy) illegal, and those convicted of the crime could be put to death. [32]

When the Roman Empire fell, laws against homosexuality and, in general, against non-procreative sex gradually were abandoned. But they returned later in the Middle Ages. Of particular concern to North Americans is the situation in England at that time, because the legal systems of both Canada and the United States derive in one way or another from British law. Laws against sodomy in England date back as far as the thirteenth century. During this period, sodomy laws were enforced by the Catholic Church. When Henry VIII broke from the Catholic Church in the sixteenth century, he developed England's secular laws, which included the *Buggery Act* of 1533. This Act outlawed "the abominable vice of buggery committed with mankind or beast." [33] It did not define buggery in precise terms, and while the term "buggery" typically refers to anal sex, over the years, enforcers of the *Buggery Act* came to interpret buggery as anal sex by a man with a man or a woman, or vaginal sex between a man or woman and an animal. Consent between the parties involved was not accepted as a defense (even if the man and the woman were married), and penalties for those convicted of buggery could include death. [34]

Canada adopted British law on sodomy in its entirety until well after Canada separated from the United Kingdom in 1867. There was some change in the law in the 1890s when Canadian courts sought to broaden the laws to include *all* forms of male homosexual sex. Later changes in the middle of the twentieth century attempted to brand all homosexual men as dangerous sexual offenders. Everett Klipper was the last victim of these laws, and his case acted as a catalyst

---

31 Plato, *Symposium*, 192a–b.

32 See Pickett, "Homosexuality."

33 Cited in George Painter, "The Sensibilities of Our Forefathers," http://www.glapn.org/sodomylaws/sensibilities/introduction.htm.

34 Ibid.

for change. During the investigation of an unrelated case (in which he was innocent), Klippert admitted to the police that he was a homosexual. Though the sexual relations he admitted to were all consensual between adult, competent men,
he was charged with "gross indecency" and sentenced to "preventative detention," which meant that his sentence was indefinite. Because he was found by
the court-appointed psychiatrist to be "incurably homosexual," he was unlikely
ever to be released from prison. Klippert appealed his conviction all the way to
the Supreme Court of Canada, but he lost. Shortly thereafter, then–prime minister Pierre Elliott Trudeau, who famously said "There's no place for the state
in the bedrooms of the nation," introduced the *Criminal Law Amendment Act
1968–1969* (Bill C-150), which decriminalized consensual homosexual sexual activity between adults. The bill passed, became law in 1969, and holds to
this day.[35]

Canada has gone further than merely decriminalizing consensual homosexual sex, however. The "Equality Rights" set out in Section 15 of the *Canadian
Charter of Rights and Freedoms*, which was introduced in 1982, states that "Every
individual is equal before and under the law and has the right to the equal protection and equal benefit of the law without discrimination and, in particular, without discrimination based on race, national or ethnic origin, colour, religion, sex,
age or mental or physical disability." Though sexual orientation is not explicitly
mentioned here, in a landmark 1995 case, *Egan v. Canada*, the Supreme Court
of Canada held that sexual orientation was implicitly included as an "analogous
ground" and therefore a prohibited ground of discrimination. This section and
ruling have been used, for example, to grant rights to same-sex couples to marry
and to adopt children.[36]

The situation in the United States has been more complicated, in part
because American states have more autonomy than do Canadian provinces. As a
result, one has to examine the law in individual states instead of simply looking
at national legislation. When we do so, we find a confusing mix of laws throughout history. Some states adopted English law, while others did not; some changed
their laws regarding sodomy quite radically over time, while again others did
not. Instead of concentrating on these differences, however, we shall point to two
U.S. Supreme Court decisions that had national significance: *Bowers v. Hardwick*
(1986) and *Lawrence v. Texas* (2003).

In 1982, when the events that eventually led to the *Bowers v. Hardwick* decisions took place, more than twenty American states still had laws against sodomy,
however that term was defined. Georgia's sodomy laws prohibited anal and oral
sex, regardless of whether it was between heterosexual or homosexual partners.
In a complicated series of events, Michael Hardwick, who lived in Atlanta, was

35 See Donald McLeod, *Lesbian and Gay Liberation in Canada: A Selected Annotated Chronology.
    1964–1975* (Toronto: ECWPress/Homewood Books, 1996); and Gary Kinsman, *Regulation of
    Desire: Sexuality in Canada* (Montreal: Black Rose, 1987).
36 See McLeod, *Lesbian and Gay Liberation in Canada*; and Kinsman, *Regulation of Desire*.

arrested for engaging in consensual oral sex in his own bedroom with a male partner. Though the local district attorney decided not to pursue the charge by bringing it before a grand jury, Hardwick himself came to sue the Attorney General of Georgia, Michael Bowers, to set a precedent for the invalidity of Georgia's sodomy laws. Hardwick reasoned that since he was an active homosexual, he would forever be in fear of prosecution under the state's sodomy laws.[37]

The American Civil Liberties Union (ACLU) sponsored Hardwick in his case, thinking that this would be an ideal test case with which to dismiss all remaining U.S. sodomy laws. They were wrong, however, as the U.S. Supreme Court, in a controversial 5-4 decision, upheld the constitutionality of the Georgia law and, by extension, all other extant American sodomy laws. The argument made by Hardwick was that his privacy rights, protected under the Constitution's Due Process Clause, had been violated. The majority of Supreme Court Justices disagreed, however, doing so essentially by an appeal to tradition. Writing for the majority, Justice Byron White wrote, "the laws of the many States that still make such conduct illegal have done so for a very long time." Chief Justice Warren Burger agreed, pointing out that condemnation of sodomy "is firmly rooted in Judeo-Christian moral and ethical standards" and, hence, to strike down the laws "would be to cast aside millennia of moral teaching." The majority of the Supreme Court Justices were also persuaded by their belief that "a majority of the electorate in Georgia [believe] that homosexual sodomy is immoral and unacceptable," even when it is performed in private and with consent between adults.[38]

There are a number of problems with the reasoning used here. The first we will discuss has to do with the nature of a Constitution and a Bill of Rights. As has been pointed out by many people, including the philosopher John Stuart Mill in his famous work *On Liberty*, democracies can be tyrannical. Because of this, we must protect individuals in various minorities against the preferences and biases of the majority. Otherwise, voting majorities could approve the enslavement, or other forms of persecution, of any minority. Bills of Rights offer such minorities constitutional guarantees of their fundamental rights. Hence, even if the majority of people in Georgia believe, or did believe in 1982, that consensual sex between men is immoral, this offers no real defense of its sodomy law. Otherwise, a majority could outlaw sex or marriage between people of different ethnic groups or codify other forms of discrimination against any vilified group. Moreover, the fact that a particular group believed something at a particular time and place does not entail that those beliefs are or were true. At one time, almost everyone believed that the world was flat and that the Sun revolved around a

---

37 See Martha Nussbaum, *From Disgust to Humanity: Sexual Orientation and Constitutional Law* (New York and Oxford: Oxford University Press, 2010); and Ellen Ann Andersen, *Out of the Closets and into the Courts: Legal Opportunity Structure and Gay Rights Litigation* (Ann Arbor: University of Michigan Press, 2006).

38 All quotations in this paragraph are cited in Painter, "Sensibilities."

stationary Earth, but this does not make either of those beliefs true. Hence, the fact that a majority believes that gay sex is immoral does not make this belief true.

Fortunately, the Supreme Court corrected its faulty reasoning in 2003, when in *Lawrence v. Texas* it overturned the ruling issued 17 years earlier in *Bowers v. Hardwick*. The majority of Supreme Court justices now agreed with the plaintiff that, on both privacy and equal protection grounds, the government could not regulate the private sex lives of consenting, competent adults, or prohibit sex acts between partners of the same sex that were permitted for those of different sexes. Hence, the sodomy laws of all fourteen states that had them in 2003 were invalidated. However, the *Lawrence* ruling was not immediately extended, either by further legal decisions or by national legislation, to guarantee the rights of all couples to marry and adopt children, unlike in Canada. The push for marriage and family equality is succeeding somewhat more slowly, and on a state-by-state basis.

Is Perverse Sex Morally Bad?

How do we determine the moral status of sexual acts that appear perverse or unnatural, and how should modern liberal, democratic states respond to behaviors that some portion of the population, perhaps the vast majority, views as immoral? The second question looks beyond the regulation of sexual activities to the broader issue of the relationship between the law and public mores.

We noted earlier that, although definitions of 'sodomy' vary across places and times, laws against it are heavily influenced by conceptions of what constitutes normal sex. Moreover, conceptions of normophilic sex are derived, in large part, by conceptions of what constitutes 'natural' sex. Normative arguments against the moral permissibility of certain sexual acts, such as homosexual ones, therefore often take the following form:

1. Homosexuality is unnatural.
2. All unnatural things or acts are immoral.
    Therefore, homosexuality is immoral.

When we assess a deductive argument, we must look at least at two things: whether the premises are true and whether the form of reasoning used is valid, that is, whether it follows an inference rule that always takes us from true premises to true conclusions. When valid reasoning is combined with true premises, we have what logicians call a "sound" argument. Sound arguments are compelling because they contain true premises, and the inference from premises to conclusion is truth-preserving. Hence, we cannot rationally refuse to accept the conclusion of a sound argument. So now let's consider whether the above argument against the morality of homosexuality is a sound argument. The form of reasoning deployed is valid because, if the premises are both true, then the conclusion must be true. The question, then, is whether the premises are true. To determine this, we need to know what the syllogism's middle term 'unnatural' means. Without knowing this precisely, we cannot determine whether the premises are true.

In an insightful article on this issue, Burton Leiser observes that, historically, at least five different meanings have been given for the term 'unnatural.' It can mean: (1) uncommon, (2) against the laws of nature, (3) artificial, (4) dysteleological, or (5) morally bad (evil).[39] To check whether the above argument is sound, then, we have to substitute one of these definitions for each instance of the word unnatural. But in order to avoid equivocating, we need to use the *same* definition in each premise when we check the soundness of the argument.

Let's start by considering how the argument fares when using definition (1). Here, the argument will look as follows: (1) Homosexuality is uncommon. (2) All uncommon things are immoral. Therefore, homosexuality is immoral. If we assume that 'uncommon' means in 'the minority' or 'statistically low,' then premise (1) of this argument is probably true. There is currently a general consensus among researchers that lesbians and gay men comprise roughly ten per cent of most populations. But premise (2) is false, because it is not the case that *all* uncommon things are immoral. There are in fact lots of examples of uncommon things—from knowing how to play the violin to having a b.a. in philosophy—that are not immoral. Indeed, many virtuous behaviors, such as generosity toward strangers, are uncommon. Hence, premise (2) is false under this definition of unnatural, and as such the conclusion does not follow.

Consider definition (2). The argument now takes this form: (1) Homosexuality is against the laws of nature. (2) All those things or acts that are against the laws of nature are immoral. Therefore, homosexuality is immoral. Once again, in assessing our argument we are faced with a definitional question: What does 'against the laws of nature' mean? Here, we must differentiate between prescriptive and descriptive laws. Prescriptive laws—such as laws against murder or driving faster than the speed limit—tell us how we *ought* to behave. Clearly, these laws can be broken—people do unfortunately murder others, and people do speed—but this is not what is meant in the above argument. There, the laws of nature apply instead to descriptive laws, which describe the way things *actually* do behave. For example, $e = mc^2$ is a law of nature that describes the relationship between energy and the mass and velocity of a body. Interestingly, laws of nature can*not* be violated. If we found a body acting inconsistently with the law $e = mc^2$, then we would have to change our formulation of the law (or limit its scope).

If we take the first premise to refer to the descriptive laws of nature, then we find that the claim being made is nonsensical, since such laws cannot be broken, but merely misdescribed. Moreover, the premise clearly overlooks much of the natural world, since many other animal species engage in same-sex sexual

---

39 Burton Leiser, "Is Homosexuality Unnatural?" Reprinted in *Sex, Morality, and the Law*, ed. Lori Gruen and George Panichas, 44–51 (New York: Routledge, 1997).

activities, not just humans.[40] Hence, without even turning to premise (2), we can see that the use of definition (2) renders the argument unsound, because at least one of the premises is false.

Under definition (3), our argument reads as follows: (1) Homosexuality is artificial. (2) All artificial things are immoral. Therefore, homosexuality is immoral. We can see quite quickly that this argument will not do since premise (2) is clearly false. Lights in our houses or apartments are artificial, as are their heating and cooling systems. Indeed, houses and apartments themselves do not appear in unadulterated nature and are therefore unnatural, as are pens, computers, cellphones, and on and on. But these things are not all immoral, at least in terms of their artificiality, and so this instance of the argument is unsound.

The fourth definition is perhaps the one that has been used most often in arguments against the morality of homosexuality based on its unnaturalness. It reads: (1) Homosexuality is dysteleological by using the sexual organs for purposes outside their primary purpose or *telos*. (2) All dysteleological uses of objects are immoral. Therefore, homosexuality is immoral. Teleological arguments of this sort, however, are problematic because they assume that a teleological account of things is correct. But this is much disputed. Modern biology, for example, denies that all things have a *telos* in the Aristotelian sense of that word. But even if we set aside this dispute, the above argument is still problematic, since it's not at all clear that premise (2) is true. Let's say that the *telos* or purpose of my nose is to smell. Surely, this doesn't entail that using my nose to hold up my glasses is an immoral use of my nose. We can say the same thing about our sexual organs. Even assuming that *a* purpose or *the primary* purpose of our genitals is to reproduce through sexual intercourse, it seems a stretch to say that using them for pleasure or to express our love to another adult human being is morally wrong. If this argument were sound, its conclusion would actually extend far beyond homosexuality to the conclusion that all uses of our sexual organs for non-procreative purposes are immoral. In fact, it's probably safe to say that the function of urination is one of the main purposes of our genitals, and that's hardly immoral either.

Finally, we have definition (5), which reads as follows: (1) Homosexuality is morally bad. (2) All morally bad things are immoral. Therefore, homosexuality is immoral. Philosophers say that this sort of argument is guilty of the fallacy of begging the question or circular reasoning. When we do this, we assume what we need to prove. In this case, we are supposed to prove that homosexuality is immoral, but instead we have simply assumed it in our definition of 'unnatural,' i.e., in the first premise. Arguments guilty of this fallacy do not, then, force us to accept the truth of their conclusions.

While proving that gay sex is immoral is quite difficult, there are some sexual activities that are immoral, and in part because they appear perverse or unnatural. We might include in this category bestiality, non-consensual sadism,

---

40 See, e.g., Michael Ruse, "Is Homosexuality Bad Sexuality?" In *Philosophical Perspectives on Sex and Love*, ed. Robert M. Stewart, 113–24 (Oxford: Oxford University Press, 1995).

non-consensual exhibitionism or voyeurism, pedophilia, and sexual fetishes that involve killing animals (e.g., so called "crush fetishes"). Anti-sodomy laws that prohibit such acts do not appear to violate any person's or minority's fundamental rights. Yet many parts of the world still have anti-sodomy laws that prohibit some forms of consensual sex between adults.

Let's return, for a moment, to our earlier discussion of British laws against sodomy since, as we said earlier, Canadian and American laws in general, and sodomy laws in particular, derived from their earlier British counterparts. By the middle of the twentieth century, little had changed in the United Kingdom from the time when Henry VIII first introduced anti-sodomy laws in 1533, except that punishments were less severe than they had once been. In the early 1950s, however, three prominent Englishmen were tried and convicted under Britain's sodomy laws, including Lord Montagu, a Conservative politician. This led to the establishment of the Departmental Committee on Homosexual Offences and Prostitution, which was tasked with examining how (and whether) homosexual "offenses" and prostitution should be treated by the law. They published a controversial report in 1957, which is typically referred to as the Wolfenden Report after the Chair of the Committee, Lord Wolfenden. The Committee, populated by academics, lawyers, judges, doctors, and clergy, recommended in its report that "homosexual behaviour between consenting adults in private should no longer be a criminal offence." The Committee did so, in brief, for the following reasons:

> [The law's] function, as we see it, is to preserve public order and decency, to protect the citizen from what is offensive or injurious, and to provide sufficient safeguards against exploitation and corruption of others.... It is not, in our view, the function of the law to intervene in the private lives of citizens, or to seek to enforce any particular pattern of behaviour, further than is necessary to carry out the purposes which we have outlined....
>
> [T]here must remain a realm of private morality and immorality which is, in brief and crude terms, not the law's business.[41]

A decade after the report was published, the *Sexual Offences Act* was passed in 1967, which decriminalized sodomy between consenting adults in private in Wales and England, with Scotland and Northern Ireland following several years after. The report and the subsequent change in law led to a famous debate between Lord Patrick Devlin, a British judge who opposed the recommendations

---

41 Committee on Homosexual Offences and Prostitution, *The Wolfenden Report: Report of the Committee on Homosexual Offences and Prostitution* (New York: Stein and Day, 1959). Cited in Ronald Dworkin, "Lord Devlin and the Enforcement of Morals," *The Yale Law Journal* 75, no. 6 (1966): 987–88.

of the report, and H.L.A. Hart and Ronald Dworkin, who supported them. At the heart of the dispute was a question regarding the extent to which the law ought to enforce "public morality" in those cases where no individuals are harmed by the "immoral" behavior.

Devlin made his point with what he called the "disintegration argument":

> Societies disintegrate from within more frequently than they are broken up by external pressures. There is disintegration when no common morality is observed and history shows that the loosening of moral bonds is often the first stage of disintegration, so that society is justified in taking the same steps to preserve its moral code as it does to preserve its government.... The suppression of vice is as much the law's business as the suppression of subversive activities.[42]

On the face of it at least, this view runs counter to the liberal view of law that was introduced by Jeremy Bentham and John Stuart Mill in the nineteenth century. Mill famously argued that

> the sole end for which mankind are warranted, individually or collectively in interfering with the liberty of action of any of their number, is self-protection. That the only purpose for which power can be rightfully exercised over any member of a civilized community, against his will, is to prevent harm to others. His own good, either physical or moral, is not a sufficient warrant. He cannot rightfully be compelled to do or forbear because it will be better for him to do so, because it will make him happier, because, in the opinions of others, to do so would be wise, or even right. These are good reasons for remonstrating with him, or reasoning with him, or persuading him, or entreating him, but not for compelling him, or visiting him with any evil, in case he does otherwise. To justify that, the conduct from which it is desired to deter him must be calculated to produce evil to some one else. The only part of the conduct of any one, for which he is amenable to society, is that which concerns others. In the part which merely concerns himself, his independence is, of right, absolute. Over himself, over his own body and mind, the individual is sovereign.[43]

Mill's position maintains that we need to separate a private from a public realm. If an action concerns myself primarily, and "harms" no one else, then that

---

42 Patrick Devlin, *The Enforcement of Morals* (Oxford: Oxford University Press, 1965), 13–14.

43 John Stuart Mill, *On Liberty* (1869; Oxford: Oxford University Press, 2008).

action should be considered private and hence beyond the interference of the state, especially through the coercive mechanism of the law. Only public actions, which by definition are ones that harm third parties, should be subject to law. Hence, to use some examples involving sex, rape is a public action and needs to be controlled by law, because it harms the victim of the rape. Consensual sexual activities committed in private by adults, however, should be considered private and beyond the control of law because no one is harmed. In general, then, Mill's principle of liberty places all consensual, private, sexual activity outside of the law's business, no matter how much the general public finds such activity, such as homosexuality in the case we are currently examining, distasteful or immoral.

Devlin's argument *could* be closer to Mill's position than it seems on first inspection, for, like Mill, he mentions harm as a justification for state interference in what might appear to be private matters. But the harms to which Devlin points are harms to society in general. To employ the analogy he uses, just as treason is harmful to the state and thus justifiably subject to law, so too are certain sexual activities that serve somehow to break the state apart—to "disintegrate" it, in his words: "There is disintegration when no common morality is observed and history shows that the loosing of moral bonds is often the first stage of disintegration." [44]

As Hart points out, however, there are a number of problems with this position. To begin, the argument is put forward as an empirical claim and yet Devlin provides no empirical evidence of societies that have disintegrated because of a change or lapse in public morality (and, more importantly, evidence that *all* societies *must* disintegrate when this happens). Associated with this problem is another regarding what Devlin means by a "society" or the "continued existence" of a society. Does every change in a society's public morality mean that one society has ceased to exist and another (and worse?) one has been created in its place? For example, women acquired the same voting rights as men in Canada in 1918 and in 1920 in the U.S. Does this mean that we had different societies in these countries after those dates? If so, were they worse societies? Had they truly "disintegrated"? Almost everyone would argue that our societies improved when women were finally granted equal voting rights with men. The suspicion, then, is that Devlin is not really presenting us with a disintegration thesis but with a variation on a conservative thesis whereby we ought to conserve what has been because it has "stood the test of time." If this is so, then we are no longer really talking about preserving society against harm—as occurs with respect to treason—but instead we are merely promoting a thesis for retaining the status quo. [45]

This is particularly problematic when we consider further what Devlin thinks forms the basis of public morality. In his view, we can determine the public morality by asking "the ordinary man, the man in the jury box, who might also be

---

44 Devlin, *The Enforcement of Morals*, 13.

45 H.L.A. Hart, "Social Solidarity and the Enforcement of Morality," *University of Chicago Law Review* 35, no. 1 (1967): 3–4.

called the reasonable man or the right minded man." [46] But for Devlin, public morality is based far more on feeling than it is on reason. This becomes patently clear when we consider that Devlin considers the limit of public morality to occur when the "ordinary man" reaches a point of "intolerance, indignation, and disgust." Devlin believed that homosexuality was "a vice so abominable that its mere presence is an offence" and as such the state had a duty to intervene through the law and regulate that behavior. Otherwise, we risked disintegration. [47]

Without any empirical evidence to support his thesis, along with questions about the appropriateness of his limits on toleration, there is good reason to reject Devlin's disintegration thesis. In its stead, we would be much better off accepting something more like the liberal position, where our concern is harm to particular individuals. We could also attempt to extend this position to groups as well, as communitarians and others do, but we must be careful in doing so to establish a demonstrable harm to the group. In justifying restrictions on bestiality and other sexual acts involving animals, we can point to the harm done to animals, although people are permitted to kill animals under some circumstances. And in the absence of a demonstrable harm to individuals coming from the consensual sexual activity of gay men committed in private, we would be better off without sodomy laws. We will, however, consider this matter further in the final chapter of this book, when we consider the limits of toleration with respect to various sexual activities.

What Are the Advantages and Disadvantages of Solitary Sex?

Speaking at a United Nations Conference on AIDS in 1994, U.S. Surgeon General Joycelyn Elders responded to a question about whether masturbation should be discussed with young people as an alternative to risky sexual practices. Because of her candid response to this question, Elders was forced to resign from her position. Elders's controversial reply acknowledged that masturbation is part of human sexuality and that it makes sense to include it in programs promoting safe-sex practices. Although there were many observers of this incident who were surprised that Elders's practical and open-minded remarks were considered controversial, a large number of people were apparently shocked by her public comments on a topic that many find embarrassing to discuss even in private. A few years later, Elders discussed the taboos surrounding masturbation—both the behavior and talking about the behavior. She speculated that future generations will judge forcing a Surgeon General from office for a public comment on masturbation to be rather foolish. [48]

---

46 Devlin, *The Enforcement of Morals*, 15.
47 Ibid., 17.
48 M. Joycelyn Elders, "The Dreaded 'M' Word," *Nerve*, June 26, 1997, http://www.nerve.com/Dispatches/Elders/mword/.

Could a comment such as Elders's provoke a similar controversy today? Numerous scientific and medical studies have found that masturbation is a near-universal practice, poses no health dangers, and offers some health benefits. Organizations of medical professionals have issued statements challenging erroneous beliefs about the harmful effects of masturbation and underscoring the safety of the practice. Many draconian devices have been invented to discourage and prevent masturbation in the course of human history, but fortunately the use of extreme methods is much less common today.[49] Nevertheless, how many parents still worry about the masturbatory habits of their children? How many people regard private masturbation as a failure of self-discipline or a pathetic substitute for sex? Or have we entered the future that Elders imagined, in which we view this topic with greater understanding and sophistication, and in which the benefits of masturbation are exploited to promote individual happiness, sex education, and the public good?

In this section, we will enumerate the potential benefits of masturbation, and then the possible disadvantages. Afterwards, we will consider whether the probable goods outweigh the probable harms, as well as other conclusions that can be derived from a simple risk/benefit analysis of masturbation.

First, engaging in solitary sex (sometimes referred to as "autoeroticism") carries a very low risk for acquiring a sexually transmitted disease (STD). If the activity is genuinely solitary, and does not involve, for example, sharing a sex toy with another person, then there is virtually no STD risk. Moreover, solitary sex carries no risk of causing an accidental pregnancy. This is, of course, why the former U.S. Surgeon General thought to recommend discussing masturbation with young people, so that they might see it as a viable alternative to more risky companion sex.

Second, another advantage of solitary sex is that it is socially and emotionally uncomplicated. A person does not need to find an appropriate social partner for sexual activities. Even if one has an appropriate social partner, at times this partner may not be available for sex, or may reject one's sexual overtures for a variety of reasons. So solitary sex is easier, socially and emotionally, because one doesn't need to seduce another when on a date, or even arrange a date. Moreover, it is not necessary to be considerate of another's sexual or romantic desires, make oneself sexually attractive to another, worry about whether sexual intimacy is (or isn't) forging a deeper social commitment, be anxious about the adequacy of one's sexual performance or skills, or a host of other concerns that attend companion sex.

---

49 Thomas Laqueur, *Solitary Sex: A Cultural History of Masturbation* (New York: Zone Books, 2003); Robert Wabash, "The Top 10 Most Brutal Anti-Masturbation Devices," *Ranker*, http://www. ranker.com/list/top-10-most-brutal-anti-masturbation-devices/robert-wabash?source=share; Matt Soniak, "Corn Flakes Were Invented as Part of an Anti-Masturbation Crusade," *Mental Floss*, December 28, 2012, http://mentalfloss.com/article/32042/corn-flakes-were-invented-part-anti-masturbation-crusade.

Third, because solitary sex is socially and emotionally uncomplicated, it poses fewer psychological risks than partner sex. One need not fear sexual rejection from another person, or having the sexual thrills of an ongoing relationship disappear. One doesn't have to worry about being unfaithful to a partner when one has sex with oneself, and if one has no partners, then there is no need to worry about whether one's partner "cheats." There will be no messy, guilt-inducing break-ups or depressing endings. Also, one need not fear sexual humiliation or reputation damage, as one can be discreet about one's solitary sexual pursuits and need not fear the betrayal of secrets and intimate moments by a sexual partner.

Fourth, solitary sex is available pretty much when one wants it or can make time for it. One has greater control over one's sexual activities and their generated benefits. One need not feel as if one is missing out on, or not getting enough of, life's sensual pleasures. Active autoerotics can become emotionally and sexually self-sufficient, making them less dependent on others for fulfilling their sexual needs, and therefore less vulnerable to sexual exploitation by others.

Fifth, solitary sex allows individuals a safe way to explore their sexual fantasies, tastes, desires, and pleasures. Such explorations are likely to enhance people's understanding of, or appreciation for, their own body and its capacities for sexual response. They also allow people to explore sexual desires that would be too uncomfortable or dangerous to explore with another person, in ways that may allow them to come to terms with initially disturbing parts of their sexual psyches. This knowledge of one's own body and sexual fantasies can be useful for future non-solitary sexual activities, as well as further autoerotic ones.

Sixth, solitary sex frees an individual from some of the social constraints and conventions of partner sex, in ways that may make future sexual activities more creative and fulfilling. The solitary pursuit of sexual pleasure can encourage creativity, role switching, and sexual experimentation without the pressure of another's judgment. Doing away with the familiar social scripts (about who does what to whom and when) may allow a person to reflect on which sexual conventions are valuable and which are possibly harmful or unnecessarily limiting.

Seventh and last, solitary sex may have considerable health benefits, such as relieving stress and thereby reducing the health risks associated with unrelieved stress, such as high blood pressure, heart disease, and cancer. Moreover, solitary sex, if pursued with moderation and safety, offers an alternative to less healthy sensual pleasures and entertainments, such as excessive eating, recreational drugs, and risky partner sex.

In a context of greater social acceptance and openness, an increase of solitary sexual activity across a community could have a significant social and economic impact, beyond the benefits to individuals. For example, the public promotion of healthy solitary sexual behaviors (along with the promotion of increased condom use, as part of comprehensive sex education) could lower STD and accidental-pregnancy rates, and reduce the psychological damage caused by bad partner sex. This could in turn lower health-care costs and reduce the social problems associated with unwanted pregnancies and children. In an atmosphere of greater tolerance for "solosexuals," new businesses or technologies might be developed, or existing industries expanded, to cater to their needs and wants. We'll leave the project of providing a full economic analysis of the displacement of risky partner sex by an increase in safe solitary sex to our readers, as it falls beyond the scope of this philosophical inquiry.

Many of the aspects of solitary sex that make it relatively risk-free (in terms of its physical, social, and emotional consequences) render it incapable of generating the benefits associated with partner sex. So let us examine the downside to masturbatory sexual activities.

First, if one wants to impregnate another, or be impregnated, solitary sex will not be effective (unless the extracted genetic material is preserved and followed by artificial insemination or embryo transfer, as happens with some fertility treatments). Moreover, frequent masturbation can reduce a man's sperm count, and therefore his ability to impregnate a woman (unfortunately not enough to be a reliable method of birth control, however).

Second, because solitary sex involves emotionally uncomplicated and, essentially, self-regarding behaviors, it does not promote the emotional growth and social skills that can occur in the context of an intimate relationship. There are few opportunities to learn about the needs and expectations of others or to access another point of view on sexuality and intimacy. A sexual life that included only solitary sex could be infantilizing in the sense of promoting self-absorption and even selfishness.

Third, a person who pursues solitary sex at the expense of companion sex may end up socially isolated and lonely. Such a person may fail to form and develop socially and emotionally beneficial sexual relationships with others, and thus fail to take part in the sharing of life experiences that keeps us connected to and involved in the lives of others. People who attempt to fulfill their sexual needs only with solitary sex and who avoid companion sex will miss out on the emotional benefits of having a private life with another person.

Fourth, solitary sex generally lacks the mystery, passion, and unpredictability of companion sex. Sex with oneself, ultimately, may not be sufficiently challenging and therefore exciting. The opportunities for romance and seduction are rather limited in solitary sex, which makes it more risk-free but also less rewarding emotionally. Solitary sex, like partner sex, may require significant imaginative effort to remain pleasurable and to keep it from becoming routine and mechanical. Partner sex has the advantage of engaging with another's imagination and fantasies to keep sex interesting.

Fifth, because solitary sex involves indulging one's sexual fantasies, there may be some risk that one will lose touch with reality. By focusing continually on one's sexual fantasies, one may misinterpret the signals and signs one receives from others. A life that included only solitary sex might fail to provide the reality checks about one's sexuality that companion sex offers.

Sixth, because it is readily available, and requires little effort or coordination with others, one needs considerable self-discipline to balance autoerotic activities with other parts of one's life. When people over-indulge in solitary sex, it can damage their relationships with others or distract them from work and other activities.

Seventh and last, solitary sex may be incomplete in the sense that it is unlikely to make a person feel attractive, desired, or loved by another. While solitary sex avoids the risks of rejection, it fails to provide the benefits of acceptance and caring attention by another human being. Companion sex provides an important avenue for developing emotionally intimate relationships and expressing deep feelings for others, which is an aspect of sexuality that is missing from solitary sex.

It is clear that solitary sex has both important benefits and a number of serious limitations or pitfalls. But rather than try to determine which is superior—solitary or partner sex—it is more useful to try to understand the place of each in a complete and full life. A life that excluded one of these types of sex is likely to be diminished in significant ways. Solitary sexual activities are a good choice for teenagers who are not emotionally ready for companion sex, adults who find themselves in circumstances without suitable partners, people with an easily transmissible infectious disease, or lovers who are physically separated from their partners. There seems to be little reason to disdain or stigmatize the activity of solitary sex or the people who enjoy it, and much to be gained from a tolerant and open-minded attitude to it. In short, solitary sex provides a genuine alternative to companion sex at appropriate times in one's life, and need not be viewed as a pathetic or embarrassing substitute.

Discussion Questions

1. How do intentionalist and reductionist accounts of sexual perversion differ?
2. To what extent is sexual desire physical and to what extent is it mental?
3. What problem(s) is/are associated with the American Psychiatric Association's definition of perverse sex as that which isn't mutually arousing and reciprocal?
4. Is gay sex dysteleogical in any important way? If it is, is that a problem?
5. Are acts that "threaten" the public morality of a state at a particular time analogous to treason?
6. Is sex inherently a social activity?
7. Why are masturbatory acts stigmatized and denigrated?

Further Reading

Freud, Sigmund. *Three Essays on the Theory of Sexuality*, translated by James Strachey. New York: Basic Books, 1905/1962.

Mill, John Stuart. *On Liberty*. Oxford: Oxford University Press, 1869/2008.

Morgan, Seiriol. "Sex in the Head." *Journal of Applied Philosophy* 20, no. 1 (2003): 1–16.

Nagel, Thomas. "Sexual Perversion." *Journal of Philosophy* 66, no. 1 (1969): 5–17.

Nussbaum, Martha. *From Disgust to Humanity: Sexual Orientation and Constitutional Law*. New York and Oxford: Oxford University Press, 2010.

Roughgarden, Joan. *Evolution's Rainbow: Diversity, Gender and Sexuality in Nature and People*. Los Angeles: University of California Press, 2004.

Soble, Alan. "Masturbation." *Pacific Philosophical Quarterly* 61 (1980): 233–44.

Chapter 6

Sex and Marriage

In the Abrahamic religions, marriage is the institution that "legitimates" sex, and therefore it is important for us to consider marriage in this text. In this chapter, we will do exactly this by considering the connection between sex and marriage, including the traditional prohibitions of premarital and extramarital sex. We will also explore which marriages the state should recognize, whether the state should penalize adulterers, and whether and when arranged marriage is a beneficial practice. Political philosophers are interested in the relationship between the state and family, and the state's role in regulating the private sphere of life. The terms of civil marriage, and its dissolution, define the legal entitlements and responsibilities of spouses and shape relationships among family members. How far should the state go in regulating the family in order to protect vulnerable members from domestic abuse and to promote broader societal goals, such as gender equality?

Must Marital Partners Be Sexual Partners?

In contemporary North America, the *legal* answer to this question is simple: no. Since there is no premarital test to prove sexual potency, then, obviously, one need not consummate one's marriage by engaging in sexual intercourse. Hence, people whose sexual organs have been so damaged that they cannot have intercourse are allowed to marry, as can anyone who, for whatever reason, is impotent.[1] Nonetheless, sex has typically been thought to be a part of marriage. Until recently, for example, a couple applying for a marriage license was required to have a blood test in many jurisdictions. Though widely believed to have something to do with the compatibility of blood types for the couple's possible future children, the tests were actually aimed (and still are in approximately seven states), at detection of various types of communicable diseases and particularly for sexually transmitted diseases (STDs) such as syphilis. The laws were constructed in the 1930s when syphilis was relatively common and there was no cure for it. But once treatments were found for common STDs, blood-test requirements for marriage slowly stopped being enforced and eventually were done away with in most jurisdictions.[2] Testing for STDs and allegedly "incompatible" blood types only made sense, of course, under the assumption that people who got married would engage in sex, including reproductive sex. Moreover, some Christian and other faiths hold that a marriage is not valid until it has been sexually consummated and husband and wife have become "one flesh," as it says in the Bible.[3] In the Roman Catholic Church, sexual intercourse between the husband and wife serves to consummate a marriage only if the spouses are not using artificial forms of birth control and are open to the possibility of creating new life.

The Bible, in fact, goes even further than this and regards sexual intercourse as a *duty* one owes to one's spouse: "The husband should fulfill his marital duty to his wife, and likewise the wife to her husband. The wife's body does not belong to her alone but also to her husband. In the same way, the husband's body does not belong to him alone but also to his wife. Do not deprive each other except by mutual consent...."[4] As a result of this edict, it was thought, at least until the late 1970s, that by getting married, a wife had consented to sex with her husband whenever he wanted; hence, spousal rape was conceptually impossible because marital sex involved implicit, if not explicit, consent. Fortunately, in many jurisdictions, the laws have changed so that it is possible for someone to bring charges against a spouse for rape.

Despite this change in the law and, in some cases, in religious obligation, marriage and sex continue to be closely linked in popular belief, as is made clear in the following playground song:

> Dave and Joy,
> Sitting in a tree,
> K-I-S-S-I-N-G
> First comes love,

---

1   Richard Wasserstrom, "Is Adultery Immoral?", in *Philosophy and Sex*, ed. Robert Baker and Frederick Elliston, 207–21 (Buffalo, NY: Prometheus, 1975).

2   Robert Shmerling, "The Truth about Premarital Blood Testing," *InteliHealth*, 2011, http://www.intelihealth.com/IH/ihtIH/WSIHW000/35320/35323/361888.html?d=dmtHMSContent.

3   Genesis 2:24; Matthew 19:5; Ephesians 5:31.

4   1 Corinthians 7:3–6.

Then comes marriage,
Then comes baby
In a baby carriage.

The song describes how the progression of intimate relationships is *supposed* to proceed. First, you fall in love (with a person of the opposite sex), then you get married, and then you have sex, which produces children. More generally, we could say that the song expresses succinctly what Frederick Elliston has called the "Western norm of sexuality." [5] This norm suggests that (1) there is a natural link between sexual intercourse and reproduction; (2) children require the stability of a "family," which is typically assumed to include one mother and one father; (3) societies are, therefore, justified in promoting the establishment of a "family" through a variety of laws and policies, which include, most prominently, restricting marriage to one man and one woman. This norm has a long history in Western thought, dating back at least to Plato in the fourth century BCE. In his late work *The Laws*, Plato maintains that marriage and reproduction are so important to society that we should think of them as social responsibilities, and not, as we tend to do today, as personal choices that aim at individual fulfillment. Indeed, Plato held that we should construct laws to enforce this responsibility. He suggested that people who hadn't married by the age of 35 be required to pay a fine, which is ironic because Plato, who lived into his seventies, never married and never had children.

The Ancient Greek historian Xenophon (c. 430–c. 354 BCE) agreed with Plato's view that the primary purpose of marriage is the production of children, and he added that marriage also efficiently divides labor between women's work inside the home and man's work outside of it. Oddly, from a contemporary perspective, love between a husband and wife was not expected or common; perhaps even odder (for us) was that marital sex was not associated with pleasure. Pleasurable sex, for the husband at least, was sought *outside* the marriage, as is made clear in the following passage taken from a court case at the time: "Mistresses we keep for pleasure, concubines for daily attendance upon our persons, and wives to bear us legitimate children and be our housekeepers." [6]

A wife's sex life, as suggested above, was dramatically different from her husband's. In order to ensure that a wife had sex and reproduced only with her husband, there were laws that were strictly enforced and provided severe penalties for adulterous women. A husband could "dismiss" or "put away" his adulterous wife. Indeed, when adulterous women were seen in public, they could be punished even by people outside the family. This view of women as dangerously, and indeed sinfully, sexual can be traced all the way back to the story of the Garden of Eden. Remember that Adam is led astray by Eve. It is she who

---

5   Frederick Elliston, "In Defense of Promiscuity," in *Philosophy and Sex*, ed. Robert Baker and Frederick Elliston, 222–46 (Buffalo, NY: Prometheus, 1975).

6   Morton Hunt, *The Natural History of Love* (New York: Bantam Doubleday Bell, 1994), 25.

encourages Adam to eat the forbidden fruit of the tree of knowledge. As the story continues in Genesis, we discover that sex and reproduction begin only *after* the fall from our state of grace; they were not part of life in the idyllic Garden of Eden. Contrast this account of the beginning of sexual sin with the depiction of the virginal Mary, whose pregnancy is the result of immaculate conception rather than sexual intercourse. In Christianity, then, we get a completely bifurcated view of woman, especially with respect to sex. Virginal women are pure, but those who engage in sexual intercourse are tainted and often thought of as the cause of men's downfall. As Saint Augustine said, "Through a woman we were sent to destruction; through a woman salvation was restored to us."[7]

For devout Christians today, marriage is the only way to contain the sin of sex for both women and men. Immanuel Kant, in the eighteenth century, had an interesting take on this matter. One of Kant's principles for moral action (which he called "the categorical imperative") was that we not use people solely as a means to an end.[8] When we do so, we turn a person into a mere object or thing, and this, Kant said, violates the inherent dignity of human beings. He maintained that sexual interactions always run the risk of immoral behavior, as we use another as a thing to gratify our sexual desires. As he put it:

> Sexual love makes of the loved person an Object of appetite;
> as soon as that appetite has been stilled, the person is cast
> aside as one casts away a lemon which has been sucked dry ...
> as soon as a person becomes an Object of appetite for another,
> all motives of moral relationship cease to function, because as
> an Object of appetite for another a person becomes a thing and
> can be treated and used as such by everyone.[9]

Only in marriage can we be absolved from this sort of immoral behavior. We do so, according to Kant, because in marriage "I yield myself completely to another and obtain the person of the other in return, I win myself back; I have given myself up as the property of another, but in turn I take that other as my property, and so win myself back again in winning the person whose property I have become. In this way the two persons become a unity of will."[10] As legally unified subjects, married people do not treat each other as disposable things, to be cast aside when their appetites have been satisfied.

Many within the Christian tradition, however, thought that even sex within marriage was clearly a distant second best to remaining pure through celibacy. Saint Paul wrote that it would be best if all men could remain celibate like him,

---

7   Saint Augustine, *Sermon* 289, ii.

8   Immanuel Kant, *The Metaphysics of Morals*, trans. Mary Gregor (Cambridge: Cambridge University Press, 1996).

9   Kant, *Lectures on Ethics*, 163.

10 Ibid., 167.

but, for those who "cannot exercise self-control, they should marry. For it is better to marry than to burn with passion [or lust]."[11] Saint Augustine even advised newly married people to refrain from sexual intercourse and, when they could not contain their sexual urges, to engage in sex only for the sake of producing children. Hence, as Morton Hunt tells us, love and sex even within marriage were seen as completely separate: love was considered God's business while sex was seen as the Devil's.[12] For great periods throughout Western history, then, Elliston's Western norm of sexuality was not in existence. Marriage allowed for the possibility of legitimate sex, but only for the purposes of reproduction, not as an expression of love, and certainly not for its intrinsic pleasure. For this reason, husbands and wives, in the past, did not look to each other for romance, and rarely for sex.

Consider courtly love in the medieval period. From a contemporary perspective, a surprising aspect of courtly love was that it wasn't directed toward one's marriage partner. In the wealthy, aristocratic classes at least, marriage was typically arranged and was done so on the basis of considerations of wealth and politics. Love was something to be pursued *outside* of marriage, a point made clearly in 1174 by the Countess of Champagne, who was considered an expert on the topic: "We declare and we hold as firmly established that love cannot exert its powers between two people who are married to each other. For lovers give each other everything freely, under no compulsion of necessity, but married people are in duty bound to give in to each other's desires and deny themselves to each other in nothing."[13]

But just as courtly love was not directed toward one's marriage partner, neither was it directed toward sexual intercourse. Rather, it was a type of "pure" devotion. The thirteenth-century Italian poet Dante is a perfect example of this sentiment in his love for Beatrice, who became his muse. In his *Vita Nuova*, he recounts that he first met her when he was nine years old and immediately began to worship her. But, as Hunt points out, "He never spoke a word to her, and scarcely hoped to; he made no efforts to meet her and saw her only at rare intervals. Even to think of sexual intimacies would have been totally impossible under this conception of love. Beatrice was perfect, goddess-like, and a source of spiritual guidance, rather than a flesh-and-blood female."[14]

Despite differences between the historical conceptions of love, sex, and marriage, one constant has been the view that the main function of marriage has been to have and raise children. That is, despite radically different views historically of the morality of adultery, the nature of men and women (and hence of the social standing of husband and wife), and the place of love within a marriage, Western societies have thought fairly consistently that marriage is primarily about children. This view about the primary purpose of marriage remained at

---

11 1 Corinthians 7:9.
12 Hunt, *The Natural History of Love*, 123.
13 Cited in ibid., 143–44.
14 Cited in ibid., 168.

least until the middle of the twentieth century. According to Robin West, at that time, marriage

> meant a lifelong union, sanctioned by state, community, and faith, between a man and a woman that hopefully would be blessed with children. A man contemplating marriage would expect to take on responsibility of being head of the household. He would be responsible for the economic support of his dependents, including his wife, and he would be charged with the duty of making decisions on behalf of his family.... A woman contemplating marriage would expect to enjoy her husband's economic support, and would be charged with the daily tasks of raising their children, as well as the domestic chores involved in maintaining a household. They would both expect lifelong, monogamous sexual intimacy and affection from the other. Both husband and wife, if this pact were honored, would achieve considerable social acceptance from their larger community in the process.[15]

While this "traditional" conception of marriage is only about 60 years old, it is drastically different from our current conception, perhaps particularly with respect to the roles to be played by husband and wife. In the U.S., "head and master" laws have been repealed so that a husband is no longer officially the sole head of household who manages the estate, nor is he expected to be the only breadwinner. Only a relatively small percentage of wives now work exclusively inside the home; in 2009 in Canada and the United States, just over 58 per cent of women over 16 were in the workforce, twice the 1976 figure.[16] And, theoretically at least, child rearing and household chores are now split between a husband and wife. While marriage partners typically plan on a lifelong, monogamous relationship, this is increasingly rare. Though statistics for adultery are quite varied, different studies indicate that between 20 and 60 per cent of married men cheat, as do about 20 to 50 per cent of married women,[17] with a combined probability of between 40 and 76 per cent that at least one member of a married couple will have an affair over the course of a marriage.[18]

Many people think that such moves away from the traditional view of marriage have placed the institution in serious peril, and some have argued that we

---

15 Robin West, *Marriage, Sexuality, and Gender* (Boulder, CO & London: Paradigm, 2007), 1–2.

16 Statistics Canada, http://www.statcan.gc.ca/pub/89-503-x/2010001/article/11387-eng.htm; United States Department of Labor, http://www.dol.gov/wb/factsheets/Qf-laborforce-10.htm.

17 David Buss and Todd Shackleford, "Susceptibility to Infidelity in the First Year of Marriage," *Journal of Research in Personality* 31 (1997): 193–221; Pamela Drukerman, *Lust in Translation: The Rules of Infidelity from Tokyo to Tennessee* (New York: Penguin, 2007).

18 A.P. Thompson, "Extramarital Sex: A Review of the Research Literature," *Journal of Sex Research* 19 (1983): 1–22.

must return to what they perceive as the core values and function of marriage. One particularly acute point of contention that has arisen recently is whether a marriage must consist of one man and one woman. We turn to this issue in the next section.

Who Should Be Allowed to Marry?[19]

The conventional answer to this question is one adult female and one adult male. But over the past two decades, LGBT (lesbian, gay, bisexual, and transgender) civil-rights groups have organized to change existing polices so that they allow people of the same sex to marry one another. John Corvino has been a leading spokesperson for the movement for "marriage equality." He writes,

> Generally speaking, it is good for human beings to commit to someone else to have and to hold, for better or for worse, and so on, for life. It is good, regardless of whether they happen to be straight or gay. It is good, not only for them, but also for their neighbors, because happy, stable couples make happy, stable citizens. And marriage helps sustain this commitment like nothing else.[20]

Some social conservatives support same-sex marriage for the reasons given in this passage. If a legally formalized commitment promotes the stability of couples and families, which in turn provides social and emotional support for individuals, then we should expand access to the institution where appropriate.

Some conservatives oppose same-sex marriage, although in North America and Europe they are quickly becoming a minority. Maggie Gallagher, co-founder of the National Organization for Marriage and an opponent of same-sex marriage, has been a leading voice in favor of the "traditional" view. In what follows, we explain her arguments in some detail and, following Corvino, point out what we take to be weaknesses in her arguments.

Gallagher's arguments fall into two broad camps: definitional *a priori* arguments and consequentialist *a posteriori* ones. The "Definitional Argument" assumes that "treating same-sex unions as marriages…is not true" (98). Just as 'giving birth to a child' is necessary for someone to be classified as a mother, to use Gallagher's example, so a 'union between a man and woman' is necessary for a couple to be classified as married. The reason for this, in turn, is that

---

19 Parts of this section were originally published in R.S. Stewart, "Review of J. Corvino and M. Gallagher, *Debating Same-Sex Marriage*," in *Metapsychology* 16, no. 36 (2012), http://metapsychology.mentalhelp.net/poc/view_doc.php?type=book&id=6624&cn=400.

20 John Corvino and Maggie Gallagher, *Debating Same-Sex Marriage* (New York and Oxford: Oxford University Press, 2012), 180; emphasis deleted. All further references in this section to this text will be given parenthetically in the text. Note that the book takes the form of an extended debate between Corvino and Gallagher on the issue of same-sex marriage.

only a union of opposite-sex couples can produce children. Hence, even if same-sex unions can be everything else a marriage can be (though Gallagher clearly doesn't believe this, given some of her consequentialist arguments, which are discussed below) they are, by definition, excluded from being "marriages."

In order for Gallagher's argument to work, she must stipulate what the term 'marriage' means. In defining 'marriage,' she does not attempt to capture its legal or social meaning, for legal and social meanings constantly shift. To use one of Gallagher's examples, a 'corporation' refers to something constructed (in this case, via the law), and its meaning can be changed simply by changing the law. According to Gallagher, terms such as 'marriage' (and 'mother') "refer to a natural phenomenon that the law does not create or control," (103), or to what philosophers call "natural kinds." 'Marriage,' on this view, is a natural-kind term, and picks out something that pre-exists language and changing human conventions.

There is a great deal of philosophical scholarship on the problem of reference, and much dispute about whether "natural kinds" exist and how the parts of a language refer to them. We won't enter into this debate here. Instead, at least for the sake of argument, let's agree that there are natural kinds. The question then becomes whether the terms 'mother' and 'marriage' refer to such entities. As Corvino argues, there is good reason to think that they do not (21–44; 180–85). For example, when we refer to a woman who has adopted a child as a 'mother,' even if she has no biological children, we do not feel as if we are stretching the meaning of the term, which Gallagher herself admits (103). So Gallagher's analogy here does not establish its point and we are left asking why 'marriage' must refer to a natural category and not a legal/customary one. Gallagher's arguments reflect the assumptions of the natural-law tradition, in which mothers and the institution of marriage have essential purposes and characteristics. The "new-natural-law theorists" claim that the essential feature of marriage is that it be a "comprehensive union which includes the biological union of coitus," and which leads to the formation of the "natural" (i.e., biological) family (188). The problem here is that heterosexual couples who are incapable of having children are not prevented from marrying, nor does Gallagher think they should be (cf. 185–87).

The definitional argument, therefore, does not establish that same-sex marriages are not true marriages, and it is difficult to imagine other *a priori* arguments that would demonstrate this. We need, then, to look at *a posteriori*, consequentialist arguments. Gallagher's consequentialist arguments take a number of forms, the most important of which focuses on the harms that she believes will befall children if we allow same-sex marriages. Here, Gallagher moves from the claim that children typically do best when they are raised by their own married biological parents to the conclusion that we shouldn't therefore allow same-sex couples to marry. Corvino, in response, maintains that there are three different forms of this argument, which he labels (1) The Emboldening Argument, (2) The Message Argument, and (3) The Stretching Argument.

The Emboldening Argument suggests that "extending marriage to same-sex couples would encourage (or 'embolden') more of them to have children" (5).

But this begs the question since it assumes that it is a bad thing for same-sex couples to have children. This is exactly what needs to be proved, however, and it can't simply be assumed. Is there any reason to believe that children reared by same-sex couples fare badly? On the whole, there is not. While there are a number of studies indicating that children do better when they are raised in stable families with two parents (as opposed to being raised, e.g., in single-parent families or families with one biological/legal parent and one step-parent), these studies *include* adoptive parents in the category "parents" (46 ff.). Moreover, there is a lot of evidence showing that children of same-sex couples do just as well as children reared by opposite-sex couples. Indeed, in the longest longitudinal study of its kind, Nanette Gartrell and others have shown that 17-year-olds of lesbian mothers rate higher in social, school/academic, and total competence, and significantly lower in social problems, such as rule-breaking and aggression, than their age cohorts raised in other settings, such as in a "typical" family of one mother and one father.[21]

In assessing arguments of this sort, we should recognize that there will be lots of variance *within* the groups being compared. Hence, some children of single parents will do exceptionally well, while some children in opposite-sex marriages will fare badly. As a result of this variance, it is difficult to make across-the-board, general claims about who should or should not have children. Indeed, if we knew that, we *might* be justified in requiring people to get a license to have children, and refuse a license to those prospective parents who are identified by current research to have high rates of bad parenting. But we simply don't have this kind of knowledge in anything but a general way, with lots of variations. One thing that does seem perfectly clear, however, is that if the interests and welfare of children are our goal, then we ought to concentrate on efforts to ensure they are free from abuse, are housed safely, fed adequately, and educated well, not on the issue of whether same-sex couples should be allowed to raise or adopt children.

The "Message Argument" also works from the claim that children do best when raised in a stable family consisting of their biological parents. According to this anti–same-sex marriage argument, attention then turns to the alleged fact that men in particular often walk away from their families, leaving their children to be raised in less than ideal circumstances—e.g., in a single-parent family or in a family with a step-parent. In order to combat this tendency in fathers, we need to ensure that adults recognize that "children need mothers and fathers, that societies need babies, and that adults have an obligation to shape their sexual behavior so as to give their children stable families in which to grow up" (23). However, if we allow same-sex marriages, we are not sending this message, according to Gallagher. Rather, she writes,

---

21 Nanette Gartrell and H. Bos, "US National Longitudinal Lesbian Family Study: Psychological Adjustment of 17-Year-Old Adolescents," *Pediatrics* (2010), http://www.nllfs.org/images/uploads/pdf/NLLFS-psychological-adjustment-17-year-olds-2010.pdf.

> Same-sex marriage would enshrine in law a public judgment
> that the desire of adults for families of choice outweighs the need
> of children for mothers and fathers. It would give sanction and
> approval to the creation of a motherless or fatherless family as a
> deliberately chosen "good." It would mean the law was neutral
> as to whether children had mothers and fathers. Motherless and
> fatherless families would be deemed just fine (24).

There is certainly something to be said for Gallagher's argument here: one need only look at the number of "dead-beat dads" to see this. Being a parent comes with a host of responsibilities that many in our society fail to meet. But as philosophers we must be careful not to extend her legitimate point to other points that don't necessarily follow. For, as we have just seen, the basic premise here—that children do best with, and therefore *need* their biological mother and father—is false, and so the argument is weak. Several other points used in the critique of the emboldening argument can also be used here, for example that there are other, and better, ways to ensure that children fare well than to oppose same-sex marriage. Additionally, we must also be wary, as Corvino cautions us (55), about moving from a claim about an ideal to claims about what is necessary or mandatory. We rarely make this move, and for good reason. Imagine moving from the claim that ideally children should be in families that are well-off financially to the claim that couples with low incomes not be allowed to marry. *One* of the reasons why such an argument would be unacceptable is that lots of children raised in non-ideal settings do perfectly well.[22]

Corvino points to additional problems with the message argument. The argument assumes that marriage has only one message to send: that children need their own biological parents. Yet marriage sends out—or can send out—important messages about lots of other things, such as the importance of love and commitment, and of providing mutual support. Finally, excluding a group from marriage also sends a message: "When we consider other groups who were once excluded from marriage—notably, slaves and prisoners—that message is pretty clear: you are less than a full citizen. Your relationships aren't 'real'; your families don't matter" (58).

Finally, the "Stretching Argument" maintains that if "marriage is expanded to include same-sex couples, norms of fidelity and other important rules will no longer be seen as core features of marriage.... The result will be more out-of wedlock births, more divorce, and more broken homes for children" (190). According to Gallagher, the norms of fidelity for heterosexual couples will be altered if we allow same-sex marriages, because the norms of gay male couples, in particular, allow for far more promiscuity and adultery. This will send a message to straight married couples that it is okay to cheat on your spouse. In response, while it may be true that gay men are less likely to require sexual

---

22 Other arguments here could focus on the rights of individuals to reproduce.

exclusivity from their long-term partners than heterosexuals and lesbians, it is hard to see, as Corvino points out, how this behavior of a very small group will alter the behavior of heterosexual couples. Certainly other norms and ideals of heterosexual marriage have remained in the face of alternative lifestyles and behavior. As Corvino writes,

> In terms of raw numbers, there are probably more straight "swingers" than there are gay men, and yet (as Gallagher documents) people still overwhelmingly expect sexual exclusivity in marriage. There are "commuter marriages," and yet people still associate marriage with co-habitation and mutual domestic care, etc. There are marriages where spouses are scarcely apart, marriages where they take separate vacations; some with frequent sex, some with infrequent sex; some with a highly gendered division of labor, some that defy gender expectations, and so on.... [M]arital norms endure even when individuals know how to think for themselves. (197)

Furthermore, the partners of gay men may value "sexual fidelity" less than the partners of straight men or lesbians, and therefore gay couples are less likely to break up over this. Straight and lesbian couples might have something to learn from gay men about the relationship between sexual and emotional intimacy.

We could also include "slippery-slope" concerns as forms of the stretching argument. Such arguments, in general, maintain that once we move from the status quo, we will slide down a slope to a position that is much worse than where we began. For example, Rick Santorum, a former Republican senator and presidential candidate, maintained that allowing same-sex marriage would inevitably lead to the acceptance of sexual acts involving a "man on child, man on dog, or whatever else the case may be" (64). For this argument to work, however, we would need to see a logical or a causal connection between allowing same-sex marriages and practices such as bestiality and pedophilia. But there is no empirical evidence supporting a causal connection, and there is certainly no necessary or logical connection between adult, loving relationships and bestiality or pedophilia.

Perhaps this is why critics of same-sex marriage who use a slippery-slope argument typically exploit worries about polygamy rather than bestiality or pedophilia. That is, some argue that, if we allow same-sex couples to marry, why not allow more than two people to marry as well? As an empirical matter, communities that now permit same-sex marriage have not generally become more tolerant of polygamy. Moreover, groups in the United States that do promote polygamy, such as Mormon fundamentalists, are strongly opposed to same-sex marriage. As a matter of principle, however, the slippery slope toward polygamy is more complex. This criticism is, in essence, that arguments supporting same-sex marriage also support polygamous marriages, so we need to revisit these arguments.

In what follows, then, we will examine the issue of polygamy in a few of its various forms and suggest that at least some forms of marriage between more than two people might be legitimate. Hence, even if it turns out factually that opening up marriage to same-sex couples leads to (or slides toward) opening up marriage to more than two people, this may not be of particular concern.

As noted above, there are both rights-based and consequentialist arguments supporting same-sex marriage. One rights-based argument rests on the premise that marriage and family rights are basic human rights.[23] One consequentialist argument (formulated by Corvino) rests on the claim that expanding marriage to include same-sex couples promotes both individual and societal good. On the face of it, these arguments do support formally recognizing those polygamous units that contribute to the well-being of their members and society. Yet, as Corvino notes, the most typical and widely practiced form of polygamy "tends almost always to be polygyny, where one man has multiple wives.... The usual result is a sexist and classist society where high status males acquire multiple wives while lower status males become virtually unmarriageable" (67). In short, patriarchal forms of polygamy (and monogamy), in which wives are subordinate to their husbands, and which leave many men unable to exercise the right to marry, are not tolerable in societies committed to gender and social equality. But we need to determine if polygamy differs from monogamy in terms of being predicated upon, or providing a foundation for, various gender and class hierarchies.

Polygamy has been around a long time. For example, many of the early prophets and the patriarchs discussed in the Old Testament had multiple wives. Polygyny was allowed in the Jewish faith until approximately 1000 CE. There is, however, no mention of polygamy in the New Testament, and the early Christian Church did not recognize it. But some Protestant sects that broke away from the Roman Catholic Church in the sixteenth century did permit polygyny. The father of the Protestant Revolution and founder of the Lutheran Church, Martin Luther, wrote, "I confess that I cannot forbid a person to marry several wives, for it does not contradict the Scripture. If a man wishes to marry more than one wife he should be asked whether he is satisfied in his conscience that he may do so in accordance with the word of God. In such a case the civil authority has nothing to do in the matter."[24] But no form of polygamy ever became common in mainstream Protestantism. It has, however, been a part of other religious groups in the West, particularly the Mormons, who accepted polygyny from the time of their origin in the early nineteenth century, until they disallowed the practice in 1890. Several splinter groups, such as the Fundamentalist Church of Jesus Christ

---

23 This right is recognized in the Universal Declaration of Human Rights, Article 16, passed by the United Nations General Assembly in 1948, http://www.un.org/en/documents/udhr/index.shtml#a16.

24 See George Joyce, *Christian Marriage: An Historical and Doctrinal Study* (London: Sheed and Ward, 1933).

of Latter-Day Saints (FLDS), left the Mormon Church and continue to practice polygyny to this day. In fact, the leader of the FLDS Church, Warren Jeffs, was found guilty of sexual assault and the aggravated sexual assault of children (some of his wives), and he is currently serving a life sentence in Texas.

Jeffs's case is instructive. His father, Rulon Jeffs, was the former leader of the FLDS and had approximately twenty wives and sixty children. When he died, his son Warren married all of his widows (presumably with the exception of his mother) in order to solidify his political power and claim as the next leader of the FLDS. He married several other women as well, and arranged a number of marriages for several of his followers. Many of these matches were between adult men and adolescent girls who had not yet reached the legal age of consent. Marriage among the FLDS offers an image of polygamy as a hierarchical and patriarchal institution in which girls are forced into marriage without consent. Clearly, if this is what all polygamy looked like, then we would have good grounds for dismissing it as a legitimate form of marriage.

A number of critics have argued along these lines against polygamy. Thom Brooks, for example, maintains that almost all forms of polygamy are cases of polygyny and, in these types of marriage, women are at great risk for a whole host of harms.[25] According to the empirical studies that Brooks cites, women in polygynous marriages have a higher risk (than women in monogamous families) of suffering from low self-esteem, powerlessness, lack of autonomy, depression, emotional abuse, and are more likely to contract STDs from their husbands. These wives thus experience less marital happiness and have more problematic mother-child relationships. Moreover, the children of such marriages are also at higher risk for developmental and behavioral issues.

While these are all serious problems for polygamy, there is room for a critical response to these arguments. Cheshire Calhoun argues that "gender inequality is a contingent, not a conceptual, feature of polygamy."[26] For example, the studies to which Brooks refers were all conducted in very patriarchal, traditional communities in the Middle East, Africa, and the U.S. Is it possible, as Martha Nussbaum asks, to find a "sex-equal polygamy," where power is not asymmetrical and the autonomy of both men and women is respected?[27] This is the sort of polygamy endorsed by groups such as "Loving More," which has advocated for decades for *polyamorous* marriage. Polyamory is, they suggest, a form of "romantic love with more than one person [which occurs] honestly, ethically, and with the full knowledge and consent of all concerned."[28]

---

25 Thom Brooks, "The Problem with Polygamy," *Philosophical Topics* 37, no. 2 (2009): 109–22, http://papers.ssrn.com/sol3/papers.cfm?abstract_id=1331492.

26 Cheshire Calhoun, "Who's Afraid of Polygamous Marriage? Lessons from Same-Sex Marriage Advocacy from the History of Polygamy," *San Diego Law Review* 42 (2005): 1039.

27 Martha Nussbaum, *Liberty of Conscience: In Defense of America's Tradition of Religious Equality* (New York: Basic Books, 2008), 197.

28 Loving More, "FAQs About Polyamory," n.d., http://www.lovemore.com/faq/.

In her article on polyamory, Elizabeth Emens describes the polyamorous relationships of four contemporary Americans, which may live up to Nussbaum's ideal of "sex-equal polygamy." They form a diverse group. April Divilbiss lives with two straight men. Although they once tried a threesome, they were dissatisfied with that and so April sleeps with her two "husbands" separately.[29] Adam is a bisexual man who is married to Amber, and he also has romantic relationships with two bisexual men. They do not all live together, though one of the male lovers lives in an apartment in the same building as Adam and Amber. They all have some relationship with other members in the group, but Amber is neither bisexual nor polyamorous, and "she does not need the person she's with to be the same way."[30] Elizabeth Joseph is a lawyer who lives in Utah with her husband and his eight other wives. Elizabeth shares a house with one other wife. Some of the wives have had group sex with their husband, but typically sex occurs between one wife and the husband, an event that is scheduled in advance by appointment. Finally, Dossie Easton, coauthor of *The Ethical Slut*, has lived openly as a bisexual polyamorist since she left her abusive husband in the late 1960s.

The relationships briefly described here vary considerably, ranging from a traditional Mormon polygynous arrangement to ones that involve sexual activity both within and outside of the committed, primary relationship. The participants in all of them say that, despite some of the challenges that maintaining simultaneous romantic relationships present, they are fully consensual and egalitarian and work better for these particular individuals than monogamous relationships would. Easton describes this when she says that she would never promise monogamy again because, in her experience, monogamy turned her into a "piece of property."[31] Elizabeth, on the other hand, finds mutual support in her relationship because it allows her to successfully juggle a demanding career with motherhood and marriage, something that many women in monogamous marriages find difficult, if not impossible, to do.

A vast majority of people remain unconvinced, however, and believe that, whatever we call it, multiple-partner sexual relationships are wrong. A 2009 Gallup Poll, for example, found that 91 per cent of Americans were opposed to polygamy.[32] We seem to believe, as the U.S. Tenth Circuit court put it, that "monogamy is inextricably woven into the fabric of our society. It is the bedrock

---

29 April and her "husbands" made the news in the late 1990s as a result of a Tennessee juvenile court taking away her child (from a previous relationship) because the judge believed that the child was being adversely affected by being raised in such an environment. The child now lives with her biological grandmother.

30 Elizabeth Emens, "Monogamy's Law: Compulsory Monogamy and Polyamorous Existence," *NYU Review of Law and Social Change* 29 (2004): 313, accessed August 5, 2012, http://papers.ssrn.com/sol3/papers.cfm?abstract_id=506242##.

31 Ibid., 291.

32 US News, "Poll: More Americans Consider Extramarital Affairs Wrong Than Polygamy," US News.com, July 2, 2009, http://www.usnews.com/opinion/articles/2009/07/02/poll-more-americans-consider-extramarital-affairs-wrong-than-polygamy.

upon which our culture is built."[33] According to Emens, this deeply ingrained view is based upon two quite different traditions—one coming from science and another from literature.

Within the scientific tradition, some evolutionary psychologists and sociobiologists have argued that there are evolutionary benefits to monogamy over promiscuity. For example, some suggest that monogamy can aid in bi-parental care. Such care is especially necessary for species whose infants are exceedingly helpless, such as many types of birds and, of course, humans. Another reason for monogamy is "reciprocity." Alternatively, promiscuity, at least for males, could have an advantage, in terms of natural selection, because it might allow men to produce more offspring. In game theory, this is called the defect, or non-cooperation, strategy. Although pursuing such strategies in the short term offers benefits, pursuing them with others over longer periods of time usually produces sub-optimal results. This is because defectors or cheaters won't be trusted enough to be allowed into cooperative ventures, such as mating. Therefore, men who behave monogamously will reap the benefits of cooperation—benefits not available to individuals on their own.[34]

In the Western literary tradition, monogamy is much valorized. One example is the speech given by Aristophanes in Plato's *Symposium*. Aristophanes recounts a mythical tale of the human past. At one time, humans were round, as each of us was joined to another. We were, Aristophanes tells us, exceptionally happy at this time, but we destroyed this by committing the sin of *hubris*. That is, we thought too highly of ourselves and even thought we were the equal of the gods. To punish us, Zeus split each of us in two. The punishment proved to be too severe, however, as people were unable to go on with their lives and eventually died from their extraordinary feelings of loneliness. Taking pity on us, Zeus moved our genitals from back to front so we could reproduce sexually (whereas previously we had reproduced by planting our seed in the ground, like grasshoppers, as Aristophanes tells us). Aristophanes makes it clear, though, that sex is a distant second best to the wholeness that we once experienced, because in sex we are only temporarily joined with another. So, if we were asked what we really want, we would reply that we desperately want to be made whole again: "to be rolled into one ... to be together, day and night, never to be parted again."[35] Therefore, according to Aristophanes, love should be defined as the desire to be made whole again with "one's other half." Encapsulated in this short tale is the longstanding belief that there is one—and only one—person in the world who is my other half, my "soul mate" who completes me, and who makes a happy and fulfilling life possible.

---

33 Cited in Emens, "Monogamy's Law," 291.

34 See David Barash and Judith Eve Lipton, *Strange Bedfellows: The Surprising Connection between Sex, Evolution and Monogamy* (New York: Bellevue Literary Press, 2009).

35 Plato, *Symposium*, 192d.

Although culturally authoritative, the scientific and literary traditions that tout the virtues of monogamy are problematic. Scientifically, there is at least as much, and probably more, evidence supporting the evolutionary advantages of promiscuity. According to David Barash and Judith Lipton, "Monogamy is extremely rare in the animal world, … it simply isn't 'natural' for animals or human beings."[36] Indeed, "out of about 4,000 mammal species, only a handful have ever been called monogamous."[37] It may be that the costs of defecting from cooperation with one partner are lower than the payoff for being promiscuous. As suggested above, promiscuity increases a male's chance of impregnating more women and thus for his genes (and the trait of being promiscuous) to be naturally selected. The case is more complex for the advantages of female promiscuity. DNA evidence shows that the offspring of animals are often not genetically related to the male half of a social pair, and some theorists conjecture that a female's promiscuity increases her chances of (i) getting pregnant, or (ii) having healthy children due to competition among genetically different sperm in fertilizing an egg, or (iii) enlisting more men in the protection of her children, and so on.[38]

Similarly, the romantic myths that circulate in literature about the undying, unique, and singularly focused love and sexual attraction between two characters provide an incomplete picture of human intimacy. Very few individuals today engage in what Emens calls "super-monogamy"—i.e., having only one sexual partner throughout one's entire life. While figures are notoriously hard to come by here, polls indicate that heterosexual men in various Western countries have between 9 and 30 female sexual partners over a lifetime, while heterosexual women in these same countries have approximately 4–17 male sexual partners over a lifetime.[39] And the percentage of men and women who have only one partner over an entire lifetime is decreasing precipitously as sexual mores change.[40] And even "simple monogamy," described as having only one sexual partner at a time, could perhaps more accurately be called serial polygamy, as larger numbers of people get married, divorced, and then remarry. In short, our ideals and expectations with respect to monogamy are becoming further and further removed from the truth of the matter, as displayed by our behavior.

---

36 Barash and Lipton, *Strange Bedfellows*, 13.

37 Ibid., 27.

38 In providing these allegedly evolutionary accounts, we should not be taken to be endorsing them. Both accounts are, in our view, guilty of a false biological determinism. Our point in raising these views is rather to show that the scientific community seems split on the issue of whether our genes favor polygamy or monogamy.

39 Kate Lunau, "Are We Blushing Yet?" *Maclean's*, June 29, 2009, http://www2.macleans.ca/2009/06/29/are-we-blushing-yet/. These figures are for heterosexuals only. Though lesbians tend to have similar numbers of sexual partners, the numbers tend to be higher for gay men. See Corvino and Gallagher, *Debating Same-Sex Marriage*.

40 Martin Beckford, "Average Man Has 9 Sexual Partners in Lifetime, Women Have 4," *Telegraph*, December 15, 2011, http://www.telegraph.co.uk/relationships/sexual-health-and-advice/8958520/Average-man-has-9-sexual-partners-in-lifetime-women-have-4.html.

We are led to ask the question, then, whether anyone truly believes in "traditional," lifelong monogamy.

David Brooks defends the ideal of a lifelong commitment to sexual exclusivity with one other person. He writes, "marriage makes us better than we deserve to be. Even in the chores of daily life, married couples find themselves, over the years, coming closer together, fusing into one flesh. Married people who remain committed to each other find that they reorganize and deepen each other's lives. They may eventually come to the point when they can say to each other: "Love you? I am you." [41] Brooks's metaphor of "fusing into one flesh" recalls Aristophanes' notion of the human longing to rejoin with one's other half to be part of a larger whole. For Brooks, married couples give up their individual and separate social identities and form a boundary around their physical and emotional intimacy that enriches their lives. [42] Polyamory transgresses the boundaries of the fused flesh and thereby weakens the marital bond by reorganizing the couple into distinct persons available for relational intimacy with others.

For instance, if A and B are lovers, and B and C are lovers, then A's private life (with B) will be more accessible to others (i.e., C), while B's private life (with C) will be less accessible to A. Even if A takes a lover D, so that A and B are in parallel situations, their intimate relationships are both exposed and closed off in ways that can damage them. In this way, if one removes "the veil from all that is private and delicate in oneself" with more than one person, then all that was private and delicate becomes "pulverized," to continue Brooks's metaphor. When this happens, the flesh presumably never fully fuses or it comes apart, along with the sacred bonds that conservatives regard as foundational to the social order.

According to many conservatives (and liberals too), marriage as the long-term union of two beings, who are stronger and better than they "deserve to be," is an impossible achievement without the commitment of sexual exclusivity. Some conservatives who accept same-sex marriage do so because they believe it will promote sexual exclusivity, i.e., monogamy, among more people. Liberals who support same-sex marriage do so primarily because they believe it promotes equality, and they typically oppose polygamy because it appears to involve intolerable forms of inequality. For these reasons, both conservative and liberal proponents of same-sex marriage often push aside slippery-slope objections and believe that permitting same-sex marriage does not logically lead to state recognition for plural marriage.

So how can polyamorists respond to the conservative marriage philosophy of David Brooks? One line of defense that Emens offers is simply that polyamory and polygamy are not for everyone; indeed, this lifestyle appears to appeal only to a small minority. Another defense is that polyamory and polygamy often

---

41 David Brooks, "The Power of Marriage," *New York Times*, November 22, 2003, http://www.nytimes.com/2003/11/22/opinion/the-power-of-marriage.html.

42 Nozick, *The Examined Life*.

involve commitment [43] and sexual fidelity, but among a group larger than two. Finally, Emens points to the fact that, for those who are polyamorous, polygamy offers a way to formalize multiple commitments of mutual care and support.

These defenses of polygamy show that many of the arguments commonly made by conservatives and liberals for same-sex marriage also apply to polygamy. One argument we often hear is that the recognition and acceptance of same-sex marriage does not threaten heterosexual marriage, or marriage itself, because same-sex marriage is not for everyone. Heterosexuals who marry can maintain those marital traditions and practices they value, and by making the institution more inclusive we underscore the symbolic and practical importance of marriage to society and its members. For the same reasons, the recognition of plural marriage should not threaten couple marriage. A second common argument in favor of same-sex marriage is that a lesbian or gay couple can make the same commitment to love and cherish each other, and uphold these commitments, as a heterosexual couple. The same would logically apply for polyamorous groups. Finally, a third common defense is that, for gay men and lesbians, same-sex marriage offers them a way to participate in what Brooks calls the culture of commitment . and fidelity, and thereby realize the personal and social goods of marriage. Again, polygamy works similarly for polyamorists.

The above defenses of polygamy do not serve to justify forms of polygamy that involve the subordination of women, or that would make marriage less inclusive by leaving out many men. It remains to be seen what forms of polygamy would develop when these marriages are based on broadly endorsed egalitarian principles. Emens mentions a number of possibilities, including the nineteenth-century utopian experiments with complex or communal marriage in the U.S. Similarly, Libby Copeland discusses the "woman-friendly roots of modern polyamory" that reach more than a century back to the "free love" ethic of a commune in Oneida, New York. She writes,

> Despite its many faults, though, the system of complex
> marriage at Oneida amounted to remarkable progress for the
> women who lived there. Older women were responsible for
> teaching young men exactly how to practice spiritual sex. Men
> were responsible for birth control by resisting orgasms during
> intercourse. Oneidan women generally had sex only with
> whom they wanted, which, as Oneida historian Spencer Klaw
> points out, "could not be said of numberless married women
> in the world outside".… Free love rejected the tyranny of

---

43 Cheshire Calhoun challenges the assumption that shaping our lives around a set of commitments makes them richer or more meaningful. She suggests that the attractiveness of commitments may depend upon a person's disposition in regard to managing her future. Though beyond the scope of this discussion, her arguments resonate well with Emens's dispositional account of polyamory. See Cheshire Calhoun, "What Good Is Commitment?" *Ethics* 119, no. 4 (2009): 613–41.

conventional marriage, and particularly how it limited women's lives to child-bearing, household drudgery, legal powerlessness, and, often enough, loveless sex.[44]

In the nineteenth century, women in complex marriages had greater equality and rights than women in monogamous marriages. The latter were expected to obey their husband "masters," and their legal and social identities were merged into his. While monogamy improved for women in the twentieth century, it may well be a mistake to assume that only this form of marriage is compatible with women's social equality. This assumption ignores the historical and ethnographic record of both monogamy and polygamy.[45]

As we can see from the above discussion, answering the question "Who should be allowed to marry?" is complex and fails to yield a single definitive answer. We have argued, however, that there are legitimate reasons for thinking that we ought to expand the notion of marriage to include same-sex couples, and, at least under some circumstances, to plural marriages as well. In the next section, we will examine the moral and legal aspects of the failure to keep marital commitments of sexual fidelity.

Should Adulterers Be Subject to Criminal or Civil Penalties?

According to Richard Wasserstrom, adultery is *prima facie* morally wrong for two reasons: (1) it involves breaking a promise, and (2) it involves lying.[46] Because both of these acts are *prima facie* wrong, so too is adultery. Let's look at this argument in a bit more detail.

When we get married, many of us promise to be sexually exclusive with our spouse. If we engage in extramarital sex, then we break this promise. Wasserstrom points out that this particular promise is both important and often difficult to keep. For this reason, the harm that can result is often much more acute than, say, breaking your promise to take out the garbage or cook supper that night. The breach of this promise can, in fact, affect our ability to trust our spouse, and that loss can be devastating to our marriage and to individual well-being.

Because we have promised to be faithful to our spouses, we must keep sexual dalliances with others secret. To do this, however, requires that we lie. The lie can either be passive, for example, when we simply don't tell our spouse what we are really doing; or it can be active, for example, when we tell our spouse that we were at a meeting when we were in fact at a hotel with someone having sex.

---

44 Libby Copeland, "Making Love and Trouble: The surprisingly woman-friendly roots of modern polyamory," *Slate*, March 12, 2012, http://www.slate.com/articles/double_x/doublex/2012/03/polyamory_and_its_surprisingly_woman_friendly_roots_.html.

45 See, e.g., Janet Bennion, *Women of Principle: Female Networking in Contemporary Mormon Polygyny* (New York: Oxford University Press, 2008); Nancy Cott, *Public Vows: A History of Marriage and the Nation* (Cambridge, MA: Harvard University Press, 2000).

46 Wasserstrom, "Is Adultery Immoral?".

Wasserstrom suggests a third, more subtle way in which committing adultery may be an instance of lying. Because in our culture we typically associate sexual relations with love and intimacy, and assume this is possible with only one person at a time, having casual sex with someone we do not love (or a spouse we no longer love) can also be considered a kind of lie.

In assessing these moral criticisms of adultery, we need to note that they occur within the context of societies that not only encourage, but also expect, monogamy. Not all societies abide by this framework, however. Moreover, within a given society, there may be spouses who do not promise to be sexually exclusive with each other. In such cases, there will be no promise breaking when one has a sexual liaison outside of the marriage. And in such cases there is far less reason to lie or to deceive one's spouse about this. If these spouses identify as polyamorous, they may be deeply committed to truth and openness, as the passage above from Loving More suggests. For so-called "open marriages," then, Wasserstrom's two moral objections to adultery do not apply. And the claim about the subtle form of deception that accompanies extramarital sex also seems inapplicable, because the people involved presumably do not believe that feelings of sex and love are only possible with one person at a time.

If the moral arguments against adultery apply only to some but not to all couples, then having criminal or civil laws against adultery in all cases is inappropriate. Such laws would need to exempt people in "open" or polyamorous marriages. This group is likely to be small, though, as Wasserstrom's 1960s model of an open marriage and its earlier versions, in which demands for sexual exclusivity are regarded as overly possessive or unrealistic, is less celebrated or endorsed in many liberal societies today. So, for marriages in which a commitment to sexual exclusivity is implicit in the marital contract, should spouses be able to bring criminal or civil charges against each other for alleged adulteries?

The Old Testament of the Bible certainly thinks we ought to have laws against adultery, since adultery violates the sixth commandment (Exodus 20:14). Indeed, adultery was thought to be such an egregious sin that the penalty for it was death, often by stoning (Deuteronomy 22:22; Leviticus 20:20, 21:9). The laws in reality, however, were applied differently to men and women. First, because, at that time, a man was permitted to marry several women, he could have sex with any of his wives without committing adultery. Second, a man was really only disallowed from having sex with a woman who was married or betrothed to another man. Interestingly, the crime of a male adulterer was considered a crime against the woman's husband, not against his own spouse. In effect, the male adulterer has used someone else's property. This is why a husband was not thought to commit adultery if he had sex with an unmarried woman, except in cases where the woman's father complained that he would receive a smaller dowry for his daughter. The husband could correct this either by paying a fine to the father of the woman, or by marrying her and paying her dowry. During the Middle Ages, adultery came to be viewed increasingly as a crime that women, and not men, committed. And secular laws allowed a husband to severely chastise his wife if he caught her committing adultery, which could include killing her.[47]

What we see, historically, is that adultery laws adversely affected women far more than they did men. This is one of the reasons why feminists have been at the forefront of campaigns to repeal laws criminalizing adultery, given their discriminatory use against women. Even where criminal laws against adultery no longer exist, or are no longer enforced, spouses can sue for divorce and civil damages in alleged cases of adultery. Often these lawsuits are expensive for both spouses, in terms of court costs and the eventual civil penalties. Several decades ago, some U.S. states began changing their laws so that couples could obtain a divorce without finding one spouse to be at fault—i.e., to have engaged in some type of wrongdoing. This was done, in part, to assist couples in uncontested cases in which the parties wished to separate without bringing charges of wrong-doing.[48] But no-fault divorce laws also reflect the idea that, while adultery is bad, it's a matter to be addressed by the couple in private, and not by the government.

While some are unhappy with the availability (now in all 50 states, and in Canada) of no-fault divorce, there is evidence that many people, and particularly women, have benefitted greatly from this change. A 2003 longitudinal study has shown that, over a twenty-year period, no-fault divorce has led to a 20-per-cent reduction in female suicide, a 33-per-cent reduction in domestic violence, and a significant reduction in domestic murders against women.[49] Critics argue that these changes make a mockery of marriage contracts[50] and increase divorce rates, but others challenge these claims and believe that the benefits far outweigh the costs.[51] Although there are many reasons why a marriage can fail to enrich people's lives and instead cause severe strain and tensions, sexual infidelity (real or imagined) is one of the main ones (though some might argue it's more often a symptom than a cause). The larger question to be addressed, however, is whether investing the state with the power to adjudicate cases of sexual infidelity, in criminal or civil courts, contributes to the creation of a just social order.

---

47 T.B. Pearce, "Adultery," in *Encyclopedia of Love, Courtship and Sexuality through History, Vol. 2: The Medieval Era*, ed. William Burns (Westport, CT: Greenwood Publishing, 2007).

48 West, *Marriage, Sexuality and Gender*.

49 Betsey Stevenson and Justin Wolfers, "Bargaining in the Shadow of the Law: Divorce Laws and Family Distress," *Stanford Graduate School Research Paper Series*, 2003, https://gsbapps. stanford.edu/researchpapers/library/RP1828.pdf.

50 Carrie Lukas, "A Marriage Contract Should Still Be a Contract," *National Review Online*, 2010, http://www.nationalreview.com/corner/232863/marriage-contract-should-still-be-contract-carrie-lukas.

51 Stephanie Coontz, "Divorce, No-Fault Style," *New York Times*, June 17, 2010, http://www. nytimes.com/2010/06/17/opinion/17coontz.html?_r=1.

Does Arranged Marriage Violate Sexual Autonomy?

In many cultures throughout history, marriages are arranged for children by their parents or by some kind of professional marriage broker. There are, for example, references to this type of marriage in the Bible, and members of the aristocracy in Europe arranged marriages for children and young adults well into the nineteenth century. In North America and Europe, today, few parents arrange marriages for their children, and few children would allow their parents to play much of a role in finding a spouse. But arranged marriage is the custom in parts of Asia, the Middle East, and Africa.

There is a significant difference between arranged marriage and forced marriage. Though there is some overlap between them, not all arranged marriages are forced. In forced marriages, the bride and groom (or just one of them) have almost no options but to accept the marriage arranged for them. When there are serious negative repercussions for refusing a marriage proposal, or when the children are betrothed at a young age, these marriages are non-consensual. Paula McAvoy explains how such practices violate girls' rights, since in most cases of forced marriage, the child is a girl:

> forcing an underage girl into a lifelong commitment to a man who assumes a position of authority over her greatly restricts her future autonomy. Further, girls from cultural groups that practice arranged marriages within liberal societies are often required to stop school in order to devote themselves to the private sphere and begin a family. This loss of a public self reinforces their second-class status and inhibits their ability to exit the marriage. Finally, arranged marriage for a minor is a violation of her right to self-protection. Because sex is an expectation within a marriage, forcing a minor into a union against her will results in a culturally orchestrated rape.[52]

Forced marriages obviously violate individual autonomy and basic human rights, and should not be allowed in a democratic state.[53] Moreover, children over 18 should not need their parents' legal consent in order to marry, and parents should not be allowed to impose a marriage or engagement before their child reaches 18. The state usually cannot prevent a parent from disinheriting a child who refuses

---

52 Paula McAvoy, "Should Arranged Marriages for Teenage Girls Be Allowed? How Public Schools Should Respond to Illiberal Cultural Practices," *Theory and Research in Education* 6, no. 5 (2008): 5–6.

53 Forced marriages occur in countries such as the U.S., where it is not the norm, because children are vulnerable to authoritarian and controlling parents. See Alyana Alfaro, "Til Death Do Us Part, the Forgotten US Victims of Forced Marriage," *Aljazeera*, January 21, 2014, http://america.aljazeera.com/articles/2014/1/21/forced-marriage-isaliveandwellintheus.html.

to cooperate with an arranged marriage, but this should define the limits of a parent's power over adult children in liberal democratic states.

Arranging a marriage, with a child's cooperation and consent, is more complicated to evaluate. How consensual it is may depend on the child's age, or whether subtle forms of coercion are used. Ideally, young adults should welcome their parents' help and advice in selecting a spouse but should be free to refuse a proposal and choose their own spouse. In practice, however, it is difficult to know the extent to which any arranged marriage is truly consensual. Some political theorists, such as Susan Moller Okin, have argued forcefully that liberal states need to protect the individual rights of vulnerable persons, such as women and children, and not tolerate the practices of religious or cultural groups that might seek to control them or limit their freedom.[54] Yet suppose a teenager is denied the right to date and participate in social activities where she might choose her own partner, and suppose her parents then pressure her to marry when she reaches 18 years old, before she has much of a chance to leave her small community. It's difficult to determine to what extent liberal states should limit parents' rights to shelter and influence their children's lives.

Some political theorists hold that liberal states should tolerate diverse cultural practices and be neutral toward different conceptions of the good, when no fundamental rights are violated. One consequence of taking cultural and religious pluralism seriously, however, is that we must tolerate certain illiberal practices, such as practices in which parents restrict a daughter's life so that she has few options but to cooperate with an arranged marriage.[55] The culturally tolerant, liberal society can prohibit practices that violate a child's or adult's civil rights, such as threats or acts that cause bodily or mental harm and which may be intended to prevent that person from exiting their community.[56] But short of this, we need to respect the rights of parents or a community to do what they think serves their children's and their members' best interests.[57]

But how do we distinguish between instances when parents are being overly but tolerably protective and when they are impairing a daughter's ability to freely and fully participate in society when she is an adult? How do we walk the fine line between protecting individual autonomy and respecting diverse community beliefs and practices? McAvoy suggests we use the notion of "overlapping consensus," which was introduced in John Rawls's influential work *A Theory of Justice*. Though Rawls's theory is subtle and complex, its basic outline is fairly clear. He has us imagine choosing the principles of justice that we would want to be governed by. In order to avoid having everyone simply choose those principles that

---

54 Susan Moller Okin, "Mistresses of Their Own Destiny," in *Citizenship and Education in Liberal-Democratic Societies*, ed. K. McDonough and W. Feinberg (New York: Oxford University Press, 2002), 346.

55 We deal at length with the issue of toleration and sexual acts and mores in Ch. 12.

56 C. Kukjathas, "Cultural Toleration," in *Ethnicity and Group Rights* (NOMOS 39), ed. I. Shapiro and W. Kymlyka (New York: New York University Press, 1997).

57 McAvoy, "Should Arranged Marriages."

benefit themselves the most, Rawls suggests that we choose behind what he calls a "veil of ignorance." This veil prevents us from knowing certain things about ourselves and our situation—for example, whether we are rich or poor, a man or a women, intelligent or not, and so on. Starting from this "original position," we will choose two basic principles of justice, the second of which is broken into two further parts. The first principle of justice maintains that there are things that we all want, whoever we turn out to be. Rawls calls these basic goods, which include fundamental liberties such as freedom of religion, thought, and expression. These basic goods will, Rawls insists under the first principle of justice, have to be divided equally amongst all citizens. The second principle of justice allows for inequalities within the social and economic sphere, but only under the two following conditions: "(a) any inequalities should benefit the least-advantaged members of society (*the difference principle*); and (b) offices and positions must be open to everyone under conditions of *fair equality of opportunity*." [58]

Let's suppose, then, that our society has been created using these two principles of justice. What sort of guarantee do we have that our society will reach agreement on specific practices, given that individuals (and groups of individuals or cultures) within our society have such substantively different conceptions of the good life, ranging from the materialistic Wall Street financier to the members of an Amish religious community living in rural Pennsylvania? This is where the notion of overlapping consensus comes to play a part. According to this notion, people can accept the same laws, but for very different reasons. In the following example, Leif Wenar explains how the (typically illiberal) Catholic Church could support a typically liberal position. He begins by citing the Church's position on religious freedom.

> This Vatican Council declares that the human person has a right to religious freedom. This freedom means that all men are to be immune from coercion on the part of individuals or of social groups and of any human power, in such wise that in matters religious no one is forced to act in a manner contrary to his own beliefs. Nor is anyone to be restrained from acting in accordance with his own beliefs, whether privately or publicly, whether alone or in association with others, within due limits. The council further declares that the right to religious freedom has its foundation in the very dignity of the human person, as this dignity is known through the revealed Word of God and by reason itself. This right of the human person to religious

---

58   John Rawls, *A Theory of Justice* (Cambridge, MA: Harvard University Press, 1971), 303; emphasis in original.

freedom is to be recognized in the constitutional law whereby society is governed and thus it is to become a civil right.[59]

As Wenar explains, "Catholic doctrine here supports the liberal right to religious freedom for reasons internal to Catholicism. A reasonable Islamic doctrine, and a reasonable atheistic doctrine, might also affirm this same right to religious freedom, each for its own reasons."[60] So how might a pluralist society reach an overlapping consensus about permissible marriage practices? What rights to marry could different groups find reasons to support?

It seems plausible that anyone would want the right to decide if and when to marry, and with whom. When arranged marriage customs infringe this basic right, they should be prohibited. The devil, of course, is in the details of determining when parental assistance in finding a marriage partner violates a child's autonomy with respect to marriage. Yet there are certain questionable practices, such as exerting pressure on a child to marry while still a teenager, or threatening to withdraw all support and cut off communication if a child's marriage does not meet with a parent's approval, and so on. Parents who respect their children's autonomy will ascertain their children's tastes and values relevant to marriage, and not substitute their own, and also not impose their help. When parents do this, there is nothing inherently wrong with using their social networks and experience to help their children negotiate complex marriage markets and find a good match. However, some recent empirical studies suggest that people who have chosen their marriage partner are more satisfied with their relationship than individuals who had little say in who they married, and that they have the ability to make more of their own choices, especially in financial matters.[61] Parents and others should consider such evidence when they are tempted to facilitate a match.

Is Virginity Valuable in a Potential Spouse?

In 2006, a French court ruled that a Muslim man could have his marriage annulled because his wife was not a virgin. Apparently, the groom wanted "out of the marriage while the wedding night party was still under way when he complained to guests that he couldn't present them with a bloodied sheet as proof of his wife's virginity.... He went to court the next day, arguing she deceived him regarding a vital part of the marriage, something to which she admitted, saying

---

59 Leif Wenar, "John Rawls," in *The Stanford Encyclopedia of Philosophy* (2008), http://plato. stanford.edu/archives/fall2008/entries/rawls/.

60 Ibid.

61 Manisha Diina, *Marital Satisfaction: Autonomous and Arranged Marriages: The Influence of Mate Selection on Marital Satisfaction* (Saarbrücken, Germany: VDM Verlag, 2009); S. Gunasekan, *Women's Autonomy and Reproductive Behaviour* (New Delhi: Kalpaz Publications, 2010); Lena Edlund and Nils-Petter Lagerlöf, "Implications of Marriage Institutions for Redistribution and Growth," *CDDRL Working Papers* (2002/2004), http://iis-db.stanford.edu/pubs/20793/ Nov27_04_No30.pdf.

she had had sexual intercourse before the wedding." The initial ruling invoked France's civil code, which says a marriage can be annulled "if there was an error about the person, or about the essential qualities of the person."[62] The event caused an uproar, with many people concerned that, if the ruling stood, many young Muslim women would seek surgery to have their hymens restored in order to ensure their marriageability and protect their reputations. Hymenoplasty, or "revirginization," is, in fact, becoming more popular in France and elsewhere. For example, Dr. Robert Stubbs, a Toronto surgeon, has performed hymen-restoration surgery for two decades and does about 25 of these surgeries a year, mainly for Middle Eastern (and not just Muslim) women, at a cost of about $3,000 each. His clients range from women who are "suicidal" after being raped to those who want to ensure that they pass the sheet test on their wedding night.[63]

For some men and their communities, then, the answer to the question posed in this section is simply yes. For many people, virginity is considered to be an important characteristic in a potential mate, and not just those from cultures in which it is a legal or social requirement for women. Indeed, virginity is making a comeback, so to speak, in the U.S., decades after the sexual revolution began in the 1960s. A decade ago, former president George W. Bush promoted "virginity until marriage" campaigns with more than 700 "abstinence" programs in high schools in all fifty states, costing approximately $135 million per year.[64] We will discuss debates over sex education in the next chapter; we refer to this statistic here simply to point out that such programs have had some impact on adolescents and single young adults, as increasing numbers of them say they want to wait until they are married to have sex.

A 2011 study conducted by the Centers for Disease Control and Prevention (CDC) found that, between 2006 and 2008, 27 per cent of young men between the ages of 15 and 24 years practiced abstinence, up from 22 per cent in 2002. Similarly, 29 per cent of young women in the same age bracket practiced abstinence, up 7 per cent from 2002. Some studies find even higher rates of abstinence and virginity. A 2007 study of the collected responses from 1,500 Duke University freshmen and seniors in Durham, N.C., found that about 53 per cent of women and 40 per cent of the men said they were virgins.[65] Importantly, the data included not only histories of vaginal intercourse, but also oral and anal sex. Hence, the rise in rates of virginity can't be explained away by saying that young people are just replacing intercourse with other

62 Susan Mohammed, "France's Virginity Fracas," *Maclean's*, June 16, 2008.

63 Ibid.

64 Debra Rosenberg, "The Battle over Abstinence," *Newsweek*, December 9, 2002: 67.

65 Sharon Jayson, "More College 'Hookups,' but More Virgins, Too," *USA Today*, March 30, 2011, http://www.usatoday.com/news/health/wellness/dating/story/2011/03/More-hookups-on-campuses-but-more-virgins-too/45556388/1.

types of sexual activity. The numbers seem to point, instead, to a real drop in sexual activity within this age group.[66]

Paradoxically, as this trend continues, so does one that seems to be its exact opposite, namely, "hooking up." Though this is a vague phrase, and can mean almost anything from kissing to having sexual intercourse, it is distinctive in that it involves "no clear mutual expectation of further interactions or a committed relationship."[67] The hooking up sexual "script" is most often contrasted with the dating script, which it has surpassed in some age groups. A date typically involves two people who arrange to meet and enjoy some activity together, such as seeing a movie or eating dinner. By contrast, hooking up typically involves two people who *just happen* to "get together" at the end of an evening. Paula England, a sociologist, has found that, by the senior college year, 72% of both sexes reported having at least one hookup, with an average of 9.7 for men and 7.1 for women. She adds, though, that these numbers can be a bit deceptive because "some people are hooking up a bunch of times with the same person but are not calling it a relationship."[68]

Can we make any sense of these contradictory trends? Is it just a matter of personal taste whether one decides to hook up frequently or remain a virgin until marriage? How much does social context shape these choices? It's somewhat hard to imagine a young woman living in a small rural village in, say, South Asia opting for a promiscuous lifestyle. Such behavior would make a different social statement than the same behavior of a university student in Boston, Montreal, or Los Angeles, and have significantly different social consequences.

In "In Defense of Promiscuity," Frederick Elliston reconstructs three arguments for why one *ought* to consider sexual experimentation with a number of partners: (1) the Classic Liberal Defense, (2) the Sex as Body Language Argument, and (3) the Authentic Sexuality, or Existential, Defense of Promiscuity.[69]

The first argument starts from the liberal position that actions which do not harm others should be a matter of private choice. Being promiscuous, then, ought to be a private matter and beyond the reach of the law, so long as one's behavior does not cause harm (e.g., by increasing rates of STDs, unwanted pregnancies, emotional trauma, and so on). Moreover, because sex can yield great pleasure, a utilitarian cost/benefit analysis supports the legitimacy, and even

---

66 See Sy Kraft, "New CDC Sex Report: Virginity is Back, Females Try Same Sex More," *Medical News Today*, March 3, 2011, http://www.medicalnewstoday.com/articles/218126.php; A. Chandra et al., "Sexual Behavior, Sexual Attraction, and Sexual Identity in the United States: Data from the 2006–2008 National Survey of Family Growth." *National Health Statistics Reports*, no. 36 (Hyattsville, MD: National Center for Health Statistics, 2011), http://www.cdc.gov/nchs/data/nhsr/nhsr036.pdf.

67 Jessie Owens et al., "Short-Term Prospective Study of Hooking Up Among College Students," *Archives of Sexual Behavior* 40, no. 2 (2011): 331.

68 Jayson, "More College 'Hookups.'"

69 Elliston, "In Defense of Promiscuity."

the advisability, of promiscuity. The second argument begins by claiming that sex is a form of communication, which uses the body rather than words to convey meaning. Most people improve their verbal communication skills by conversing with a number of different people, and similarly, most will improve their nonverbal communication skills by engaging in sex with different partners. And of course, good communication skills are valuable. Finally, the third argument begins by drawing a distinction between an authentic and an inauthentic life. Following in the footsteps of existential philosophers such as Jean-Paul Sartre, Elliston maintains that living authentically involves understanding that our choices are not completely constrained by our circumstances or ordinary social expectations, and that we have more freedom than we typically acknowledge when choosing our path. He suggests that teenagers and young adults are under a lot of pressure to conform in one way or another, including sexually. Those who understand that conformity and nonconformity are choices they have, and then self-consciously choose one option, are living authentically. Because promiscuity is often socially stigmatized, choosing this option can be a sign that one is not merely following social convention and is living more authentically.

Elliston concludes his essay with what he calls an "unscientific postscript" (à la Kierkegaard). Although he doesn't retract his earlier arguments, he does suggest that the issue of promiscuity is complex and that his arguments might have limitations. For example, the existential defense of promiscuity demands only that we actively choose the sex life we want, as opposed to letting the prevailing social norms dictate our behavior. But this leaves open the possibility that one could choose any number of different sex lives, including celibacy before marriage and monogamy after it, or we might choose to live differently at different stages in our lives. With respect to the body language argument, Elliston considers the counterpoint that sex with a wide variety of people may be analogous to a series of shallow conversations at a big social gathering, where one says or hears nothing of particular importance. It may be that our truly deep conversations are held with one person, such as a long-term sexual partner. Speaking to the same person need not mean that the same conversation is held over and over again; indeed, for some, an extended conversation with a single interlocutor may be the only way to move beyond exchanging platitudes and to feel comfortable enough to take risks and experiment.

Finally, the liberal argument is built on the assumption that a promiscuous life isn't harmful to anyone when the right precautions are taken, and that it provides its participants great pleasure. While these two claims may be true, they might also be false. Research on hooking up, in particular, has provided conflicting evidence regarding harms and benefits. Moreover, some of these harms and benefits differ between men and women. Men have consistently rated casual sex more highly than women, and hence men tend to look more favorably on hooking up than women do. Part of the explanation for this seems to be that women more frequently look for things that hooking up typically does not provide, such as companionship and intimacy.[70] Furthermore, though the sexual double standard isn't as powerful or as acute as it used to be, women are still much more likely to be denigrated for promiscuous behavior than are men. This may in turn explain why women often experience depression and feelings of regret after hooking up, while men experience such feelings less often.[71] On the other hand, some women report many benefits from hooking up. For one, they can initiate a hookup, whereas, in the dating script, men almost always take the lead or active role.[72] They also report further benefits from hooking up, such as an enjoyable sexual experience, feeling wanted and cared for, and feeling excitement. Both men and women report that hooking up is less likely to lead to a "broken heart."[73] For whatever reasons, though, women begin to lose interest far sooner than men in hooking up. Women have typically had enough of hooking up by their early twenties, while men are likely to continue for many years after.[74]

While both virginity and extensive sexual experience are valuable in a potential spouse (and, of course, one cannot have both), sometimes these are valued for the wrong reasons. There is no good reason to think that women (or men) who are virgins are more morally or spiritually pure than those who are not. And there is no good reason to think that men (or women) who have a great deal of sexual experience will make better lovers or domestic partners than those without such experience. Both virginity and promiscuity have risks. One risk of long periods of abstinence is that one can miss out on rewarding experiences and relationships, which provide us with important insights about others and ourselves. The risks of promiscuity include contracting an STD, and dealing with the awkwardness or emotional turmoil created when one frequently changes partners or has several simultaneous partners. Perhaps, as with other indulgences, moderation is a good thing, however we come to define it with respect to sex.

---

70 P. Mongeau et al., "Defining Dates and First Date Goals: Generalizing from Undergraduates to Single Adults," *Communication Research* 34 (2007): 526–47.

71 E.M. Eshbaugh and G. Gute, "Hookup and Sexual Regret Among College Women," *Journal of Social Psychology* 148 (2008): 77–89.

72 Carolyn Bradshaw et al., "To Hook Up or to Date: Which Gender Benefits?" *Sex Roles* 62 (2010): 661–69.

73 E.L. Paul and K.A.Hayes, "The Casualties of 'Casual' Sex: A Qualitative Exploration of the Phenomenology of College Students' Hookups," *Journal of Social and Personal Relationships* 19 (2002): 639–61.

74 Kathleen Bogle, *Hooking Up: Sex, Dating, and Relationships on Campus* (New York: New York University Press, 2008).

Discussion Questions

1. Are celibate marriages problematic in some way? Explain your answer.
2. Should close relatives (e.g., cousins) be allowed to marry?
3. Summarize and evaluate the "slippery-slope" objection to same-sex marriage.
4. Is sexual exclusivity "natural" for humans?
5. What kinds of formal or informal sanctions should we impose on people who commit adultery?
6. Would you want your parents to arrange your marriage? Why or why not? Would you want to help your children find a suitable marriage partner?
7. Is there a connection between sexual abstinence and moral virtue?

Further Reading

Barash, David, and Judith Eve Lipton. *The Myth of Monogamy: Fidelity and Infidelity in Animals and People.* New York: W.H. Freeman, 2001.

Calhoun, Cheshire. "Who's Afraid of Polygamous Marriage? Lessons for Same-Sex Marriage Advocacy from the History of Polygamy." *San Diego Law Review* 42 (2005): 1023–42.

Corvino, John, and Maggie Gallagher. *Debating Same-Sex Marriage.* New York & Oxford: Oxford University Press, 2012.

Elliston, Frederick. "In Defense of Promiscuity." In *Philosophy and Sex*, edited by Robert Baker and Frederick Elliston, 222–46. Buffalo, NY: Prometheus, 1975.

Emens, Elizabeth. "Monogamy's Law: Compulsory Monogamy and Polyamorous Existence." *NYU Review of Law and Social Change* 29 (2004): 277–376. http://papers.ssrn.com/sol3/papers.cfm?abstract_id=506242##.

Wasserstrom, Richard. "Is Adultery Immoral?" In *Philosophy and Sex*, edited by Robert Baker and Frederick Elliston, 207–21. Buffalo, NY: Prometheus, 1975.

Chapter 7

Sex and Children

What, if anything, should children and adolescents be taught about sex? And who should be responsible for providing this instruction: professional educators, medical providers, or parents? More controversially, is it okay for adolescents, or even children, to engage in some kinds of sexual activities with other adolescents (or children), and, if so, at what age? How should parents, teachers, and other community authorities address inappropriate or harmful sexual conduct involving adolescents or children? These questions raise deeper issues about the basic civil rights of adolescents and children (e.g., to an education, to a safe environment, etc.) and about the limits of parents' authority over any minors in their custody (e.g., to deny life-saving medical treatment). Moral and political philosophers often focus on the rights of adults, but some have focused on the moral and legal rights of minors and, correspondingly, on the duties and responsibilities that these rights impose on adults. Because adolescents and children need to learn about how to protect their health, and to protect themselves against various kinds of abuse, we cannot wait until they are adults to teach them about STDs or what constitutes inappropriate sexual behavior. Moreover, because many adolescents and children do not wait until they are adults to begin engaging in sexual activities, we need to consider how or when parents and other adults should limit these activities.

What Should Children and Adolescents Be Taught about Sex?

A researcher studying sex education in the U.S. provides an indication of how controversial this issue has become: "community discussions … morphed into disagreements, then flared into furious public displays of feeling. I heard neighbors scream at each other and saw angry shoving outside of public meeting halls. School board members told me about receiving death threats."[1] The forced resignation of Surgeon General and pediatrician Joycelyn Elders in 1994, after comments she made at a United Nations conference on AIDS (see Ch. 5), also reflects public sensitivities around the topic of sex education for children. Responding to a question about whether teaching children about masturbation should be included in programs that promote safer forms of sex, she said: "I think that is something that's part of human sexuality and it's part of something that perhaps should be taught. But we've not even taught our children the very basics. And I feel that we have tried ignorance for a very long time and it's time we tried education."[2] Yet some opponents of having sex education in public schools think it is not simply wrong, but evil. For example, Randy Engel maintains that whatever those in favor of sex education may say, this sort of education is "really about sterility, death, killing, vice, genital stimulation, infidelity, sexual idolatry, the cannibalism of innocence and purity, and immorality." Indeed, she sees sex education as a *"legalized form of child seduction and molestation."*[3]

The public was not always this polarized. When sex education was first introduced into U.S. schools in the early part of the twentieth century, there was actually a great deal of agreement about both the necessity of such education and the content of it. The push for sex education came from a group called the American Social Hygiene Association (ASHA). Although the group's initial membership came mostly from the wealthy classes of New York society, it included suffragists, physicians, and industrialist philanthropists. ASHA received support from organizations as diverse as the Young Men's Christian Association (YMCA), the Young Men's Hebrew Association, Metropolitan Life Insurance Company, the General Federation of Women's Clubs, the National Congress of Parents and Teachers (the forerunners of today's PTA), and the federal government.[4] Its goals, expressed in the society's name, were all about "social hygiene," which embraced a panoply of concepts but focused especially on the need to fight venereal disease. And this fight, in turn, was focused on eradicating prostitution, which was thought to be the primary cause of the spread of these diseases.

---

1   Janice Irvine, *Talk about Sex: The Battles over Sex Education in the United States* (Berkeley: University of California Press, 2002), xiii.

2   Ibid., 1.

3   Randy Engel, *Sex Education: The Final Plague* (Gaithersburg, MD: Human Life International, 1989), 8; emphasis in original.

4   Kristin Luker, *When Sex Goes to School: Warring Views on Sex—and Sex Education—Since the Sixties* (New York & London: W.W. Norton, 2006), 40–41.

ASHA and other members of the social-hygiene movement thought there was far more involved in the fight against prostitution than keeping it illegal. To be successful, the fight also required a radical alteration in beliefs about the nature of sexuality. In particular, the movement felt that it had to attack the widespread belief that there is a radical and *natural* difference between men's and women's sexuality. According to the generally accepted views of the day (and still true today to a lesser extent), men were thought to *need* sex in a way that women did not. The influential nineteenth-century British medical doctor William Aston wrote in the early twentieth century, "The majority of women (happily for them) are not very much troubled with sexual feeling of any kind.... As a general rule, a modest woman seldom desires any sexual gratification for herself. She submits to her husband's embraces, but principally to gratify him; and, were it not for the desire of maternity, would far rather be relieved from his attentions."[5] This picture of women's sexuality, when combined with the then-common belief that masturbation is both immoral and detrimental to one's health,[6] would suggest that prostitution is perhaps the least bad alternative for dealing with men's unrelenting lustful desires. Indeed, one common view that persists to some degree today is that sex with "bad women" is a necessary evil, in part so that men do not try to corrupt and ruin "good women."

Women in the social-hygiene movement, however, were unconvinced by this reasoning. In 1910, Lavina Dock pointed out that "the double standard tacitly permits men to indulge freely and unchecked in sexual irregularity without consequent loss of social standing, but it dooms the women who are necessarily involved in these irregularities to social ostracism and even to complete degradation."[7] Another movement leader, Anna Garlin Spencer, called attention to how prostitution imperiled all women: "The ancient denial of full equality to womanhood has thus taken its stand in the last refuge of infamy, the sex-slavery of a minority of outcaste women. Let no woman think she is safe from ignominy, however praised and beloved, while any other woman is bought and sold in the auction-mart of vice! Let no man believe, however, pure and upright his own life may be, that he can wipe from his forehead the brand of despotic class-morality while any other man buys and sells women in sex-slavery!"[8] In short, all women were potential victims of what was called "white slavery"—i.e., human trafficking.

The social-hygiene movement sought to do away with these double standards of sexual morality for men and women. In particular, the movement's leaders thought that men had to be "raised" to the level of sexual morality expected of 'good' women. G. Stanley Hall, the father of developmental psychology, concurred with this goal and proposed the following for the sexual education of boys:

---

5   Quoted in ibid., 45.

6   See, e.g., Jean Stengers and Anne Van Neck, *Masturbation: The History of a Great Terror*, trans. K. Hoffman (New York: Palgrave Macmillan, 2001).

7   Quoted in Luker, *When Sex Goes to School*, 42.

8   Quoted in ibid., 43.

"We must make no degree of concession whatsoever in the ideals of chastity for boys at this [adolescent] stage any more than we do for girls. Apart from the social stigma, there is now some reason to think that lapses from chastity for boys at this age are physiologically and biologically worse in their effect on the last, highest, and always most precarious stages of the psychophysical development of the individual. Hence, we must never let down our ideals of purity, innocence, modesty...."[9] Social reformers promoted this agenda by introducing education about sexuality into the public schools.

Over time, sex education morphed into a form of "family life education," which covered topics as diverse as the roles of both sexes in a marriage, the value of "family councils," how to budget, the dangers and immorality of premarital sex, and the difficulties of interracial and interfaith marriages.[10] In other words, sex education was deployed to promote middle-class norms and "traditional family values." Sex education, however, became controversial after the "sexual revolution" of the 1960s, when young people started to seriously question the traditional values—sexual and otherwise—of their parents. This revolution coincided with the introduction of highly reliable contraception (e.g., the birth-control pill), significant progress in fighting venereal diseases (e.g., by using penicillin for syphilis), and successful state-by-state efforts to legalize abortion (culminating in the *Roe v. Wade* ruling in 1973). For the first time, sex did not inevitably lead to pregnancy, or to disease; prevention was a real possiblity, and this eventually became the focus of much sex education.[11]

But a number of groups in the U.S. equate sex education about prevention with the promotion of premarital and extramarital sex (i.e., sex without costs or penalties), and with changes in traditional gender roles. Women, who had been especially burdened by the threat or actuality of an unwanted pregnancy, began in the 1970s to pursue advanced education and work outside the home in much greater numbers. These changes led to other social upheavals. In 1960 in the U.S., the median age of first marriage was 22.8 for men and 20.3 for women; by 2012,

---

9   Quoted in ibid., 50.

10 See ibid., 60–63.

11 The situation in Canada is somewhat similar, but different in some important respects. Canada first introduced the *Criminal Law Amendment Act* in 1968, which allowed hospitals to set up "Therapeutic Abortion Committees," although hospitals were free not to establish one. A legal abortion could occur only if approved for "therapeutic" reasons by such a committee. Some committees almost always approved requests for abortions, while others almost never did, and, of course, hospitals without such a committee did not perform abortions at all. This law was struck down as unconstitutional in the 1988 *R. v. Morgentaler* case. A subsequent government tried briefly to construct a new abortion law, but it was narrowly defeated by the Senate, the upper house of Parliament. As a result, Canada is currently one of very few countries that has absolutely no abortion law, thus making an abortion a decision entirely a matter between a pregnant women and her doctor. Subsequent cases made clear that the father of the child could not stop a women from having an abortion (e.g., *Tremblay v. Daigle*, 1989), and that abortions would be paid for by Canada's public health-care system, whether it was performed in a hospital or in an abortion clinic.

it was 28.6 for men and 26.6 for women.[12] Moreover, as more people delay getting married, fewer are remaining abstinent until marriage. For example, according to a survey conducted in 2002 in the U.S., 89 per cent of men and 92 per cent of women had engaged in sexual intercourse by the time they reached the ages of 22–24, and the average age of first intercourse was 16.9 for men and 17.4 for women.[13]

The widespread shift in sexual, marital, and gender norms has substantially altered how sex educators view the purpose of sex education. In 1968, Mary Calderone, founder of the Sex Information and Education Council of the United States (siecus), wrote that we have to "reframe our moral values in terms relevant to the needs and conditions of a world that grows more complex and demanding every day."[14] In 2007, Lawrence Finer wrote, "Almost all Americans have sex before marrying. These findings argue for education and interventions that provide the skills and information people need to protect themselves from unintended pregnancy and sexually transmitted diseases once they become sexually active, regardless of marital status."[15] In short, sex educators see it as their responsibility to provide instruction about disease and pregnancy prevention.

For social and religious conservatives, this change in curriculum, however, sends the wrong message: that sex outside of marriage is acceptable. Many conservatives, according to Luker,[16] hold that sex is "sacred" and involves forms of intimacy that can be protected only in marriage. By contrast, sex educators usually recognize that there is a broad range of views about sexual morality, from conservative to liberal. Although liberals might well think that sex is best within a committed relationship such as marriage, many see nothing wrong per se with enjoying sex in a variety of contexts. Moreover liberals are generally more tolerant about somewhat stigmatized sexual activities, such as masturbation and homosexuality, and think that these topics, along with methods of disease and pregnancy prevention, should be part of a comprehensive sex education.

Through the 1970s and 1980s in the U.S., liberals won many battles over sex education, and there was a considerable increase in the number of schools offering comprehensive sex education. However, in the last two decades there has been a reversal in this trend. For example, while only 2 per cent of public-school teachers taught that abstinence was the sole means of pregnancy avoidance in 1998,

---

12 Sheri Stritof and Bob Stritof, "Estimated Median Age at First Marriage, by Sex: 1890 to 2012," *About.com: Marriage*, 2013, http://marriage.about.com/od/statistics/a/medianage.htm. In Canada, the changes are even more profound: in 2012 the mean age for first marriage was 31.1 for men and 29.1 for women.

13 W.D. Mosher et al., "Sexual Behavior and Selected Health Measures: Men and Women 15–44 Years of Age, United States, 2002," *Advance Data from Vital and Health Statistics*, no. 362 (Hyattsville, MD: National Center for Health Statistics, 2005).

14 Quoted in Luker, *When Sex Goes to School*, 84.

15 Lawrence Finer, "Trends in Premarital Sex in the United States, 1954–2003," *Public Health Report* 122.1 (Jan–Feb 2007): 73–78, http://www.ncbi.nlm.nih.gov/pmc/articles/PMC1802108/.

16 Luker, *When Sex Goes to School*, 99.

23 per cent of teachers were using "abstinence only" curricula in 1999. This figure jumped to 30 per cent by 2003.[17] The move away from comprehensive sex
education in public schools to "abstinence only" (until marriage) programs was
strongly endorsed and promoted by the George W. Bush administration. While
abstinence-only programs received $10.9 million in funding in 1982, they received
$120 million in 2003, with a promise of $1.5 billion to be spent from 2005–2010.[18]
Throughout the first decade of the twenty-first century in the U.S., the battle line
over sex education was drawn primarily between those who supported abstinence-only programs and those who wanted a comprehensive curriculum.

Despite these battles, sex education has largely failed to achieve the goals set
by any group. For example, studies show that U.S. adolescents are quite ignorant
about pregnancy prevention. A 2000 study by Carrera et al. found that, even
before the abstinence-only program hit full stride, almost 75 per cent believed
that letting semen drip out of the vagina after intercourse prevented pregnancy,
roughly 25 per cent believed that birth control was unnecessary if one engaged
in sexual intercourse only occasionally, and more than 70 per cent thought that
douching provided effective contraception.[19] At the heart of debates over sex
education are fundamental differences about who should provide sex education
to children and adolescents (parents or schools), and how to balance the rights
of parents to instill their values about sex, the rights of children to sexual-health
information, and the interests of society in controlling the spread of disease, the
costs of health care for STDs and unwanted pregnancies, and the social costs
of unwanted and uncared-for children. These questions will be explored in the
following sections of this chapter.

Who Should Provide Sex Education: Parents, Schools, or Health-care Providers?

In a 2011 op-ed piece in the *New York Times*, George and Moschella argue that
mandatory public-school sex-education programs, even when families can opt
out, are unconstitutional and violate the right of parents to teach their children
about private moral and religious matters. They write:

> Parenting, especially in moral and religious matters, is very
> important and highly personal: while parents enlist others' help
> in this task, the task is theirs. They are ultimately responsible
> for their children's intellectual and moral maturity, so within
> broad limits they must be free to educate their children,
> especially on the deepest matters, as they judge best. This is
> why parental rights are so important: they provide a zone of

---

17 Irving, *Talk About Sex*, xv.
18 Ibid, xvi.
19 Cited in ibid., 5.

sovereignty, a moral space to fulfill their obligations according to their consciences.

The right to parent is rather like the right to exercise one's religion. Like parental duties, religious duties are serious and highly personal. This is why, absent the most serious reasons, it would be a grave violation of individual rights if the state prevented people from honoring what they regarded as their religious obligations. To subject children to indoctrination in deeply personal matters against their parents' consciences is no less a violation than forcing Muslim parents to send their children to a Catholic Mass.

True, the state needs to protect children from abuse and neglect. It is also true that the state has a legitimate interest in reducing teenage pregnancy and the spread of sexually transmitted diseases. But it is not abuse or neglect to protect the innocence of preteenage children or to teach one's children more conservative, as opposed to more liberal, moral values.[20]

The argument presented by George and Moschella hinges on what they see as the special obligation that parents have to care for their children, especially through their most formative years. This part of their argument is uncontroversial. What is controversial is the application of this claim to the issue of sex education in public schools. Here, their argument is based upon an analogy between parental rights and the right to practice one's religion. They note that both kinds of rights are fundamental, and therefore the state may infringe these rights only when doing so serves a compelling interest. If a parent refuses a life-saving blood transfusion for a child, on religious grounds, or chooses to forego traditional medical interventions in favor of prayer only, the state may intervene to protect the child's life or health. Similarly, on the basis of a comprehensive review of constitutional cases on the matter, Dittersdorf writes, "nothing in the [U.S.] Constitution guarantees parents complete control over the children's education. In some instances parental interests in the child's values, individuality, and behavior, may have to be compromised."[21]

George and Moschella recognize the state's compelling interest in protecting "children from abuse and neglect," as well as its "legitimate interest in reducing teenage pregnancy and the spread of sexually transmitted diseases." So if government programs, including sex education, were narrowly tailored to these aims, the state would not be overstepping its authority. But George and Moschella

---

20 R.P. George and M. Moschella, "Does Sex Ed Undermine Parental Rights?" New York Times, October 18, 2011, http://www.nytimes.com/2011/10/19/opinion/does-sex-ed-undermine-parental-rights.html?_r=0. All further references in this section to George and Moschella are to this piece and will not be footnoted further.

21 N. Dittersdorf, "Public School Sex Education? Does It Violate Parents' Rights?" Review of Law & Social Change XII: S91 (1983–84): 591–616.

imply that some sex-education programs go further and can damage "the inno-cence of preteenage children" or attempt to instill liberal values. How do we determine when educating children about sex does this? Some might think that teaching children about their sexual anatomy, or about safe and consensual sex, robs them of innocence or promotes liberal attitudes. Christian theology has long taught that sex is inherently "dirty" or sinful, and any knowledge about it causes a loss of innocence. Yet should the public schools limit their curricula to topics that are acceptable to conservative Christian moralists? Or can the schools take a neutral approach, and teach sex as part of their instruction in human biology, health, social studies, and humanities? It's difficult to see how schools can pro-vide students with the information they need to protect themselves without going into some detail about sexual health, reproduction, and the difference between acceptable and unacceptable sexual acts.

George and Moschella claim that, for the government to be truly neutral in regard to sex education, it must allow parents "to teach [their] children more conservative, as opposed to more liberal, moral values." Schools undermine a parent's ability to do this when the content of the curricula contradicts a parent's beliefs and values. For this reason, sex-ed programs tend to cover topics that can be approached objectively or represented as a set of facts, and they unfortunately avoid consideration of unpopular or controversial views, liberal or conservative. Yet even deciding what facts to share with children and adolescents is contro-versial. A national U.S. survey in 2000 indicated that, in regard to what sex ed should cover, parents "want it all." Although the vast majority of parents want their children to wait to have sex, "two-thirds said ... [they want their children to] use birth control and to practice safe sex if they do not wait." Moreover, "at least 75% of parents said that classes should cover a wide range of other topics, including homosexuality, abortion, proper condom use, and how to get tested for HIV and other sexually transmitted diseases." [22] In sum, parents want sex-ed programs to cover disease and pregnancy prevention, and even controversial sub-jects such as homosexuality, abortion, and rape. Of course, when schools try to include such topics, they may face the kind of school-board meetings described at the beginning of this chapter.

One reason why schools may need to do part of the job of sex education is that many parents are not sufficiently informed about sexual health and policy to educate their children properly. Also, many parents may feel uncomfortable dis-cussing sex with their children, and therefore they may avoid the topic. In addi-tion, there is the important issue of parental bias. For example, because racist parents might teach their children that people who look different from them are inferior, formal schooling is needed to challenge such biases and ignorance. Similarly, formal schooling is needed to address irrational social prejudices and ignorance about sexual behavior. A further, and perhaps the most important,

---

22 Todd Zwillich, "Parents Want More Comprehensive Sex Education in Schools," Reuters, November 27, 2000, http://cig.salk.edu/extra_html/sex_and_school.html.

point to be made in response to George and Moschella is that they recognize only the rights of parents, and not those of children. Is this correct, or do children have a right to be educated about sex when they are old enough to inquire about it? And how should societies protect a child's right to be educated and prepared for life as an adult? We will consider this question in the next section.

Do Public Sex-education Programs Serve the Public Good?

There is a longstanding tension between the public good and individual rights. This tension is especially felt when there is a threat to public health. Ronald Bayer notes: "Early advocates of public health in the USA ... in the late nineteenth and early twentieth centuries, were unabashed as they defended the legitimacy of coercion in the face of public health threats ... those things which are, strictly speaking, detrimental to health or dangerous to life, may become the subject of action on the part of the Board of Health."[23] The use of coercion by governmental agencies to protect people's health continues to be controversial. Whether it's the *Affordable Care Act*, or laws mandating helmets for cyclists or immunization for children, many believe that the government is overly restricting individual choice when it forces us to protect our health. Others believe that individual health is a public matter, because some illnesses are contagious and some are costly to employers and taxpayers. The case for comprehensive sex education is often predicated on the need to protect public health.

First, there are many who argue for the necessity of comprehensive public sex education on the basis of children's right to information necessary to protect their health. Some point out that if children are not given proper information, they may obtain inaccurate or misleading information.[24] The UN Convention on the Rights of the Child holds

> that effective HIV/AIDS prevention requires States to refrain from censoring, withholding or intentionally misrepresenting health-related information, including sexual education and information, and that, consistent with their obligations to ensure the right to life, survival and development of the child (art. 6), State parties must ensure that children have the ability to acquire the knowledge and skills to protect themselves and others as they begin to express their sexuality.[25]

---

23 Ronald Bayer, "The Continuing Tensions between Individual Rights and Public Health. Talking Point on Public Health Versus Civil Liberty," *EMBO Reports* 8, no. 12 (2007): 1099–1103, http://www.ncbi.nlm.nih.gov/pmc/articles/PMC2267241/.

24 S. Shaw, "The Child's Right to Sex Education," *Planned Parenthood Challenges* 1 (1995): 2–3.

25 Quoted in *Child Rights International Network* (CRIN), "Sexuality" (2009), http://www.crin.org/en/library/publications/sexuality.

This international agreement puts pressure on governments to develop programs that ensure that children will be educated about HIV/AIDS prevention, at a minimum. Not only should governments avoid censoring sexual-health information, but they should also take positive steps to make this information accessible to children. Many U.S. state-level educational policies incorporate this minimal mandate.

Do states and federal governments that implement abstinence-only programs meet their obligation to ensure that children can "acquire the knowledge and skill to protect themselves and others"? Current research indicates that they do not. According to Debra Hauser,

> Abstinence-only programs show little evidence of sustained (long-term) impact on attitudes and intentions. Worse, they show some negative impacts on youth's willingness to use contraception, including condoms, to prevent negative sexual health outcomes related to sexual intercourse. Importantly, only in one state did any program demonstrate short-term success in delaying the initiation of sex; none of these programs demonstrates evidence of long-term success in delaying sexual initiation among youth exposed to the programs or any evidence of success in reducing other sexual risk-taking behaviors among participants.[26]

Abstinence-only programs are far more prevalent in the U.S. than in other industrialized democracies, and reliance on them may partly explain the relatively high incidences of STDs and teenage pregnancies in the U.S., when compared to similar industrialized countries. For example, the Urban Child Institute reports that 10 per cent of births in the U.S. are to mothers younger than 19,[27] and the U.S. teen birth rate is 39.1 births per 1000 teenage girls between the ages of 15–19,[28] compared to 4.3 births per 1000 teenage girls between the ages of 15–19 in Switzerland.[29] In a study comparing the differences in contraceptive use among teens in the United States, France, Sweden, Canada, and Great Britain, researchers found that teens from the U.S. were more likely than their

---

26 Debra Hauser, "Five Years of Abstinence-Only-Until-Marriage Education: Assessing the Impact" [Title V State Evaluations] (Washington, DC: Advocates for Youth, 2004), http://www.advocatesforyouth.org/publications/623?task=view.

27 Guttmacher Institute, "In Brief: Facts on American Teens' Sexual and Reproductive Health" (January 2011), http://www.guttmacher.org/pubs/FB-ATSRH.html.

28 B.E. Hamilton et al., "Births: Preliminary Data for 2009," *National Vital Statistics Reports* 59, no. 3 (2010): 1–29.

29 M.S. Kearney and P.B. Levine, "Why Is the Teen Birth Rate in the United States so High and Why Does It Matter?" *Journal of Economic Perspectives* 26 no. 2 (2012): 141–66, http://www.ncbi.nlm.nih.gov/pubmed/22792555.

international counterparts *not* to use contraceptives (and even more unlikely to use more than one method of contraception).[30]

The relatively low use of prevention methods, including condoms, by U.S. teens, may stem from the fact that abstinence-only programs do not provide much information about contraceptive devices. When they do, they often emphasize their failure rates, and their figures are typically false or at best skewed. For example, *The Big Talk*, part of the Illinois abstinence-only program, understates the effectiveness of condoms in preventing pregnancy by claiming that "14 percent of women who use condoms scrupulously for birth control become pregnant within one year." *Choosing the Best Way Leader's Guide* also provides misleading information. The curriculum states, "couples who use condoms to avoid a pregnancy have a failure rate of 15%."[31] Both works, however, fail to differentiate properly between "scrupulous" and "typical" use of condoms. Scrupulous use means "correct use of a condom during every episode of intercourse," whereas typical use of a condom is "using it improperly and/or not all the time." Inconsistent and incorrect use is associated with a 15-per-cent failure rate within a year, while scrupulous use results in less than a two-per-cent pregnancy (or failure) rate within a year.[32]

In addition, abstinence-only programs often mislead and misinform students about the effectiveness of condoms in preventing the transmission of STDs. Two abstinence-only texts, *Choosing the Best Life* and *Choosing the Best Path*, state that condom use reduces the risk of HIV transmission by only 69 per cent.[33] This statistic (and the one concerning pregnancy) appears to be taken from Susan Weller's 1993 study, which conflates consistent and proper use of condoms with improper and inconsistent use.[34] In fact, the Department of Health and Human Services issued a statement in 1997 urging that Weller's study not be used in instructional materials because of its false and misleading claims and the false conclusions that could be drawn from it. Indeed, a special investigation in 2004 by the U.S. House of Representatives' Committee on Government Reform into

---

30 J.E. Darroch et al., "Differences in Teenage Pregnancy Rates among Five Developed Countries: The Roles of Sexual Activity and Contraceptive Use," *Family Planning Perspectives* 33, no. 6 (2001): 224–50.

31 Advocates for Youth, "Illinois Abstinence-Only Programs—Disseminating Inaccurate and Biased Information," http://www.advocatesforyouth.org/publications/599?task=view.

32 See J. Trussell, "New Research in Contraceptive Failure Rates," *Contraception* 70 (2004): 89–96; A. Spruyt et al., "Identifying Condom Users at Risk for Breakage and Slippage: Findings from Three International Sites," *American Journal of Public Health* 25 (1998): 239–44; and D.L. Warner, "Male Condoms," in *Contraceptive Technology*, 17th rev. ed., ed. R.A. Hatcher et al. (New York: Ardent Media, 1998); 325–55.

33 Advocates for Youth, "Illinois Abstinence-Only Programs."

34 Similarly, the abstinence-only text by Libby Gray, *A.C. Green's Game Plan* (Project Reality, 2001) states on page 34 of the teacher's manual that, "[T]he popular claim that 'condoms help prevent the spread of STDs,' is not supported by the data." But again, the claim here is highly misleading: evidence suggests that rates of infection are reduced tremendously when condoms are used consistently and properly. See Centers for Disease Control and Prevention, "Condoms and STDs," http://www.cdc.gov/condomeffectiveness/latex.htm.

federally funded abstinence-only programs concluded that abstinence-only programs are filled with inaccuracies.

There is, however, an overwhelming amount of evidence on the effectiveness of condom use in helping prevent the spread of HIV. Condoms also provide exceptional protection against gonorrhea, chlamydia, and trichomoniasis, since these are transmitted through semen. Though condoms provide protection against genital herpes, syphilis, chancroid, and human papillomavirus (HPV), they are less effective with these diseases because the latter are transmitted primarily through contact with infected skin or with mucosal surfaces, which are not covered or protected by the condom.[35]

Finally, there is considerable evidence to suggest that just giving children a scientific account of sex (e.g., the biology of STDs and pregnancy) can fail to prepare them for the challenges involved in negotiating a sexual relationship. This can make them more susceptible to an STD, because it generally takes training in sexual negotiation and communication to get a partner to cooperate with condom use and STD testing, or to disclose relevant facts about their sexual history. Children need to be educated about many aspects of sex, including how to determine when an act is consensual, the responsibilities entailed by sexual relationships, and diverse moral and religious perspectives on sexual expression and behavior.[36]

Is Sex Always Harmful for Children?

Let's re-examine the ancient Greek practice of pederasty, which we discussed in Ch. 5. You will recall that pederasty is the practice in which an older man (*erastes*) romantically pursued, in a ritualistic and rule-governed fashion, a boy (*eromenos*) typically in his early to mid-teens. In exchange for providing the boy with gifts, mentoring, and an introduction to powerful people in the city's society, the boy would submit to the older man's sexual advances. Kenneth Dover describes the terms of this relationship in his influential book, *Greek Homosexuality*, as follows: "acceptance of the teacher's thrusting penis between his thighs or in his anus is the fee which the pupil pays for good teaching, or alternatively, a gift from a younger person who has come to love an older person."[37]

---

35 See articles cited in Advocates for Youth, "Illinois Abstinence-Only Programs," including Centers for Disease Control & Prevention, *Male Latex Condoms and Sexually Transmitted Diseases* (Atlanta: Dept. of Health & Human Services, 2002); Centers for Disease Control & Prevention, *Sexually Transmitted Disease Surveillance, 2001* (Atlanta: Dept. of Health & Human Services, Division of STD Prevention, 2002); W. Cates and K.M. Stone, "Family Planning, Sexually Transmitted Diseases and Contraceptive Choice, Parts I and 2," *Family Planning Perspectives* 24 (1992): 75–84 and 122–28; L.C. d'Oro et al., "Barrier Methods of Contraception; Spermicides and Sexually Transmitted Diseases: A Review," *Genitourinary Medicine* 70 (1994): 410; S. Weller, "A Meta-analysis of Condom Effectiveness in Reducing Sexually Transmitted HIV," *Social Science & Medicine* 36 (1993): 1635–44.

36 See Advocates for Youth, "Illinois Abstinence-Only Programs."

37 Dover, *Greek Homosexuality*, 90.

According to the etiquette of this ritualized seduction, the older man was always the pursuer, and the boy remained the passive one pursued. Dover explains, "That the eromenos should initiate a homosexual act for its own sake is not a possibility admitted by … any … Greek enthusiast or apologist for homosexual eros."[38] The distinction between the active pursuer and passive pursued actually existed in all forms of sexual encounter; indeed, it was very rare in ancient Greece for either homosexual or heterosexual pairings to be composed of people of the same age or social status. For example, marriages in ancient Greece typically paired a man in his late twenties or thirties with a girl approximately fourteen years old.[39] Moreover, the goal of sex wasn't really a matter of satisfying reciprocal desire.[40] The older man, whether he pursued a male or a female, was thought to be the one who enjoyed the sex itself. Hence, when a man pursued sex with any female, from his wife to a slave or prostitute, he always took the role as the active participant, with the other adopting a passive and receiving role.

Oddly, scholars remained silent on the issue of sexual activity among the ancient Greeks for centuries. This may have been due to the belief that such discussion would sully the reputation of a culture that we consider the birthplace of Western civilization, and from which we inherit both our democratic ideals and many intellectual traditions, such as philosophy. Even more odd, perhaps, is the nonjudgmental treatment given to this practice by scholars, when they began studying it in the late twentieth century. For example, Vernon Provencal says that

> Pederasty (both ancient and modern) should not be confused
> with our meaning of pedophilia to designate the sexual
> exploitation—whether heterosexual or homosexual—of a
> child's immaturity. The distinction between the two is observed
> socially by recognizing an appropriate age for the erotic on
> the part of the adult and the sexual consent on the part of the
> adolescent. The ideal age of the eromenos depicted in vase
> paintings and described graphically as the age of a first beard is
> that of a 14–17-year old.[41]

Part of Provencal's point here is that the pederast chooses from an older age group—between 14 and 17—while the pedophile typically chooses prepubescent children who are under 12.[42] Yet, according to Dover, there is a lot of evidence

---

38 Ibid.

39 Enid Bloch, "Sex between Men and Boys in Classical Greece," *Journal of Men's Studies* 9, no. 2 (2001): 183–204.

40 Dover, *Greek Homosexuality*, 16.

41 Quoted in Beert Verstraete and V. Provencal, "Introduction," *Journal of Homosexuality* 38, no. 3–4 (2005): 3.

42 See, e.g., APA, *DSM-IV-TR*, 973.

to suggest the boys sought in Ancient Greece were 12–16, rather than 14–17. Moreover, from a contemporary perspective, men in their thirties having sex with 15-year-olds is somewhat concerning, although for much of history this age difference caused little concern if the 15-year-olds were girls. Provencal thinks the fact that a boy's consent was sought before the sexual interchange legitimates the practice. Yet in the twenty-first century we usually define the age of sexual maturity—when consent can be meaningfully given—as higher than 15, and certainly higher than 12.[43] Consent involves at least two things: lack of coercion, and adequate knowledge. Today many would regard the intellectual and social advantages typically possessed by the older person as rendering any sex with a teenager coercive, and few think that young teens comprehend sex and its potential consequences sufficiently to meaningfully give consent.[44] For these reasons, the legal age of consent in many countries has been raised, especially over the last century.

In ancient Greece, in some instances, there was considerable pressure put on the boy by his own family, particularly when they were promised great things from the man pursuing their boy.[45] Mark Golden describes the practice of gift giving in his defense of Ancient Greek pederasty:

> There is little disagreement [among scholars] on the benefits that were said to accrue to the boys themselves or on the role of male homosexuality as an institution of transition between boyhood and maturity. Broadly speaking, regular intimacy with an older member of the citizen elite provides a boy with a model of appropriate attitudes and behaviors, a source of wisdom.... [For individual boys], involvement with a particularly well connected or gifted partner may prove socially and politically valuable, not just for the boy but for his whole family.[46]

Of course, parents today who permitted others to have sex with their children for such mercenary reasons would be charged with prostituting them. Golden's defense here seems to serve as a *reductio ad absurdum* of this ancient practice. But his description of the transfer of social capital involved also shows how difficult it is to judge a practice from one cultural context by the standards of another. Once again, if the exchange of social capital described by Golden pertained to a marriage arrangement between an older man and an adolescent girl, it might seem less culturally strange.

---

43 See Stephen Robertson, "Age of Consent Laws," *Children and Youth in History*, http://chnm. gmu.edu/cyh/teaching-modules/230; and "Age of Consent Laws [table]" http://chnm.gmu. edu/cyh/primary-sources/24.

44 Susan Clancy, *The Trauma Myth: The Truth about the Sexual Abuse of Children and Its Aftermath* (New York: Basic Books, 2011).

45 Bloch, "Sex between Men and Boys."

46 Mark Golden, *Children and Childhood in Classical Athens* (Baltimore: Johns Hopkins University Press, 1990), 59.

Before we can judge the ancient practice of pederasty, we need to try to see it as those who practiced it saw it. The concepts and categories they used to evaluate and classify it may be radically different from our own, especially their pre-Christian ideas about the nature of sexuality or childhood. There is also evidence that pederasty was not accepted by all members of the societies in which it occurred. This may be why Plato, in his classic work on the nature of love, *The Symposium*, feels called upon to defend the practice while also calling for its reform. In particular, he suggests that the *eromenos*, or teenage boy, ought to be older than the practice typically dictated. A recent article by Enid Bloch makes the interesting and very plausible argument that almost all we know about ancient Greek pederasty comes from the writings and perspectives of the older men who engaged in it. But this may tell us no more about how it was experienced by the boys they pursued than would the writings of contemporary ephebophiles about their sexual exploits with adolescents.[47]

While ancient pederastic practices may not have been seriously harmful to adolescents in Ancient Greece, they would very likely be so to adolescents today, given modern attitudes and understandings about sex and children. Despite this, the North American Man/Boy Love Association (NAMBLA) appeals to the practice of Ancient Greek pederasty in order to defend contemporary "man–boy" sexual relationships and to argue for changes in the law. In particular, NAMBLA wants to see the age of consent for sex lowered so that man–boy sexual encounters are not prosecuted as statutory rapes. Their website states that, since their inception in 1978, they have been engaged

> with the basic work of identifying, assembling and/or
> analyzing the most recent and relevant statistics and peer-
> reviewed research on subjects including the character and
> outcomes of man/boy love relationships, the realities of
> child neglect and abuse, the true effects of policies which
> criminalize love and reward authoritarianism, the misleading
> nature of mainstream media on these subjects, and the lies
> and distortions promulgated by various parties with vested
> interests in fuelling the anti-man/boy-love hysteria—including
> an analysis of what they stand to gain.[48]

They are doing so, according to their mission statement, in order "to end the extreme oppression of men and boys in mutually consensual relationships by: building understanding and support for such relationships; educating the general public on the benevolent nature of man/boy love; cooperating with lesbian,

---

47 Bloch, "Sex between Men and Boys." Yet some older lovers (*erastes*) were presumably themselves once young beloveds (*eromenos*) too.

48 North American Man/Boy Love Association (NAMBLA), http://www.nambla.org/, All further references to NAMBLA refer to this website and will not be footnoted further.

gay, feminist, and other liberation movements; supporting the liberation of persons of all ages from sexual prejudice and oppression." NAMBLA cites several recent studies to support the claim that non-coercive sexual relationships between men and boys are not inherently harmful, and can be of positive benefit to boys. If consensual man–boy sexual relationships in fact do not harm boys, then despite public perceptions to the contrary, there may be nothing morally wrong with them (at least, for consequentialist moral theorists). Let's consider, then, some of the empirical evidence to which NAMBLA refers to see if it can withstand close scrutiny.

On their website, NAMBLA refers to a 1997 literature review by Rind and Tromovitch, which argues that

> in the general population, CSA [child sexual abuse] is not associated with pervasive harm and that harm, when it occurs, is not typically intense. Further, CSA experiences for males and females are not equivalent; a substantially lower proportion of males report negative effects. Finally, we found that conclusions about a causal link between CSA and later psychological maladjustment in the general population cannot safely be made because of the reliable presence of confounding variables. We concluded by cautioning that analysis at the population level does not characterize individual cases. When CSA is accompanied by factors such as force or close familial ties, it has the potential to produce significant harm.[49]

Rind and Tromovitch's second article, which made similar points, produced much publicity and a storm of controversy.[50] This was, in part, because the article was published in the prestigious *Psychological Bulletin*, which is the official journal of the American Psychological Association. Roughly nine months after the article was published, the popular radio talk show host Dr. Laura Schlessinger told her 18 million listeners that the study "could be used to normalize pedophilia, [and] to change the legal system."[51] While NAMBLA is attempting to change the legal system, it does not promote "pedophilia" (adult sexual interest in prepubescent children), but rather ephebophilia (adult sexual interest in mid- to late-adolescent teenagers). Eventually, the House of Representatives and Senate both unanimously approved a resolution that rejected "the conclusions of [the Rind et al.] ... article published in the *Psychological Bulletin*, ... that suggests that

---

49 B. Rind and P. Tromovitch, "A Meta-Analytic Review of Findings from National Samples on Psychological Correlates of Child Sexual Abuse," *The Journal of Sex Research* 34, no. 3 (1997): 237.

50 B. Rind, P. Tromovitch, and R. Bauserman, "A Meta-Analytic Examination of Assumed Properties of Child Sexual Abuse Using College Samples," *Psychological Bulletin* 124, no. 1 (1998): 22–53.

51 J. Duin, "Critics Assail Study Affirming Pedophilia," *Washington Times*, March 23, 1999: A1.

sexual relationships between adults and children might be positive for children." The resolution explained why Congress took action on this: "elected officials have a duty to inform and counter actions they consider damaging to children, parents, families, and society."[52] Many scientists and scientific organizations, such as the American Psychological Association itself, also published statements rejecting the claims of Rind et al.

There is a wealth of evidence supporting the harmfulness to both children and adolescents of sexual activities with adults. According to the American Academy of Child and Adolescent Psychology, sexual contact between children or adolescents and adults can cause a host of psychological and physical problems.[53] These include lacerations to the vaginal and anal areas as well as STDs, depression, post-traumatic stress disorder, attention deficit/hyperactivity disorder (ADHD), conduct disorder, and oppositional defiant disorder (ODD).[54] Moreover, children who have been sexually abused tend in much higher numbers than the general population to become abusers themselves.[55] Three earlier meta-analyses of the relationship between CSA and maladjustment reach the exact opposite conclusion to the one drawn by Rind et al.[56] According to Dallam, "little support can be found for Rind et al.'s conclusion that the significant relationship they found between CSA and maladjustment was likely spurious due to confounding between CSA and family environment. [A number] ... of large scale representative studies, prospective studies, and co-twin studies using non-clinical samples ... almost uniformly reported significant associations between reporting CSA and a wide variety of mental, physical, behavioral problems which

52 House Congressional Resolution 107. Cited in S.J. Dallam, "Science or Propaganda? An Examination of Rind, Tromovitch and Bauserman (1998)," *Journal of Child Sexual Abuse* 9, no. 3/4 (2002): 112–13.

53 American Academy of Child and Adolescent Psychology (AACAP), "Child Sexual Abuse," http://www.aacap.org/AACAP/Families_and_Youth/Facts_for_Families/Facts_for_Families_Pages/Child_Sexual_Abuse_09.aspx.

54 M.E. Herman-Giddens et al., "Underascertainment of Child Abuse Mortality in the United States," *JAMA* 282, no. 5 (1999): 463–67; M.W. Roosa et al., "The Relation of Child Sexual Abuse and Depression in Young Women: Comparisons across Four Ethnic Groups," *Journal of Abnormal Child Psychology* 27, no. 1 (1999): 65–76; C.S. Widom, "Posttraumatic Stress Disorder in Abused and Neglected Children Grown Up," *The American Journal of Psychiatry* 15, no. 8 (1999): 1223–29; G. Hornor, "Child Sexual Abuse: Consequences and Implications," *Journal of Pediatric Health Care* 24, no. 6 (2010): 358–64; K. Walsh and D. DiLillo, "Child Sexual Abuse and Adolescent Sexual Assault and Revictimization," in *The Psychology of Teen Violence and Victimization*, ed. Michael A. Paludi, 203–16 (Santa Barbara, CA: Praeger, 2011).

55 T.L. Messman-Moore and P.J. Long, "Child Sexual Abuse and Revictimization in the Form of Adult Sexual Abuse, Adult Physical Abuse, and Adult Psychological Maltreatment," *Journal of Interpersonal Violence* 15, no. 5 (2000): 489.

56 S.A. Jumper, "A Meta-Analysis of the Relationship of Child Sexual Abuse to Adult Psychological Adjustment," *Child Abuse & Neglect* 19 (1995): 715–28; D.A. Neuman et al., "The Long-Term Sequelae of Childhood Sexual Abuse in Women: A Meta-Analytic Review," *Child Maltreatment* 1 (1996): 6–16; and E. Oddone and M.L Genuis, *A Meta-Analysis of the Published Research on the Effects of Child Sexual Abuse* (Calgary: National Foundation for Family Research and Education, 1996).

persist even after controlling for family dysfunction."[57] In short, sexual contact with adults is harmful to children and adolescents even when it is not compounded by incest or other forms of child abuse from family members. Other criticisms of Rind et al. include charges of sample bias. This charge focuses mainly on Rind et al.'s exclusive use of college students in their sample. This would potentially miss all those people who were so psychologically traumatized by their childhood sexual abuse that they didn't make it to college,[58] or dropped out soon after entering.[59]

NAMBLA also cites Susan Clancy's *The Trauma Myth: The Truth About the Sexual Abuse of Children—and Its Aftermath*. Clancy argues that the way we typically understand childhood sexual abuse is that it is traumatic and analogous to rape, since its victims only engage in such sexual activity when forced or threatened. On the basis of extensive interviews with adults who had been sexually abused as children, however, she found that the children "did not fight it. It was not done against their will. They went along … only 5% tried to stop it."[60] Clancy concludes that, because the sexual abuse of children is not typically violent and because the child victims are too young to fully understand sex, the victims do not see the event as traumatic and rarely report it.

NAMBLA sees this as an endorsement of adult–child sexual relationships. But this grossly misrepresents Clancy's work. The fact that child sexual abuse does not typically involve violence or threats, and is not analogous to rape, does not mean that it produces no harm in children. These children will eventually grow up and come to realize what happened to them, and so the resulting trauma is often delayed. As Pinker (2010) writes in her review of Clancy's book, it is the "co-opting of a child's loyalty and 'participation' that prompts great distress in victims later, … by reinforcing their sense of culpability and isolation. [Clancy] argues persuasively that, for most victims, we need to shift our concept of abuse from the violent rape model to something more varied and subtle if we want to succeed at treatment and prevention."[61] In other words, Clancy's book shows that we need to better understand the harms of childhood sexual abuse in terms of how adults can abuse the authority they have over children and adolescents, and the consequent feelings in children of tremendous guilt and betrayal, as they grow up.

Studies of sexual harassment show that persons in positions of authority and power cannot assume that consent is genuine when it is given by persons who

57 Dallam, "Science or Propaganda?", 115.

58 D. Spiegel, "The Price of Abusing Children and Numbers," *Sexuality and Culture* 4 (2000): 63–66.

59 R.D. Duncan, "Childhood Maltreatment and College Drop-Out Rates: Implications for Child Abuse Researchers," *Journal of Interpersonal Violence* 15 (2000): 987–95.

60 Clancy, *The Trauma Myth*, 41.

61 Susan Pinker, "A New View of Child Abuse," *Globe and Mail*, Feb. 19, 2010, http://www.theglobeandmail.com/arts/books-and-media/review-the-trauma-myth-by-susan-a-clancy/article4308015/.

are subordinate to, or dependent upon, them. Someone can hold authority and power over another because of their age, job title, or their position of leadership in a community. The sexual abuse of children and adolescents is not unique to man/boy love societies, and, as we have seen recently, it happens in churches, youth sports organizations, detention centers for children, schools, and so on. The perpetrators are often trusted individuals, such as priests, coaches, security guards, and teachers. There is little justification for such behavior, and many reasons to condemn it, including the probability of harm to the minor, and because it constitutes a violation of the minor's right to personal safety, bodily control, sexual autonomy, and dignity. In Ch. 4, we considered "Romeo and Juliet" cases, in which the difference in age between the minor and adult was only a few years, and of course, exceptions can be made when there is little evidence of coercion. But the greater the difference in age, the greater the possibility that some form of social coercion is involved, which the minor may not realize until they are an adult. While the correct age for legal consent to sex can always be disputed, the historical trend toward increasing this age is, in all likelihood, a good development.

Discussion Questions

1. What forms of sexual autonomy and privacy should we grant to children and adolescents?
2. Should instruction on how to prevent STDs and pregnancy be mandatory for all students, and, if so, at what age should it be introduced into school programs?
3. Should schools provide information in sex-education courses about diverse sexual orientations, the criteria of consensual sex, or different religious perspectives on sexual morality?
4. Should schools refer both students and their parents to the many websites that sex and health educators have now designed for teenagers, such as Scarleteen (http://www.scarleteen.com/) or Sex, Etc. (http://sexetc.org/)?
5. Some anthropologists and historians speculate that the pederastic practices of ancient Greece were less harmful to adolescents in that context than the same practices would be to boys today. Why might this be true?

Further Reading

Drexler, Peggy. "Gay Parents Raising Kids: How Will They Fare?" *Psychology Today*, May 29, 2012. http://www.psychologytoday.com/blog/our-gender-ourselves/201205/gay-parents-raising-kids-how-will-they.fare.

George, R.P., and M. Moschella. "Does Sex Ed Undermine Parental Rights?" *New York Times*, October 18, 2011. http://www.nytimes.com/2011/10/19/opinion/does-sex-ed-undermine-parental-rights.html?_r=0.

Irvine, Janice. *Talk About Sex: The Battles Over Sex Education in the United States*. Berkeley: University of California Press, 2002.

Luker, Kristin. *When Sex Goes to School: Warring Views on Sex—and Sex Education—Since the Sixties*. New York & London: W.W. Norton, 2006.

Stengers, Jean, and Anne Van Neck. *Masturbation: The History of a Great Terror*. Translated by K. Hoffman. New York: Palgrave Macmillan, 2001.

Chapter 8

Sexual Speech and the Freedom of Expression

Are some forms of pornography so objectionable that they should be banned, and if so, which kinds? What dangers arise when we invest our government with the power to ban certain kinds of speech and expressive materials? Many philosophers are interested in understanding what it takes to maintain robust democratic institutions, and one important part of this involves determining which restrictions on speech are desirable and which are pernicious. In this chapter, we will explore the kinds of restrictions that often exist on sexual speech, and whether they are justified. We will also explore the value of sexual speech, including sexual humor.

How Is Child Pornography Harmful?

Most people agree that child pornography is harmful and should be banned. In this section, we will explore what is objectionable about child pornography in order to see if some of these objectionable qualities are found in other forms of pornography, such as adult pornography or violent pornography.

First, child pornography in which an actual child is used in the making of the material involves the sexual abuse of a child. Second, child pornography of this sort records and disseminates a child's victimization, for the benefit of others who might view it. In this way, viewers abet and vicariously participate in the sexual violation of a child, in ways that can amplify the harms done. These include damage to the victim's mental and physical health, sense of self-worth or dignity, ability to form supportive social relationships, and ability to exercise the right to privacy. Third, the content of child pornography is offensive to all decent people and contains nothing of redeeming social, artistic, or scientific value.[1] Fourth, pornography that depicts children as appropriate sexual objects trivializes the harms caused by child sexual abuse and thereby implicitly condones and encourages sex crimes against children.

The first two reasons here focus on the harm that the producers, distributors, and consumers of child pornography do to a particular child. The third and fourth reasons focus on the noxious content of child pornography and its ill effects. Some child pornography is made with animation or only adult actors (e.g., 18-year-olds who look younger), and therefore the first two objections would not apply to this kind of material. So, in thinking about the wrongs of child pornography, we need to distinguish child pornography that is produced using actual children from that which is not. We also need to determine what kinds of representations involve the sexual abuse of a child, and when patently and universally offensive content with no redeeming social value is present, in order to develop fair and effective social policies. For example, is a photograph of a child's nude body a type of child pornography? Or must the child be posed in a sexually flirtatious or alluring fashion? Is a film of two 17-year-olds having consensual sex a type of child pornography if these teenagers made and disseminated the film themselves (e.g., can they be both the victims and perpetrators)? Is a sexually suggestive drawing or cartoon of a child that is done in a non-realist style a type of child pornography? Is a novel that depicts the sexual violation of a child in a way intended to arouse rather than repel readers a kind of child pornography, or must pornography involve visually graphic sexual content? Courts often have to consider such types of pornographic material and then determine whether to prosecute those who produce, sell, or possess them.

The existence of borderline cases of child pornography does not show that the laws restricting this material are unreasonable; it merely shows that these laws are challenging to formulate and apply. Sometimes the application of a law may be based on subjective interpretations about the existence or offensiveness of the sexual content in an expressive artifact, and for this reason, laws in the U.S. that restrict obscene materials set fairly high standards for restricting them based on their content. It is generally easier to prosecute and punish child pornographers when they use minors in the making of their works. But with the introduction of sophisticated digital editing and illustration tools, even this can sometimes be difficult to prove.

---

1   These criteria echo the current legal standards for classifying materials as obscene, which will be discussed in more detail below.

In 2002, the U.S. Supreme Court struck down provisions in a federal law (the *Child Pornography Prevention Act* of 1996) that banned virtual child pornography.[2] Writing for the majority, Justice Anthony Kennedy argued that the government should not restrict "speech that records no crime and creates no victims by its production." Furthermore, he wrote, "the statute prohibits the visual depiction of an idea—that of teenagers engaging in sexual activity—that is a fact of modern society and has been a theme in art and literature throughout the ages."[3] Although Justice Sandra Day O'Connor concurred that the First Amendment protected sexually explicit content in which adults were costumed to look like children, she agreed with those in the minority that realistic computer-generated images with similar content should be banned. She reasoned that the availability of sophisticated computer simulations might allow child pornographers to avoid liability by claiming in court that their works were generated without child, or any, actors. O'Connor's distinction recognizes that, when the actors in a film are adults, this should be easy for the defendant to prove. But how does the defendant prove that no actors were used, or, conversely, how do the prosecutors prove that child actors were indeed used, if it is possible to create the same images without actors? What evidence should the prosecutors or defendant be allowed to present to support their case? If the prosecutors cannot establish the identities of the alleged child actors and the defendant does not have convincing evidence of the digital production process, what then?

In 2008 the U.S. Supreme Court upheld a provision in the revamped 2003 "PROTECT Act" that prohibits pandering in virtual pornography if the seller promotes the material as actual child pornography. According to one news report, Justice Antonin Scalia explained that "an offer to provide or a request to receive virtual child pornography is not prohibited by the PROTECT Act and continues to have First Amendment protection." In Scalia's words: "A crime is committed only when the speaker believes or intends the listener to believe that the subject of the proposed transaction depicts real children."[4] This provision prevents a pornographer from marketing a product as real child pornography, and then later deploying the legal defense that it was only virtual, or digitally produced, material.

What if people *pander* in virtual child pornography by misrepresenting their fake goods as the real, illegal stuff? What then is the criminal intent of such persons: to induce potential buyers to buy legal, virtual materials that the buyers falsely believe to be illegal material made with real children? Surely such sellers are guilty of catering to the vices and weaknesses of others, but they are doing so without involving or harming a real child. Perhaps they are misguidedly

---

2   David L. Hudson, Jr., "Virtual Child Pornography," *First Amendment Center*, September 13, 2002, http://www.firstamendmentcenter.org/virtual-child-pornography .

3   Linda Greenhouse, "'Virtual' Child Pornography Ban Overturned," *New York Times*, April 17, 2002, http://www.nytimes.com/2002/04/17/us/virtual-child-pornography-ban-overturned.html.

4   Warren Richey, "Ban Upheld on Offering Child Porn," *Christian Science Monitor*, May 20, 2008, http://www.csmonitor.com/USA/Justice/2008/0520/p01s10-usju.html/%28page%29/3.

attempting to corner the market on child pornography, so that less non-virtual stuff will be produced, and so that alleged pedophiles will satisfy their base desires without hurting real children. Should acts with such intentions be criminalized? The sellers are involved in fraudulent business practices, but for an allegedly good purpose, from which they also profit. Of course, if using such materials is likely to provoke the buyers to harm real children—something quite difficult to prove scientifically—then the sellers' acts are not benign.

Given the difficulty of determining the origins of a specimen of child pornography, is the Court saying in 2008: if you describe it as real for purposes of selling it, then you will be prosecuted as if the materials are the real thing, without the Court attempting to investigate and decide this matter? Courts generally do not do this with other kinds of fake materials. For example, suppose I attempt to sell bags of blue sugar crystals that I represent as "meth," and not as candy, to some naïve person who is addicted to the TV series *Breaking Bad*. Am I guilty of pandering in virtual meth? Should I be charged only with perpetrating a deceptive transaction in which someone is essentially robbed of her money? Or does a person who sells (or attempts to sell) a fake illegal substance commit a different crime than a person who sells (or attempts to sell) a fake that, if it were not a fake (or was truthfully represented as fake) would be legal (a fake Van Gogh, for example)? In the fake meth case, the courts should have a relatively easy procedure for determining whether the material being sold is real or fake, unlike with virtual child pornography or fake art. But if we could come up with a procedure for determining whether child porn was real or virtual, should there be enhanced penalties for trying to sell a legal substance (virtual child pornography, sugar crystals) when it is falsely represented as something that it would be illegal to sell or buy? Do people who sell virtual child porn, but fraudulently represent it as the real thing, have the *mens rea* (criminal intent) that justifies charging them with violating child pornography laws? Their buyers who falsely believe that the material was made with real children do, but do the sellers, if they know their product was made with virtual technology?

People who pander in prostitution (e.g., pimps and other intermediaries) are attempting to sell something that is illegal (in the U.S.) and not a fake substitute. In virtual child pornography cases, the sellers and buyers would be doing something legally permissible, if their acts reflected the belief that what they were selling or buying was virtual pornography (under the 2003 PROTECT Act). The dissenting opinion in 2008 points out that the PROTECT Act goes against the long-standing principle that restrictions on freedom should be put in place not after ascertaining "the private understandings of speakers or listeners, but only after a critical assessment of practical consequences."[5] But in cases of realistic virtual child pornography, where there is no clear test yet for ruling out whether real children were used, courts may just have to let the private understandings of the participants define reality. Alternatively, the courts can attempt to restrict

---

5   Ibid.

expressive material, such as virtual child pornography, based on its "obscene" content by applying the relevant legal standards.

In the U.S., pornography is regulated as a form of "obscene" speech, which can be restricted without violating constitutional guarantees to free speech (as stated in the First Amendment). In a 1973 case (*Miller v. California*), the legal standards for identifying obscene speech were refined into the following test:

1. The work in question must depict or describe sexual CONDUCT.
2. The prohibited conduct must be specifically described in the law.
3. The work, taken as a whole, must lack SERIOUS literary, artistic, political, or scientific value (the "SLAPS" test).
4. The work, taken as a whole and applying CONTEMPORARY COMMUNITY STANDARDS, must appeal to PRURIENT INTEREST in sex.
5. The work must portray sexual conduct in a PATENTLY OFFENSIVE way, applying contemporary community standards.[6]

When legal experts refer to the Miller Test, they typically shorten it to the last three "prongs" (3, 4, and 5). In theory, some virtual child pornography could meet the criteria of the Miller Test, and those who produce, distribute, or possess it could be prosecuted under various obscenity statutes.[7] A few countries have laws specifically restricting child pornography in any form, including simulated child pornography and non-realistic depictions, such as in cartoons or video games. In the U.S., content-based restrictions on speech receive various levels of judicial scrutiny, and generally they must be shown to serve a compelling public interest. Speech that aims to incite violence is another category identified by the Supreme Court as not protected under the First Amendment, when it meets the standard of presenting "a clear and present danger." Although virtual child pornography could conceivably incite sexual crimes against children (objection 4 at the beginning of this chapter), this would not be sufficient to ban or prosecute such speech, unless the danger posed was imminent. That is, the First Amendment protects the expression of ideas that may be considered dangerous, irresponsible, disgusting, and reprehensible, as long as the danger is not immediate and can be addressed with less restrictive means. Free-speech

---

6 "The 'Miller Test' for Obscenity," *Exploring Constitutional Conflicts,* http://law2.umkc.edu/faculty/projects/ftrials/conlaw/millertest.html (emphasis in original); see also "Regulation of Obscenity," *Exploring Constitutional Conflicts*, http://law2.umkc.edu/faculty/projects/ftrials/conlaw/obscenity.htm.

7 "Virtual Child Pornography—an International Issue," *criminal law in the virtual context* (blog), http://virtualcrimlaw.wordpress.com/2010/11/22/virtual-child-pornography-an-international-issue-2/.

advocates defend these protections because, when the public is allowed to freely access information and robustly debate controversial and disturbing ideas, those ideas may be usefully reconsidered (e.g., speech advocating the elimination of slavery, promoting LGBT rights, legalizing drugs or prostitution, etc.).[8] Speech that does not pose an immediate danger can be restricted without censorship, for example by laws that regulate the minimum age for buying pornography or that restrict fully nude dancing to establishments that don't sell alcohol.[9] The recent passage of legislation in Russia that designates speech depicting nontraditional sexual relationships in positive ways as illegal propaganda serves to remind us of the importance of limiting the government's power to restrict speech.[10]

Are Child and Adult Pornography Significantly Different?

One of the main differences between child pornography (involving real children) and other forms is that, if no children are involved in the production of pornography, then a pornographic product does not involve the criminal and sexual violation of a child. In the U.S., people reach the "age of consent" at age 18, which is when their consent to participate in a sexual act carries legal weight.[11] Therefore, all legal forms of pornography in the U.S., which record sex acts performed by real actors, use actors who are over the age of 18. But because much legal pornography involves "barely legal" actors, we might ask whether a typical 18-year-old has the knowledge and social skills to give genuinely free and informed consent about participating in commercial pornography. Can a typical 18-year-old understand the consequences of her participation, and the nature of the activity to which she is giving her consent? Is the adult entertainment business sufficiently regulated so that young and inexperienced adults (inexperienced in terms of both sex and waged employment) are not subject to undue coercion and manipulation

---

8   "Freedom of Speech," *fact-index.com*, http://www.fact-index.com/f/fr/freedom_of_speech.html.

9   "Strip Club Laws and the Regulation of Sexually Oriented Business," *FindLaw*, http://smallbusiness.findlaw.com/business-laws-and-regulations/adult-entertainment-law-zoning-and-other-regulations.html.

10 Andrew E. Kramer, "Russia Passes a Bill Targeting Some Discussion of Homosexuality," *New York Times*, June 11, 2013, http://www.nytimes.com/2013/06/12/world/europe/russia-passes-bill-targeting-some-discussions-of-homosexuality.html.

11 Stephen Robertson, "Age of Consent Laws," *Children and Youth in History*, Item #230, http://chnm.gmu.edu/cyh/teaching-modules/230. The age of consent for sexual activity in Canada was 14 until 2008, when it was raised to 16. However, there are exceptions. For activities like prostitution and pornography, where there is a risk that the young person may be exploited, the age of consent is 18. Finally, there are "close-to-age" provisions that allow people under the age of consent to engage in sexual activity without legal consequence if their partner is close in age. For example, a 14- or 15-year-old can consent to sex with someone less than 5 years older where there is no relationship of trust, authority, or dependency or any other exploitation of the young person. Children aged 12 and 13 can consent to sex only with those less than two years older. See Government of Canada, Department of Justice, http://www.justice.gc.ca/eng/rp-pr/other-autre/clp/faq.html.

when they enter this industry? Finally, if we determine that it is not possible to regulate the industry in order to adequately protect young adults from unfair exploitation, should the age of consent for participating in a commercial sexual activity be higher than the age of consent for participating in non-commercial sexual activities?

One of the main risks of acting in a porn film is contracting a sexually transmitted disease (STD). Surprisingly, few jurisdictions require that actors in porn films use condoms, and instead most pornography producers rely on regular STD screening tests for their actors in order to minimize the spread of STDs in their industry.[12] Given these practices, the risks of an STD infection are typically higher for a person acting in a porn film than for a person working (legally) as a prostitute, where condom use is more common. Actors who contract an STD typically find themselves unable to work, while they simultaneously face long-term health problems and expenses. Returning to our earlier question, is the average young adult likely to be able to estimate the health risks that acting in a porn film involves? The question we are raising here is similar to a question that some are beginning to ask about the sport of football (both American and Canadian styles). Given what we now know about the significant risk of brain injuries for players, is the average young adult athlete (often a college student) in a position to adequately understand the pros and cons of participating in this sport? What kinds of policies should we have to protect the health of young men if this sport cannot be made reasonably safe? If young adult football players are given accurate information about the risks and consequences of brain injuries in their sport, should they be allowed to choose to play football, even if the risks remain quite high? Should the same hold for young adults who want to act in a porn film?

Another question to raise about adult pornography is whether some of it involves filming criminal sexual assaults. There is a significant amount of violent sex and rape depicted in commercial pornography, most of which is simulated, much like the violence in mainstream movies. Some feminist theorists have questioned, though, whether the sexual violence against women shown in pornographic films is always consensual. Are normal contract procedures followed when hiring actors, or are illicit forms of pressure used to get women to cooperate with filmmakers? When a woman is economically dependent on her male partner, is she genuinely free to say "no" to his sexual demands, on or off the porn set? When she does say "no," does her male partner respect her refusal to participate? Given background social conditions that render many women vulnerable to sexual exploitation by men, can we conclude that women in porn are acting autonomously and are freely pursing their own ends? Or, is much commercial pornography simply a record of men's sexual subordination

---

12 Susan Abram, "STDs in Porn Industry Higher than Reported," *Huffington Post*, November 2, 2012, http://www.huffingtonpost.com/2012/11/02/stds-porn-industry_n_2064639.html.

and exploitation of women?[13] Some films that graphically depict the sexual abuse of adult women may document the victimization of actual persons for the benefit of others, much like child pornography. One of the most famous cases of this was the 1972 movie *Deep Throat*. Many years after the movie was a big hit, the star of the film, Linda Lovelace, alleged that she was forced by her husband to make the film, and that viewers are essentially watching her be raped.[14] Lovelace's story reminds us that, as viewers, we don't always know the conditions under which a film was made, and that we have some responsibility to be more informed about the materials we view. Those who enjoyed watching *Deep Throat* in the 1970s may now feel somewhat uncomfortable about the pleasure they took in watching the sexual exploits of an actress who may have been coerced and exploited during the production of the film. Today, when any person with a cell phone can make a porn film and share it with friends, and where websites feature "revenge porn,"[15] we need to be sure that our viewing does not aid and abet a crime. Amateur pornography may, in some cases, provide willing actors with decent working conditions, but, in other cases, it may be produced or released without the actors' consent.

In terms of the content of violent pornography, some films trivialize the sexual abuse of women, often by failing to show the serious harm it causes. These films can appear to condone and encourage sexual assaults against vulnerable people, much like child pornography. The legal theorist Catharine MacKinnon argues that material eroticizing and promoting the sexual abuse of women is similar to hate speech, which aims at socially marginalizing and inciting violence against members of a particular group. She proposed that, rather than violent pornography being prosecuted as a form of obscene speech, it should be prosecuted as hate speech that infringes the civil rights of women to personal security and to be treated with equal respect. Several decades ago, she led efforts to legally redefine 'pornography' as:

> the graphic sexually explicit subordination of women, whether
> in pictures or in words, that also includes one or more of
> the following: (1) Women are presented as sexual objects
> who enjoy pain or humiliation; or (2) Women are presented
> as sexual objects who experience sexual pleasure in being
> raped; or (3) Women are presented as sexual objects tied up

---

13 For a summary of feminist criticisms of pornography, see Shrage, "Feminist Perspectives on Sex Markets."

14 Tom Leonard, "Abused by the Porn Industry AND Her Feminist Saviours: How Deep Throat Star Linda Lovelace's Tragic Life Was a Very Modern Morality Tale," *Daily Mail*, March 26, 2012, http://www.dailymail.co.uk/femail/article-2120823/How-Deep-Throat-star-Linda-Lovelaces-tragic-life-modern-morality-tale.html.

15 "Fighting Back Against Revenge Porn," *New York Times*, October 12, 2013, http://www.nytimes.com/2013/10/13/opinion/sunday/fighting-back-against-revenge-porn.html?smid=pl-share.

or cut up or mutilated or bruised or physically hurt, or as dismembered or truncated or fragmented or severed into body parts; or (4) Women are presented as being penetrated by objects or animals; or (5) Women are presented in scenarios of degradation, injury abasement, torture, shown as filthy or inferior, bleeding, bruised, or hurt in a context that makes these conditions sexual; or (6) Women are presented as sexual objects for domination, conquest, violation, exploitation, possession, or use, or through postures or positions of servility or submission or display.[16]

A law of this sort was approved in the city of Indianapolis in 1984, and it allowed for men, children, and transsexuals, as well as women, to seek redress for harms caused by pornographic works.

The Indianapolis ordinance prohibited trafficking in pornography and coercing another to perform in or watch a pornographic work. People could bring charges against pornography producers or distributors for injuries caused by an assailant who viewed their work. The ordinance did not censor all pornographic speech, but only those works that, in a graphic and sexually explicit way, depicted the subordination of women, and it aimed to hold pornographers accountable for some of the ill effects of their works. However, the Sixth Circuit Court of Appeals struck down the Indianapolis ordinance in 1986 as an attempt by the government to restrict speech to particular approved views.[17] While MacKinnon argued that the message of much pornography is equivalent to an incitement to rape, the court did not find pornographic speech to pose an immediate danger or present the kind of threat that could not be dealt with by less restrictive means. Unlike some countries that have passed laws restricting forms of hate speech, U.S. policies reflect the view that the best way to respond to noxious speech is with more speech, and not by chilling the free exchange of ideas, even false or disgusting ideas.[18]

Some viewers of violent pornography understand that what they are viewing is a performance, and they do not necessarily interpret such material as instruction on how to commit rape. As with violence in mainstream entertainment products, most viewers would not find the material enjoyable if they believed they were viewing real abuse or propaganda promoting abuse. Those who defend violent popular culture often claim that it allows people to explore disturbing desires and fantasies in a relatively safe way. Nevertheless, some

---

16 "American Booksellers Association v. William H. Hudnut, III, Mayor, City of Indianapolis," *Exploring Constitutional Conflicts*, http://law2.umkc.edu/faculty/projects/ftrials/conlaw/amerbookseller.html.

17 "Regulation of Fighting Words and Hate Speech," *Exploring Constitutional Conflicts*, http://law2.umkc.edu/faculty/projects/ftrials/conlaw/hatespeech.htm.

18 Franklyn Haiman, "The Remedy Is More Speech," *American Prospect*, December 4, 2000, http://prospect.org/article/remedy-more-speech.

anti-pornography advocates hold that our regulations should take into account the existence of mentally unstable and impressionable viewers.

Some psychologists contend that hard-core pornographic materials are comparable to drugs. Most people who view them do not become addicted, but some users of hard-core pornography will find such materials addictive.[19] Moreover, addicts typically need more and more of a substance to achieve the same high, and this may eventually lead some porn addicts to attempt in real life the acts they viewed in violent pornography in order to achieve the same levels of excitement. Some studies attempt to demonstrate a connection between viewing violent pornography and committing rape, but such studies are controversial and inconclusive. The Internet has made pornography, including violent porn, more available than ever before, and yet there is some evidence that rates of sexual assault are declining.[20] Those who subscribe to the porn-addiction model usually hold that sex is itself addictive (see Ch. 10), and that excessive viewing of pornography is an unhealthy way for some people to pursue their sex addiction. On the other hand, skeptics of the addiction model of pornography argue that this theory absolves people of responsibility for their behavior by placing the blame on something that they have consumed.[21] While there may be a few people with mental illnesses who are adversely affected by viewing violent materials, most people are able to critically process and evaluate works of pornography as they do with other expressive works.[22] One compromise between prohibition and unregulated access would be to require buyers to have a prescription before purchasing violent hard-core porn. If you find such policies implausible, it may be because you are unconvinced of the analogy between violent hard-core pornography and addictive drugs.

Are Stripping and Lap-dancing Art Forms, and Should They Be Protected Forms of Self-expression?

While the First Amendment proscribes the passage of laws "abridging the freedom of speech," the U.S. Supreme Court has expanded this idea to include "freedom of expression."[23] The latter phrase includes non-verbal artistic works (e.g., drawing, sculpture, music, and so on), as well as non-verbal acts of communication (e.g., flag burning, tattoos, and so on).[24] That is, the speech protected by

---

19 A quick search of the Internet will turn up many websites about porn addiction, which discuss its effects, treatment programs, and the medical validity of treating excessive porn use as an addiction.

20 Steve Chapman, "Is Pornography a Catalyst of Sexual Violence?" *Reason*, November 5, 2007, http://reason.com/archives/2007/11/05/is-pornography-a-catalyst-of-s.

21 David Ley, "Porn Is Not the Problem—You Are," *Psychology Today*, May 20, 2013, http://www.psychologytoday.com/blog/women-who-stray/201305/porn-is-not-the-problem-you-are.

22 "Album Cover of Blizzard of Ozz," *Art on Trial*, http://www.tjcenter.org/ArtOnTrial/ozzy.html.

23 "Freedom of Speech."

24 "Art as 'Speech,'" *Art on Trial*, http://www.tjcenter.org/ArtOnTrial/bodyart.html.

the First Amendment is not limited to utterances spoken or written in a human language, in the narrow sense of that concept. Nonverbal speech is sometimes used for political commentary (e.g., comics, satirical painting, and so on) and frequently contains sexual content intended to mock political officials and public figures.[25]

According to the legal scholar Erwin Chermerinsky, "the Court has indicated that some types of sexually oriented speech, although protected by the First Amendment, are deemed to be of 'low value,' and thus are more susceptible to government regulation."[26] Sexual speech can fall into the category of obscene speech, and as such it is exempt from First Amendment protection. Otherwise, sexual speech can be regulated by content-based or content-neutral restrictions. The latter receive a lower level of judicial scrutiny and, therefore, are more likely to be upheld if challenged as unconstitutional. Content-neutral regulations define the "time, place, and manner" in which a product can be sold, displayed, or used.[27] Content-neutral restrictions are justified when they serve an important government objective, and the restriction narrowly aims at that objective and therefore does not overly interfere with people's use and enjoyment of that product.

Stripping and lap-dancing involve sexual speech that is often regulated with content-neutral restrictions.[28] Cities and other jurisdictions classify establishments featuring nude dancing as "adult businesses" and, as such, they are subject to a variety of restrictions.[29] These include special zoning and licensing requirements, mandatory buffer zones between clients and performers, and bans on the sale or use of alcohol on the premises. State legislators, city officials, and residents who support such laws usually believe that adult businesses raise crime rates in a neighborhood, which negatively impacts the quality of life for residents and lowers their property values. The U.S. Supreme Court ruled in 2000 that states and cities may even ban nude dancing as a strategy to prevent crime and other ill effects. According to Linda Greenhouse, an earlier ruling established that "the government could essentially assume that 'pernicious secondary effects' would result from the presence of nude dancing establishments," and the new ruling reaffirms this standard.[30] Greenhouse reports that Justice Sandra Day O'Connor

---

25 "Satire and Political Commentary," *Art on Trial*, http://www.tjcenter.org/ArtOnTrial/ officials.html. See also Lynn Hunt, ed., *The Invention of Pornography. Obscenity and the Origins of Modernity, 1500–1800* (New York: Zone Books, 1993).

26 E. Chermerinsky, *Constitutional Law* (New York: Aspen Publishers, 2006), 986.

27 "Time, Place, and Manner Regulations," *Exploring Constitutional Conflicts*, http://law2.umkc. edu/faculty/projects/ftrials/conlaw/timeplacemanner.htm.

28 David L. Hudson, Jr., "Nude Dancing," *First Amendment Center*, September 13, 2002, http:// www.firstamendmentcenter.org/nude-dancing.

29 For example, see: "Municipal Regulation of Adult Uses," *New York State General Counsel*, http:// www.dos.ny.gov/cnsl/lu03.htm.

30 Linda Greenhouse, "Justices Uphold Laws Banning Nude Dancing," *New York Times*, March 30, 2000, http://www.nytimes.com/2000/03/30/us/justices-uphold-laws-banning-nude-dancing.html.

offered the following explanation: "the case was governed by the lower level of First Amendment scrutiny the court applies to content-neutral laws that regulate conduct and have only an incidental effect on expression."[31]

A law that prohibits nude dancing that expresses contempt and disrespectful attitudes toward women, for example, would face a higher level of scrutiny because it aims to ban specific content rather than prevent various secondary effects. Of course, some feminists argue that speech expressing high levels of contempt toward women promotes behaviors that cause harm to women, but this is difficult to prove. Even so, there are other kinds of secondary effects that are less difficult to prove, such as the impact of adult-themed theaters or bars on neighborhood crime rates and property values.

However, the anthropologist Judith Hanna claims that there is actually an absence of studies demonstrating the negative impact of nude-dancing establishments on their communities.[32] It appears that U.S. courts do not require governmental authorities to defend their restrictions by providing much evidence that nude-dancing establishments negatively impact their neighborhoods. Few studies prove any hypothesis conclusively, and even when a correlation exists between the opening of sex businesses and an increase in crime in a particular neighborhood, we know that showing a correlation is not equivalent to proving causation. So it's unclear what Hanna and others would take as "proof" that sex-oriented businesses have a negative impact on their communities. Yet it's also unclear what to count as a sex-oriented business, and if we include establishments such as Hooters or condom and sex-toy emporiums, their impact may be more mixed.

In a recent book, Sarah Kingston considers how the most controversial kind of sex-oriented business (prostitution) can impact communities.[33] Kingston studies communities' reactions to both licit and illicit sex work that occurs within their borders, and provides a balanced and nuanced approach. Because adult businesses can stimulate the economies of otherwise poor communities, Kingston identifies both positive and negative effects, from the perspectives of her community informants. The effects, of course, are not independent of how sex work is regulated in a community, as the regulations affect whether sex workers are integrated into their communities or outcasts associated with the criminal elements of a community. In other words, how much crime sex-oriented work brings into a community is a function of what types of activities are criminal (e.g., prostitution, alcohol and drug use, and so on). Unfortunately, it is not always easy to tease out the ill effects caused by an activity from the ill effects caused by attempts to control it.

---

31 Ibid.

32 Peter Monaghan, "Stripping as an Art Form," *Chronicle of Higher Education*, May 23, 2012, http://chronicle.com/blogs/pageview/stripping-as-an-art-form/30473.

33 Sarah Kingston, *Prostitution in the Community: Attitudes, Action, and Resistance* (New York: Routledge, 2013).

Another problem is when ordinary health-and-safety regulations protecting both workers and customers are not enforced in sex-oriented businesses. For example, in bars featuring stripping and pole- and lap-dancing, workers are often sexually harassed and assaulted. Due to the nature of the businesses, some clients and business owners, as well as law-enforcement officials, think that existing regulations pertaining to sexual harassment and sex discrimination can be relaxed or ignored. However, in settings where nude and erotic dancing takes place, there is probably a greater need to protect workers from unwanted forms of sexual attention, even if much of the attention they get is actually wanted. Some sex workers argue that the negative effects of sex-oriented businesses can be largely eliminated if the owners are held to the same standards as more respectable establishments, while others contend that there is a need for special safety regulations for different kinds of industries, such as food production, health care, and also sex work.[34] The common thread of these approaches is that it is better to let these businesses operate in the open, with appropriate restrictions, rather than to push them to the margins of society where they will operate without much public oversight.

One form of nude dance that may call out for special regulation is lap-dancing. Unlike other forms of erotic dance, lap-dancing involves physical contact between the performer and the customer. In some jurisdictions, lap-dancers may perform with rather minimal clothing, and they can touch their customers with their bodies in ways that may be sexually arousing. In fact, some legal experts question whether lap-dancing is a form of prostitution.[35] The primary difference seems to be that the customer of the lap-dancer generally remains clothed, and skin-to-skin contact involving the genitals of any participant is not permitted. This difference is probably sufficient to prevent the spread of most STDs, which is one of the main rationales for prohibiting prostitution. However, prostitution with mandatory condom use is probably equally safe and prevents skin-to-skin contact in the genital areas, so does it make sense to criminalize one activity and not the other? In many jurisdictions, the legal definition of 'sex' involves penetration of a bodily orifice, and so, technically, lap dancing does not count as 'paid sex.' The FBI uses the following definition of forced sex for the purpose of prosecuting rape: "The penetration, no matter how slight, of the vagina or anus with any body part or object, or oral penetration by a sex organ of another

---

34 For an interesting exploration of the labor issues of women in the exotic-dancing industry, see the film *Live Nude Girls UNITE!* Also see "Exotic Dancers: Resources and Advocacy," *Prostitutes' Education Network*, http://www.bayswan.org/EDAindex.html. For an interesting Canadian perspective on the labor issues for exotic dancers and porn actors, see the controversial National Film Board documentary *Not a Love Story*, which follows the tale of Linda Lee Tracey, an exotic dancer from Montreal, on her journey of discovery regarding the sex industry (http://onf-nfb.gc.ca/en/our-collection/?idfilm=13558). After the film was made, Tracey claimed that the film's anti-pornography message was not consistent with her views. On this last point, see http://www.collectionscanada.gc.ca/women/030001-1268-e.html.

35 Bridget Crawford, "Is Lap Dancing Prostitution?" *Feminist Law Professors*, July 17, 2009, http://www.feministlawprofessors.com/2009/07/is-lap-dancing-prostitution/.

person, without the consent of the victim."[36] This definition is an improvement over earlier ones, in which rape was understood more narrowly to involve only the penetration of a woman by a man, and sometimes of a man by another man. And, for the purpose of distinguishing the crime of rape from other crimes, the new definition makes sense. But for the purpose of distinguishing one type of paid sexual activity from another (e.g., a lap dance vs. a "hand job" or penetrative sex), we may need an even broader legal definition of 'sex'. Under a broader definition, lap-dancing could be prohibited as a form of paid sex or, conversely, other kinds of paid sex (generally lumped together as "prostitution," including escort services, brothel work, street soliciting, etc.) could be permitted and regulated like lap-dancing.

Why Does the Topic of Sex Make Us Laugh?

Jokes and comedy routines often focus on sex. Why is this? Is there something inherently funny about human sexuality, or is there something about the nature of humor that explains our tendency to laugh about sex?[37] Psychologists, linguists, and other scientists have sought to identify the sources and mechanisms of humor, and so have some philosophers. In philosophy, there are four recognized approaches to explaining humor: Superiority Theory, Relief Theory, Incongruity Theory, and Play Theory.[38] Some philosophers and psychologists are exploring another approach, called the Benign Violation Theory."[39] These theories are not mutually incompatible and, taken together, they may explain different kinds of humor. In this section, we will briefly explore each theory and see if it can expand our understanding of humor about sex.

The Superiority Theory holds that humor is often a tool for mocking or humiliating other people. Laughing *at* someone allows us to feel superior to others, which may give us a momentary ego boost. We also laugh at earlier stages of ourselves, which may allow us to feel more grown up and sophisticated. How might this apply to sexual humor? Consider, for instance, humor that deploys sex

---

36 Federal Bureau of Investigation, "UCR Program Changes Definition of Rape," March 2012, http://www.fbi.gov/about-us/cjis/cjis-link/march-2012/ucr-program-changes-definition-of-rape.

37 "Laughter" is a behavior caused by many things, including things that are genuinely funny or humorous, and therefore some philosophers distinguish laughter from humor. See Richard C. Richards, *A Philosopher Looks at the Sense of Humor*, createspace.com, 2013, https://www.createspace.com/4323079.

38 John Morreall, "The Philosophy of Humor," *Stanford Encyclopedia of Philosophy* (2012), http://plato.stanford.edu/entries/humor/; Aaron Smuts, "Humor," *The Internet Encyclopedia of Philosophy*, http://www.iep.utm.edu/humor/.

39 Nina Rastogi, "5 Leading Theories for Why We Laugh—and the Jokes that Prove Them Wrong," *Slate*, May 13, 2011, http://www.slate.com/blogs/browbeat/2011/05/13/5_leading_theories_for_why_we_laugh_and_the_jokes_that_prove_them_wrong.html; Jeanna Bryner, "Study Reveals Why We Laugh at Disgusting Jokes," *LiveScience*, August 10, 2010, http://www.livescience.com/8466-study-reveals-laugh-disgusting-jokes.html.

in order to take down a notch someone in a position of power and authority. This would include jokes about the sexual habits of our political leaders, clergy, teachers, and bosses. Such jokes are leveling and often convey that those in positions of power are no better than us, or they call attention to the hypocrisy of people considered moral authorities. But some sexual jokes are more mean-spirited and aim to further humiliate a socially stigmatized group, such as women, lesbians, gay men, the elderly, and racial, national, and religious minorities. Such jokes may express feelings of social superiority by members of the socially dominant group. Additionally, some sexual humor may be aimed at people whom we see as naïve and sexually inexperienced. Laughing at them in this way may allow us to feel more knowledgeable about an important part of human life.

The Relief Theory holds that humor is a device for releasing nervous energy or tension. We often laugh when we feel anxious or tense, and humor, which prompts laughter, simply aids in the release of built-up nervous pressure. How might this work with sexual humor? Sexual encounters, as well as simply discussing sex, can be anxiety inducing, and so focusing on the humorous aspects of our sexual interests and experiences may relieve this anxiety. There are many ways in which we may feel tense or uncomfortable about sexuality in general, and our own sexuality or relationships in particular. We may feel insecure about our sexual attractiveness or skills, we may feel uncomfortable about particular desires, we may feel emotionally vulnerable to others because of our sexual needs, we may have unresolved moral qualms about sexual activities, we may feel judged by others for our sexual activities, and so on. All of our "sexual issues" contribute to making us feel tense, and sexual humor may be a useful therapy for enabling us to cope with the messiness of sexual desire and relationships. When we laugh at sexual jokes, we are releasing a reservoir of nervousness that inevitably builds up around our sexual thoughts and experiences. Moreover, sexual humor often involves heightening levels of nervous tension around sex by exploring taboo sexual topics. By violating the norms of polite discourse to engage in humorous "dirty talk," we perhaps release some of the nervousness we feel about the boundary violations involved in ordinary sexual activities, and in talking about sex more broadly.

The Incongruity Theory holds that humor is often produced when we observe that two or more things are misaligned, or don't fit, in ways that violate our expectations. According to this theory, our laughter expresses our momentary surprise or confusion at how the world really is, and at the gap between our ideas and reality. This theory might help to explain the humor we find in stories about sex that have a twist at the end. We might laugh at stories of failed seduction when we thought submission was inevitable, or stories of awkward seduction attempts that unexpectedly succeed. We often make misassumptions about what others find sexually alluring, and this can produce humor. We might especially laugh at people with unusual and surprising erotic tastes. This theory may also explain why we find funny sexual pairings that run counter to our expectations, such as a big woman with a small man, a gay man with a female date, a man with a robot girlfriend, and so on. This theory may also illuminate why we laugh at images of men with abnormally large phalluses or women with abnormally large breasts or buttocks. Sometimes we laugh at things that are absurd or don't make sense to us, such as bestiality, science-fiction sex machines, or depictions of goofy sexual feats. In all these cases, our expectations are defeated, and laughter may express our momentary inability to resolve the incongruous elements we perceive.

The Play Theory holds that humor is often produced when we pretend to be or do something. Playing at doing something, or imitating someone, can generate excitement and elicit laughter. For example, imitating someone giving a speech can be funny, while simply giving a speech might not. Similarly, imitating a fight can come off as funny, while engaging in a real fight usually isn't, for both participants and observers. In order for this kind of humor to work, we have to be able to distinguish when another's acts are a form of play or imitation, and when they are sincere or serious. One of the rules of play is that we are not supposed to take ourselves, or the situation, too seriously, because we are engaged in a kind of imitation or mockery. When someone does take us too seriously during a moment of play, we often say, "I was only joking." The Play Theory of humor may explain why imitations of sex—but not sex itself—make us laugh. A comedian might imitate someone having sex, and we find this funny only if we recognize it as someone pretending to have sex, and not really having it. Similarly, we often laugh at staged or filmed performances of sex when they call attention to themselves as a form of play or imitation, and not the real thing. Burlesque humor often uses this technique, so that the audience remains titillated by the ambiguity between whether it is watching real or only pretend sex. Watching real sex may make us feel like voyeurs, and therefore uncomfortable and awkward, whereas watching pretend sex may allow us to laugh at ourselves.

The Benign Violation Theory holds that humor often involves breaking sacred rules in ways that are harmless. For example, we may find it enjoyable to watch violence, as long as we know it's not real and real people are not being hurt. Slapstick often involves this kind of humor, where people engage in pranks that could have catastrophic consequences. We laugh once we understand that no one is harmed (unless we're sadists). Because sex can often involve violating sacred rules about what kinds of acts are permissible and who is an appropriate sexual partner, benign violations of these rules can often be funny. For example, instances where someone engages in a form of dangerous or reckless sex, but emerges unscathed, might offer occasions for humor. In the movie *Clerks*, a woman enters a dark bathroom in a convenience store and later emerges in a state of ravishment, thinking she just had great sex with her boyfriend. We soon learn she has had sex with the corpse of a customer who died masturbating prior to her entering the bathroom. When the woman learns who was in the bathroom, she goes into a state of shock but otherwise is not too harmed. This scene is hilarious, in part, because of all the taboos it violates.

It may be that the best sexual humor exploits multiple conventions that require more than one theory to explain. For example, several scenes from the *American Pie* films depict young adults engaged in elaborate schemes to view other people having sex or undressing. The humor we find in these scenes may be due to the feeling of superiority we have when watching the characters in the film, until of course we realize that we ourselves are engaging in an act of vicarious voyeurism. The humor might be due to the tension that builds during the scenes between the sympathy we feel for the victims and our desire for the perpetrators to succeed. The humor might also be due to the narrative twists that defeat some of our (and the movie characters') expectations, such as when what they manage to see is not what they expected to see. The humor may also be produced by the fact that we understand ourselves to be watching a playful imitation of voyeurism, and the exaggerated efforts taken to pull it off, and not the real thing. Finally, the humor may derive from the exploitative actions of the characters, which violate the rules of sexual decency, but in ways that turn out to be harmless to the movie's characters.

An interesting controversy involving sex and humor erupted in 2012 when the comedian Daniel Tosh enraged many with his comments about rape jokes. At a live show, Tosh began talking about how funny rape jokes are, and one audience member objected and yelled out that rape jokes are never funny. In response to this, Tosh allegedly said something like this: "Wouldn't it be funny if that girl got raped by like, five guys right now? Like right now? What if a bunch of guys just raped her ..."[40] Not surprisingly, a number of people were appalled and strongly criticized Tosh in the mainstream press and online social media. Tosh later issued an apology where he added, "The point I was making before I was heckled is there are awful things in the world but you can still make jokes about them."[41]

Tosh has a point here, but when someone makes jokes about "awful things," the object of the jokes needs to be evident and, in particular, the humor should not come at the expense of the people who have been victimized by those things. If Tosh meant to make fun of himself, as a guy who just doesn't get what's wrong about rape (or rape jokes), then that might be funny. Or if Tosh meant to make fun of the twisted humor in rape jokes, that could be funny. But his comments suggest that he thinks jokes about rape are funny, even when they exploit our feelings of superiority toward the victims in a mean-spirited way (according to the first theory of humor above). This type of humor can serve to trivialize or desensitize people to rape, which is why many people take such jokes seriously. If Tosh was trying to be edgy and make fun of the ways we are all confused about rape (e.g., the difference between aggressive seduction and rape, or rough sex and rape), then this could be funny as a "benign violation" of our cherished

40 "So, a Girl Walks into a Comedy Club," http://www.democraticunderground.com/11397719.
41 Hollie McKay, "Comedy Central Star Daniel Tosh Slammed for Gang Rape Joke, Tweets, Apology," Fox News.com, July 11, 2012, http://www.foxnews.com/entertainment/2012/07/11/comedy-central-star-daniel-tosh-slammed-for-rape-joke/point.

values about sex and love. Or he might make fun of rape fantasies and generate humor in ways that help us relieve our anxieties about such fantasies or see the incongruities in our beliefs about sex.

Given Tosh's clumsy or clueless remarks, *The Onion* was able to deliver a funny rape joke, which ironically supports Tosh's point, but at his expense:

> HOLLYWOOD, CA—Embroiled in controversy following comments he made during a recent performance at the Laugh Factory in Los Angeles, comedian Daniel Tosh chuckled this afternoon while being violently raped by a group of men in a Hollywood alley. "You have to admit, this is pretty hilarious," said the teary-eyed 37-year-old, his bloodied face slamming against a brick wall as he was brutally and repeatedly penetrated against his will for the 53rd straight minute. "Sure, I'll be forever tormented by images of my attackers tearing off my pants and holding a knife against my throat as they viciously tear into my rectum, but c'mon, you gotta have a sense of humor about this sort of thing." As of press time, sources said a disheveled Tosh checked into a nearby treatment center, where he quietly smirked after being diagnosed with HIV.[42]

The Superiority Account can partly explain the humor in *The Onion*'s "rape story" and joke, in that the joke makes fun of someone who makes fun of rape, and thereby takes that person down a notch. This joke manages to show the awfulness of rape and its consequences by allowing the audience to imagine someone's rape and then, somewhat awkwardly, laugh about it. But what *The Onion*'s audience is likely to find funny is not the act of rape itself, but an imagined situation in which a person who makes fun of rape is forced to reckon with the awfulness of it. Importantly, the readers know that they are laughing at an imagined rape and not a real one (a benign violation for this reason), and would probably react differently if Tosh were really raped. But, if he were really raped, we would probably not read about it in *The Onion*.

Does Sexual Speech in a Workplace Generally Involve Sexual Harassment?

Some people find speech with explicit or graphic sexual content disturbing or offensive and may choose to avoid it. But what if such speech occurs at their workplace or in their classroom, places they cannot avoid without consequences? Must we sanitize such public spaces of all sexual speech (both verbal and nonverbal) in order to accommodate people who are made uncomfortable by it?

---

42 *The Onion*, July 12, 2012, http://www.theonion.com/articles/daniel-tosh-chuckles-through-own-violent-rape,28769/.

In the previous section, we focused on why sex is frequently the subject of humor. Another question regarding sexual humor is: when does it cross the line from being edgy and funny to offensive and not funny? Sexual humor can be vulgar, in bad taste, rude, disrespectful, and degrading. Some sexual humor may be offensive because of its content, or because of the social context into which it is injected. When sexual speech is used in political and social commentary, it can be offensive to some, but the content may be more about politics than sex. Should our right to free speech in the workplace be limited by what others generally find offensive?

Employers are typically permitted to limit speech that undermines their mission, such as hate speech, without infringing their employees' First Amendment rights. Can sexual speech undermine an employer's or organization's mission, and could other kinds of speech (e.g., about religion, politics, etc.) eventually come to be viewed as disruptive of the workplace? A court case in Tennessee in 1996 illustrates the conflict that can exist between one person's First Amendment rights and another's right to work in an environment free of sex discrimination and sexual harassment. In this case, an employee found offensive a painting of a female nude exhibited in a building where she worked, and she filed a sexual-harassment complaint. The employer had the painting removed, and then the artist filed a lawsuit alleging that removing her painting from the building violated her First Amendment rights. This case was decided on a technicality in favor of the artist, and it did not resolve the issue of when a painting or other expressive work on display in a workplace potentially violates an employer's sexual-harassment policy.[43]

Under U.S. law, the government may restrict speech with sexual content in order to prevent harm to minors. "Harm to minor" laws generally restrict speech with sexual content in public venues where children are normally present. But workplaces are often private spaces where minors are unlikely to be present. Employers may restrict speech with sexual content that potentially creates a "hostile environment" for some workers in order to limit their legal exposure in sexual-harassment cases. In such cases, courts typically invoke a "reasonable person" standard—what would a reasonable person find abusive or demeaning—so that the outcome of a complaint does not rest on the quirky tastes or sensitivities of a few individuals. In the Tennessee case, we would need to ask whether a reasonable person would find the painting in question offensive or degrading. Given that this painting depicted a nude in a representational style that few adults would probably find offensive,[44] or sexually explicit, expression of this sort in the workplace will likely remain permissible.

There are workplaces in which speech with sexual content is relevant and important to the mission of the organization. For example, an institution with

---

43 "The Issue: Sexual Harassment and Artistic Expression," *Art on Trial*, http://www.tjcenter.org/ArtOnTrial/sexharass.html.

44 Ibid.

a mission of promoting the arts, such as a museum, might find that restrictive policies governing speech with sexual content—even controversial or potentially offensive speech—would undermine its ability to fulfill its purpose. "Hostile environment" complaints at such places would need to balance the mission of the institution against both the First Amendment rights of artists and the civil rights of employees. Similarly, an institution with the mission of providing education, including education about human sexuality, would need to tolerate open and serious speech with sexual content. Of course, employers can accommodate employees who are offended, by assigning them to jobs in the workplace where they are less likely to be exposed to such speech.

We've considered in this chapter how speech with sexual content is often treated differently than other forms of speech that some might find offensive, such as speech glorifying violence or communism. Is this a good thing? Or do the special restrictions on sexual speech promote the idea that there is something inherently shameful and evil about sex? Moreover, do they inhibit open and wide public discussion of sexual issues that would be educative and beneficial? Perhaps we should restrict sexual speech in the same ways that we do for other types of speech, for example, when it amounts to "fighting words" or libel, and get rid of the legal category of "obscene speech."[45] In earlier eras, speech with sexual content was thought inappropriate for "polite company," or mixed company, which often meant when women were present. This notion is rather outdated, and both formal and informal restrictions on sexual speech need to change in order to fit new social norms that pertain to women. But whether the standards for public sexual speech should descend to locker-room levels, or be raised to protect both men and women from the raunchy impulses of others, is still an open question.

---

45 For an interesting discussion of whether the idea of an obscenity is too subjective to apply in a consistent, non-arbitrary way, see Abraham Kaplan, "Obscenity as an Esthetic Category," *Law and Contemporary Problems* 20 (1955): 544–59, http://scholarship.law.duke.edu/cgi/viewcontent.cgi?article=2651&context=lcp.

Discussion Questions

1. Should a parent who takes nude pictures of her pre-adolescent children and shares them with friends and family be charged with creating and distributing child pornography?
2. If a job requires serving alcohol, a few jurisdictions require that the person employed be 21 or over. Should the same restriction apply when someone works for a company that makes hard-core pornographic films? If the job requires acting, filming, editing, etc., a hard-core scene, should the government set a minimum age of 21?
3. Are visually graphic depictions of sex more powerful and problematic than visually non-graphic (soft-core, cartoons, etc.) or non-visually graphic (novels, music lyrics) depictions of sex?
4. Are films containing excessively violent and graphic sexual content more objectionable than films containing excessively violent and graphic non-sexual content?
5. Find a cartoon, joke, comedy routine, or funny movie/TV scene with sexual content. Explain why it's funny, and then propose which theory of humor can best account for the source of the humor.
6. Find or describe one or more examples of sexual speech that you think should not be allowed in most workplaces, and explain why.
7. In order to avoid the use of arbitrary and subjective criteria when determining if an expressive work meets the legal definition of obscenity, the Miller Test invokes the notion of "contemporary community standards." In the age of the Internet, how do we determine the boundaries of our community?

Further Reading

Brake, Elizabeth. "Sex Skeptics: Speech Is Free but Thought Remains in Chains." *Reason Papers: A Journal of Interdisciplinary Normative Studies* 25 (2000): 101–12.

Estlund, David M. *The Visit and The Video: Publication and the Line Between Sex and Speech.* New York: Oxford University Press, 1997.

Fokt, Simon. "Pornographic Art—a Case from Definitions," *British Journal of Aesthetics* 52, no. 3 (2012): 287–300.

Langton, Rae. *Sexual Solipsism: Philosophical Essays on Pornography and Objectification.* New York: Oxford University Press, 2009.

Maes, Hans. "Drawing the Line: Art Versus Pornography." *Philosophy Compass* 6, no. 6 (2011): 385–97.

Mikkola, Mari. "Illocution, Silencing, and the Act of Refusal." *Pacific Philosophical Quarterly* 92, no. 3 (2011): 415–37.

Patridge, Stephanie L. "Pornography, Ethics, and Video Games." *Ethics and Information Technology* 15, no. 1 (2013): 25–34.

Chapter 9

Sexual Privacy

In this chapter, we examine the idea of privacy rights and why they are especially important in the sphere of sexual relationships and activities. Privacy can take at least three forms: (i) control over who has access to sensitive information about us (informational privacy), (ii) access to physical spaces where our activities are not visible to others (physical privacy), and (iii) control over important life decisions without undue interference from others (decisional privacy). In terms of our sexual lives, we generally want to protect all three types of privacy. For example, the decision to use birth control and engage in non-procreative sex is one that, some argue, should be encompassed under the third form of privacy. Being able to keep from public view information about our sexual interests and relationships, or images of our intimate activities, involves the first two forms of privacy. In this digital age, where images and information can travel great distances in a matter of seconds, it is becoming especially difficult to protect the first two types, so we will focus below on violations of informational and physical privacy. Moral and political philosophers are especially interested in understanding when our expectations of privacy are reasonable, and when these expectations should be respected by others and protected by our government. For example, are there situations in which people deserve to be "outed," that is, have some potentially damaging piece of information about their sexual interests or conduct made public? Similarly, when someone takes and sends images of us to others that show us in our so-called "private moments" (e.g., in bed, getting undressed, kissing someone, etc.) is this always wrong?

Why Is Sexual Privacy Important?

Political theorists draw a distinction between the public and private spheres. Simply put, in a democratic state, there should be a domain of activity beyond the government's reach. A robust private sphere or "civil society" is necessary for a democracy, where citizens have the freedom to communicate about public matters, criticize their government, practice their faith, organize their family lives, and so on. The civil society includes private, nongovernmental organizations and associations, such as the press, houses of worship, and the family, and is a "public" sphere, in the sense that it can be a space for democratic deliberation and non-market exchanges.

There are many meanings to the term 'private,' including "nongovernmental" and the three senses identified in the introduction to this chapter. Similarly, the term 'public' has different meanings, and very often these terms overlap. For example, a news organization may be private in the sense of not being owned or sponsored by the government, but it can be publicly owned, in the sense of selling ownership shares to members of the public, and it mainly exists to serve the general public. Reporters claim the right to keep their sources private (informational privacy), and to make decisions about what to publish without undue government interference (decisional privacy). Sexual conduct can be both private and public, in these different ways. Most sexual conduct is not visible to third parties (e.g., is physically private), but it can occur in public venues, such as beaches or "adult" clubs, and, in these places, such conduct may be visible to others. Information and decisions about our sexual lives are generally beyond the reach of the government (and other third parties), except when our sexual conduct poses a nuisance to, or threatens to harm, others. In this chapter, we shall explore why protecting the privacy of our sexual lives is important.

It will be helpful at the outset of this discussion to consider why privacy, in general, is important. The philosopher James Rachels has isolated three distinct, though connected, views about this matter: the conventional view, the core person view, and the view that privacy is necessary for maintaining a variety of personal relationships.[1]

Conventional view:
On this view, privacy is important because it enables us to keep our secrets. This is significant, in turn, because revealing these secrets could be harmful or detrimental to us in some way. Revealing our sexual secrets might merely embarrass us or others, but in some cases it could damage our reputations, cause tensions

---

1   James Rachels, "Sex and Personal Privacy," paper delivered in Cape Town, South Africa, August, 1999, http://www.jamesrachels.org/sex.pdf; James Rachels, "Why Privacy Is Important," *Philosophy and Public Affairs* 4, no. 4 (1975): 323–33, http://www.jstor.org/stable/pdfplus/2265077.pdf?acceptTC=true.

among our families or friends, or make us more vulnerable to discriminatory treatment.

Core person view:
On this view, there are integral parts of myself that I show to only some of the people with whom I interact. Thomas Nagel presents a view of this sort when he explains that, if we couldn't keep private a lot about ourselves and what goes through our heads in a typical day, life would be impossible. Making ourselves transparent to others takes work, and it isn't necessary for much of our dealings with people, so we generally don't share many aspects of our core self with others—especially sexual aspects. According to Nagel,

> most of us, when sexually engaged, do not wish to be seen by anyone but our partners; full sexual expression and release leave us entirely vulnerable and without a publicly presentable "face." Sex transgresses these protective boundaries, breaks us open, and exposes the uncontrolled and unpresentable creature underneath; that is its essence. We need privacy in order not to have to integrate our sexuality in its fullest expression with the controlled surface we present to the world.[2]

Nagel here suggests that privacy is important so that the unruly or unvarnished aspects of ourselves can be detached to some degree from our public selves. Rachels points out, however, that it isn't just our beastly, "uncontrolled and unpresentable" selves that we want to keep separate from our public personas; we also want to leave out some very mundane aspects of ourselves, such as how often we do or don't have sex.[3]

The view that privacy is necessary for maintaining
a variety of personal relationships:
Personal relationships are defined, in part, by how much we share about ourselves. Without the ability to close off parts of ourselves to others, there would be little distinction between friends with whom we are intimate and acquaintances with whom we are not. In "Why Lovers Can't Be Friends," James Conlon[4] suggests that different types of relationship—from the most intimate to the casual—ought to be compared to different genres of literature, each with its own definitional and evaluative criteria. This isn't to claim, according to Conlon, that our relationships form a hierarchy of intimacy or shared secrets, starting with acquaintances at the bottom and lovers at the top. Such hierarchies imply that

---

2   Quoted in Rachels, "Sex and Personal Privacy," 9.

3   Ibid.

4   James Conlon, "Why Lovers Can't Be Friends," in *Philosophical Perspectives on Sex and Love*, ed. Robert M. Stewart (Oxford & New York: Oxford University Press), 295–300.

those at the top know more about us than anyone else. Yet it is possible that our long-time best friend knows things about us that our lover does not, and that even our colleagues, at least with respect to our work lives, know things about us that our lover or best friend does not know. What Conlon's (and Rachels's) view does imply is that the various relationships we have are, in part, defined by the *kinds* as well as the *amounts* of information we share. Hence, a lover typically has more information about our sex life than a friend, while a long-time friend may know more about our childhood.

Rachels prefers this third view of the value of privacy. The conventional view implies that privacy is about keeping secrets, or preventing others from knowing the truth about us in order to avoid harm. The core person view suggests that there are aspects of ourselves we need to keep hidden because they are too raw or unprocessed. By contrast, the third view suggests that privacy is less about hiding ugly truths or primitive selves, and more about differentiating relationships with others and understanding the kinds of sharing that are appropriate or inappropriate to each.

Of course, sometimes people share personal aspects of themselves indiscriminately, such as when someone writes a memoir about a past love relationship, or performs as an exotic dancer. Privacy rules are valuable not so much to restrict sharing, but rather to prevent forced sharing. We often appreciate writers and performers (and even friends) who share things that most of us keep private, as they have trusted us with their story or creativity so we might learn something or be entertained. Yet even writers and entertainers maintain different levels of intimacy with different people and audiences. In the remainder of this chapter, we will assume that Rachels's third view best explains the value of privacy.

Is It Wrong to Force Someone "Out of the Closet"?

"Outing" another usually means making more public someone's gay or lesbian identity, or past same-sex sexual activities, without their permission.[5] Although anyone can be forced "out of the closet," when a prominent public figure is outed, this is often done to challenge the latter's moral hypocrisy, and to further the rights of a disparaged minority. For these reasons, some philosophers and activists defend outing in such circumstances. Here, we will examine three cases in which conservative evangelical ministers were outed.

Ted Haggard was a Colorado-based evangelical minister who was also the leader of the National Association of Evangelicals (NAE) from 2003 until November 2006. During much of that time, he held weekly meetings with then–U.S. president George W. Bush on a number of spiritual and policy issues. Although he did not oppose the rights of lesbians and gay men as stridently as

---

5   "Outing" can also include disclosing other potentially stigmatizing sexual proclivities, or indeed any kind of potentially damaging information. The cases we consider here, however, all deal with gay men.

others in the evangelical movement, Haggard has gone on record to state that the Bible explicitly condemns homosexuality as a sin. Also, he and his church publicly supported a Colorado Constitutional Amendment prohibiting same-sex marriage. Yet, in November 2006, Mike Jones, a professional escort and masseur, alleged that Haggard had paid him over a three-year period for Jones's sexual services, and had also purchased crystal methamphetamine from him. Though Haggard initially denied the claims, mounting evidence eventually forced him to admit to these allegations; this, in turn, led him to take an administrative leave from his church and to step down as head of the NAE.[6]

Jonathan Merritt is an up-and-coming evangelical leader. He has published widely in respected national outlets such as USA Today, the Atlantic, the Washington Post, and CNN.com. He is the author of A Faith of Our Own: Following Jesus Beyond the Culture Wars (2012), and Green Like God (2010), which Publisher's Weekly called "mandatory reading for churchgoers."[7] As a respected religious commentator, he has been interviewed by ABC World News, CNN, NPR, PBS, Fox News, Time, and the New York Times. When compared with others within the evangelical movement, Merritt is a moderate, although he is associated with the Southern Baptist Convention. His father, James Merritt, was that organization's president from 2000–2002, and it has been hostile to gays and lesbians. Indeed, the Southern Baptist Convention passed a "Resolution on Homosexuality" that claims homosexuals have a "depraved nature" and have "wrought havoc in the lives of millions," including the introduction and spread of AIDS, which has affected not only people "within the homosexual community but also many innocent victims." Homosexuals, they continue, engage in a "deplorable" activity that is a "perversion of divine standards and … a violation of nature and natural relations."[8] Jonathan Merritt has argued for the toleration of homosexuals, maintaining that though we must hate the sin, we must also love the sinner.[9]

In July 2012, an ex-evangelical blogger, Azariah Southworth, outed Merritt by revealing that the two had sexted each other, had engaged in some erotic Skype sessions, and had once had sex together.[10] Merritt eventually admitted that he and Southworth had "physical contact that went beyond the bounds

6   "The Last Temptation of Ted," GQ, February 2011, http://www.gq.com/news-politics/newsmakers/201102/pastor-ted-haggard?printable=true.

7   "About Jonathan Merritt," Religion News Service, http://jonathanmerritt.religionnews.com/about-jonathan-merritt/; "Jonathan Merritt," Huffington Post, 2013, http://www.huffingtonpost.com/jonathan-merritt/.

8   Southern Baptist Resolutions, "Resolution on Homosexuality," 1998, http://www.sbc.net/resolutions/amResolution.asp?ID=610.

9   Jonathan Merritt, "An Evangelical's Plea: 'Love the Sinner,'" USA Today, April 20, 2009, http://usatoday30.usatoday.com/printedition/news/20090420/column20_st.art.htm.

10   Azariah Southworth, "Why I Outed a Christian Star," Salon, August 12, 2012, http://www.salon.com/2012/08/12/why_i_outed_a_christian_star_2/.

of friendship."[11] Merritt continues to deny, however, that he is gay. Rather, he says, he is "broken," the result of being sexually assaulted by a gay man when he was a boy. Merritt writes, "I don't identify as 'gay' because I believe there can be a difference between what one experiences and the life that God offers. I'm a cracked vessel held together only by God's power. And I'm more sure each day that only Christ can make broken people whole."[12] He continues to be an active writer in the evangelical movement.

Tom Brock is a pastor at the Hope Lutheran Church in Minneapolis. The congregation is socially conservative, and it broke away from the Evangelical Lutheran Church in America (ELCA) around the turn of the century over the latter's increasingly liberal direction on homosexuality, among other issues. Brock was and is a firm believer that homosexuality is a sin.[13] In fact, he went so far as to blame the occurrence of a tornado in the Minneapolis area on a meeting of the ELCA in which the group passed a motion to allow gay clergy.[14] He was outed by a reporter, John Townsend, who managed to infiltrate a confidential Catholic support group for people "struggling" with same-sex attraction. According to Townsend, at one meeting Brock admitted that during a mission to Slovakia, he had been "weak" and "fell into temptation." Moreover, Brock said, "I just got weak, and I had been so good for a long time."[15] Brock has taken some time off from the pulpit, but he has indicated that he plans to return in the future.

The cases of Haggard, Merritt, and Brock share some important features. All three outed men are public figures who have taken a public stand that homosexuality is immoral, while at the same time they engaged in (or were tempted to engage in) gay sex. Moreover, all three men suffered personal setbacks, most obviously in terms of their careers, but also in terms of their relationships with colleagues, friends, and family members. There are also some differences in the cases. Haggard and Merritt were outed by men with whom they had sex, whereas Brock was outed by someone he hardly knew and with whom he did not have a sexual relationship. Furthermore, it is not clear whether Brock actually engaged in sex with another man, or merely desired to do so.

Can any or all of these cases of outing be defended as morally acceptable? Richard Mohr argues that outing someone—whether they be a public figure or not—is not morally wrong, and instead those who keep secret their

---

11   Jason Farago, "Jonathan Merritt Profits from Gay Hatred. He Deserved to Be Outed," *Guardian*, August 14, 2012, http://www.theguardian.com/commentisfree/2012/aug/14/homophobe-jonathan-merritt-deserves-outed.

12   Ed Stetzer, "Jonathan Merritt Shares His Story," *Christianity Today*, July 26, 2012, http://www.christianitytoday.com/edstetzer/2012/july/jonathan-merritt-shares-his-story.html.

13   Lillian Kwon, "'Outed' Pastor Says No to Homosexuality: Follows Jesus," *Christian Post*, August 3, 2010, http://www.christianpost.com/news/outed-pastor-46157/.

14   Queerty, "Lutheran Pastor Tom Brock Blamed ELCA's Tornado on Homosexuality," August 3, 2010, http://www.queerty.com/lutheran-pastor-tom-brock-blamed-elcas-tornado-on-homosexuality-which-uh-he-suffers-from-20100618/.

15   Quoted in ibid.

gay or lesbian orientation are participating in the oppression of lesbians and gay men, which is itself morally objectionable. He argues that we don't have a right to privacy in regard to our sexual orientation, in the same way that we don't have a right to privacy about our marital status, even though much about these parts of our lives are private. To argue that people have the right to protect such information perpetuates the idea that some sexual orientations are shameful.[16] Thus, when we out someone, we don't violate their rights or harm them, but rather prevent them from living in a way that is degrading to themselves and others like them.

Mohr assumes that keeping one's gay identity a secret is in a sense being untruthful about oneself to one's friends, family, and colleagues. So by outing someone we are simply telling the truth about that person and refusing to participate in that person's lie. Mohr does not see this as forcing people to share information that they may see as inappropriate for others to have. Yet imagine that some high-school students discover another student is gay and decide to out him to the school via Facebook. The consequences of outing this student will depend partly on where he lives, but it is unlikely that that there would be no negative fallout. When people are outed, we take away from them some amount of control over their lives and relationships. Even though being gay is not shameful, in some places it is still stigmatizing, and in these contexts a person might wish not to be a target of scorn, especially if avoiding that place is not an option.

Mohr assumes that if one is not out about being gay, then others will assume they are straight, and therefore they will be living a lie. This is true to some degree, but not in all contexts. In contexts in which not much is known about a person's "private" life, and in which a person is not "out" as straight or gay, then sometimes people will not make this assumption. Sometimes, it may not be appropriate to the relationship for others to have information about a person's sexual orientation, whether one is gay or straight, such as potential employers, teachers, or public officials. Perhaps straight people should be less out about their sexual orientation and less fearful that others might assume they're gay.

Let's assume that by respecting someone's wish not to have his or her sexual orientation known we are not participating in a lie, but instead we are simply respecting that person's wish to differentiate how socially intimate they are with us and others. On this view of privacy, we do have a right not to share information about our sexual orientation (*contra* Mohr), and thus outing another is *prima facie* wrong.[17] Is there anything that could change this general assessment

---

16 Richard Mohr, *Gay Ideas: Outing and Other Controversies* (Boston: Beacon Press, 1992).

17 At the end of this section, we will consider a sort of counterargument which maintains that celebrities who are gay or lesbian have an obligation to out themselves and that, if they don't, others are justified in outing them.

to morally justify particular instances of outing? In this regard, consider the following from Azariah Southworth in his own defense for outing Jonathan Merritt:

> Outing Jonathan was not an easy decision. I mulled it over
> for more than a year and discussed it with friends. Those
> conversations always ended in, "Yeah, it's probably not a good
> idea." So, what changed my mind?
> I was tired of the lies. I was tired of hearing Jonathan say
> that being gay is not "God's best." Meanwhile he enjoys the
> company of men. Jonathan's approach to LGBT people and
> issues may be less extreme than that of the late Jerry Falwell,
> but in the end the results and message are the same: Your
> sexual orientation is a sin and you need to change with God's
> help. It's all lies—and the conversation not only needs to
> change but the leaders as well. I'm tired of my humanity as a
> gay man being invalidated by hypocritical leaders like Jonathan,
> who then expect my support in return.[18]

There are two strands to Southworth's argument. In his last sentence, he makes a Kantian-type claim[19] that he was justified in outing Merritt because Merritt's disputable claims equating homosexuality with sin constitute attempts to strip Southworth and all gay men of their humanity. The second strand involves claims about lies and hypocrisy, which are related—but not equivalent—concepts. Lying is broader than hypocrisy, since all instances of hypocrisy involve some sort of lie, but not all lies are instances of hypocrisy. For example, if I claim that Canada has a larger population than the United States, I am lying—since the claim is false and I know that it is false—but I am not being hypocritical. Hypocrisy is a particular type of lie or deception that is particularly loathsome. As Judith Shklar writes, hypocrisy is "the only unforgivable sin, inexcusable even for those who can justify almost any other vice."[20]

Plato writes about the evil of hypocrisy when he tells the story of the Ring of Gyges, at the beginning of his most famous work, *The Republic*. According to the story, the ring allows the wearers to become invisible so they can do anything they want, without the risk of getting caught. Although Plato uses this myth to show, ultimately, that justice is not simply about power, it also serves as an indictment of hypocrisy: anyone who wears the ring can pretend in public to be a paragon of virtue, while secretly doing evil under the cloak of invisibility. People who attempt this, typically without a magical ring, are hypocrites, in that

---

18 Southworth, "Why I Outed a Christian Star."

19 This is not something Kant would agree with since he thought homosexuality was a sin. But there is at least some semblance of this line of thought in his general theory.

20 Judith Shklar, "Let Us Not Be Hypocritical," *Ordinary Vices* (Cambridge, MA: Belknap Press of Harvard University Press, 1984), 45.

they try to appear virtuous according to the values they profess, while furtively being vicious. They are also liars, because they wish to deceive others about their moral character and beliefs. Some hypocrites may not be fully aware of the disconnection between their words and actions, and in these cases we might say that they deceive themselves too.[21] For Plato, those who take advantage of the power of the ring to get away with being bad become victims of their own weaknesses, and are less happy than those who live by the standards to which they hold themselves and others.

The three outed ministers we discussed earlier are probably ordinary, and not self-deluded, hypocrites. They all publicly preached the immorality of homosexual acts—and indeed advanced their careers by condemning them—while secretly they pursued sex with men. In doing so, each minister deceived his followers by promoting the false belief that he lived by the values he preached. Outing each of them, then, denied them the ability to go on deceiving their followers, and it undermined their moral authority and, thereby, their ability to marginalize gay men and lesbians. Arguably, gay men and lesbians have a duty to prevent forms of hypocrisy so toxic to them, or, at least, they have no obligation to protect the privacy of such hypocrites.

In response to these charges, Haggard, Merritt, and Brock could claim that their actions show only that they are weak-willed and not hypocrites. Aristotle recognized this failing, which he called *akrasia*, and described it as the lack of control over oneself: you know what is best for you, but lack the will to do it. For example, a cigarette smoker typically knows that it is unhealthy for her to smoke, but can't stop herself. Haggard tried this defense by claiming that he was "addicted" to certain sexual activities (and hence unable to stop doing what he knew was wrong), and he compared himself to a dieter who can't maintain a restricted diet.

If these men were merely weak and tried, but failed, to live by the values they preached, then we might feel more sympathy for them. But did Haggard and the others simply do the equivalent of falling off their diets? A more accurate comparison would be, not with an ordinary weak-willed dieter, but with a professional diet therapist who secretly resorts to cosmetic surgery or stomach pumping in order to lose weight, rather than moderate eating, while condemning others for committing the sin of gluttony. This professional diet therapist is a hypocrite and deceiver who contributes to the marginalization of those who do not meet current (and possibly irrational) standards of thinness.

Having said this, there might be some reason to think that Brock's outing was morally different from the other two. Remember that Brock was outed after he attended a confidential therapy session for men who want to resist their sexual attraction to other men. The person who outed him was not a former lover, but

---

21 For a detailed description of various types of hypocrisy, along with lots of fabulous examples of it, see Bela Szabados and Eldon Soifer, *Hypocrisy: Ethical Investigations* (Peterborough, ON: Broadview Press, 2004).

a reporter, who entered a space in which people have a reasonable expectation of privacy with the express purpose of violating a participant's privacy in order to damage that person's reputation. Whatever one might think of the morality or effectiveness of therapeutic groups such as this, Brock's case is made substantially different by this feature. To defend the outing of Brock, then, we must provide a stronger justification. Our defense must identify and explain the circumstances in which breaking the confidentiality of a therapeutic setting is acceptable. Even Mohr might defend Brock's right to keep private what he shared in this session.

There are sometimes legitimate reasons for breaking confidentiality, even in therapeutic, medical situations. The legal precedent for this was set in the U.S. by a 1974 case, *Tarasoff v. Regents of California*. This ruling concluded that mental-health professionals have an obligation to break confidentiality in order to protect individuals from a threat to their life or health posed by one of their patients. In the case, a student, Prosenjit Poddar, had sought counseling by a psychologist employed by the University of California, Berkeley, and, in their sessions, Poddar confided that he planned to kill another student, Tatiana Tarasoff. Tarasoff was never informed of the threat to her, and Poddar did end up killing her. Tarasoff's mother successfully sued the University of California.

The circumstances in Brock's case are quite different from those in the Tarasoff one. Perhaps the most important of these differences is that, in the Tarasoff case, confidentiality needed to be broken in order to protect a particular person's life. Nothing similar was at stake in Brock's case, since he did not confess an intention to seriously harm another person. Yet, one might argue that Brock's public condemnations of homosexuality promote hostility and intolerance against gay men and lesbians, and that gay men and lesbians face an increased threat of violence and hate crimes when others incite hate. Rates of violence toward gay men and lesbians appear to spike during periods of heated public debate over their rights. For example, when Californians were debating Proposition 8, a ban on same-sex marriage, many evangelical ministers (among others) spoke out strongly in its favor, and some research shows that an increase in hate crimes occurred.[22] On the basis of such findings, one might argue that outing people who abet hate and intolerance is necessary in order to reduce hate crimes against the LGBT community, even when this requires violating patient/therapist confidentiality. In other words, protecting an implicit promise of confidentiality in Brock's case may be outweighed by the need to protect others from an increased risk of serious harm that he indirectly causes. The issue here is not whether speech that incites hate should be censored (when the threat of violence is not immediate), but whether public figures who regularly engage in such speech have the same rights to privacy as ordinary citizens.

One might go further and argue that outing any lesbian or gay man who is a celebrity or respected public figure is acceptable, even if this person is not

---

22   Dan Aeillo, "DA Blames Prop 8 for Anti-Gay Violence," *The Bay Area Reporter*, April 2, 2009, http://www.ebar.com/news/article.php?sec=news&article=3839.

a hypocritical liar or does nothing to incite homophobia. Two kinds of arguments are typically offered to defend this stance. One is a consequentialist argument: that the benefits of outing such persons, on balance, outweigh the harms. The other is a rights-based argument: that public figures don't have the same right to privacy as ordinary citizens, primarily because they can influence public opinion, and therefore the public has the right to know more about them. We'll examine these in reverse order.

Reporter Louis Peitzman rejects the "right to privacy" argument for reasons similar to Mohr's:

> It equates sexual identity with sexual behavior—and though the two do go hand in hand, they're not one in the same.... Sexual identity isn't private. It's a characteristic as intrinsic as race and should be treated accordingly.... Unfortunately, not publicly identifying as gay means society sees you as straight—you are essentially "passing."[23]

Like Mohr, Peitzman holds that one's sexual identity is a social status, similar to one's race, marital, or citizenship status, and while we might have a reasonable expectation of privacy with regard to our sexual behavior, we don't with regard to our social identities. Also like Mohr, Peitzman sees someone who is not out as "passing" as a heterosexual, and therefore living a lie in order to claim the privileges of straight people. Peitzman's (and Mohr's) points carry more weight when they pertain to public figures. As private citizens, we should be able to decide who has knowledge of both our sexual behaviors and identities, in part, so that we can control how we are identified. For example, someone may identify another as a lesbian who herself identifies as bisexual. Sexual and racial identities are not "intrinsic" or objective facts; rather, we construct our sexual identities in part by determining when and how we share that information with others. Moreover, as we mentioned earlier, the presumption of heterosexuality does not operate in all contexts. A straight person at a gay-pride parade may be presumed to be gay. Yet, with respect to public figures, who must function in a predominantly heterosexual cultural space, if they don't come out publicly as gay, then their constituents are likely to assume they are straight. Whether they are candidates for political office, or sports or entertainment celebrities, public figures can significantly influence public opinion and policies. While public figures have a right to privacy, when they choose to participate in public-policy discussions, the public may have a greater right to relevant information about that person than they would about a private citizen. For example, public figures who participate in public debates about immigration policies may be expected

---

23 Louis Peitzman, "Why the Right to Privacy Doesn't Apply to Coming Out," Louispeitzman.com, July 2, 2012, http://louispeitzman.com/2012/07/02/why-the-right-to-privacy-doesnt-apply-to-coming-out/.

to share information about their citizenship status or immigrant background, so the public can determine how much weight to give their public statements. Outing a public figure so that the public can decide how to measure their influential statements is therefore different from outing an ordinary private citizen. Similarly, outing a public figure who is benefiting from "passing" and then using those benefits to harm others is different from outing a private citizen who does no harm to others by remaining somewhat closeted.

The consequentialist argument for outing is reflected in the following comment by Anderson Cooper, the well-known CNN reporter: "I've begun to consider whether the unintended outcomes of maintaining my privacy outweigh personal and professional principle. It's become clear to me that by remaining silent on certain aspects of my personal life for so long, I have given some the mistaken impression that I am trying to hide something—something that makes me uncomfortable, ashamed or even afraid. This is distressing because it is simply not true."[24] Cooper here is not defending the right of someone else to out a person like him; rather, he is recognizing his own moral and social duty to come out, given the inadvertent harm that can result when a public figure like him is believed to be gay but is unwilling to publicly acknowledge it. But one might take Cooper's point further and argue that, when someone like Cooper is unwilling to do what's right and come out, and this has the unintended consequence that many people then infer that Cooper is ashamed about being gay, others are entitled to out such persons in order to block such inferences, as well as the possible further implication that being gay is shameful.

Another consequentialist argument for outing gay public figures is the need for high-profile gay role models. Kate Aurthur makes this point: "[H]aving been a teenager in the 1980s, I remember when there were no—as in zero—out role models for gay, lesbian, bisexual and transgender kids to emulate. Instead, we survived on rumors of Sapphic superstar love triangles and A-list leading men who joined cults that helped keep their gay secrets. Gossip has its own power, not to mention pleasure, but let's face it: The world is a better place when people aren't lying."[25] This role-model argument points to the positive consequences especially on gay teens, who have high suicide rates and who are often subject to bullying from their peers. Protecting isolated gay teenagers from suicide and bullying may be of sufficient benefit to outweigh any harm done to a celebrity who is outed.

Moral philosophers draw a distinction between "erogatory" actions, which are morally required, and "supererogatory" ones, which involve good deeds that go above and beyond our obligations. For example, donating a sizable portion of my income to charitable organizations that help relieve suffering is probably

---

24 Quoted in ibid.

25 Kate Aurthur, "Be a Hero, Not Part of the Problem," *New York Times*, July 2, 2012, http://www.nytimes.com/roomfordebate/2012/07/02/do-gay-celebrities-have-an-obligation-to-come-out/be-a-hero-not-part-of-the-problem.

supererogatory, although some utilitarian philosophers argue that such acts are erogatory if, on balance, they reduce others' misery while causing little hardship to myself. For gay celebrities, is the duty to come out erogatory or supererogatory, and similarly, if others have a duty to out them, is this erogatory or supererogatory? If the duty of any celebrity to come out is only supererogatory, then when others force that person to do what is admittedly good, but not morally obligatory, they are violating that person's autonomy (even if we agree that there is no right to privacy in regard to our social identities). So to justify outing public figures, we need to show that they have failed to do what was morally required of them, and here a consequentialist or utilitarian approach will probably be the most useful in supporting the erogatory nature, in some circumstances, of coming out and outing others.

When Does "Sexting" Violate a Person's Privacy?

"Sexting" involves using electronic messaging to send text, photos, or video that contain sexual content.[26] Most of the uproar over sexting is over the sharing of nude or sexually explicit images.[27] Although adults can engage in sexting—for example, former U.S. congressman Anthony Weiner was caught sexting in 2011—sexting creates more concern when it occurs among minors.[28] Sexting surveys offer us some idea of the prevalence of sexting, though their figures vary. Some report that only 4 per cent of cell-owning teens (12–17) have sexted, while others maintain that as many as 20 per cent of teens (13–19) and 33 per cent of young adults (20–26) have done so. The surveys also suggest that more teens and young adults have received a sext message than have sent one, with the numbers ranging from 15 to 31 per cent.[29] Teens most frequently sext with a current boyfriend or girlfriend, but they sometimes sext with someone they are romantically pursuing, a close friend, or someone they barely know or only know online.[30]

---

26 See, e.g., Elizabeth Eraker, "Stemming Sexting: Sensible Legal Approaches to Teenager Exchange of Self-Produced Pornography," *Berkeley Technology Law Journal* 25 (2010): 555–671, http://www.btlj.org/data/articles/25_1/0555-0596%20Eraker_Web.pdf.

27 Richard Chalfen, "'It's Only a Picture': Sexting, 'Smutty' Snapshots and Felony Charges," *Visual Studies* 24, no. 3 (2009): 258–68.

28 K. Albury, K. Crawford, and P. Byron, *Young People and Sexting in Australia: Ethics, Representation and the Law*, ARTC Centre for Creative Industries and Innovation/Journalism and Media Research Centre, The University of New South Wales, Australia, 2013, http://www.cci.edu.au/node/1522.

29 See Amanda Lenhart, "Teens and Sexting: Pew Internet Survey," 2009, http://www.pewinternet.org/Reports/2009/Teens-and-Sexting/Main-Report/1-The-PIP-Study.aspx; and National Campaign to Prevent Teen and Unplanned Pregnancy, *Sex and Tech: Results from a Survey of Teens and Young Adults*, 2008, http://www.thenationalcampaign.org/sextech/PDF/SexTech_Summary.pdf.

30 Luke Gilkerson, "Sexting Statistics: What Do the Surveys Say?" Covenanteyes.com, January 10, 2012, http://www.covenanteyes.com/2012/01/10/sexting-statistics-what-do-the-surveys-say/.

Sexting among teenagers raises a whole host of issues. We will focus on concerns about the sexualization of teens, lack of consent, and whether sexting among teens amounts to producing, distributing, and viewing child pornography. The recent case of Rehtaeh Parsons is becoming too common. Rehtaeh was a teenager from Dartmouth, Nova Scotia, who committed suicide when she was 17 years old. In November 2011, when she was 15, she attended a party with a friend where she was allegedly raped by four young men. According to many reports, she was so intoxicated that she had trouble standing and walking, when one man allegedly sexually assaulted her. It was during that assault that a photo was taken, which then circulated widely within three days of the event. As a result of the electronic messaging showing her assault, Rehtaeh became, bizarrely, the victim of "cyberbullying" by other teenagers in her school, who called her a "slut." A year after the incident, the Royal Canadian Mounted Police (RCMP) stated that there was "insufficient evidence to lay charges."[31] The distribution of photos of her rape is believed to have led to Rehtaeh Parsons's suicide.

One issue is whether the police mishandled the investigation of the rape, which is controversial. What is uncontroversial, however, is that those who took photos of the rape and then distributed them widely by electronic means, without Rehtaeh's consent, acted unethically and with appalling meanness and callousness. Moreover, many recipients of the images compounded her assault by publicly attacking her, thereby escalating her humiliation and the psychological damage it caused. Fortunately, most cases of sexting do not involve rape and, generally, they do not trigger the kind of cyberbullying to which Rehtaeh was subjected. Yet sexts exchanged among teenagers frequently involve violations of privacy. Given the nature of the technology, it is exceedingly easy for a "private" interchange between two people to get communicated publicly to a great number of people at an incredibly fast rate.[32] According to some recent surveys, 14 per cent of teens (13–19) said they have shared a sext message with someone other than the person it was originally meant for, and 29 per cent of teens said they have had sext messages shared with them that were not meant for them to see.[33]

These revelations are disturbing, and they show that communication technologies have advanced much faster than the ability of people to think through the ethical issues and establish appropriate rules and policies. In addition to multiplying possibilities for privacy violations, sexting by teens contributes to the sexualization of children. This can have a number of negative effects on children, such as feelings of shame or guilt or reduced self-confidence, according

---

31 Selena Ross, "Who Failed Rehtaeh Parsons?" *The Chronicle Herald*, April 9, 2013, http://thechronicleherald.ca/metro/1122345-who-failed-rehtaeh-parsons.

32 Chalfen, "'It's Only a Picture,'" 261.

33 See, e.g., National Campaign to Prevent Teen and Unplanned Pregnancy, *Sex and Tech*.

to the American Psychological Association.[34] The sexualization of children raises other worries, especially that it sends the message that sexual contact with them is acceptable, much like child pornography. The following warning, which is taken from a brochure constructed and distributed by a law-enforcement agency, explains that minors can indeed be prosecuted under child pornography statutes when they sext:

> In addition to damaging your reputation, you could be charged with a crime for making such a photograph. If you are under 18, any photograph you take of yourself in a nude or provocative pose is technically considered child pornography. And if you send that photo to someone, you are disseminating child pornography. Teens in some states have been charged with felony crimes! If you are found guilty, a felony record could follow you for life and you may have to register as a sex offender. This registration requirement will follow you to college or university campus and your future places of employment.[35]

Oddly, in some cases, the perpetrator and victim of child pornography can be the same person: the child herself. One such case involved a 17-year-old Pennsylvania girl who had semi-nude photos of herself on her phone, which were discovered by the school principal after her teacher confiscated her phone.[36] In other cases, the victim and perpetrator are different: a 16-year-old girl in British Columbia who sent a nude photo of her boyfriend's ex-girlfriend to another girl;[37] a 17-year-old boy from Wisconsin who was charged with child pornography after posting naked pictures of his girlfriend, who is a year younger, on the Internet; and a 16-year-old boy from Rochester, New York, who faces seven years in jail for circulating an image of a girlfriend to friends.[38]

While prosecuting under child-pornography statutes teens who sext may be overly harsh and punitive, charging them under existing privacy laws may not be sufficient to address the harm that they can cause to another minor. But do we really want teens who sext to be treated as sex offenders? Perhaps privacy laws could be strengthened, with stiffer penalties for infringing a minor's right to privacy by making, circulating, or viewing nude or sexual images of them.

34 American Psychological Association, "Report of the Task Force on the Sexualization of Girls," 2007, http://www.apa.org/pi/women/programs/girls/report.aspx.

35 Quoted in Chalfen, "It's Only a Picture,'" 546.

36 CBS News, "'Sexting' Leads to Child Porn Charges for Teen," June 5, 2010, http://www.cbsnews.com/8301-18563_162-6552438.html.

37 CBC News, "Sexting Victoria Teen Girl to Be Tried on Child Porn Charge," September 19, 2013, http://www.cbc.ca/m/touch/canada/british-columbia/story/1.1861288.

38 Ed Pilkington, "Sexting Craze Leads to Child Pornography Charges," Guardian, January 14, 2009, http://www.theguardian.com/world/2009/jan/14/child-pornography-sexting.

Some recent studies suggest that teens sext for a wide variety of reasons, including peer pressure and to engage in a form of "safe sex."[39] Some teen sexters, like many teens before them, wonder why adults are making such a fuss. In a recent Australian study, a number of teenagers interviewed thought that the word itself, 'sexting,' was nothing but a media label deployed to raise unnecessary alarm about teen behavior. Some of these teenagers indicated that they never use the term because it now has the connotation of something sinister or offensive, and so they opt instead for the more neutral term 'pictures.'[40] These Australian teens have a point: most media commentary about teen sexting includes a lot of hyperbole and, at times, reflects or promotes mass hysteria.[41] Yet can teens exchange sexy "pictures" in responsible ways that avoid violating another's privacy and that avoid damaging their own or another minor's mental health and reputation?

Teenagers in the Australian study recognized that sext messages often get shared, and that this could cause problems for the person who originally sent the message, and especially for any females whose bodies and sexual behavior are exposed.[42] These teenagers were also adamant that charging them with child pornography was completely unwarranted, at least in most cases. Child pornography charges were only appropriate, they thought, when there was a significant age difference between the people exchanging sexts and when one of them was well beyond his (or sometimes her) adolescence. There was some ambivalence regarding how educators should deal with sexting, though they noted that simply telling teenagers not to sext was both ineffective and inappropriate.

Many within the legal profession recognize the need to find ways to address sexting among teenagers who are close in age, without resorting to the criminal justice system. The lawyer for the 16-year-old girl in British Columbia, mentioned in an earlier paragraph, points out that sexting is lawful for adults, and then raises the following question about using criminal statutes against child pornography: "The provisions were created to protect children. So is it now appropriate to use those provisions to prosecute children? ... On a common sense level, does it make sense to charge youth with child pornography if they are not engaged in pedophiliac behaviour?"[43] It does not seem to make sense when the sexting is consensual and the acts recorded are not themselves criminal acts, unlike in the Rehtaeh Parsons case. Marsha Levick, legal director of the nonprofit Juvenile Law Centre, makes a similar point when she asks, "Why should we criminalize a kid for taking and possessing a photo of herself.... There is no

---

39 Albury, Crawford, and Byron, *Young People and Sexting in Australia*; Chalfen, "'It's Only a Picture.'"

40 Albury, Crawford, and Byron, *Young People and Sexting in Australia*.

41 Chalfen, "'It's Only a Picture.'"

42 Albury, Crawford, and Byron, *Young People and Sexting in Australia*.

43 CBC News, "Sexting Victoria Teen Girl."

problem that needs to be solved."[44] Shaheen Shariff, from McGill University's education faculty, agrees: "I don't think putting kids through the criminal justice system is the answer, especially under child pornography laws." Shariff continues, "Schools have always been reactive to bullying and cyberbullying, and occasional anti-bullying programs haven't worked. We need to address the root societal issues of rape culture, misogyny, homophobia and objectification of women—and get kids to realize the long-term impact of their postings."[45] One issue is why sexting is so much more damaging to girls or women than to boys or men? How does sexting get used to stigmatize women for their sexual behavior ("slut" labeling), and also gay men and lesbians?

As a form of speech between adults, most sexting is protected by free-speech guarantees. So when adults consensually exchange sext messages, even misogynist or homophobic ones, or ones that trivialize rape, this is mostly legal. But when the sexting involves sexual images of children, it is no longer protected speech, even when children are producing and disseminating images of themselves. We need to find ways to limit the speech of minors without criminalizing their sexually explicit messages about themselves, especially when they share these consensually with others of similar age. In her recent article "Why Kids Sext," Hanna Rosin mentions that approximately 20 states in the U.S. have approved "sexting" laws that treat initial offenses as misdemeanors and repeat violations as felonies, with lighter penalties for the former. She writes,

> Where they've been passed, the new laws have helpfully taken ordinary teen sexting out of the realm of child pornography and provided prosecutors with a gentler alternative. But they have also created deeper cultural confusion, by codifying into law the idea that *any* kind of sexting between minors is a crime. For the most part, the laws do not concern themselves with whether a sext was voluntarily shared between two people who had been dating for a year or was sent under pressure: a sext is a sext. So as it stands now, in most states it is perfectly legal for two 16-year-olds to have sex. But if they take pictures, it's a matter for the police.[46]

Rosin proposes that laws regulating sexting should target those who forward a sext to a third party without the consent of its author, and also anyone who gains access to nude "selfies" and circulates or publishes them without the permission

44 CBS News, "'Sexting' Leads to Child Porn Charges for Teen."

45 Quoted in Karen Seidman, "Child Pornography Laws 'Too Harsh' to Deal with Minors Sexting Photos without Consent, Experts Say," *National Post*, Nov. 16, 2013, http://news.nationalpost.com/2013/11/16/child-pornography-laws-too-harsh-to-deal-with-minors-sexting-photos-without-consent-experts-say/.

46 Hanna Rosin, "Why Kids Sext," *The Atlantic*, October 14, 2014: http://www.theatlantic.com/magazine/archive/2014/11/why-kids-sext/380798/?single_page=true

of the author and those depicted in the photograph.[47] Rosin's research shows that approximately 1/3 of teens in the U.S. sext, and thus laws that criminalize an increasingly common behavior among teenagers represents an overreaction to the harm typically done, and compounds the damage to the minors whom the laws are meant to protect. Parents and law enforcers have other ways to minimize the harms of sexting, such as by making teens more aware of the rights and wrongs, and benefits and costs of sexting, and how to protect themselves and others against such violations of their privacy.

How Should Violations of Sexual Privacy Be Treated and Punished?

As we noted in the introduction to this chapter, there are different kinds of privacy that we value and want protected. One form involves controlling who has access to sensitive information about ourselves, such as our medical or school records, our sexual tastes and history, or any history of criminal charges or convictions. Another form of privacy involves the ability to make decisions about one's personal life without undue interference from others. A third form of privacy involves being able to control who can see or hear, or otherwise monitor, our ordinary, daily physical acts.[48] In many countries there are laws or constitutional provisions that aim to protect informational, decisional, and physical privacy. For example, many countries restrict access to a person's medical or school records, limit the government's authority to search our homes or our cell phones, limit the government's power to spy on its citizens, and limit the government's power to interfere with the decisions people make about their non-public sexual activities or their reproductive options.

In 2012, a Rutgers University student was convicted of invading the privacy of his roommate when he used a webcam to spy on his roommate's intimate activities with another man.[49] Tragically, the victim committed suicide several days after the incident. In this case, the victim's informational and physical privacy were violated. The perpetrator disclosed, without consent, his roommate's sexual orientation and dorm-room activities to others, by sharing a webcam video stream from his computer with friends over the Internet. This case was probably more vigorously prosecuted than others because the violations of privacy contributed to a suicide, although the link to the suicide was difficult to prove. However, had the victim not committed suicide, the accused's actions still involved a criminal invasion of privacy, as the victim had the "reasonable

---

47 "'Why Kids Sext' Describes Nude Photos as 'Social Currency' Among Teens," *NPR*, October 15, 2014: http://www.npr.org/blogs/alltechconsidered/2014/10/15/356393531/why-kids-sext-describes-nude-photos-as-social-currency-among-teens.

48 Judith De Cew, "Privacy," *The Stanford Encyclopedia of Philosophy* (2013), http://plato.stanford.edu/entries/privacy/.

49 Emily Bazelon, "Dharun Ravi Found Guilty," *Slate*, March 16, 2012, http://www.slate.com/articles/news_and_politics/crime/2012/03/rutgers_spying_verdict_dharun_ravi_found_guilty_of_invading_the_privacy_of_tyler_clementi.html.

expectation of privacy" (under U.S. law) regarding his actions or property in his dorm room.

Determining when and where a person should have a reasonable expectation of privacy is somewhat complicated.[50] Should we have it in a store dressing room, a public restroom, a hospital waiting room, or the office space our employer provides? Do we have a reasonable expectation of privacy with regard to our phone-call records, our library borrowing records, or our bank-account records? And when can this expectation or right be denied: when someone is on parole, when there are signs posted that security cameras are operating, or when we've discarded our personal materials in a public wastebin? The Rutgers case was not a difficult one in terms of privacy: we generally have a reasonable expectation of privacy in our own homes, even when our curtains are not drawn or someone is using a camera, and a dorm room is analogous to a home.

Sexual privacy involves all three forms of privacy mentioned above. We should be able to restrict access to information about our non-public sexual activities and thoughts—information that could be gleaned from medical or other institutional records, or from documents in our homes, such as photos, personal letters, or books. We should also be free from coercion or interference by others when we make decisions about our non-public sexual activities. Furthermore, we should have a high degree of control over who can view our non-public sexual acts. When these forms of privacy are violated by governmental or non-governmental agents, we should be able to seek remedies under our criminal or civil law.

But there are many borderline cases. Consider, for example, whether people should have a legally protected expectation of privacy in the following situations. Suppose someone shares personal information on Facebook, and restricts access using various privacy settings, but the information leaks to those who were not given permission to view it. Or suppose someone takes a picture of two people kissing in a car, but viewable from a public street, and then makes the picture public. Suppose someone sees you buy gay porn in a public venue, and then casually mentions this in front of your friends. Suppose a former lover tells stories about what you were like in bed in his next novel, but does not use your name? Suppose he posts nude photos of you that you once gave him?[51] Suppose your employer announces that he disapproves of premarital sex and adultery, and will fire any employee who is found to engage in such practices. Suppose your employer disapproves of non-procreational sex and will not offer health insurance that covers contraception. Suppose you inadvertently discover that a friend of yours is transgender and you disclose this to another person, who later physically assaults your friend. Suppose your roommate thinks you're asleep

---

50 See Electronic Frontier Foundation, "Surveillance Self-Defense," https://ssd.eff.org/your-computer/govt/privacy.

51 See http://www.huffingtonpost.com/2013/10/02/jerry-brown-revenge-porn_n_4030175.html.

and begins to have sex with her partner, but you're only pretending to be asleep so you can watch?

All of the cases above involve invasions of privacy, but the difficult issue is whether these invasions are serious enough to warrant criminal or civil action. How serious we take them to be will probably depend on how damaging they are to the victims and how reasonable we find a person's expectation of privacy in such circumstances. Another issue concerns who should be charged in any given privacy violation: a commercial website that publishes an image and that may stand to profit from it, or an individual who shares information or material received legally and who does not benefit financially from sharing it? The constant introduction of new technologies will make it increasingly difficult to protect the forms of privacy we value. Nevertheless, ethicists, legislators, legal scholars, and concerned citizens will need to devise new rules and procedures for protecting our privacy, including our sexual privacy.

Discussion Questions

1. What kinds of information about our sexual lives do we typically want to keep private, and why might this be important to us?
2. Was outing Tom Brock morally justified? Why or why not?
3. How is outing a person who is trangender similar to or different from outing a person who is gay?
4. What restrictions should parents place on teenagers' sexting habits?
5. Should sexting ever be a criminal offence for an adult, and for a minor? If so, when?
6. What makes an expectation of privacy reasonable?
7. In most cases, is it morally erogatory or supererogatory for a celebrity to come out?

Further Reading

Halwani, Raja. "Outing and Virtue Ethics." *Journal of Applied Philosophy* 19, no. 2 (2002): 141–54.

MacLachlan, Alice. "Closet Doors and Stage Lights: On the Goods of Out." *Social Theory and Practice: An International and Interdisciplinary Journal of Social Philosophy* 38, no. 2 (2012): 302–32.

Mill, John Stuart. *On Liberty*. Edited and introduced by Gertrude Himmelfarb. Harmondsworth, UK: Penguin Classics, 1859/1982.

Mohr, Richard. *Gay Ideas: Outing and Other Controversies*. Boston: Beacon Press, 1994.

Mohr, Richard. "Why Sex Is Private: Gays and the Police." *Public Affairs Quarterly* 1 (1987): 57–81.

Murphy, Timothy. *Gay Ethics: Controversies in Outing, Civil Rights, and Sexual Science,* New York: Routledge, 1994.

Chapter 10

Sex and Responsibility

Our moral responsibilities as sexual actors are sometimes unclear, even though sexual acts expose people to significant physical, emotional, and social risks. In this chapter, we will explore the contours of our moral and legal responsibility for sharing various kinds of information with sexual partners, as well as our responsibility for managing a common consequence of sex: pregnancy. We will also investigate whether our sexual obsessions can diminish both our capacity to make free choices and, consequently, our moral responsibility for our sexual behaviors. Lastly, we'll consider what our basic sexual duties are to our long-term or marital partners. While the answers to the moral questions debated in this chapter may, at times, seem elusive, we need to find a rational basis and enough common ground for approving social policies that can maintain civil peace.

What Should We Be Required to Disclose about Ourselves to Our Sexual Partners before Engaging in Sex?

In many domains of life, we find ourselves weighing the benefits of transparency against the value of privacy. For example, voters probably should know who is funding particular political campaigns, but some donors believe they have the right to make contributions anonymously. Governments want to monitor bitcoin transactions in order to block illegal trades in drugs or weapons, but some entrepreneurs want to be able to spend money without any government oversight. Employers and landlords often request information about an applicant's background that the applicant may have an interest in shielding. It's not always clear when one person's right to privacy outweighs the needs of others to know things about us, and when protecting public safety and assigning individual responsibility require greater transparency.

There are few legally enforceable transparency requirements with respect to sexual transactions, though there are many types of information that we are often expected to divulge to partners, such as our marital status, fertility status, sexual orientation, the depth of our affection, and so on. However, in a majority of states in the U.S. and in several other countries, people who are HIV-positive can be criminally prosecuted if they fail to be transparent about their status with their sex partners.[1] In many jurisdictions, the failure to disclose that one is HIV-positive to a sex partner is punishable even when there has been no transmission of an HIV infection, and when the violator has acted without the intent to harm. Some HIV exposure and disclosure laws include other STDs, but typically only HIV-positive persons, and generally only those who know that they are HIV-positive, can be charged with a felony.

HIV-specific criminal statutes are controversial for a number of reasons. Medical experts point out that HIV-exposure laws are outdated because there are now drug therapies that lower a person's viral load to a level where the risk of transmitting the virus to another person is negligible. Moreover, we now know that many intimate acts do not involve a substantial risk of transmission (e.g., kissing, penetrative sex with a condom, etc.). Patient advocates argue that HIV laws stigmatize and promote discrimination against people who are HIV-positive, which imposes unnecessary social burdens on individuals who have a serious but manageable health condition. Public health officials argue that HIV laws discourage people from getting tested and treated for HIV, because criminalization creates a culture of blame and fear. Criminalization does little to prevent the transmission of HIV, while testing and treatment do.[2]

Legal scholars in the U.S. and elsewhere argue that most HIV statutes are overly broad and can lead to punishing acts that pose no substantial risk of harm, or where there is no criminal intent. Most cases of transmission occur when the parties involved underestimate the risks of their activities. Underestimating the risks of transmission is not good, but it's not criminal. Cases in which people know they are HIV-positive and are not in treatment, and engage in risky sex with a partner with the intent to harm or with criminal negligence are rare. Laws that punish people for reckless endangerment or assault are sufficient to deal with

---

1   "State HIV Laws," *The Center for HIV Law and Policy,* http://www.hivlawandpolicy.org/state-hiv-laws; "Criminalization of HIV Transmission," *AIDS-Free World,* April 2012, http://www.aidsfreeworld.org/PlanetAIDS/Transmission.aspx.

2   "HIVMA Urges Repeal of HIV-Specific Criminal Statutes," *HIV Medicine Association,* October 16, 2012, http://www.hivma.org/uploadedFiles/HIVMA/FINAL%20HIVMA%20Policy%20Statement%20on%20HIV%20Criminalization.pdf; Michael Hobbes, "Why Did AIDS Ravage the U.S. More Than Any Other Developed Country?" *New Republic,* May 12, 2014, http://www.newrepublic.com/article/117691/aids-hit-united-states-harder-other-developed-countries-why.

such cases, and we do not need special laws to deal with the specific threat of HIV transmission. Many researchers estimate that half of all new HIV infections are transmitted by people who do not know their status, and HIV disclosure laws do not apply in such cases. Of course, we could modify existing HIV laws so that they applied to people who know they have engaged in behaviors that put them at significant risk for HIV, and not only to those who have (responsibly) been tested and know their status. We might also exclude from prosecution those who are receiving treatment and have a low viral load. Some state laws exempt those who use condoms, and perhaps they also should include exceptions for other relatively safe sex acts (generally most non-penetrative sex acts, or acts in which there is little contact with another's semen, vaginal secretions, or blood). Furthermore, laws could be modified so that charges could only be brought in cases of actual transmission and not for alleged exposure to HIV. Finally, there seems to be no good reason for criminalizing HIV transmission and not the malicious transmission of other incurable diseases (when there is criminal intent or negligence), even ones that are not sexually transmitted. In other words, there is no reason our laws should single out people who are HIV-positive, rather than treat all people with serious and incurable infectious diseases alike.

In a 2010 report, the Obama administration recommended that "State legislatures … consider reviewing HIV-specific criminal statutes to ensure that they are consistent with current knowledge of HIV transmission and support public health approaches to preventing and treating HIV."[3] The report notes that mandatory-disclosure laws may make people less willing to disclose their HIV status when it might be needed, because of the intolerant and punitive environment such laws help to maintain. Moreover, the report emphasizes the need to protect the civil rights of people living with HIV and to increase prevention efforts in communities where transmission rates are the highest. While the report underestimates the risk of HIV transmission in prison settings, it notes some of the ways in which incarceration can impede access to adequate health care.[4]

There is a growing debate among scholars, policy analysts, and activists over whether HIV laws should be reformed or repealed. Reformers recommend that laws criminalizing HIV transmission should no longer focus on a person's HIV status. This is because the risk of HIV transmission depends on a person's overall viral load, the different viral loads of the bodily fluids exchanged, and the particular body parts exposed. Margo Kaplan argues that prosecutors need to investigate these facts in order to gather "evidence

3   "National HIV/AIDS Strategy for the United States," Whitehouse.gov, July 2010, http://www. whitehouse.gov/sites/default/files/uploads/NHAS.pdf.

4   Centers for Disease Control and Prevention, "HIV in Correctional Settings," http://www. cdc.gov/hiv/risk/other/correctional.html; "Sexual Violence in Detention Spreads Infectious Diseases," Just Detention, October 2007, http://www.justdetention.org/en/factsheets/ Disease.pdf.

of substantial and unjustifiable risk of transmission."[5] Advocates for repeal generally argue that we should use public-health measures to deal with public-health threats, and that existing laws are adequate for dealing with the rare cases that involve the malicious transmission of a potentially lethal and incurable virus.[6] In 2013, Senator Chris Coons of Delaware introduced the *Repeal Existing Policies that Encourage and Allow Legal ("REPEAL") HIV Discrimination Act*, "a bill to require an interagency review of federal and state laws that criminalize certain actions by people living with HIV."[7]

Policy reformers may be getting ahead of public opinion in the U.S. on the issue of HIV laws. Many people appear to believe that HIV laws are necessary to protect the health of HIV-negative persons, and to protect the latter's right to make informed and free choices about their sexual partners. Those who are not infected with HIV may feel that they need to know the HIV status of potential sex partners, and they may be glad that the threat of criminal prosecution exists so they can demand transparency on these matters. People who are HIV-positive may be reluctant to disclose their status due to the legitimate fear of being persecuted for relatively harmless acts. So how do we balance the rights of each group? Do we want to live in a world where people can bring criminal charges against former lovers when they acquire an HIV infection? While the newly infected may understandably want to blame their former partners, they too will face the possibility of criminal prosecution with future lovers.

Canada has recently taken a different path than the U.S. with respect to the sexual activity of HIV-positive persons who have not disclosed. In fact, Canadian courts have recently taken a position quite similar to the one endorsed by Kaplan above. In Canada, people living with HIV commit a criminal offence only if they engage in sexual activity without disclosing their HIV status when that status poses a "significant risk" to their sexual partner. While "significant risk" has not yet been defined completely, there have been some interesting recent cases that have helped achieve some clarity. For example, it is considered a "substantial risk" for a person with HIV to have *unprotected* vaginal or anal sex. But it has also been made clear that "no risk" activities, such as kissing and mutual masturbation, are not subject to criminal prosecution. Oral sex when a condom or other latex barrier is used is considered a "negligible risk," and hence such sexual activities are unlikely to be prosecuted. But this leaves a wide variety of sexual activities poorly categorized and in need of being decided on a

---

5   Margo Kaplan, "Rethinking HIV-Exposure Crimes," *Indiana Law Journal* 87 (2012): 1517–70, http://ilj.law.indiana.edu/articles/87/87_4_Kaplan.pdf.

6   "Criminalization of HIV Transmission and Exposure," The Center for HIV Law and Policy, 2013, http://www.hivlawandpolicy.org/resources/criminalization-hiv-transmission-and-exposure-research-and-policy-agenda-american-journal.

7   Chris Coons, "Outdated Laws Preserve HIV Stigma," *Huffington Post*, December 10, 2013, http://www.huffingtonpost.com/chris-coons/outdated-laws-preserve-hi_b_4419360.html; Scott Simon, "HIV Disclosure Requirement Called Discriminatory," NPR, December 14, 2013, http://www.npr.org/templates/story/story.php?storyId=250990132.

case-by-case basis at the provincial level. For example, in 2010 a trial court in British Columbia acquitted an HIV-positive man who had unprotected anal sex, because he was the receptive partner. Another case in 2010, this time in Manitoba, acquitted an HIV-positive man for engaging in vaginal intercourse while using a condom. And, finally, cases in both Manitoba and Quebec have acquitted persons with HIV who engaged in unprotected vaginal sex without prior disclosure because they had undetectable viral loads.[8]

There is a concept in the law of 'rape by deception,' and several years ago there was a controversial case in Israel in which a woman brought charges against a man for failing to disclose his true ethnic status.[9] Such charges depend on treating sex as nonconsensual when consent is given under false pretenses. But is sex without transparency, or *informed* consent, the same as sex without any form of consent? For example, has someone who has had sex with a person who is HIV-positive, and without knowing that person's status, been raped? Should people be able to charge a former lover with rape when they find out that the person withheld their true sexual orientation or transgender status? What about failures to disclose one's true fertility status or use of birth control, one's marital status, or the number of one's current sexual partners? Should a person be required to disclose one's current or past sexual offender status? These failures of disclosure potentially violate a person's right to make a free and informed choice when choosing to participate in a sexual transaction. Moreover, such failures of disclosure can result in an unwanted pregnancy, serious emotional trauma, as well as the transmission of a serious illness. While discussions about transparency in sexual interactions should not be limited to HIV exposure, we should probably be careful about equating failures of disclosure with rape, or sex without consent. Treating such cases as equivalent to rape fails to appreciate the difference between cases in which no form of consent was given and those in which consent was given but with incomplete information.

Laws that treat all HIV-positive persons as felons when they fail to disclose their status to their sex partners are tantamount to treating such acts as a type of sexual assault. Perhaps we need to treat failures of HIV disclosure in the same way we treat other failures of disclosure. In most cases we take a "buyer beware" attitude and expect sexually active adults to take steps to protect themselves from the potential risks of sex, or to choose to avoid sex in situations where there is a lack of transparency. In other words, we distribute responsibility between the parties for making sex safe, and we do not place all the responsibility on one partner. People who are HIV-negative, or want to avoid emotionally traumatic sex, or creating a pregnancy, and so on, can avoid sex that they know to be risky or take steps to make it less risky, such as by using condoms or avoiding casual sex.

8   Canadian HIV/AIDS Legal Network, "Criminalization of HIV Non-Disclosure: Current Canadian Law," http://www.aidslaw.ca/publications/publicationsdocEN.php?ref=847; see also http://www.aidslaw.ca/publications/interfaces/downloadFile.php?ref=2291.

9   Newman, "Unraveling the Israeli Arab 'Rape by Deception' Case."

In short, policies that ignore and infringe the privacy rights of HIV-positive people in order to protect the health of others need to be re-evaluated.[10]

Can Sex or Porn Be Addictive?

When we think about addictions, what generally comes to mind is someone becoming psychologically or physically dependent on a substance such as heroin, nicotine, or alcohol. When people become addicted to a substance, they become unable to stop using it, even when its use may be causing harm to their health, work, or relationships with others. Addictive substances have a sufficiently powerful effect on us that those who become addicted often seek help from therapists and support groups in order to control or be cured of their addictions. When people are unable to overcome an addiction that is contributing to self-destructive behavior, they often appear to be not fully in control of their behavior. That is, addicts may lack free will or the ability to choose among different options, and therefore lack the capacity to exercise moral restraint. Can sex or porn be addictive in this way? And if so, should the possibility of a sex addiction be taken seriously when someone commits adultery or a violent sexual offense?

Some scientists and researchers believe that people can lose their ability to control their urges for sex or porn. In the deliberations leading up to the revised *Diagnostic and Statistical Manual of Mental Disorders* (DSM-5), some mental health professionals proposed adding "Hypersexual Disorder" (HD). Two of the multiple criteria that some therapists use to diagnose HD are "A lack of ability to reduce or stop sexual activities the patient believes are problematic; and evidence of 'personal distress' caused by the behavior, like interference with work or relationships."[11] While there are some self-identified sex addicts who have sought treatment for their condition, and some therapists and self-help groups who offer treatment, there has not been enough scientific research about HD to find out how many people suffer from it and what factors might put one at risk. Because of the lack of research, HD was ultimately not included in the DSM-5.[12]

Some medical researchers claim that there is a neurological basis for HD in that both sex and porn can cause the release of pleasure-inducing brain chemicals. These chemicals can rewire neural pathways or circuits in ways that shape

---

10 Some of the ideas and arguments in this section were previously published in L. Shrage, "Sex Crimes that Shouldn't Be," *New York Times*, June 1, 2014, http://nyti.ms/1tA5bCP.

11 Rebecca Boyle, "Science Says Sex Addiction Is For Real. Here's How to Diagnose It," *Popular Science*, October 22, 2012, http://www.popsci.com/science/article/2012-10/science-says-sex-addiction-real-disorder-and-here%E2%80%99s-how-diagnose-it; "Hypersexual Disorder: Diagnostic Criteria for *DSM-5* Tested in New Study," *Huffington Post*, October 23, 2012, http://www.huffingtonpost.com/2012/10/23/hypersexual-disorder-dsm-5-diagnostic-criteria_n_2005933.html.

12 John M. Grohol, "Final *DSM 5* Approved by the American Psychiatric Association," *PsychCentral*, http://psychcentral.com/blog/archives/2012/12/02/final-dsm-5-approved-by-american-psychiatric-association/.

a person's future behavior.[13] According to Cristian Bodo, with the emergence of modern neuroscience,

> scientists started investigating the changes that substances of abuse provoked in patterns of neuronal firing and neurotransmitter release. This led to the description of the mesolimbic reward system: essentially a group of neurons that release dopamine into a specific brain area (the nucleus accumbens) in response to pleasurable stimuli. In fact, it was discovered that what made these stimuli pleasurable was precisely this focalized release of dopamine, and that certain drugs had the ability to stimulate this system even in their absence. Addiction was thus redefined in terms of the neurochemistry of the brain. Any substance and/or stimulus that was capable of over-stimulating the system normally responsible for our experience of pleasure was in principle potentially addictive. Notice, however ... the difference between a normal, well-adjusted individual and an addict becomes, under this new definition, only a matter of degree. We all experience dopamine highs routinely, but the addict lives for them.[14]

Bodo points out that this new definition has led to a proliferation of addictions, which encompass the "usual suspect" substances, such as alcohol and cocaine, as well as behaviors that over-stimulate the brain's pleasure system, such as shopping, gambling, sex, and porn. Bodo discusses the work of Judith Reisman, who describes pornography as an "erototoxin that produces an addictive drug cocktail of testosterone, oxytocin, dopamine and serotonin with a measurable organic effect on the brain."[15] Reisman believes that when people consume too much pornography, their brains are restructured so that they become dependent on pornography and will start to abuse it. Pornography, on this model, is addictive in the same way that alcohol or cocaine are.

Bodo ultimately finds the scientific evidence for sex and porn addiction rather thin. Since most people experience pleasure through some activities, the new and expansive model of addiction fails to explain why some people can resist or discipline their impulses to seek pleasure while others cannot. Other critics have described the theories of sex and porn addiction as "junk science."

---

13 Matthew Herper, David Whelan, and Robert Langreth, "The Shadowy Science of Sex Addiction," *Forbes*, November 22, 2009, http://www.forbes.com/2009/12/22/sex-addiction-science-lifestyle-health-tiger-woods.html.

14 Cristian Bodo, "Does Sex Addiction Have Any Basis in Science?" *AlterNet*, December 18, 2008, http://www.alternet.org/story/114024/does_sex_addiction_have_any_basis_in_science.

15 Quoted in ibid.

David Ley, author of *The Myth of Sex Addiction*, claims that ideas about sex addiction are rooted in various anti-masturbation movements from earlier eras.[16] We derive pleasure from many habit-forming activities, but the sex-addiction movement singles out sex as potentially dangerous to our health because of societal attitudes toward it. In contrast, Ley underscores some of the dissimilarities between drug use and sex:

> Drugs and alcohol introduce a foreign substance into the brain. Sex doesn't introduce anything. During sex the brain is working the way it's supposed to work. There's also no evidence of what [is referred to as] the "tolerance effect." With alcohol, when you start drinking, a little can have a big effect, but later on you need more to have the same effect. There's no evidence of a tolerance effect with sex. An orgasm never stops feeling good.[17]

Ley points out that no one has died from having too much sex, or from quitting suddenly, which can happen with alcohol abuse.

Ley alleges that many so-called sex addicts are men who have engaged in stereotypical masculine behaviors such as sexual cheating, patronizing prostitutes or strip clubs, having cybersex, or using porn.[18] By viewing these behaviors as symptoms of an addiction, Ley argues that we fail to send the message that men can make responsible choices about their sexual behavior. While desires for sex can be distracting, these desires are normal and under our control, and most people can function well with or without sex. Ley argues that when people do engage in destructive sexual behaviors, such as risky or predatory sex acts and sexual infidelity, the reasons are socially and psychologically complex and cannot be reduced to the loss of self-control due to addiction. The disease model too easily absolves of moral responsibility those people who engage in problematic sexual acts, while at the same time the model stigmatizes them.

Marty Klein suggests that many people who are candidates for sex addiction are suffering from either narcissistic character structure, obsessive-compulsive disorder, or some other kind of psychological problem, such as post-traumatic stress syndrome.[19] In other words, someone who regularly makes imprudent or selfish choices about sex may have an underlying psychological disorder. Klein mentions that the main evaluation tool is the Sexual Addiction Screening Test (SAST), which contains questions about culturally stigmatized behaviors that

---

16 Emma Gray, "Sex Addiction: Why You're Not Addicted to Sex, According to Dr. David J. Ley," *Huffington Post*, March 9, 2012, http://www.huffingtonpost.com/2012/03/09/sex-addiction-myth-david-ley_n_1335132.html.

17 Ibid.

18 "Myth of Sex Addiction," *New York·Post*, March 4, 2012, http://nypost.com/2012/03/04/myth-of-sex-addiction/.

19 Marty Klein, "You're Addicted to What?" *Humanist*, June 28, 2012, http://thehumanist.com/magazine/july-august-2012/features/youre-addicted-to-what.

can invoke feelings of shame or guilt. Klein concludes that "the diagnosis of sex addiction is in many ways a diagnosis of discomfort with one's own sexuality, or of being at odds with cultural definitions of normal sex, and struggling with that contrast."[20]

Despite the lack of scientific support for the existence of sex or porn addiction, there are many organizations and professionals offering services to help with these addictions, such as Sex Addicts Anonymous or Sexaholics Anonymous. Klein suggests that deploying the metaphor of addiction for certain patterns of sexual behavior or porn use is not merely benign or false. He writes, "calling this behavior an 'addiction' validates the idea that these people are out of control. Instead, we need to say that *feeling* out of control isn't the same as *being* out of control."[21] While Ley worries that the addiction model relieves men of responsibility for their culturally conventional masculine behaviors, Klein worries that it will be used to promote public policies aimed at controlling unconventional, but harmless, sexual behavior and expression.

Sexual addiction theories are part of a phenomenon often referred to as "the medicalization of sexuality," which involves the propensity to turn ordinary sexual problems into medical disorders. Treating a person's poor decision-making in regard to sex or porn as a disease may make it easier for that person or his partners to confront and discuss the problem. But the medicalization of sexuality also opens up avenues for self-described experts and drug companies to promote useless services and products by exploiting people's fears. In Ch. 11, we will look at the medicalization of other sexual problems, such as the inability to have pleasurable sex. If medicine is to be a science and not merely an art, its diagnoses and treatments should be based on solid evidence. Ley points out that supporters of the sex-addiction hypothesis refuse to acknowledge or define the kinds of evidence that would count against this theory.[22] Ley notes that many philosophers of science hold that scientific accounts should not only be supported by empirical evidence, but should also be potentially refutable by new evidence and experiments. In Ch. 11, we will investigate whether much of the science of sex counts as good or bad science.

Should Fatherhood Be a Choice?

Historically, men avoided responsibility for their biological offspring when they were born to women they had not married. Such children were deemed "illegitimate" and they had no rights to their father's support or inheritance. Unless another man adopted them (and married their mother), they and their mothers

---

20 Ibid.

21 Ibid.; emphasis in original.

22 David J. Ley, "Sex Addiction: The Null Hypothesis," *Psychology Today*, December 6, 2011, http://www.psychologytoday.com/blog/women-who-stray/201112/sex-addiction-the-null-hypothesis

were socially scorned and marginalized. In the past century, however, advocates for children's and women's rights have organized to remove the stigma of "bastardy" and unwed motherhood, and to give children "born out of wedlock" rights comparable to those born to married parents. In the U.S. and elsewhere, courts can now assign legal paternity to a man, against his wishes, if he impregnates a woman to whom he is not married and who then gives birth to their biological offspring.[23] Imposing the legal status of "father" is typically a mechanism that allows the state to make men financially liable for their biological children. In some countries, a man who impregnates a girl or woman by raping her may find that he is obligated to pay child support, with or without legal paternity or parental rights.[24] The primary rationale for compulsory paternity policies is to relieve taxpayers of the burden of financial support for fatherless children, by forcing men to take responsibility for the consequences of their nonmarital sexual activities.

On the surface, these policies seem to distribute responsibility for a child born to unmarried parents appropriately. Not all women will choose to abort in these circumstances, and not all women will be able to secure abortions, even when they seek them. Moreover, the biological father should not be able to force a woman to have an abortion against her will, in order to avoid financial responsibility. Raising a child is expensive, and few women can afford to do so without the financial support of a second parent. Involuntary legal paternity means that the father is not permitted to avoid financial responsibility by waiving his parental rights. The availabilty of DNA testing makes it more difficult for biological fathers to challenge paternity assignments, and the greater ability of governments to track their citizens across state and national borders makes it increasingly difficult for legal fathers to avoid paying child support.

In general, in cases of an unplanned pregnancy, women have two options that are not open to men: either terminating the pregnancy (when this is permitted and affordable), or not identifying the father and then releasing the child for adoption.[25] Some states now have "infant safe haven" laws that permit a mother

---

23 If the woman is married to someone else, and her husband seeks legal paternity with her support, often the biological father will be denied paternity status and rights, should he happen to seek them. In this section, we will focus on involuntary paternity, rather than the denial of paternity, which is an important issue that concerns the scope of men's reproductive rights.

24 A proposed bill in Brazil that would "force a rapist to provide child support for any offspring of his crime" aims to mitigate the effects of broadening abortion restrictions; Lourdes Garcia-Navarro, "Brazil's Restrictions on Abortion May Get More Restrictive," NPR, October 28, 2013, http://www.npr.org/blogs/parallels/2013/10/29/241410709/brazils-restrictions-on-abortion-may-get-more-restrictive. In the U.S., many states not only impose child-support obligations, but also assign paternity to rapists, which entitles them to sue for custody rights; Ed Payne and Ted Rowlands, "Child Custody Rights for Rapists? Most States Have Them," CNN, August 1, 2013, http://www.cnn.com/2013/08/01/us/rapist-child-custody/; Laura Bassett, "Bill to Block Rapists' Parental Rights Remains Stalled in Ohio Senate," Huffington Post, March 18, 2014, http://www.huffingtonpost.com/2014/03/18/rapists-parental-rights_n_4988394.html.

25 If the biological father is eventually identified and decides to exercise his paternal rights, this can disrupt an adoption process.

to leave a newborn at a designated facility without being charged with abandonment or child endangerment.[26] However, when a father is identified, a biological mother is typically not permitted to give her child up for adoption without the father's permission; and, if he chooses to raise the child, she might be assigned legal maternity involuntarily, with child-support obligations.[27]

Given the asymmetries that still exist between the options that men and women have when faced with an unplanned pregnancy and child, we might ask if court-ordered paternity policies are fair to men.[28] In the past, men in many societies had the choice of whether or not to recognize their "bastard" children, while motherhood for women was often not a choice. Women's rights advocates have long struggled for motherhood to be a voluntary condition, and for every child "to be a wanted child." With access to effective birth-control technologies for both single and married women, including some access to abortion services, and infant safe-haven laws so that desperate birth mothers are not charged with child abandonment, these advocates have achieved much of their goal. Should fatherhood also be a voluntary status or condition? Do men today have enough control over their reproductive destinies when they have access to condoms or vasectomies, or should men too be able to relinquish the legal duties and rights of fatherhood when they conceive a child with a woman?

Elizabeth Brake argues that the case against compulsory fatherhood is much the same as that against involuntary motherhood. She writes, "if women's partial responsibility for pregnancy does not obligate them to support a fetus, then men's partial responsibility for pregnancy does not obligate them to support a resulting child."[29] Brake claims that men who have unintentionally conceived a fetus should have the choice to waive their parental rights, just as women do. Men do not, and should not, have the right to choose abortion for a partner whom they accidentally impregnate, and therefore they may not be able to avoid biological fatherhood. But, according to Brake, they have no moral duty to co-parent or assume the social responsibilities of fatherhood, if they opt out from the beginning. Brake favors holding men responsible for the medical expenses and other costs of a pregnancy they have caused. But, if a woman chooses to continue a pregnancy, when the biological father has informed her upon learning of the pregnancy that he does not wish to be her child's legal father, she should not

---

26 "Infant Safe Haven Laws," *U.S. Department of Health and Human Services*, 2013, https://www.childwelfare.gov/systemwide/laws_policies/statutes/safehaven.cfm.

27 Mary Shanley argues that a biological father's right to veto an adoption should depend on the nature of the relationship he had with the mother, and should take into consideration any reservations the mother has about his ability to parent. Mary Shanley, "Fathers' Rights, Mothers' Wrongs: Reflections on Unwed Fathers' Rights and Sex Equality," *Hypatia* 10 (1995): 74–103.

28 Some of the ideas and arguments in this section were previously published in L. Shrage, "Is Forced Fatherhood Fair?" *New York Times*, June 12, 2013, http://opinionator.blogs.nytimes.com/2013/06/12/is-forced-fatherhood-fair/?smid=pl-share.

29 Elizabeth Brake, "Fatherhood and Child Support: Do Men Have a Right to Choose?" *Journal of Applied Philosophy* 22 (2005): 55–73.

have recourse to court-ordered paternity in order to force the biological father to pay child support. Brake does not believe that women should be reduced to poverty in such situations, but with an adequate social safety net, and with the option of finding another partner who is willing to share parental responsibilities, women and their children might not be much harmed.

Indeed, compulsory paternity may not serve a child's best interest. Although children's rights advocates aimed to end the practice of denying children born out of wedlock the right to a father's support and protection, their goals reflect patriarchal assumptions. First, the idea that a child needs to have a father—i.e., to be acknowledged by some man as his progeny and given his surname—in order to gain social legitimacy and support is somewhat sexist. While children greatly benefit from having more than one loving and supportive parent, many today would argue that a second parent need not be genetically related to the child or be a man. Second, involuntary legal fathers burden a child with a forced relationship that is likely to lead to feelings of rejection and resentment, without much benefit to the child. In the worst cases, such forced familial and legal relationships may be a source of constant conflict, including violent conflict. Countries that now assign paternity to a rapist burden the rape victim and her child with a legal relationship to a man who has committed a crime against the child's mother. Many forced fathers repeatedly go back to court to disestablish their legal bond to the child, which is emotionally difficult for all, especially for the child. Because of this, the legal and court costs of imposing paternity may be sufficiently high that there is no net gain to taxpayers when compared with the costs of various kinds of social assistance to single mothers and their children, or greater tolerance for same-sex parenting and second-parent adoptions (by adults of either sex, regardless of their marital status). For these reasons, compulsory paternity is not the best way to remedy past policies that classified children born to unwed parents as illegitimate and denied them rights to support.

There have been cases in which a mother, or the state, has sought to establish a sperm donor as the legal father. Sperm donors typically donate their gametes to help a woman or couple conceive a child, with the understanding that the child will belong to them and not the donor. It seems wrong for the state not to recognize or honor the agreement between the donor and the parents and, similarly, wrong for a woman to try to back out of an agreement that she entered into in order to obtain the man's sperm. A man who accidentally impregnates a woman, without any prior promise to procreate with her, has accidentally become a sperm donor. George Harris argues that a man in such circumstances is free of responsibility to co-parent the child with the mother because "he has not given his consent to the use of his body for the pursuit of her interest in procreation."[30] Agreeing to have sex with someone is not tantamount to agreeing to raise a child with them.

---

30 George Harris, "Fathers and Fetuses," *Ethics* 96 (1986): 597.

We need to balance the rights of both men and women to reproductive autonomy, and the rights of all children to support and care, with the interests of society in distributing the costs of raising children fairly. Are there better ways to balance these rights and interests than by forcing fatherhood on men and their children when these bonds amount to no more than a piece of paper and a legal burden? Reproductive rights activists point out that a pregnancy can happen when a woman is unable to support or raise a child, such as when she is very young, or when she faces various medical or social hardships. Boys and men, too, can find themselves faced with an accidental pregnancy when they are unable to assume the responsibilities of fatherhood. Of course, once anyone assumes the reponsibilities of parenting and establishes a parental relationship with a child, the terms of backing out must be much more stringent. But whether there should be a window of time during a pregnancy when both the biological mother and the father can back out is a topic that needs greater public debate.

Are We Responsible for the Fetuses We Unintentionally Create?

In the U.S. and elsewhere, many people believe that a pregnant woman should not have the right to choose to abort her pregnancy. Some are absolutists on this issue and hold that abortions are always impermissible, independent of the circumstances. Those who are not absolutists will make exceptions for cases in which there is serious hardship, for example, when a pregnancy threatens a woman's life or health or was caused by a sexual assault, or when a fetus has an incurable disability that is likely to severely reduce the quality or length of its life. Often the abortion debate is couched in terms of whether the fetus's right to life should outweigh the woman's right to control what happens to or in her own body, or whether the woman's "right to choose" trumps the fetus's "right to life," in most cases. Below we will evaluate these two basic positions and consider objections to them.

The philosophical case for the moral permissibility of abortion rests on the idea that people have the right to defend themselves against threats to their basic interests (e.g., physical and economic security, health, the ability to use and enjoy things and capacities that are theirs, and so on). When a pregnancy threatens harm to a woman's basic interests, she has the right to defend herself. Even if the agent who poses the threat is morally innocent (such as the fetus), acts of self-defense are still morally justified. However, in a situation of self-defense, one is morally permitted to use only an amount of force proportional to the anticipated harm. For example, it is not morally permissible to use lethal force to defend one's car or a tree on one's property, as the loss of such things is not sufficiently damaging to one's basic interests to justify killing a human being. The question about the morality of abortion turns on whether an unwanted pregnancy can cause sufficient harm to a woman's basic interests to justify aborting the pregnancy and, along with it, the fetus. Those who support a woman's right to choose abortion believe that it can, and therefore that our policies should give women sufficient time and resources to obtain abortions when they (possibly together with others) determine that a pregnancy poses a significant threat.[31]

There are three common objections to this argument. First, the pregnant woman is responsible for bringing her "attacker" into existence, and therefore her fetus is her child and is entitled to her support, even if fulfilling this claim involves sacrificing some of her basic interests. Second, having an abortion, in most cases, poses a greater threat to a woman's basic interests than carrying an unwanted pregnancy to term. Third, the option of giving a baby up for adoption can alleviate almost all serious threats to a woman's basic interests, except in the rare and most serious cases, such as a life-threatening pregnancy.

Defenders of the right to choose abortion have a number of responses to these objections. First, in the case of an accidental pregnancy, the fetus's existence is simply an accident for which the pregnant woman is, at most, only partially responsible. Although the fetus's existence is partly due to actions taken by the pregnant woman, in many cases these actions occur under conditions of limited reproductive and sexual self-determination. Women and girls often do not have access to adequate contraception, or cannot get their partners to cooperate in the use of contraception, which deprives them of reproductive autonomy. Inadequate, and even adequate, contraception can fail, and generally one is not responsible for all the unintended consquences of one's actions. Furthermore, many girls and women do not have complete control over when and with whom they have sex, which deprives them of sexual autonomy and limits their moral responsibility for the consequences of their sexual activities.

Second, studies claiming to prove that having an abortion poses serious risks to a woman's basic interests (e.g., by damaging her mental health, increasing her cancer risk, or reducing her fertility) are controversial among scientists, and their conclusions have been refuted by other studies. There is no consensus among health providers and medical researchers that having an abortion under the supervision of a qualified medical provider carries significant risks to a woman's heath. Indeed, for decades, abundant medical research has shown that the abortion procedures now in use in hospitals and clinics pose minimal risks to a woman's health, and the level of risk is typically lower than the risk to her health by carrying a pregnancy to term. Furthermore, the objection overlooks how compulsory pregnancy and birth can pose serious mental health and psychological burdens on a woman, just as a compulsory abortion might. Of course, when and where safe and sanitary abortions are not available (e.g., outside a modern medical facility), they pose a serious health risk.

Third, giving birth to a baby and then putting it up for adoption is very difficult emotionally and psychologically for many women. If aborting a pregnancy is not morally objectionable, then it is wrong for others to coerce a woman to undertake an action that might cause her lifelong regret and emotional pain.

---

31 The basic outline of this argument was offered by Judith Thomson in her now classic essay "A Defense of Abortion," *Philosophy and Public Affairs* 1 (1971): 47–66.

It is also true that having an abortion that one did not truly want can cause lifelong regret and emotional pain, which simply highlights the importance of protecting a woman's reproductive autonomy. Each woman, in consultation with her family, friends, and medical providers, is in the best position to decide whether adoption or abortion is the best option.

While these responses address many objections to making abortion services available, they do not justify an unlimited right to abortion services. Given that the case for abortion rights appeals to a woman's right to protect her basic interests, the amount and kind of access she should be granted need only be sufficient to allow her to do this. For example, policies that give women access to abortion in all cases where a pregnancy poses a serious threat to their life or health, as well as some period of unrestricted access in the early stages of a pregnancy so women can defend themselves against threats that deprive them of control over their bodily capacities or family size, would arguably be adequate to respect a woman's right to self-defense.

Deciding, though, how to limit access to abortion is a complicated matter of public policy, one that involves balancing competing views about what constitutes a "serious threat" to a woman's life or health, and how long into a pregnancy a woman typically needs to plan for an abortion. The longer the period of access, the more developed the fetus will be, and therefore the more complicated, costly, and risky the abortion procedure will be. Moreover, as the fetus gets older and more developed, the more morally troubling the choice to abort it becomes. Once the fetus is viable, or can survive on its own, a woman can terminate her pregnancy without killing her fetus, although by choosing a premature birth, she may cause lifelong and serious disabilities to her infant, which is morally unacceptable. For this reason, most jurisdictions limit "elective" abortions, or those that are not medically necessary, in the last half or third of a pregnancy. Such policies seem more morally justified than policies that would permit any and all abortions before a pregnancy reaches its normal term, or policies that would permit euthanizing viable fetuses (when ending a pregnancy is not medically necessary).

The philosophical case against abortion rests on the idea that the fetus is a potential person with a future that is very valuable to it. Killing persons is generally wrong because the act robs them of their future; and this is the same for potential persons. Therefore, on this view, feticide is wrong.[32]

One common objection to this argument is that it fails to distinguish intentionally causing a death from unintentionally causing one. Unintentional (but foreseeable) deaths occur, for example, when we decide to discontinue (or not to offer) life-saving aid to others in many circumstances. Abortion, some argue, involves causing an unintentional (but foreseeable) fetal death by terminating a fetus's nonconsensual use of a woman's body, which it uses to sustain its life. The woman (or doctor) who initiates an abortion aims to terminate a pregnancy, not

---

32 See Don Marquis, "Why Abortion Is Immoral," *Journal of Philosophy* 86 (1989): 183–202.

to kill a fetus, but she thereby denies the fetus continued use of her body, which will result in the fetus's demise. Sometimes our acts of refusing life-saving aid are ungenerous and callous, but often they are prudent decisions about where we can best invest our time and resources.

This objection to the case against abortion is partly right and partly wrong. An abortion that takes place before the fetus reaches viability involves an unintentional death. The fetus dies when it is removed from the uterus because it cannot survive on its own and because safe fetal transfer to an alternative life-support system is not yet possible. But when a viable fetus (a fetus that can be kept alive outside the womb) is removed and euthanized (or euthanized and then removed), intentional killing is involved. For this reason, the U.S. Supreme Court ruled in 1973 that, at the stage of viability, an abortion too closely resembles infanticide and can therefore be prohibited, as long as there are exceptions for life- and health-threatening pregnancies.

Some circumstances other than pregnancy that involve withholding live-saving support include the following: someone's refusal to make a bone-marrow donation when he or she is the only available genetic match, the failure of many to contribute to blood banks when there are shortages, the failure of many to contribute money to charities that save lives, and so on. Societies rarely punish people when they fail to save lives in these kinds of circumstances, even when doing so poses minimal burdens to the donor, and even when the donors belong to the imperiled person's family. Does a society treat pregnant women unequally when it restricts access to abortion and thereby forces them to donate their bodily capacities and other resources to support vulnerable human lives? Public discussion of abortion should include the full range of situations in which people are morally obligated to make some sacrifice in order to save another's life.

Canada has taken a different legal stance on abortion than the U.S. has. Canada's former abortion laws were struck down in 1998 as unconsitutional. A subsequent government attempted to create a new abortion law, but that bill was defeated by the (unelected) Senate. This is quite rare in Canada, but when it does happen, the (elected) House of Commons typically alters the original bill and resends it to Senate. But that did not happen in this case due to a change in government, and as a result Canada is one of the few countries in the world that has no abortion laws at all. This means that the decision to have an abortion is entirely a matter between a pregnant woman and her doctor. Legally speaking, this allows a woman to get an abortion very late in her pregancy, when a fetus is usually viable. In practice, however, the chances of a woman finding a doctor to perform an abortion at such a late stage are slim to none: terminations of late-stage pregnances in Canada occur only when continuing the pregnancy poses a substantial risk to the health of the mother or when the fetus has a catastrophic medical condition. Though not all Canadians are happy with this situation, many would argue that it has worked relatively well and has avoided unnecessary and unhelpful litigation.

Do Commited Relationships Entail Special Moral and Sexual Duties?

When people moralize about sex, they often ask under what circumstances is sex morally permissible, and between whom? Some philosophers take a rather restrictive view on these questions and limit permissible sex to marital coitus that aims at procreation. Others take a more tolerant view and rule out only those sex acts that are nonconsensual or harmful in some way. There are a range of views in between these two, such as limiting sex (perhaps good or dignifed sex) to acts among social equals or affectional partners that aim at reciprocal pleasure. Parents, concerned citizens, educators, and policy-makers have sought guidance on these issues for centuries.

There are other moral questions regarding sexual acts and relationships that remain unanswered. Many questions can be raised about the harms of sexual infidelity, and the appropriate forms of redress that should be available to the injured parties. In Ch. 6 we considered the morality of adultery, but sexual cheating can be an issue for unmarried partners as well. Another issue concerns sexual selfishness, and whether we have a moral duty to help our partner(s) achieve sexual fulfillment. This question may be more important in the context of a monogamous relationship. If we expect our partner to sacrifice the pursuit of other sexual partners, does this create a reciprocal duty to be sexually available to one's partner, within reason, and to make reasonable efforts to satisfy one's partner's sexual interests and tastes? Finally, a more basic question, captured by the phrase "all's fair in love and war," is whether the ordinary rules of morality apply to sexual acts, that is, whether sex inevitably involves a kind of competition in which players seek their own advantage, or personal victories over others. Schopenhauer's account of sexual attraction (see Ch. 2) suggests that our motives in choosing particular partners or in having sex are hidden to us, which would make imposing any moral rules rather difficult.

In this section, we will assume that people have the capacity to control their sexual behaviors, and therefore we will explore the second question about selfishness. Selfishness, in general, is considered a moral flaw, and selfish people are characteristically insensitive to the needs of others and lack kindness and generosity. Our societies and religions teach us to be concerned about the welfare of others and not only about fulfilling our own needs. Nevertheless, when we are asked to make self-sacrifices for the sake of others, it is usually to help people meet their basic needs. Few of us feel morally obligated to help the unfortunate among us acquire a Mercedes Benz or a yacht. The question, then, is whether having sexual satisfaction in one's life should be compared to enjoying a yacht, or to meeting a basic need for shelter, food, and so on. Even with our partners, we probably feel a greater obligation to insure that their basic needs are met rather than to address their need for luxury goods.

If we treat having a fulfilling sex life as a luxury—and sometimes an unaffordable one, given one's other time and work commitments—then we will probably feel less responsible for assisting our partners in this sphere of life, regardless of their perspectives about the place of sex in their own lives. Alternatively, if we treat sexual satisfaction as a basic need, then we will probably assume greater responsibility for helping a sexual partner in a monogamous relationship secure an adequate level of satisfaction. This responsibility may be part of an overall duty to strive to enrich the lives of our loved ones, and it may be also a matter of prudence—to keep our personal bonds strong and to minimize conflict.

The advice columnist and social critic Dan Savage maintains that we should make significant efforts and sacrifices to satisfy the sexual interests and tastes of a partner in a committed and monogamous relationship. Moreover, if we are not willing or able to handle our partner's needs, then we should tolerate his (or her) seeking other partners in ways that are not disruptive to the primary relationship. Mark Oppenheimer summarizes Savage's views as follows:

> It is for the sake of staying together—not merely for the sake of orgasms—that Savage coined his famous acronym, "G.G.G.": lovers ought to be good, giving and game (put another way, skilled, generous and up for anything). And if they cannot fulfill all of each other's desires, then it may be advisable to decide to go outside the bounds of marriage if that is what it takes to make the marriage work.[33]

The gist of Savage's advice is that we need to be flexible in terms of what we are willing to do or permit, so that our partners can secure sexual fulfillment. He contends that we should judge the health or success of a marriage on the degree of honesty and joy in it, rather than on the ability to remain sexually exclusive. Savage recognizes that his advice depends on people's ability to compartmentalize their needs so that, when they have extramarital sex, it does not threaten their marriage. And his advice also depends on spouses being able to discern this ability in their partners, in order to avoid feeling jealous or insecure. Nevertheless, Savage recognizes that not everyone will be capable of these emotionally protective mental feats, especially in a culture that equates sexual "fidelity" with romantic love, and infidelity with its loss. Consequently, many partners who aim to stay together must work out between them how they will fulfill each other's sexual desires, even those that they find frightening or disgusting, or just awkward and inconvenient. Sexual indifference or selfishness, for Savage, is not an option.

Savage is questioning the idea that partners in a marital or commited relationship have a basic, and generally understood, moral duty to be sexually monogamous. He suggests, instead, that marital partners recognize a moral duty to be honest and to try to understand each other's sexual desires. If we accept this, then our duty to help our partner achieve sexual fulfilment will take precedence over

---

33 Mark Oppenheimer, "Married, with Infidelities," *New York Times*, June 30, 2011, http://www.nytimes.com/2011/07/03/magazine/infidelity-will-keep-us-together.html.

our need for sexual exclusivity. If we have a strong need for a sexually exclusive relationship, then it is incumbent upon us to understand our partner's desires and to make a robust effort to fulfill them. Conversely, people with partners who prioritize sexual exclusivity over other goods will need to make an honest assessment of their own needs and whether they can be satisfied in a monogamous relationship. When conflict arises around these issues, Savage recommends that couples try to resolve their differences in non-judgmental ways.

Historically, wives were expected to tolerate their husband's infidelities, especially if the husbands fulfilled their duties of support and provided enough sexual attention for the purpose of procreation. But in more egalitarian relationships between partners of the same or opposite sex, the terms of relationship fidelity, sexual and otherwise, need to be worked out by each couple. Savage points out that gender equality does not necessitate that men restrict their sexual behavior to patterns of behavior once expected of women. Nor does gender equality mean that women will find happiness and fulfillment by behaving like men. Lesbian, gay, and heterosexual couples can work out the terms of their relationships differently, and diversity in this realm of life is acceptable. Perhaps we must primarily avoid coercive or hierarchical relationships, in which one partner gets to formulate the terms and the other can only accept or refuse. Savage's approach to marriage and committed relationships offers a way to balance sexual selfishness and generosity, assuming that we are capable of rethinking our romantic and sexual expectations.

Discussion Questions

1. In a society that places a high value on female chastity, are women morally obligated to disclose to potential spouses, or to family members, whether or not they are virgins?

2. In your community, what types of personal information require disclosure in order to make sexual encounters reasonably transparent, and to assign responsibility for any potential negative effects?

3. If getting treatment for "sex addiction" helps people cope with sexual behaviors that make them or others uncomfortable, should we accept this approach to addressing sexual problems, even if the theory on which it is based is currently unsupported by scientific research?

4. Does the availablity of relatively inexpensive and safe contraception, such as condoms, give men adequate reproductive autonomy?

5. Imagine that we had the technology to safely transfer a fetus at any stage of pregnancy into an incubator that could support its life until birth, and without posing greater risk to the pregnant woman's health than a standard abortion. Would there ever be a reason to deny a woman's request to terminate her pregnancy, if her fetus could be transferred and incubated elsewhere? Would all embryos, including those created and stored for assisted reproduction purposes, have a right to incubator support until birth?

6. Is the idea that each committed couple must work out the terms of their sexual relationship too individualistic? Is it better to have these terms debated and worked out by our communties, especially those groups that share our basic values (such as the religious or political organizations to which we belong)?

Further Reading

Alward, Peter. "Abortion Rights and Paternal Obligations." *Public Affairs Quarterly* 26, no. 4 (2012): 273–91.

Brugger, E. Christian. "The Problem of Fetal Pain and Abortion: Toward an Ethical Consensus for Appropriate Behavior." *Kennedy Institute of Ethics Journal* 22, no. 3 (2012): 263–87.

Francis, Leslie P., and John G. Francis. "Criminalizing Health-Related Behaviors Dangerous to Others? Disease Transmission, Transmission-Facilitation, and the Importance of Trust." *Criminal Law and Philosophy: An International Journal for Philosophy of Crime, Criminal Law and Punishment* 6, no. 1 (2012): 47–63.

Gupta, Kristina. "Protecting Sexual Diversity: Rethinking the Use of Neurotechnological Interventions to Alter Sexuality." *American Journal of Bioethics: Neuroscience* 3, no. 3 (2012): 24–28.

Harbin, Ami. "Sexual Authenticity." *Dialogue: Canadian Philosophical Review* 50, no. 1 (2011): 77–93.

Porter, Lindsey. "Adoption Is Not Abortion-Lite." *Journal of Applied Philosophy* 29, no. 1 (2012): 63–78.

Varden, Helga. "A Feminist, Kantian Conception of the Right to Bodily Integrity: The Cases of Abortion and Homosexuality." In *Out from the Shadows: Analytical Feminist Contributions to Traditional Philosophy*, edited by S. Crasnow and A. Superson, 33–57. Oxford: Oxford University Press, 2012.

Chapter 11

The Scientific and Medical Study of Sex

In this chapter we shall redirect our attention to the scientific study of sex and the "medicalization of sex"—when ordinary problems are transformed into medical issues. First, we examine what philosophers call the "demarcation problem": how is scientific knowledge different from other forms knowledge? Here we will consider two different conceptions of how science works: positivism and social constructionism. Second, we briefly review the history of sexology and try to determine whether research in this field offers us a scientific understanding of sex. Third, we turn to some contemporary debates over the best scientific explanation for particular sexual phenomena. One such debate involves the biological or reproductive function of the female orgasm, which seems far more mysterious than the function of the male orgasm. We then look at scientific research on sexual dysfunction, and its connection to the medical treatment of sexual disorders. Philosophers and other social critics have questioned whether sexual disorders typically require medical intervention, or whether the medicalization of sex is driven by its profit potential to pharmaceutical companies. Some sexual problems may involve health issues, but some appear to involve only the failure to conform to social norms. If research on sexual dysfunction is strongly influenced by market and cultural norms, then this raises questions about the legitimacy of such scientific research.

Can Sex Be Studied Scientifically?

One popular view of science is that it tells us what *is* the case as opposed to what *ought* to be the case. For example, while different religions may tell us which sexual activities are permissible, science tells us which sexual activities are common, and when, where, and for whom, regardless of their religious significance. The *Oxford English Dictionary* points to this descriptive aspect of science by defining the scientific method as "a method of procedure that has characterized natural science since the 17th century, consisting in systematic observation, measurement, and experiment, and the formulation, testing, and modification of hypotheses." There are a number of things to note about this definition. First, science is limited to things or events that are observable, even when we have to use powerful instruments to observe them, or when we observe them only indirectly by detecting their effects. In other words, science can only investigate physical objects, forces, and events, and not immaterial ones. Second, science does more than merely observe the physical world; scientists measure and perform experiments upon it. As we shall see, however, there has been a great deal of controversy, among both scientists and philosophers, regarding how these experiments work and what, exactly, they are supposed to signify.

A nineteenth-century English scholar, William Whewell, developed an influential account of the experimental method of science, which he called the "hypothetico-deductive method."[1] His account has been endorsed in various forms by many contemporary thinkers. According to Whewell, scientists must begin by formulating a hypothesis, which is a conjecture about or anticipated answer to a question under investigation. Scientists then determine what the hypothesis logically implies, or what *would* be true about the world *if* the hypothesis were true. The implication derived from the hypothesis is then tested in an experiment. If the experiment is successful, the hypothesis is (inductively) confirmed; but if it is not successful, the hypothesis is proved false and must be rejected.[2]

Consider a simple example. Imagine that your car won't start. You think that it may be out of gas. We will call this your hypothesis regarding the car's inability to start. If this is indeed the cause of your problem, then putting gas in the car should enable the engine to start. We can call this the implication of the hypothesis. In this case, it's a prediction of sorts: if the car had gas, it would start. To test this, you put gas in the car. If the car starts, your hypothesis is confirmed; if it does not, then your hypothesis is falsified and you have to come up with an alternative hypothesis regarding the car's failure to start. For example, it might have a faulty starter, or the battery could be dead.

While actual hypothesis formation and experimental testing can be quite complex, the above simple example points to a number of important features of

---

1   See William Whewell, *History of the Inductive Sciences* (1837) and *Philosophy of the Inductive Sciences* (1840).

2   See, e.g., Carl Hempel, *Aspects of Scientific Explanation* (New York: Free Press, 1965).

science and how it differs from other areas of inquiry, such as philosophy, religion, or poetry. According to the influential philosopher of science Karl Popper, scientific doctrines must be "falsifiable."[3] This means that the hypotheses that scientists put forward must be empirically testable, and it must be possible, in principle, for any given hypothesis to fail some test. The hypothesis in our example above is falsifiable. A conjecture such as the car won't start because it is out of gas is empirically testable by filling the gas tank and trying to start the car. If this does not work, the hypothesis is proven false. But if this works, the experiment provides some confirmation for the hypothesis. Note that the experiment does not prove the hypothesis with certainty, as it could be that the driver hadn't previously turned the key all the way, or pressed the clutch down, and then was more careful to do these after filling the tank with gas. Philosophers use different names to refer to the view that science involves something like the hypothetico-deductive method, including positivism, scientism, or scientific realism. This view of how science works came under attack by the middle of the twentieth century, but despite the criticism it has received, many scientists and students of science continue to subscribe to it, especially in fields such as chemistry, physics, and biology.

Thomas Kuhn, whose highly influential *The Structure of Scientific Revolutions* was published in 1962, offers an alternative account of how science works. Kuhn alleges that scientific inquiry can occur only within a worldview or conceptual framework, which he called "a paradigm."[4] A paradigm provides a set of answers, to which scientists generally agree, to some fundamental questions in an area of science. For example, contemporary biology assumes (roughly speaking) a Darwinian framework: species evolve through "natural selection."[5] This is not to say that biologists agree on everything. In fact, they disagree, sometimes quite radically, about any number of things. But they subscribe to the same paradigm, and indeed believe that disagreements only make sense within that framework. The critics of positivist accounts of science claim that a paradigm represents a social fact and not an objective truth about the external world. In other words, scientists do not approach the world as independent, neutral observers; instead, scientific investigations are shaped by intersubjective agreements about how the world basically works. From time to time, there are "paradigm shifts" in science, that is, substantial changes in the set of fundamental beliefs about how the world works. These shifts change the epistemic lenses through which scientists view the world—lenses that are colored not only by prevailing scientific opinion but also by prevailing religious and cultural beliefs. Because religious and cultural beliefs produce distortions in the lenses, they are sometimes isolated and removed. Yet, because the community of scientists has, historically, been mostly

---

3   Karl Popper, *The Logic of Scientific Discovery* (London: Hutchinson, 1959); Karl Popper, *Conjectures and Refutations*, 2nd ed. (New York: Routledge, 2011).

4   Thomas Kuhn, *The Structure of Scientific Revolutions* (Chicago: University of Chicago Press, 1962).

5   Natural selection is a process commonly explained as "the survival of the fittest."

composed of men with similar cultural backgrounds, they often fail to perceive their own cultural biases. Therefore, much science has been put in the service of proving erroneous cultural beliefs, such as beliefs about race-based differences among humans.[6] Human sexuality has mostly been studied by male scientists, and this has similarly produced culturally biased explanations. In a later section we will discuss scientific studies of the female orgasm, and how debates among scientists reflect norms pertaining to male sexuality.

Kuhn's account of how science works is associated with anti-positivist, social-constructionist accounts of science. On this view, we construct the world from a variety of beliefs, including uncritical cultural assumptions. Ruth Hubbard notes that, due to this aspect of science, we must always be conscious of who the "factmakers" are.[7] In Europe and its former colonies, these factmakers have mostly been affluent, white, heterosexual, Christian men. As a result, the so-called "objective" claims of science have often been constructed by members of socially dominant groups who aim to justify their socially privileged position.

We can evaluate scientific studies of sexuality from both positivist and social-constructionist perspectives on science. The approaches taken by scientists themselves often reflect one of these understandings of science. Positivists try to approach the study of sex as neutral observers who study what happens in the brain and other parts of the body during sex. Social constructionists position themselves as participant observers and culturally comparative interpreters of sexual practices. Each approach can produce good or bad science.

Is Sexology a Science?

Sexology, or the study of human sexuality and relationships, began in the late nineteenth century. While the first generation of sexologists tried to deploy scientific methods, they were overly constrained by the morality of their day. These scientific pioneers were particularly interested in examining sexualities that were considered psychologically deviant and morally troubling, and this encompassed almost everything except procreational sex between a wife and husband. Some theorists argued, though, that *all* sex is somewhat problematic. For example, Elizabeth Osgood Goodrich Willard, who coined the term sexology, thought sex for women was inherently dangerous. An orgasm, she said, was more debilitating to the system than a hard day's work. We must be vigilant, therefore, to stop the waste of energy

> through the sexual organs, if we would have health and
> strength of body. Just as sure is that the excessive abuse of

---

6   In the twentieth century, social and humanist critics of science documented the history of "scientific racism," i.e., ordinary racist beliefs bolstered by allegedly scientific studies.

7   Ruth Hubbard, "Science, Facts, and Feminism," in *Feminism and Science*, 2nd ed., ed. Nancy Tuana, 120–31 (Bloomington: Indiana University Press, 1989).

the sexual organs destroy their power and use, producing inflammation, disease, and corruption, just so sure is it that a less amount of abuse in the relative proportion, injures the parental function of the organs, and impairs the health and strength of the whole system. Abnormal action is abuse.[8]

In the nineteenth century, two major preoccupations and worries about sex were masturbation and homosexuality. A century earlier, the Swiss physician Samuel-Auguste Tissot (1728–97) had argued that, because semen was vitally important to male health, excessive sex and onanism (his term for all non-procreative sex, including masturbation) could lead to anything from unclear thinking and acne to tuberculosis, intestinal disorders, and impotence. He thought these vices were even worse in women since, in addition to all the above problems, onanism could lead to lesbianism. Moreover, in prepubescent adolescents, Tissot believed that excessive sex and masturbation could lead to insanity.[9]

Richard von Krafft-Ebing (1840–1902), who published *Psychopathia Sexualis* in 1886, was perhaps the most significant writer about sexuality in the nineteenth century. A medical doctor and psychiatrist, Krafft-Ebing shared many of the negative attitudes of his time toward sex, while he nevertheless struggled to think of it, and of sexual "deviancy," in newer, less judgmental ways. For example, while he believed that homosexuality was not necessarily degenerate and perverse, and that homosexuals could be "normal" in the nonsexual parts of their lives, he also believed that sexual desire was always potentially dangerous and therefore had to be tightly controlled. Uncontrolled sexual desire, he thought, was like a "volcano which scorches and eats up everything, or an abyss wherein everything is walled up—honor, property, health. [By establishing monogamous marriage] Christian peoples obtained a spiritual and material pre-eminence over other peoples, particularly those of Islam."[10] Here Krafft-Ebing crosses over the line between describing sexual behavior and morally pontificating about it. Claims such as this are not scientific in any recognizable sense of that term.

The most significant figure in the second generation of sexologists was Sigmund Freud (1856–1939), the Austrian neurologist and father of psychoanalysis. His theories had the greatest impact within psychiatry for at least half a century, and he continues to be influential in fields as disparate as literature and sociology. Freud believed that sexual desires were at the root of almost all human behavior and that the vast majority of psychological problems stemmed from the failure to channel these desires toward appropriate ends. Freud's overarching theory is complex and the subject of intense debate, and so we won't be

---

8 Cited in V.L. Bullough, *Science in the Bedroom: A History of Sex Research* (New York: Basic Books, 1994), 26.

9 Ibid., 20–22.

10 Quoted in ibid., 48.

exploring it in any detail here. Instead, we will focus on whether Freud's theories about sex can be supported scientifically.

The historian of sexology Vern Bullough summarizes Freud's central ideas:

> [At the end of] his own self analysis ... (about 1902), Freud emerged with the conviction that he had discovered three great truths: that dreams are the disguised fulfillment of unconscious, mainly of infantile wishes; that all human beings have an Oedipus complex in which they wish to kill the parent of the same sex and possess the parent of the opposite sex; and that children have sexual feelings. He later added two ideas to these emerging principles of psychoanalytic thought, namely the division of the human mind into superego, ego, and id, and the concept of the death instinct (thanatos).[11]

The data for Freud's theories about mental illness came primarily from clinical case studies of patients undergoing "analysis," a process in which people become conscious of problematic desires or thoughts that they keep repressed. Many of the early sexologists relied heavily on case studies when formulating or defending their views about sex. While case studies provide a wealth of empirical information, they primarily tell us a lot about particular individuals.[12] Their use becomes problematic when (1) they are treated as evidence for claims about large groups of people or all people, and (2) they are not properly done. The use of case studies by the first and second generation of sexologists suffered from both of these problems.

Regarding problem (1), consider the example of the influential English sexologist Havelock Ellis (1859–1939). His theories were drawn largely from case studies of himself, his wife, and their friends. Unfortunately, from a research perspective, these interesting individuals formed an unrepresentative sample. Ellis's wife was a lesbian, and Ellis himself suffered through long periods of impotence and had a fascination with urolagnia (sexual arousal caused by urine). And their friends, especially his wife's, were sexual dissidents who lived outside the mainstream society of Victorian England.[13] It is therefore unlikely that the data acquired through case studies of these persons would be generalizable to the population as a whole. Freud made a similar mistake by drawing almost all of his empirical data from patients who suffered from some neurosis or other disorder. In regard to such uses of case studies, Beatrice Faust observed:

---

11 Ibid., 88.

12 See, e.g., Roy Levin, "Single Case Studies in Human Sexuality—Important or Idiosyncratic?" *Sexual and Relationship Therapy* 22, no. 4 (2007): 457–69; and Carl Elliott, "The Tyranny of Happiness: Ethics and Cosmetic Pharmacology," in *Enhancing Human Traits*, ed. Eric Parens, 177–88 (Washington, DC: Georgetown University Press, 1998).

13 Phyllis Grosskurth, *Havelock Ellis: A Biography* (London: Allen Lane Publishers, 1980).

"it is always possible to discover a few case histories to support any particular argument but case histories only illustrate—they don't verify."[14] And even Freud himself said of this method, "It strikes me as strange that the case histories I write should read like short stories and that, as one might say, they lack the serious stamp of science."[15] Today, medical researchers largely reject the individual case-study method as well as claims that rely mostly or exclusively on the physicians' clinical experience. Instead, they promote "evidence based medicine," in which experimenters randomly sample large populations and use control groups to test theories. Yet getting this kind of data about the sexual lives and desires of large numbers of people can prove difficult.

Regarding the second problem with the use of case studies, Freud is a prime example of how individual case histories can be seriously flawed due to researcher bias. Social constructionists point out that scientific inquiry does not exist in a vacuum, and all researchers bring to their investigations a particular view of the world or paradigm. Freud's worldview resulted in his refusing to believe his patients' testimony when his female patients told him that they had been victims of sexual abuse, typically by close family members. Instead, he speculated that these women were delusional and their testimony was evidence of repressed oedipal desires. As we shall discuss in greater detail in the next section, Freud also refused to believe women about the anatomical location of their orgasms.

The third wave of sexologists attempted to avoid the problems of the previous generation by eschewing case studies and instead using large, allegedly representative samples. The most important figures who pioneered this approach were Alfred Kinsey (1894–1956), and William Masters (1915–2001) and Virginia Johnson (1925–2013).

Trained as a biologist, Kinsey was adamant that human sexuality could be studied scientifically. To this end, he set out to collect data by conducting long and intricate interviews, which he designed and which he taught to only three other investigators who worked with him at Indiana University.[16] These four men interviewed approximately 18,000 individuals, and the data they collected formed the basis of Kinsey's two major works: *Sexual Behavior in the Human Male* (1948) and *Sexual Behavior in the Human Female* (1953). These reports turned out to be incredibly popular, and both of them became bestsellers. Given the subject matter, they were also highly controversial. The book on male sexuality was criticized for claiming that a fairly high percentage of American males had engaged in at least one homosexual experience (37 per cent, according

---

14 Beatrice Faust, *Women, Sex, and Pornography* (New York: MacMillan, 1980), 125.

15 Cited in Bullough, *Science in the Bedroom*, 136.

16 These interviews could last for hours, with the longest one lasting more than 17 hours. See Bullough, *Science in the Bedroom*, 174–75.

to Kinsey[17]), and that bisexuals were not really homosexuals who had adapted to a homophobic society. The book on female sexuality raised doubts about the widely held belief that most women remained virgins until marriage. According to Kinsey, 50 per cent of American women had intercourse before marriage.[18] Also, Kinsey's claim that approximately 26 per cent of American women and 50 per cent of American men had engaged in extramarital or adulterous sex was somewhat shocking to people at the time. Kinsey's work demonstrated to Americans that they were not nearly as conservative and constrained in their sexual behavior as the majority appeared to believe.

Kinsey's work was far more scientific and rigorous than the work of most of his predecessors. Nevertheless, his critics alleged that his informants were not randomly selected, and therefore his findings could not support broad conclusions about human sexuality. Although Kinsey did not rely on a small number of case studies as many of the earlier sexologists had, his samples were not as representative or diverse as they should have been. First, Kinsey relied on volunteers, and this raises questions because people who self-select to be interviewed about their sexual life may have more positive attitudes about sex than the general populace. Second, his subjects were mostly from the Midwest region of the United States—in fact, not far from Indiana where he was based. Finally, the male study, in particular, contained a disproportionate number of prisoners and homosexuals. So while his large data sets are helpful, their failure to match the characteristics of the population about which he made generalizations undermines the scientific credibility of his studies.[19]

William Masters was an obstetrician with a clinical background, something that Kinsey did not have. As a doctor, he was as interested in helping patients as he was in accumulating data and advancing knowledge about human sexuality. He and his research partner (and eventual wife), Virginia Johnson, made important innovations in the treatment of sexual dysfunction, in part by defining a new occupation: the sex therapist. Sex therapy, as conceived by Masters and Johnson, provides an alternative to Freudian psychoanalysis, which dominated the treatment of sexual dysfunction at that time. Most sex problems were not, they argued, the result of some deep neuroses that had to be overcome by years of analysis.

Masters and Johnson maintained that most sexual problems were relatively easy to resolve, as they were largely the result of ignorance about human sexual anatomy and physiology or the specific sexual preferences of one's sexual partner.[20] Masters and Johnson made sexual arousal and climax less mysterious by describing a sexual response cycle with four phases: excitement, plateau, orgasm,

---

17 Alfred Kinsey, W. Pomeroy, and C. Martin, *Sexual Behavior in the Human Male* (Bloomington: Indiana University Press, 1998).

18 Alfred Kinsey, W. Pomeroy, C. Martin, and P. Gebhard, *Sexual Behavior in the Human Female* (Bloomington: Indiana University Press, 1998).

19 Bullough, *Science in the Bedroom*, 176–77.

20 See ibid., 203–05.

and resolution.[21] This model is still widely used today. They also pointed out that men and women differ in their sexual response capacities. For example, women can more easily than men return to the plateau phase and experience multiple orgasms. While Kinsey's research relied on the reports that his informants gave about their sexual practices, Masters and Johnson pioneered the technique of direct laboratory observation of people having sex, and they were somewhat controversial for this reason. Students interested in learning more about the sex research of Masters and Johnson can now watch the TV series *Masters of Sex*.[22] Similarly, there have been a number of recent films about the sex research of Kinsey.[23]

We can see, even from this brief examination of the history of sexology, that researchers have used quite different methods to study sex. Vern Bullough argues at the end of his history of sexology that scientific studies of sexuality do not fit into a coherent pattern. Today, sexologists represent a wide array of fields (including biology, neurology, medicine, psychology, sociology, and anthropology) and deploy diverse methodological approaches. The Society for the Scientific Study of Sexuality (ssss) holds annual meetings and sponsors the *Journal of Sex Research*, both of which provide forums for the interdisciplinary exchange of work among sex scientitists.[24] These investigators work within various paradigms (evolutionary psychology, interpretive anthropology, etc.) that shape the questions they pursue and the methods they use. In some cases, they test hypotheses and provide empirical confirmation for (or falsify) them. So sexology fits both positivist and social-constructionist models of how science works and is an interdisciplinary field of science, much like cognitive science.

Why Does the Female Orgasm Puzzle Scientists?

In this section, we examine two debates about the female orgasm: (1) whether it results primarily from clitoral or vaginal stimulation, and (2) whether it serves any reproductive purpose. The first issue has implications for whether penile-vaginal penetration—the paradigm of heterosexual sex—is as satisfying for women as it is for men. The second issue has implications for whether female sexual pleasure increases a woman's chances of becoming pregnant. In the Middle Ages, many experts believed that a woman's orgasm was necessary for conception to occur, a view that received attention recently when Todd Akin, a former Republican Representative from Missouri, maintained that women would not get

---

21 W.H. Masters and V.E. Johnson, *Human Sexual Response* (Boston: Little, Brown, 1966).

22 Dave Itzkoff, "Don't Mind Us. We'll Just Watch: 'Masters of Sex' Recalls the Work of Masters and Johnson," *New York Times*, July 26, 2013, http://www.nytimes.com/2013/07/28/arts/television/masters-of-sex-recalls-the-work-of-masters-and-johnson.html?smid=pl-share.

23 See especially the 2004 film *Kinsey*.

24 SSSS: The Society for the Scientific Study of Sexuality, http://www.sexscience.org/resources/journal_of_sex_research/.

pregnant in what he called "legitimate" rape.[25] Men who wanted children had to learn how to induce orgasms in their wives. This belief also led to the conviction that, if a woman became pregnant through an act of rape, then this was evidence that she experienced pleasure. Since people typically do not experience pleasure when they are being forced to do something against their will, pregnancy was also taken to be evidence of consent or that the impregnating act was not a rape. For evolutionary biologists today, the question is whether women's capacity to have orgasms would give individual women, or the species, some kind of advantage. If so, then this would be a trait that is naturally selected, in the sense that women with this capacity would give birth to and raise more children.

Freud was highly influential on the issue of which parts of a woman's body were at the center of her libidinal desires and pleasure. According to Freud, humans, ideally, pass through five stages of psychosexual development: (i) the oral, (ii) the anal, (iii) the phallic, (iv) the latent, and (v) the genital (see Ch. 5). Aside from the latent stage, the names of these stages indicate the primary body parts through which children and adolescents seek or receive sexual pleasure. Freud maintained that the last stage of this process represented full adult maturity, when sexual desire was focused on penis-vagina intercourse and reproduction. Failure to reach this end stage, he alleged, was often an indication of a neurosis or mental illness.

According to Freud, adult (i.e., post-pubescent) women whose sexual pleasure is focused on their clitoris are stuck in the immature, childish, phallic stage of development, when children become aware of the differences between male and female genitals and girls develop penis envy, and when sexual pleasure is primarily sought through masturbation. In his *New Introductory Lectures in Psychoanalysis*, Freud wrote, "With the change to [adult or mature] femininity, the clitoris should wholly or in part hand over its sensitivity, and at the same time its importance, to the vagina."[26] In other words, mature, feminine women are supposed to seek and receive sexual pleasure through heterosexual intercourse.

Contemporary studies show, however, that the vast majority of women don't reach orgasm through vaginal stimulation alone. Unfortunately, Freud's theory of psychosexual development tells women that they are unfeminine and psychologically immature when they pursue sexual pleasure via clitoral stimulation, especially via masturbation. An interesting historical case study of a woman who considered herself sexually deviant in this way involves Princess Marie Bonaparte, the great-grand niece of Napoleon Bonaparte. Although she could attain orgasm through masturbation, she could not do so via intercourse with men. She came to believe that the problem was with her: specifically, that there

---

25 Jennifer Tucker, "The Medieval Roots of Todd Akin's Theories," *New York Times*, August 23, 2012, http://www.nytimes.com/2012/08/24/opinion/the-medieval-roots-of-todd-akins-theories.html?smid=pl-share.

26 Sigmund Freud, "The Psychology of Women," in *The Standard Edition of the Complete Psychological Works of Sigmund Freud*, translated by James Strachey, 24 vols. (London: Hogarth, 1953–74), Vol. 22: 118.

was too great a distance between her clitoris and her vaginal opening, which in her case was almost three centimeters. Evidently, Princess Bonaparte collected data (eventually published in a medical journal in 1924) that led her to conclude that women with a space of 2.5 centimeters (about an inch) or more between their vagina and their clitoris almost never reach an orgasm through intercourse alone. Women below this 2.5-centimeter range generally can attain orgasm through intercourse alone, while women at the borderline can only occasionally achieve orgasm in this manner. These data have in fact recently been confirmed.[27] The truly remarkable thing about this story is that Bonaparte had her clitoris removed and reattached closer to her vagina. Of course, the surgery did no good in terms of her inability to achieve orgasm through intercourse, as it may have left her with painful scar tissue and damaged nerves. Moreover, the clitoris is not simply the small visible tip that protrudes between the labia, but it contains nerves that extend approximately ten centimeters (four inches) along the vaginal wall. So once her clitoral tip was removed, it was separated from these nerves, thus leaving it rather numb.

Kinsey was—here as elsewhere—one of the first to investigate the matter of female orgasm empirically. According to Kinsey, 39 to 47 per cent of women reported that they always, or almost always, had an orgasm during intercourse.[28] But, according to Elisabeth Lloyd, this figure is misleading because Kinsey included women who reached orgasm when assisted by clitoral stimulation as well as vaginal penetration. Lloyd maintains that although research in this matter is still ongoing, only about 20 per cent of women can reach orgasm without direct clitoral stimulation.[29] The rate at which women achieve orgasm through intercourse alone is relevant to the issue of whether the female orgasm is an adaptation that contributes to reproductive success. Most evolutionary biologists have said that it is. But after reviewing all 21 published adaptionist accounts of this trait, Lloyd concludes that they are wrong for one reason or another. Following the biologist Donald Symonds,[30] she claims instead that female orgasm is a "by-product" of evolution, like nipples on men. Obviously, these claims need further explanation and defense. Let's begin with her preferred by-product account.

In the earliest stages of human fetal growth, males and females have the same anatomical parts, except for, of course, different chromosomes. So male and female fetuses have the same genital protostructures, which begin to differentiate only at around eight weeks of gestation, when the male fetus releases hormones that start the process of sexual differentiation. If no hormones are released, then the fetus will continue to develop into a female. Hence, according

27 Mary Roach, *Bonk: The Curious Coupling of Science and Sex* (New York: W.W. Norton), 65–71.

28 Kinsey et al., *Sexual Behavior in the Human Female*.

29 Elisabeth Lloyd, *The Case of the Female Orgasm: Bias in the Science of Evolution* (Cambridge, MA: Harvard University Press, 2005).

30 Donald Symonds, *The Evolution of Human Sexuality* (New York & Oxford: Oxford University Press, 1979).

to Lloyd, the clitoris and the penis "are the same organ in men and women; there is an organ in the undifferentiated embryo that turns into a penis if it receives a dose of a particular hormone, otherwise it matures into a clitoris. In other words, the penis and the clitoris have the same embryological origins and thus are called 'homologous' organs. Similarly, the nervous and erectile tissues involved in orgasm in both sexes arose from a common embryological source."[31]

Despite their common embryological origin, orgasms in men and women have, on the face of it, quite different reproductive functions. The male orgasm functions as a delivery system for depositing sperm in a female's vaginal canal, in order to fertilize an egg. The female orgasm does not serve a similar ejaculatory function. Thus, while the clitoris and penis are homologous and each is involved in the generation of orgasms (and orgasms can be pleasant and meaningful for both men and women), their *biological* roles are quite different. Similarly, although nipples and breasts for both men and women are associated with erogenous zones, they have dissimilar biological functions, because male nipples and breasts cannot deliver milk to an infant. For Lloyd, then, both male nipples and female orgasms are merely a by-product of the fact that all human fetuses share a common early developmental history (apart from their DNA of course).

Now let us to turn to the adaptionist accounts of female orgasm and to Lloyd's rejection of them. These accounts vary considerably, but they fall into three broad camps: (1) pair bonding, (2) non-pair bonding, and (3) "sperm selection" accounts. Very briefly, pair bonding accounts maintain that female orgasm promotes long-term bonds between males and females. Many reasons have been offered for why the ability to form stable pair bonds would be naturally selected. One reason is that human children are quite helpless and require significant amounts of care over extended periods of time. The assumption behind this account is that it is beneficial to a woman to have a male mate who supports and assists her in raising her (or their) children. Another reason pair bonding may be adaptive is that it provides some assurance to the male that her offspring are his, and so he will protect them. Because males have never been able to tell, with certainty, whether any offspring are theirs (until recently with DNA paternity testing), they rely on a woman's sexual fidelity. Allegedly, sexual pleasure with a man, in the form of orgasms, displays her satisfaction with him, and thus the likelihood that she won't seek other mates.[32]

The primary problem with all these pair-bonding adaptionist accounts, Lloyd argues, is that they assume that women are like men and always or usually attain orgasm during intercourse. But this is simply not the case. As we said earlier, only about 20 per cent of women attain orgasm through intercourse alone. Indeed, Lloyd surveys 32 studies conducted between 1929 and 1994 on the frequency of female orgasm during intercourse: "The mean value [of women who said they 'always' had orgasm with intercourse] was 25.3% while the median value

---

31 Lloyd, *The Case of the Female Orgasm*, 108.
32 Ibid., 44–76.

was 23.5%."[33] The two most reliable studies,[34] which used "probabilistic sampling techniques," respectively found that 18 and 28.6 per cent of women reported usually having an orgasm with intercourse.[35]

Compare these results with women's reports about orgasms achieved through masturbation, which is done mostly by direct clitoral stimulation and not by vaginal penetration alone. Here the large majority of women achieve orgasm and do so much more quickly than they do during intercourse. Indeed, men and women take approximately the same length of time to reach orgasm through masturbation. Lloyd concludes: "The chief empirical problem with [pair bonding adaptionist accounts of female orgasm] is the presence of the substantial gap between the occurrence of intercourse and the occurrence of female orgasm."[36] The odd fact that most researchers have failed to see this, Lloyd contends, is that these researchers have typically been men and have therefore looked at the matter from a man's point of view. Men almost invariably achieve orgasm during intercourse (unless they have a health problem) and so they assume that women do as well, or if women don't, something is wrong with them. That is, male bias has greatly skewed the investigations.

Non-pair bonding accounts of female orgasm typically begin by noting what pair bonding accounts miss, namely, that most of the time the majority of females do not experience orgasm through intercourse alone. Researchers working within this framework point to the gap between intercourse and female orgasm as evidence of an adaptation that has evolutionary fitness. Time and space permit us to mention only a couple of these research studies, and readers are encouraged to examine Ch. 4 of Lloyd's book to get her full account.[37]

Sarah Blaffer Hrdy, for example, maintains that female sexual pleasure is adaptive.[38] This is because women will seek to continue copulation until they are satisfied. But, because women typically take more time to reach orgasm through intercourse than men do, women will have to be promiscuous and mate with several males in quick succession in order to achieve orgasm. Hrdy's account is diametrically opposed to pair bonding accounts because it implies that women will be genetically disposed to be promiscuous rather than sexually monogamous. Hrdy argues that promiscuity achieves the same end as monogamy—acquiring male support and protection—and, in fact, promiscuous women will

---

33 Ibid.

34 L. Stanley, *Sex Surveyed, 1949–1994* (London: Taylor & Francis, 1995); E.O. Laumann et al., *The Social Organization of Sexuality: Sexual Practices in the United States* (Chicago: University of Chicago Press, 1994).

35 Lloyd, *The Case of the Female Orgasm*, 27.

36 Ibid., 75.

37 Ibid., 77–106.

38 S.B. Hrdy, *The Woman That Never Evolved* (Cambridge, MA: Harvard University Press, 1981); S.B. Hrdy, "The Primate Origins of Human Sexuality," in *The Evolution of Sex*, ed. R. Bellig and G. Stevens, 101–36 (San Francisco: Harper & Row, 1988); S.B. Hrdy, "The Evolution of Female Orgasms: Logic Please but no Atavism," *Animal Behavior* 52 (1996): 851–52.

have *a number of men*, rather than just one, to help rear their children. Because none of the men knows which child is theirs, and each male is potentially the father of some child, they are all willing to help out.

One obvious response to non-pair bonding accounts is that most women engage in pair bonding. Hrdy acknowledges this and claims that this sort of promiscuity is not currently adaptive for humans; it is, rather, a vestige of a behavior that was once adaptive but no longer is (like a tailbone in people). Yet this claim is hard to corroborate one way or the other. Another problem for Hrdy's account is that the length of intromission (the time the penis is inside the vagina) appears to make little difference in terms of whether a female achieves orgasm, for the majority of women.[39]

There are several versions of the "sperm selection" account, but the most widely held is the "upsuck hypothesis." The idea is quite simple: female orgasm causes the uterus to "upsuck" sperm through the vaginal canal, thus increasing the chances of fertilization. Lloyd writes, "If the sperm-upsuck theory is correct, then it would constitute the much sought after connection between female orgasm and a feature, fertility, which might be connected to reproductive success, which would thus make it more plausible that female orgasm serves an adaptive function."[40] Yet the empirical studies done so far (by Masters and Johnson)[41] provide no evidence for an upsuck of sperm when a woman experiences an orgasm. In fact, quite the opposite seems to be the case. Lloyd writes, "the contractions of orgasm start at the back or the top of the uterus and go down through the middle, ending in the cervix. In other words, these contractions might have the effect of expulsion rather than ingestion. Masters and Johnson also note that the sperm-suction theory wouldn't seem to work because the upper end of the vagina around the cervix expands during orgasm, and lifts the cervix away from the pool where the semen would be deposited."[42]

Lloyd concludes that adaptionist accounts of the female orgasm are not confirmed by existing studies and that the best explanation is that the female orgasm is not related to reproductive success but is simply "for fun" (i.e., a by-product effect, like male nipples). That many researchers have thought otherwise, she claims, is largely the result of male bias, which leads them to assume that there is a strong relationship between heterosexual intercourse and orgasms in women. Even if Lloyd is correct, and the female orgasm has little evolutionary significance, there are some recent studies that support a stronger connection between vaginal penetration and female orgasms. That is, these studies appear to show that vaginal penetration can stimulate the base of the clitoris and also the tip, producing different patterns of blood flow and sensation than when

---

39 Lloyd, *The Case of the Female Orgasm*, 98.

40 Ibid., 180.

41 Masters and Johnson, *Human Sexual Response*, 123.

42 Lloyd, *The Case of the Female Orgasm*, 182.

the tip alone is stimulated.[43] It may be that the low rates of vaginal orgasm that women report are due to the sexual position many heterosexual couples appear to prefer (men on top), and to women not taking a more active role in sex, which can affect stimulation to the "root" of the clitoris. If more women find ways to achieve orgasm through penile-vaginal penetration (i.e., potentially reproductive sex), then this will likely re-open debates about whether the female orgasm is somehow adaptive—the second question we raised at the beginning of this section. Regarding the first question, these new studies confirm Freud's thesis that women can achieve orgasm via different body parts (clitoris and vagina), though, *contra* Freud, both types involve the clitoris—but different ends of it. However, they do not confirm Freud's view that women who seek sexual pleasure only through penile-vaginal sex are more feminine or psychologically mature. Perhaps future research on the female orgasm will involve scientists who are women and also lesbians, and who will thus bring new perspectives to this kind of scientific research.

What Are the Criteria of Sexual Dysfunction and When Is Medical Intervention Appropriate?

The *Oxford English Dictionary* defines the verb 'medicalize' as: "to give a medical character to; ... to view or interpret in (*esp. unnecessarily*) medical terms" (emphasis added). The psychologist Leonore Tiefer describes the 'medicalization' of sexuality, in particular, even more negatively, as

> a process of establishing universal norms, and then declaring all variations disordered and in need of treatment ... [typically tracking the following pattern:] expensive meetings, books and journals underwritten by drug companies, new disorders discovered to be treated by expensive drugs, health and medical journalists alerting the public to their quick-fix cures, drug-company sponsored epidemiological studies creating and identifying new markets, urgent government and commercially funded consensus conferences. Meanwhile, the factors that account for the lion's share of women's [and, we would argue, men's] sexual problems (economic, social, political) will be ignored, avoided, and generally said to be "not about sexuality."[44]

---

43 Jodie Gummow, "How Many Types of Orgasms Can a Woman Have? You May Be Surprised," AlterNet, March 18, 2014, http://www.alternet.org/sex-amp-relationships/how-many-types-orgasms-can-woman-have-you-may-be-surprised.

44 Leonore Tiefer, "Female Sexual Dysfunction (FSD): Witnessing Social Construction in Action," *Sexualities, Evolution & Gender* 5, no. 1 (2003): 35.

As Tiefer's description implies, drug companies stand to make big profits from the medicalization of any problem, including sex, and, accordingly, fund much of the medical research on "sexual disorders" and then promote their "quick fixes." Instead of promoting "talk therapy," including the non-professional kind, to address the common social causes of sexual problems, medical researchers collaborate with commercial drug companies for material gain, and perhaps benefit more than their "patients."

For example, Pfizer, the company that makes Viagra, has been involved in research about "erectile dysfunction" (ED). Currently, several drug companies are attempting to develop and win FDA approval for a "female Viagra" but, according to Tiefer, they first need to frame and conceptualize the disorder that they claim it will fix. Of course, Viagra has some benefits for some men, but it is unclear whether a pill to address female sexual dysfunction—however it's understood—has much of anything positive to offer women. Unfortunately, there are huge financial interests at stake in any quest to find a medical cure, but especially one as supposedly common as female sexual dysfunction. In this section, we will first discuss the medicalization of male sexual problems and then review some current debates about female sexual disorders.

The word 'impotence' has a long history and literally means powerlessness, which has many negative connotations. The problem of "male impotence" was re-described as "erectile dysfunction" in the early 1990s, when sildenafil (Viagra) was proposed as a possible treatment. According to Roy Moynihan and Barbara Mintzes, this phrase sounded "more clinical, more physical, ma[de] no judgement about the man's potency ... [and] implied the problem was that a man's penis wasn't functioning properly." [45] The DSM-IV-TR describes erectile disorder or dysfunction (ED) as "a persistent or recurrent inability to attain, or to maintain until completion of the sexual activity, an adequate erection," which causes the person "marked stress or interpersonal difficulty." [46] ED is distinguished from "premature ejaculation" and other ejaculation disorders, as well as disorders of desire.

Sildenafil, or Viagra, was initially tested in the late 1980s and early 1990s as a potential anti-angina drug. Angina is severe chest pain caused by a lack of blood flow and oxygen to the heart and is generally caused by an obstruction in the coronary arteries. But sildenafil failed these tests. However, among the many side-effects of the drug—flushing, headaches, indigestion, muscle aches, and distortion of color vision—researchers noticed a further one: it produced penile erections. So, in 1993, Pfizer began to test sildenafil as a treatment for ED. Over the next four years, sildenafil underwent 21 clinical trials, exposing approximately 4,500 test subjects to the drug. The results, according to these trials, appeared very good, with an overall success rate of around 70 per cent

---

45   Roy Moynihan and Barbara Mintzes, *Sex, Lies & Pharmaceuticals: How Drug Companies Plan to Profit from Female Sexual Dysfunction* (Vancouver: Greystone, 2010), 123.

46   APA, *DSM-IV-TR*, (Washington, DC: American Psychiatric Association), 545.

for men with ED, and the drug was approved in the U.S. in March 1998 and in Europe later that year. One million men in the U.S. were given prescriptions for Viagra in its first few weeks on the market and, by 2006, it was estimated that 750,000 physicians had prescribed either sildenafil (Viagra) or one of the other "PDE5 inhibitors"—vardenafil (Levetra) and tadalafil (Cialis)—to more than 23,000,000 men in the U.S.[47] By 2008, U.S. sales had reached $1.5 billion, representing 19,000,000 prescriptions. Part of the reason for the tremendous sales was evidently the fact that many elderly people started having sex again: 57 per cent of 70-year-old men and 52 per cent of 70-year-old women now report being sexually active compared to 40 and 35 per cent, respectively, 30 years ago. And when the "baby boomers," with their disproportionately large numbers, begin to enter this age range, the numbers will surge ever higher.[48]

All of the PDE5 inhibitors are "vasodilators," which are drugs that dilate the blood vessels. They treat ED by improving blood circulation to the penis, allowing the penis to become engorged and achieve an erection. If a man's sexual problems are primarily psychological (such as, anxiety, depression, stress, or guilt) rather than physiological, then Viagra and its variants will not be effective. Or if his problems are interpersonal, such as a loss of affection for and sexual attraction to his partner, then Viagra will not be of much help here either. Some studies indicate that about the same percentage of men are affected by a loss of sexual desire as are those affected by ED. By far the biggest sexual problem that men report is premature ejaculation (at 21 per cent), and Viagra and the other PDE5 inhibitors similarly offer little help for this problem.[49]

Nevertheless, the number of men who have taken one or more of these new drugs suggests that many men are happy to have them on the market. Current estimates are 150 million worldwide, with the expectation this will rise to 300 million men by 2025, even though many drug plans do not cover the cost (or the full cost) of these pills (usually between $10 and $20 per pill).[50] Besides helping men have and sustain erections, many men taking PDE5 inhibitors report an increase in self-esteem and a decrease in guilt and depression. Moreover, the majority of men taking these drugs were satisfied with them.[51] The current treatment of ED is remarkably better than previous physiological treatments for impotence. Consider, for example, the testicular grafts and implants first employed by the Turkish obstetrician Skevos Zervos, in 1909. A few years later,

---

47 All figures in this paragraph are from Hossein A. Ghofrani et al., "Sildenafil: From Angina to Erectile Dysfunction to Pulmonary Hypertension and Beyond," *Nature Reviews* 5 (2006): 689–702.

48 Deborah Kotz, "Sex, Health & Happiness," *US News & World Report*, September 15, 2008.

49 John Leland et al., "The Science of Women & Sex," *Newsweek*, May 28, 2000, http://www.newsweek.com/science-women-sex-160071.

50 H. Padman-Nathan, "Sildenafil Citrate (Viagra) Treatment for Erectile Dysfunction: An Updated Profile of Response and Effectiveness," *International Journal of Impotence Research* 18 (2006): 423–31.

51 Ibid.

the implant—in which a third testis is added to the scrotum—was introduced in the United States. Of course, finding donors willing to forgo one of their testicles was difficult, and so treatments were developed that used the testes of cadavers. Other researchers tried xenotransplantation, using the testes of everything from sheep to chimpanzees. Unfortunately, none of these worked, for a number of reasons, including the rejection by the body of these foreign objects. Men in some societies concoct drinks made from a variety of male animal parts, but these generally do not work well either.[52] By comparison, then, Viagra and other similar medications are a tremendous improvement.

Yet is the popularity of these drugs due, in part, to the aggressive advertising campaigns launched by Pfizer and other drug companies, and not to the widespread prevalence of health problems that cause ED? The direct marketing of pharmaceutical drugs happens only in a few countries (but includes the U.S. and, to a lesser extent, Canada) and is a recent phenomenon, dating back only to 1996. Nevertheless, advertising drugs directly to consumers (and not only to doctors) has had a huge effect on sales of pharmaceuticals, almost tripling them over a ten-year period, from $11.4 billion in 1996 to $29.9 billion in 2005.[53] When Viagra was first marketed, the ads targeted men and couples in their "senior" years. Bob Dole, a former U.S. senator and presidential candidate, was one of the first to appear in a commercial for Viagra. Dole was at that time in his seventies and was recovering from prostate surgery, which is known to cause difficulties with getting and sustaining an erection. Soon Viagra was increasingly marketed to younger and younger men who had no obvious health problems or had not been diagnosed with ED. Consider Moynihan and Mintzes' discussion of a magazine advertisement, depicting a

> ruggedly handsome man around the age of 40 with the bold
> headline: "Viagra. It works for older guys. Younger guys.
> Even skeptical guys." The ad then asks its readers: "Think you're
> too young for Viagra? Do you figure, 'It only happens once
> in a while so I'll live with it?' Then nothing's going to change,
> especially your sex life." The message was clear: even the most
> occasional erection problems could benefit from being treated
> with a drug.[54]

This ad implies that the occasional failure to achieve an erection could be a sign of ED and therefore treatable with a drug, even when such failures could be due to unreasonable expectations (e.g., multiple erections over a short period of time),

52 Roach, *Bonk*, 177–92.

53 Julie Donahue et al., "A Decade of Direct-to-Consumer Advertising of Prescription Drugs," *New England Journal of Medicine* 357, no. 7 (2007): 673–81, http://content.nejm.org/cgi/content/full/357/7/673.

54 Moynihan & Mintzes, *Sex, Lies & Pharmaceuticals*, 125.

or simply to being tired and overworked. Such overdiagnosis also shows up in surveys that claim that more than half of men over forty experience ED.[55]

Proper erectile functioning has come to be defined by what is normal for a healthy, 20-year-old man, and deviations from this norm are viewed as sexual dysfunctions in need of treatment.[56] Ads that promote concern about ED to men over 30 exploit culturally entrenched stereotypes of men. In one poll sponsored by Pfizer, for example, two of the top ten characteristics of "manliness" were "potency" and being "always ready for sex." [57] Because the inability to perform sexually, on demand, is equated with a loss of virility, men make easy targets for Pfizer's sales pitches. In this context, then, it is not that odd to see so many men taking Viagra and reporting satisfaction with it, especially when merely popping a pill can help avoid the social stigma of impotence. Some physicians even promote the overdiagnosis of ED alongside the drug companies that often pay them to promote their products. Consider the following from a New York urologist, who is also a paid spokesman for Pfizer: "People think that they have to have severe ED to take Viagra. But that's not true. It works well for men who can get erections, but the erections aren't as rigid as they once were. Or they don't last as long as they used to. Or there may be longer intervals between erections. Now, I prescribe Viagra for men of all ages. But I think just about every sexually active man over 50 could benefit from Viagra." [58] An executive at Bayer, which markets Levetra, maintains that "it's going to be important to communicate to men that it's okay ... [to take a drug since] ED is just a natural consequence of aging. Kind of like when you reach the age of 40 and you start to need eyeglasses." [59] Perhaps it's more important to communicate to men that their capacity for sexual response may change as they age, and this is normal too. Do Viagra and Levetra offer "better living through chemistry," to echo an old DuPont ad, or is this just an industry trying to make a buck by promoting unrealistic standards for men so they will buy its products in order to meet these standards?

A number of researchers have begun to investigate how satisfied women are when their partners use Viagra (and similar drugs). They have found that some women are disappointed that they have not been included in the ED drug studies, since ED is a problem for couples, not just individuals. Some women also fear that Viagra will increase the chances that their partner will have extramarital affairs. And, finally, some women aren't happy about the amount of sex that their partners expect after taking a pill. As one woman expressed it: "He'd kill me for saying this, but if he takes a tablet at night before we go to bed ... we might have

---

55 H.A. Felman et al., "Impotence and Its Medical and Psychological Correlates: Results of the Massachusetts Male Aging Study," *Journal of Urology* 151 (1994): 54–61.

56 See Moynihan & Mintzes, *Sex, Lies & Pharmaceuticals*, 122–30.

57 C. Asberg and E. Johnson, "Viagra Selfhood: Pharmaceutical Advertising and the Visual Formation of Swedish Masculinity," *Health Care Analysis* 17 (2009): 144–57.

58 Quoted in Moynihan & Mintzes, *Sex, Lies & Pharmaceuticals*, 126.

59 Quoted in ibid.

intercourse that night, then sometimes in the morning … and then if it doesn't necessarily appeal to me I think oh no … he's going to try again."[60] This comment suggests that women lose some control over when and how often they have sex when this depends on a pill rather than on mutual desire or seduction.

To summarize, then, while drugs like Viagra have an important role to play in the treatment of genuine erectile problems, difficulties abound. First, these drugs have been vastly overprescribed and are often used as an enhancement technology rather than a medical cure. Second, the marketing of the drugs has taken advantage of men's anxieties about their manliness to sell them a product that most do not need, and which, like any drug, poses some health risks.[61] Third, the existence of the drugs encourages men to reduce complex sexual problems to mechanical ones and to treat common life problems (e.g., aging) or unrealistic social expectations as medical problems for experts to fix. And fourth, these drugs have been tested only in particular populations for treating ED, and the safety of their long-term use for enhancing normal sexual performance is unknown. As with any drugs, they can be dangerous when used in combination with other medicines, or with various recreational or party drugs that men may be using right before they have sex.[62]

Given the enormous success of Viagra for men, pharmaceutical companies are now trying to develop a Viagra pill for women. Indeed, some women have used the Viagra pill designed for men. Because Viagra relaxes the smooth muscle tissue of the penis to allow it to engorge with blood during arousal, some users and researchers think that Viagra can also relax the smooth muscle tissue of the clitoris to allow it to engorge with blood during arousal. But so far tests have shown Viagra to work no better than a placebo in women, so drug companies are searching for other medications.[63]

The search for a female potency pill reflects the assumption that the capacity for sexual response in women is basically similar to men's, which is the same assumption behind most attempts to explain how the female orgasm is adaptive. John Bancroft, the current head of the Kinsey Institute, makes a similar point: "We are still in a culture which has defined sexuality, sexual pleasure, and sexual goals in male terms. Then we apply the same paradigm to women. That is a mistake."[64] One difference between women and men can be explained in terms of Masters and Johnson's four-stage "human sexual response cycle." The DSM

---

60 Quoted in ibid., 139.

61 Some men have "overdosed" on Viagra, by not following the instructions or heeding the warnings on the label, and some of these men have had to have their penis amputated. One can find a number of news stories about such cases by searching the Internet, or ask an Emergency Room physician how many such cases they see. While any drug can be misused, the promotion of Viagra as an enhancement to one's sex life, rather than a strong medicine with potentially serious side effects, may influence users not to take the warnings seriously.

62 Moynihan & Mintzes, *Sex, Lies & Pharmaceuticals*, 140–41.

63 Leland et al., "The Science of Women & Sex."

64 Quoted in ibid.

defines this cycle as follows: (1) "Desire," which "consists of fantasies about sexual activity and the desire for sexual activity;" (2) "Excitement," which "consists of a subjective sense of sexual pleasure and accompanying physiological changes," such as erection in men and "vasocongestion in the pelvis, vaginal lubrication and expansion, and swelling of the external genitalia" in women; (3) "Orgasm," and (4) "Resolution."[65] Viagra works during the "excitement" stage, as erectile disorder involves blood-flow mechanisms. However, women's sexual disorders are more likely to overlap with stages (1) or (3); that is, women report more problems with desire and reaching orgasm, rather than with the problems characteristic of stage (2). Sometimes drug companies re-describe what their product does to fit women's physiology. Moynihan and Mintzes write, "If Pfizer is promoting a drug that enhances blood flow to the genitals, then the condition might best be described as an 'insufficiency' of vaginal engorgement. If Proctor & Gamble is pushing its testosterone patch as a cure for women, the sexual disorder is discussed as a 'deficiency' of hormones. And if Boehringer has a pill that affects the mind's neurotransmitters, women with low libido may have a 'chemical imbalance' in their brains. In a strange way, the disease seems designed to fit the drug."[66] These drug companies are designing women's sexual diseases to fit the drugs originally developed for men.

Carl Elliott, along with others, has exposed the ways in which "Big Pharma" is involved in both medical education and research on the effectiveness of its own drugs.[67] Some drug companies have created subsidiary companies to do their educational courses and research for them in order to avoid the appearance of conflicts of interest. This means that the research behind many papers published in scientific journals is sponsored by drug companies. Elliott points out that more than half of the research studies on, for example, the new SSRI antidepressant drugs (Selective Serontonin Reuptake Inhibitors) are sponsored by for-profit drug companies. Moreover Pharma-sponsored research typically generates more optimistic results than non–Pharma-sponsored research—i.e., it shows the drugs to be more effective and have fewer side-effects. Over 50 per cent of the mental-health professionals who decide what will be included in each edition of the DSM are on Big Pharma's payroll.[68] Indeed, Steven Sharfstein, writing as the President of the American Psychiatric Association, has acknowledged that "as a profession we have allowed the biopsychosocial to become the bio-bio-bio model." As a result, he says, "a pill and an appointment" is too often the preferred (or only) treatment offered.[69] Allen Frances warns that the new "DSM 5 will give drug companies running room to continue their disease mongering

65 American Psychiatric Association, *DSM-IV-TR*, 536.
66 Moynihan & Mintzes, *Sex, Lies & Pharmaceuticals*, 3.
67 Elliott, "The Tyranny of Happiness."
68 Carl Elliott, "Pharma Goes to the Laundry," *Hastings Center Report* 34, no. 5 (2004): 18–23.
69 Steven Sharfstein, "Big Pharma and American Psychiatry: The Good, The Bad, and The Ugly," *Psychiatric News* 40, no. 16 (2005): 3.

of female sexual disorders—hyping this DSM diagnosis as a means of pushing pills."[70] This claim implies that the mental-health professionals who vote on what goes into the DSM—many of whom receive funding from drug companies— permit drug manufacturers to engage in "disease mongering," that is, selling diseases so they can then "push pills" to treat them. Frances also suggests that many "female sexual disorders" (FSD) in the most recent DSM have been designed to fit the drugs that Big Pharma is pushing.

As discussed above, in their book *Sex, Lies & Pharmaceuticals*, Moynihan and Mintzes have detailed how Big Pharma has promoted the development of a female Viagra. The first part of this process is to define a disease that they believe their medication can cure. In the 2009 film *Orgasm, Inc.*, the filmmaker Liz Canner interviews a drug-company manager, Darby Stephens, who admits that female sexual dysfunction is somewhat new and unknown: "In order for us to develop drugs, we need to better and more clearly define what the disease is…. We're hoping to be able to expedite the process… of disease development."[71] The aim of the drug companies is to define the disease in a broad enough way so that a great many people will experience the symptoms, even if their problem is slight and occasional. For example, the DSM-IV includes "Hypoactive Sexual Desire Disorder," which is defined as "a deficiency or absence of sexual fantasies and desires for sexual activity."[72] It also includes "Female Sexual Arousal Disorder," which is defined as "a persistent or recurrent inability to attain, or to maintain until completion of the sexual activity, an adequate lubrication-swelling response of sexual excitement."[73] Another FSD is "Sexual Aversion Disorder," which is "the aversion to and active avoidance of genital sexual contact with a sexual partner."[74] Given this broad set of relatively common symptoms, an article published in the prestigious *Journal of the American Medical Association* (JAMA) found that 43 per cent of women suffer from some type of female sexual dysfunction.[75] This statistic was cited more than 1000 times in scientific papers, and tens of thousands of times in the popular media.[76] Yet, this figure is misleading, given that it was derived by defining female sexual disorders in terms of commonly experienced situations, even when these happened infrequently. The JAMA authors posed a short series of questions to women, asking them, according to Moynihan and Mintzes,

---

70 Allen Frances, "Female Sexual Dysfunction and Disease Mongering," *Psychology Today*, March 4, 2013, http://www.psychologytoday.com/blog/dsm5-in-distress/201303/female-sexual-dysfunction-and-disease-mongering.

71 Liz Canner, *Orgasm, Inc.: The Strange Science of Female Pleasure* (Astrea Media, 2009).

72 APA, *DSM-IV-TR*, 539, 541.

73 Ibid., 543.

74 Ibid., 541.

75 E.O. Laumann et al., "Sexual Dysfunction in the United States," *JAMA* 281 (1999): 537–44.

76 Moynihan & Mintzes, *Sex, Lies & Pharmaceuticals*, 44–45.

whether they had experienced any of seven common difficulties for several months or more during the past year: The questions asked things like whether they'd ever lacked interest in sex, ever felt anxious about their sexual performance, ever had trouble with lubrication, had ever failed to orgasm, came to orgasm too quickly or ever experienced pain on intercourse. By simply answering yes to just one of these questions, women were then categorized as having a sexual dysfunction. ...[77]

They were categorized as having an FSD even when the problem was minor, happened just once, or caused them no distress. Of course, the JAMA article carefully qualified its findings by stating that they were "not equivalent to clinical diagnosis" of dysfunction.[78] But this caveat was largely ignored both by the scientific community and by the wider public. Readers also overlooked the fact that the article's lead author had been paid by Pfizer, the drug company that markets Viagra and that is investigating treatments for FSD.

FSD is not only an example of an "invented" disorder, but it is also one modeled to fit drugs designed for men. This is not to say that women never experience sexual difficulties, but instead that many of their problems stem from social rather than physiological sources: lack of communication with partners about sexual matters or poor sexual negotiation skills, exhaustion from "double-shift" responsibilities, and, as Kinsey observed, ignorance about their own bodies and how they work. A pill is unlikely to address these problems. Because scientists and medical doctors have a great deal of cultural authority, their theories about sexual desire, pleasure, and disorders significantly influence how many of us understand these aspects of our lives. It's therefore important that scientists and physicians use respected research methods and are transparent about any conflicts of interest. Philosophers of science and medicine, along with other humanist critics, social theorists, science journalists, and patient advocate groups, all play an important role in challenging the claims of scientists, including sex scientists.

---

77 Ibid., 46–47.
78 Ibid., 48.

Discussion Questions

1. Is sex more difficult to study scientifically than other human behaviors, such as eating habits or workplace practices? Explain your answer.
2. Discuss the methodologies of different fields of science as they might be applied to the study of sex, especially biology, neuroscience, chemistry, physics, medicine, psychology, sociology, economics, and anthropology.
3. The *DSM* no longer includes "homosexuality" among its catalog of sexual disorders. Why do you think this was once included, and what does this show about sex science and medicine?
4. Do you think that women's capacity for sexual pleasure and orgasm is something that is adaptive and therefore a trait that would be "naturally selected"?
5. Are erectile dysfunction and female sexual dysfunction partly due to unrealistic social expectations about sex?
6. What conflicts of interest exist for drug manufacturers and medical researchers when they research sexual disorders, and how can we minimize these?

Further Reading

Elliott, Carl. *A Philosophical Disease: Bioethics, Culture, and Identity*. New York: Routledge, 1998.

Foucault, Michel. *The History of Sexuality, Vol. 1*. Translated by Alan Sheridan. New York: Pantheon, 1976/1988.

Freud, Sigmund. *Three Essays on Sexuality*. 1905. New York: Basic Books, rev. ed. 2000.

Lewontin, Richard. *Biology as Ideology: The Doctrine of DNA*. New York: HarperCollins, 1993.

Lloyd, Elisabeth. *The Case of the Female Orgasm: Bias in the Science of Evolution*. Cambridge, MA: Harvard University Press, 2005.

Tuana, Nancy, ed. *Feminism and Science*. 2nd ed. Bloomington: Indiana University Press, 1989.

Chapter 12

Sex and the Limits of Tolerance in Secular Democratic Societies

In pluralist societies, we acknowledge that there are different but equally valid "conceptions of the good," which the philosopher John Rawls defined as what we think is valuable in life.[1] For this reason, we promote tolerance toward the different views and practices of others, as long as these are relatively harmless. When they are not harmless, though, societal intolerance is appropriate and justified. In this book we have discussed violent and nonconsensual sexual behaviors, such as sexual assault and harassment, and such practices are clearly harmful and should not be tolerated. But are there any nonviolent or consensual sexual practices that we should also not tolerate? In this chapter, we consider some practices involving sexual conduct or sexual health that are not typically violent or nonconsensual but are nevertheless controversial. We then explore whether such practices should be tolerated. For example, should political leaders be removed from office when they commit adultery or otherwise engage in sexual conduct that is legal but widely viewed

---

1   Leif Wenar, "John Rawls," *The Stanford Encyclopedia of Philosophy* (2012), http://plato.stanford. edu/entries/rawls/.

as immoral? Should parents be allowed to practice genital cutting on their daughters, when they believe that doing so is necessary for their daughters' well-being? Should someone be able to physically restrain another, or inflict minor bruises on another, if such activity is consensually pursued for sexual excitement and release?

Political and moral philosophers have attempted to define the limits of tolerance in societies that value freedom and equality. Some are concerned that a society can become too tolerant, or too respectful of cultural diversity, so that it will fail to defend widely shared, basic values and rights. Questions about which marriages we should recognize, whether sexual commerce should be decriminalized, or how abortion should be restricted also raise questions about the limits of tolerance. One thorny issue is whether liberal states should tolerate the practices of groups that are authoritarian, elitist, or ethnocentric and therefore conflict with the basic ideals of pluralist democracies. In this final chapter of the book, we consider whether tolerating political leaders with scandalous sexual lives, or the body modifications that some parents choose for their children, or the practices of various BDSM communities, accords or conflicts with our general commitment to maximizing freedom and equality.

Should We Care about the Sexual Improprieties of Our Political Leaders?

Let's examine some recent political scandals in various countries. The president of France from 1981 to 1995, François Mitterrand, had a mistress for many years, with whom he had a daughter. At his funeral, his wife, mistress, and "illegitimate" daughter all stood together. For a high-profile male politician, having one or more mistresses was acceptable in France at the time.[2] Even today, there is a general social expectation, in France and elsewhere, that powerful men will have affairs.

Silvio Berlusconi, who stepped down from office in 2011, was the longest-serving prime minister of Italy since World War II. He has also been at the center of several sex scandals, including one involving a teenage Moroccan nightclub dancer and alleged prostitute, Karima El Mahroug, better known as "Ruby the Heartstealer." Allegedly, Berlusconi gave El Mahroug $10,000 to attend "bunga bunga" parties and dance nude at his private villas when she was 17. After a widely publicized trial, he was convicted on charges of paying for sex with a minor and abusing his authority. The latter charge was for arranging to have El Mahroug released from a juvenile detention center in Milan, where she was being held on theft charges. Recently, an appeals court overturned these verdicts. Berlusconi had been sentenced to seven years in prison and also had been banned from holding public office.[3]

---

2   C. Deloire and C. Debois, *Sexus Politicus* (Paris: Albin Michel Littérature, 2006).

3   Ilaria Polleschi and Silvia Aloisi, "Italy Appeals Court Clears Berlusconi in Sex Trial," Reuters, July 18, 2014, http://www.reuters.com/article/2014/07/18/us-italy-berlusconi-idUSKBN0FN1AS20140718.

Pierre Elliott Trudeau, the prime minister of Canada from 1968–79 and 1980–84, allegedly had a long-standing affair with Liona Boyd, a famous Canadian classical guitarist. His wife, Margaret, who was thirty years younger, allegedly had affairs with Mick Jagger of the Rolling Stones and U.S. Senator Ted Kennedy. After his divorce from Margaret, Trudeau had a child out of wedlock with Deborah Coyne, a lawyer and politician. These "indiscretions" by Trudeau seemed to add to his mystique, and they didn't harm his political career at all. Unfortunately, his wife was subjected to far more public scrutiny of her private life and was often ridiculed in the press.

Bill Clinton, the 42nd president of the United States, famously had an affair with a White House intern, Monica Lewinsky, between 1995 and 1997 (see Ch. 1). This affair, and a lawsuit charging sexual harassment by a former Arkansas state employee, led to his impeachment by the House of Representatives for perjury and obstruction of justice. The Senate, though, acquitted him of both charges. Nevertheless, Clinton's second term as president was consumed by the scandal. One indication of how obsessed people, particularly Americans, were by the charges and trial is that, when Monica Lewinsky appeared on the Barbara Walters show, it drew an audience of 70 million viewers. ABC claimed this set a record for a television news show in the U.S. at that time.

There have been literally dozens and dozens of sex scandals involving federal-level U.S. politicians since the late eighteenth century. In contrast to France, Canada, and Italy, most of these scandals have forced politicians out of office or ruined their political careers. The controversial conduct in these cases ranges from consensual adultery to sexual harassment. It's not too far-fetched to conclude, then, that U.S. citizens are quite intolerant of sexual indiscretions on the part of their politicians.

Is it reasonable to judge politicians on the basis of their private sexual conduct, if the conduct is not illegal? Historical figures such as King Henry VIII of England or Cleopatra of Egypt are famous (or infamous) for their affairs, and they have, as a result, garnered a lot of attention on the basis of their sex lives. Importantly, their sexual relationships had political and social repercussions far beyond the individuals directly involved. In England, for example, Henry VIII's decision to marry Anne Boleyn required an annulment from his first wife, Catherine of Aragon. Because the Pope would not grant such an annulment, the king separated the Church of England from the Roman Catholic Church. This, in turn, caused many thousands of deaths as England's Protestants and Catholics fought religious wars for years, both internally and externally. In sum, King Henry's private sexual and marital life had serious public consequences. Had he and Anne Boleyn been satisfied with carrying on an affair—as the king had with a number of other women, including Anne's sister, Mary—the social disruption might have been more limited and not long-lasting. Yet the political subjects of this English king had good reason to be concerned about their ruler's love life.

None of the sex scandals involving U.S. politicians has caused anything that amounts to this kind of turmoil. A few cases have involved alleged criminal sexual assault or sexual harassment, so, of course, the public has every right to be concerned about such criminal behavior on the part of their leaders. However, in a secular democracy, a political leader does not need the approval of a religious official for a divorce, and, today, criminal prosecution for adultery or gay sex is unlikely.[4] So one might ask whether the social disruption and consequent harm to society that currently result from an office holder's adulterous or same-sex relationship is caused by the public's intolerance? Or is the illicit, but legal, sexual conduct on the part of a high-profile person inevitably a "weapon of mass distraction" that prevents the person from carrying out the duties of their office?

When a married person has an affair, often there are harmed third parties, such as the non-adulterous spouse and the couple's children. Hillary Clinton was personally and perhaps politically harmed by her husband's affair with Monica Lewinsky, and their daughter, Chelsea, also probably suffered emotionally, as well as from all the media attention devoted to her father's affair. Yet Clinton asserted, once he finally admitted publicly to his indiscretions, that ultimately his adultery was a private matter between him and his wife, and had nothing to do with the public business of running the government. Some empirical studies support Clinton's assertion that his private sexual behavior need not have undermined his public service, had the public not been so responsive to the dirty political maneuvers of his opponents. For example, the research of Robert Murray and Tim Blessing on U.S. presidents shows that "many of the qualities that make for a good presidential candidate or that contribute to his electability (physical appearance, educational and geographic background, religious belief, marital infidelity, and so on) have had little to do with ensuing success in the White House."[5] While the public may believe that adulterers are bad people in some respects, they can be effective leaders, if the public allows them to lead.

Many moral conservatives reject the idea that the public should tolerate or ignore the sexual improprieties of public leaders. According to Patrick Devlin, as discussed in Ch. 5 above, societies need to uphold general moral principles in order to keep from disintegrating. In his words,

> Societies disintegrate from within more frequently than they
> are broken up by external pressures. There is disintegration
> when no common morality is observed and history shows
> that the loosening of moral bonds is often the first stage of

---

4   Ethan Bronner, "Adultery, an Ancient Crime that Remains on Many Books," *New York Times*, November 14, 2012, http://www.nytimes.com/2012/11/15/us/adultery-an-ancient-crime-still-on-many-books.html?smid=pl-share.

5   Robert Murray and Tim Blessing, *Greatness and the White House: Rating the Presidents from George Washington through Ronald Reagan*, 2nd ed. (University Park: Pennsylvania State University Press, 1994), 98. See also S. Rubenzer and T. Faschingbauer, *Personality, Character, & Leadership in the White House* (Dulles, VA: Brassey's, Inc., 2004). We thank Stewart McCann for pointing out these works and this passage to us.

disintegration, so that society is justified in taking the same steps to preserve its moral code as it does to preserve its government.... The suppression of vice is as much the law's business as the suppression of subversive activities.[6]

Today, few secular democratic countries have laws criminalizing the "vice" of adultery. Over the last century, almost all countries in Europe, especially in the north, have decriminalized adultery. Similarly, in Canada adultery itself is no longer a crime, although it can still be used as grounds for a divorce and for determining the division of assets and child custody in civil-law cases.[7] However, in the U.S. there are approximately two dozen states that still have criminal adultery statutes.[8] According to Ethan Bronner, "This is yet another example of American exceptionalism: in nearly the entire rest of the industrialized world, adultery is not covered by the criminal code."[9] A little over half of U.S. states, though, have decriminalized adultery, and, while many states retain adultery laws with penalties varying from a life sentence in Michigan to a $10 fine in Maryland, they are rarely enforced. After the 2003 Supreme Court ruling (*Lawrence v. Texas*) that decriminalized private consensual sex between adults, some legal theorists believe that criminal adultery statutes are no longer enforceable. Yet, Bronner notes, "the question of how that ruling affects adultery remains unanswered because others may be harmed by adultery—a spouse and children. Several courts have alluded to the constitutionality of adultery laws since the Lawrence decision."[10]

Fortunately, few people will be forced from political office today if they are outed as gay, though they might be if they were elected primarily by conservative voters whom they courted, in part, by opposing LGBT equality. But over the past decade we have seen many men forced out of political office in the U.S. when the media has shone a spotlight on their acts of adultery, and many progressive as well as conservative voters have called for their removal. Are voters being too judgmental about the messy private lives of their political leaders? Those who think not can point out that some political leaders who commit adultery are breaking the law in their state, even if these laws are not often enforced. Perhaps there are some good practical reasons to prefer political leaders with neater private lives, so that their private problems do not become fodder for smear campaigns that undermine their political effectiveness and influence. But whether there are good moral reasons for being intolerant of such leaders remains an

---

6 Devlin, *The Enforcement of Morals*, 13–14.

7 See *Divorce Act*, Revised Statutes of Canada, 1985, Chapter 3 (2nd Supplement), canlii.com/ca/sta/d-3.4/.

8 Jonathan Turley, "Adultery, in Many States, Is Still a Crime," *USA Today*, April 26, 2010, http://usatoday30.usatoday.com/news/opinion/forum/2010-04-26-column26_ST_N.htm.

9 Bronner, "Adultery."

10 Ibid.

open question. In addressing it, we might ask whether the dictum "let him who is without sin cast the first stone" has any relevance to the improprieties of those in positions of power.

Should Genital Cutting Practices Be Tolerated?

Female Genital Mutilation (FGM) is defined by the World Health Organization (WHO) as "all procedures that involve partial or total removal of the external female genitalia, or other injury to the female genital organs for non-medical reasons."[11] The WHO has classified four different types of FGM:

1. *Clitoridectomy:* partial or total removal of the clitoris (a small, sensitive and erectile part of the female genitals) and, in very rare cases, only the prepuce (the fold of skin surrounding the clitoris).

2. *Excision:* partial or total removal of the clitoris and the labia minora, with or without excision of the labia majora (the labia are "the lips" that surround the vagina).

3. *Infibulation:* narrowing of the vaginal opening through the creation of a covering seal. The seal is formed by cutting and repositioning the inner, or outer, labia, with or without removal of the clitoris.

4. *Other:* all other harmful procedures to the female genitalia for non-medical purposes, e.g. pricking, piercing, incising, scraping and cauterizing the genital area.[12]

The WHO reports that FGM is practiced in 29 countries, mainly in Africa and some countries in the Middle East and Asia, and among migrants from these countries. The WHO estimates that 125 million women and girls around the world have undergone some form of the procedure, which is typically performed on girls between 1 and 15 years old. The WHO's fact sheet states that FGM procedures "can cause severe bleeding and problems urinating, and later cysts, infections, infertility as well as complications in childbirth and increased risk of newborn deaths."[13] FGM is performed for a variety of reasons: to make girls' bodies more feminine by removing "male" or "unclean" body parts, to discourage women from having illicit sexual relationships by impairing their capacity for sexual response, to ensure that one's daughters will be desired for marriage, to continue a practice perceived to be part of one's ethnic traditions and identity, and to conform to the perceived requirements of one's religion.

---

11 World Health Organization (WHO), "Female Genital Mutilation: Fact Sheet," updated February 2014, http://www.who.int/mediacentre/factsheets/fs241/en/.

12 Ibid.

13 Ibid.

Xiaorong Li suggests that we need to separate two issues in regard to FGM: how to address it when it occurs within our own country, and how to respond to it when it is performed in other countries.[14] Since 1996, performing a clitoridectomy on underage persons in the U.S. has been a crime. The U.S. has also condemned the practice in other countries and has, at times, placed economic sanctions on countries that have not outlawed FGM. In addition, the U.S. has granted asylum to some who have fled from their home countries in order to escape coerced FGM.

Those who see FGM as a violation of the human rights of girls and women applaud the U.S. stance toward FGM within and outside its borders. But some commentators on FGM see such condemnation and intervention as a form of cultural imperialism.[15] Some anthropologists argue that the term "mutilation" exaggerates the harms caused by various forms of genital cutting, and that most injuries can be avoided when the procedures are performed using modern medical techniques. Fuambai Ahmadu compares such cutting to male circumcision, which is done for ethnic, aesthetic, and hygienic reasons.[16] Moreover, male circumcision is typically performed on boys before they reach adulthood. Li argues for an intermediate view: that we work to ban the practice in countries where it is very difficult for women of any age to refuse the procedure, and where girls are subject to the procedure when they are minors and cannot meaningfully consent. Within our own countries, she argues, we ought to be tolerant of the practice so long as it is performed on adults who have provided informed consent.

Not all body modifications "mutilate" the body, and cultural preferences and beliefs influence our thinking on which ones are acceptable. Consider, for example, labiaplasty, hymenoplasty, vaginal "rejuvenation" surgery, breast or buttocks augmentation, sex reassignment surgeries and therapies, rhinoplasty, blepharoplasty, piercing, or tattooing. Such body modifications are popular all around the world. Yet these modifications all involve procedures that carry some risk. For instance, breast implant surgery can result in a number of complications, including breast pain, breast tissue atrophy, capsular contracture, deflation or rupture, infection, and necrosis, and it can also interfere with mammograms and breast-feeding.[17] Still, many women get these surgeries in order to feel more attractive and feminine, and, in some cases, because of social pressure from boyfriends and others. "Genital cutting" (GC)—to use a more neutral expression for the practices referred to as FGM—may appear to be unnecessary

---

14 Xiaorong Li, "Tolerating the Intolerable: The Case of Female Genital Mutilation," *Philosophy and Public Affairs Quarterly* 21, no. 1 (2001): 2–8.

15 Nowa Omoigui, "HB 22 Bill and Genital Mutilation," *Vanguard Daily* (Lagos), Feb. 20, 2001, http://www.circumstitions.com/FGM-defended.html.

16 "Yes to Female Circumcision?" Antropologi.info, February 15, 2010, http://www.antropologi.info/blog/anthropology/2010/female-circumcision.

17 U.S. Food and Drug Administration (FDA), "Risks of Breast Implants," updated September 25, 2013, http://www.fda.gov/MedicalDevices/ProductsandMedicalProcedures/ImplantsandProsthetics/BreastImplants/ucm064106.htm.

or performed for reasons that reflect sexism and ethnic chauvinism, but this could be said for many other procedures on the list above.

There are practices that are unacceptable from any reasonable or fair-minded perspective—such as widow burning, honor killing, female infanticide, and human slavery.[18] And no cultural practice is immune from critical investigation. But the difficulty is how to investigate the practices of others without letting our own cultural assumptions and biases get in the way. Is GC like honor killing, or is it more like male circumcision? Honor killings reflect assumptions that are not fair-minded (i.e., about female sexuality) and that violate a girl's right to life and personal security. Does GC reflect sexist assumptions about female sexuality, and does it violate a girl's or woman's right to protect her health, and even life? If it does, then the burden of proof is on those who want to continue GC practices.

Fuambai Ahmadu, mentioned above, is an American anthropologist who is originally from Sierra Leone and who as an adult underwent a clitoridectomy. According to her, "women who uphold these rituals do so because they want to—they relish the supernatural powers of their ritual leaders over against men in society, and they embrace the legitimacy of female authority and particularly the authority of their mothers and grandmothers."[19] Ahmadu maintains that, in the Kono ethnic group (to which she belongs), both male and female circumcision symbolically represent the separation of child from the parent(s), and the feminization or masculinization of the child. The initiation of women in particular

> is highly organized and hierarchal: the institution itself is
> synonymous with women's power, their political, economic,
> reproductive, and ritual spheres of influence. Excision ... is
> a symbolic representation of matriarchal power ... [by]
> activating the women's "penis" *within* the vagina (the clitoral
> 'shaft' or 'g-spot' that are subcutaneous). During vaginal
> intercourse, women say they dominate the male procreative
> tool (penis) and substance (semen) for sexual pleasure and
> reproductive purpose, but in ritual they claim to possess the
> phallus autonomously.[20]

Female circumcision achieves this, she argues, without harmful effects, sexual or otherwise. She writes,

---

18 Li, "Tolerating the Intolerable," 5.

19 F. Ahmadu, "'Ain't I a Woman, Too?' Challenging Myths of Sexual Dysfunction of Circumcised Women," cited in John Tierney, "A New Debate on Female Circumcision," *New York Times*, Nov. 30, 2007, accessed Jan. 6, 2012, http://tierneylab.blogs.nytimes.com/2007/11/30/a-new-debate-on-female-circumcision/.

20 F. Ahmadu and R. Shweder, "Disputing the Myth of the Sexual Dysfunction of Circumcised Women," *Anthropology Today* 25, no. 6 (2009): 14.

> According to the women I interviewed, sexual foreplay is
> complex and requires more than immediate physical touch:
> emphasis is on learning erotic songs and sexually suggestive
> dance movements; cooking, feeding and feigned submission, as
> powerful aphrodisiacs, and the skills of *aural* sex (more than
> *oral* sex) are said to heighten sexual desire and anticipation.
> Orgasms experienced during vaginal intercourse, these female
> elders say, must be taught and trained, requiring both skill
> and experience on the part of both partners (male initiation
> ceremonies used to teach men sexual skills on how to 'hit the
> spot' in women—emphasizing body movement and rhythm
> in intercourse, and importantly, verbal innuendos that titillate
> a woman's senses). Thus, from the viewpoint of these women
> elders, vaginal intercourse is associated with womanhood and
> adult female sexuality.[21]

The women elders whom Ahmadu interviewed are in agreement with Freud about vaginal intercourse and mature female sexual pleasure. Moreover, as we saw in our discussion of the female orgasm in Ch. 11, new studies indicate that vaginal intercourse produces a different kind of orgasm in women by stimulating the base of the clitoris. So there is now some scientific research that supports the views of women elders from the Kono. Ahmadu's claims challenge the view that GC reflects sexist assumptions about female sexuality, and instead she asserts that GC practices have to do with matriarchal power and the achievement of a particular form of sexual pleasure in women.

Yet what about the health risks associated with GC? Ahmadu cites some studies in her work indicating that the risks are lower and less serious than the risks associated with maternal smoking. However, a comprehensive WHO study shows that GC significantly increases the risks of bladder and urinary-tract infections, infertility, and complications in childbirth, including postpartum hemorrhage and stillbirth.[22] In addition, some opponents argue that GC greatly reduces the capacity for sexual pleasure in women. Clitoridectomy, in particular, prevents women from achieving orgasm through direct stimulation to the outer tip of the clitoris. Some opponents of GC allege that reducing women's sexual pleasure is the main reason for the practice, so that women will be less promiscuous.

Yet Ahmadu rejects much of this. Her research indicates that, while sexual pleasure changes and is differently focused for women after a clitoridectomy, their pleasure is just as, if not more, intense and satisfying. But we need to note

---

21 Ibid., 16.

22 World Health Organization (WHO) Study Group on Female Genital Mutilation and Obstetric
    Outcome, "Female Genital Mutilation and Obstetric Outcome: WHO Collaborative
    Prospective Study in Six African Countries," Original Text, *The Lancet* 367, no. 9525 (2006):
    1835–41, http://www.thelancet.com/journals/lancet/article/PIIS0140-6736(06)68805-3/
    abstract.

that her claims in this regard require that both women and men must commit to a complex set of prescriptions about the nature of sexuality—including its aural elements—and that there is a further commitment by men to learn techniques to pleasure women who do not possess an external clitoris. Outside of groups that practice these sexual rituals, GC would make little sense. Regarding the health risks and complications, a lot rests on how the procedures are performed, and on the type of procedure itself. Some of the more serious health risks are associated primarily with type 3 procedures, and approximately 90 per cent of the genital surgeries done in Africa are type 1 or 2.[23] Moreover, just as with "back alley abortions," when any kind of surgery is done outside of a modern health clinic there is a much greater likelihood of infection and other serious complications. When trained medical providers perform GC under sterile conditions, the risks are considerably lower.

Some respond to the outcry over GC by arguing that human rights activists from North America and Europe are too preoccupied with sexual pleasure and orgasm and overlook other important life goods and goals. Yael Tamir makes such an argument:

> Nuns take an oath of celibacy, but we do not usually condemn the church for preventing its clergy from enjoying an active sex life. Moreover, most of us do not think that Mother Teresa is leading a worse life than Chichulina [a former pornographic star and former Member of the Italian Parliament], though the latter claims to have experienced an extensive number of orgasms. It is true that nuns are offered spiritual life in exchange for earthly goods, but in the societies where clitoridectomy is performed, the fulfilling life of motherhood and child bearing are offered in exchange. Some may rightly claim that one can function as a wife and a mother while experiencing sexual pleasures. Others believe that full devotion to God does not require an oath of celibacy. Yet, these views are, after all, a matter of convention.[24]

Martha Nussbaum agrees with some of Tamir's points, but she points out that Tamir overlooks the fact that Mother Teresa and other nuns freely *choose* to live a celibate life, whereas young girls who undergo GC do not freely choose to have their genitals altered. Nussbaum writes,

---

23 The Public Policy Advisory Network on Female Genital Surgeries in Africa, "Seven Things to Know about Female Genital Surgeries in Africa," *Hastings Center Report*, no. 6 (2012): 19–27.

24 Yael Tamir, "Hands Off Clitoridectomy," *The Boston Review* 21, no. 3/4 (2006): 21. Though we won't pursue the matter here, one could argue that the Roman Catholic Church's obsession with the celibacy of its nuns, and especially its priests, has caused all sorts of problems, and that its unhealthy views on sex have contributed to the many sexual-abuse cases that currently haunt that institution.

> There is a great deal of difference between fasting and
> starvation; just so, there is also a great difference between
> a vow of celibacy and FGM. Celibacy involves the choice not
> to exercise a capability to which nuns, insofar as they are
> orthodox Roman Catholics, ascribe considerable human
> value.... FGM, by contrast, involves forgoing altogether the very
> possibility of sexual functioning—and ... well before one is of
> an age to make such a choice.[25]

Ahmadu's clitoridectomy was very much an anomaly since she freely consented to the practice as an adult. In addition, she made the decision to have her clitoridectomy when she was living in the U.S. and therefore could have decided, with little consequence, not to have it done. Her clitoridectomy, then, is analogous to a nun choosing a celibate life, but disanalogous to the vast number of women subjected to GC. In regard to cases like Ahmadu's, Li maintains that we should accept the decision of adult women to have a clitoridectomy when that decision is made within the borders of free, democratic, and secular nations. We should not, however, accept GC practices in illiberal, undemocratic countries, even when performed on adult women, because the social consequences of not submitting to GC are too great, and they deny girls and women a genuinely free choice.[26] Li recognizes that a woman living within a minority immigrant community in a liberal democratic country may also face significant social pressure to conform to her ethnic group's customs. But, she says, we are all under social pressure of some sort and we must trust that people in liberal societies have the freedom to leave their ethnic communities without the fear of reprisal.

In her discussion of GC, Nussbaum considers three other strategies for defending the cultural autonomy of groups that practice GC:

1. It is morally wrong to criticize the practices of another
    culture unless one is prepared to be similarly critical
    of comparable practices when they occur in one's own
    culture....
2. It is morally wrong to criticize the practices of another
    culture unless one's own culture has eradicated all evils of a
    comparable kind....
3. Female genital mutilation is morally on a par with practices
    of dieting and body shaping in American culture....[27]

Nussbaum acknowledges that the claim made in (1) is true; however, she argues, there is no reason to think that those criticizing GC are not prepared to criticize

---

25 Martha Nussbaum, *Sex and Social Justice* (Oxford: Oxford University Press, 1999), 127.
26 Li, "Tolerating the Intolerable."
27 Nussbaum, *Sex and Social Justice*, 121.

comparable practices in their own societies. Indeed, many feminist critics in particular have criticized comparable practices in their own societies, such as breast augmentation, labiaplasty, and eyelid surgery. And many feminists and others are critical of the medical use of clitoridectomy to "correct" the genitals of intersex infants with large clitorises. The second claim, however, is false, according to Nussbaum. No culture can ever attain moral perfection, but this should not block all legitimate criticism. If it did, we would not have been able to criticize the apartheid policies of South Africa, or the genocides perpetrated in various countries, such as Germany, Cambodia, or Rwanda. Moreover, Nussbaum writes, "the fact that a needy human being happens to live in Togo rather than Idaho does not make her less my fellow, less deserving of my moral commitment. And to fail to recognize the plight of a fellow human being because we are busy moving our own culture to greater moral heights seems the very height of moral obtuseness and parochialism."[28] Here, Nussbaum expresses the cosmopolitan view that all human beings deserve our moral regard and respect, and not merely the members of our own religious, ethnic, or national group.[29]

In regard to the third claim, Nussbaum argues that GC is not morally on par with dieting and body shaping.[30] They differ, in part, because GC is irreversible, is associated with lifelong health problems, is often performed in unsanitary conditions, and is typically performed on children, and in cultures where illiteracy rates, particularly among girls and women, are very high. GC also limits the capacity for sexual enjoyment in women, while promoting heterosexist, if not necessarily sexist, norms. Most forms of dieting and other body modification procedures (e.g., rhinoplasty, piercing, tattoing, etc.) can be done with greater safety. But there are some body modifications, as we have suggested, such as breast augmentation, that cause lifelong health problems. Moreover, breast-implant surgeries are irreversible because removing the implants leaves women with damaged breasts, and they limit women's capacities for sexual enjoyment by causing, in some cases, severe nipple sensitivity or nipple numbness. Some diet medications have been shown to increase the risk of heart attacks, and to have other serious side-effects. Furthermore, GC can be done under sanitary conditions and by trained surgeons, which significantly reduces the health risks, and the extent to which it is currently done under unsanitary conditions is controversial.[31] But the primary morally relevant difference between GC and dieting and other body modification procedures is that GC is generally performed on children.

---

28 Ibid., 122.

29 Pauline Kleingeld and Eric Brown, "Cosmopolitanism," *The Stanford Encyclopedia of Philosophy* (2013) http://plato.stanford.edu/entries/cosmopolitanism/.

30 Nussbaum, *Sex and Social Justice*, 123–24.

31 The Public Policy Advisory Network on Female Genital Surgeries in Africa, "Seven Things to Know about Female Genital Surgeries in Africa."

Male circumcision, too, is typically done on infants or young boys. If we object to GC when it is performed on female children, should we also object to circumcisions that are performed on male children? In other words, is male circumcision morally on a par with female GC? The WHO estimates that 664,500,000 males aged 15 and over are circumcised (30 per cent of all males around the world). The countries and regions that have the highest prevalence of male circumcision include Israel, most Islamic countries in the Middle East, the U.S., parts of Southeast Asia and Africa, the Philippines, and South Korea. It is much less common in Europe, Latin America, Southern Africa, and most of Asia and Oceania.[32] While the WHO estimates that approximately 75 per cent of American males and 30 per cent of Canadian males (i.e., from newborns to seniors) are circumcised, these statistics are beginning to change quite drastically. In Canada, rates of circumcision for newborns have dropped from about 50 per cent in 1998 to about 20 per cent in 2000, and 14 per cent in 2003.[33] In the U.S., the drop in rates has been more recent. Until 2006, more than 50 per cent of newborn males were being circumcised, but that fell to 32 per cent in 2009.[34]

Although some types of male circumcision are highly invasive, such as "superincision" and "subincision," which are practiced in some small pockets of the Pacific Islands and among some Aboriginal groups in Australia,[35] male circumcision is typically a very minor procedure in which the foreskin (prepuce) is removed. Male circumcision is not associated with long-term, serious health problems, or a significant loss in the capacity for sexual response. Some men believe that it reduces the sensitivity of their penis and, as a result, they can engage in sexual intercourse for longer periods of time before they reach orgasm. Because the health and sexual side-effects are minimal, Nussbaum rejects the analogy between male and female circumcision. Instead, she points to the more relevant analogies drawn by Nahid Toubia: "The male equivalent of the clitoridectomy [type 1 FGM] would be the amputation of most of the penis. The male equivalent of infibulation [type 3 FGM] would be 'removal of the entire penis, its roots of soft tissue, and part of the scrotal skin.'"[36] Ahmadu might take issue with these analogies, since a woman who has been circumcised can still engage in penile-vaginal intercourse (although with a loss of sensation and, in some cases, pain). A man whose penis has been amputated would not be able to do so. Moreover, if the health risks and sexual side-effects of male circumcision

32 World Health Organization (WHO), "Male Circumcision: Global Trends and Determinants of Prevalence, Safety and Acceptability" (2007), http://whqlibdoc.who.int/publications/2007/9789241596169_eng.pdf.

33 Canadian Children's Rights Council, "Circumcision" (2011), http://www.canadiancrc.com/Circumcision_Genital_Mutilation_Male-Female_Children.aspx.

34 Circumcision Reference Library, "Circumcision Statistics" (2010), http://www.cirp.org/library/statistics/USA/.

35 Kirsten Bell, "Genital Cutting and Western Discourses on Sexuality," *Medical Anthropology Quarterly* 19, no. 2 (2005): 125–48.

36 Nussbaum, *Sex and Social Justice*, 119.

are minimal, there are still some risks. So why do we accept circumcision for male children, rather than urge parents and doctors to wait until boys reach adulthood and can choose for themselves?

There seem to be several health benefits from male circumcision. In 2012, the American Academy of Pediatrics issued the following policy statement: "Evaluation of current evidence indicates that the health benefits of newborn male circumcision outweigh the risks and that the procedure's benefits justify access to this procedure for families who choose it. Specific benefits identified included prevention of urinary tract infections, penile cancer, and transmission of some sexually transmitted infections, including HIV."[37] In 2007, the WHO endorsed male circumcision as "an important intervention to reduce the risk of heterosexually acquired HIV."[38] The main risks of male circumcision, according to the AAP's recent report, are "bleeding, infection and penile injury. Procedures performed on infants had lower complication rates than those performed later in life."[39] The report notes that male circumcision is relatively safe when done in a sterile environment by trained professionals.

Given the health benefits of male circumcision, and the fact that there are no major health risks or loss of sexual sensation, there seems to be little reason to interfere with the right of parents to choose this medical procedure for their child. Some parents may decide to wait until their sons are old enough to choose for themselves, or at least participate in the decision, but some may feel it is better to have it done in the first year or so after birth. Given that there are no known health benefits of GC, and given the health risks, the irreversibility, and the loss of sexual sensation and autonomy, GC is only acceptable when an adult woman freely chooses it, as Li has argued. Human rights activists should urge ethnic groups that practice GC to stop performing it on children, and to respect a woman's right to choose not to have GC.

Should BDSM Be Restricted?

The initialism BDSM stands for bondage and discipline (BD), dominance and submission (DS), and sadomasochism (SM). These terms have replaced the single term 'sadomasochism' (or S/M, S&M, etc.) because they cover a larger number of activities, and because they focus on roles defined by the type of power

---

37 "Circumcision Policy Statement," The American Academy of Pediatrics, 2012, http://pediatrics. aappublications.org/content/130/3/585.

38 C.R. Rubin, "Steep Drop Seen in Circumcision in the U.S.," *New York Times*, Aug. 16, 2010, http:// www.nytimes.com/2010/08/17/health/research/17circ.html?ref=health&pagewanted=2.

39 Catherine Pearson, "Circumcision Guidelines by the AAP Have Been Revised for the First Time Since 1999," *Huffington Post*, August 27, 2012, http://www.huffingtonpost.com/2012/08/27/ new-circumcision-guidelin_n_1826069.html.

one accepts or gives up, rather than on psychological dispositions toward pain.[40] These power roles and exchanges can include rituals of sadomasochistic play, the use of restraints, social role play, and props such as paddles, handcuffs, costumes, and scenery.[41] While a fairly small percentage of people identify as members of the BDSM community, BDSM activities are becoming more popular and mainstream in North America and Europe. In the U.S., some studies suggest that up to 14 per cent of men and 11 per cent of women have engaged in some form of BDSM activities, and the number of people who report having BDSM-type fantasies is much higher.[42]

One can also assess the current popularity of BDSM by considering how it has entered popular culture; for example, pop-music idols from Madonna and Lady Gaga to Marilyn Manson often wear clothing associated with BDSM. BDSM imagery has infiltrated advertising campaigns for items ranging from clothing, jewelry, and fragrances to automobiles.[43] The store Hot Topic, which sells BDSM-inspired accessories, can be found in many suburban shopping malls in the U.S. A recent advertisement for the Mini Cooper car featured a woman dressed in latex and black leather brandishing a whip and standing beside a Mini car, with the caption "Mini Dominates Winter."[44] The novel *Fifty Shades of Grey* has made best-seller lists around the world and has now been made into a film.

Despite its current popularity, many people continue to be disturbed by BDSM because some activities aim to cause pain or humiliation, and some simulate acts of sexual violence. Defenders of BDSM point out that all activities are consensual, and participants use safety measures to make sure that no one is injured. Despite appearances to the contrary, "bottoms" or submissives can control the interaction, because they communicate their limits to the "top" or dominant person.[45] The BDSM community summarizes its ethic with phrases such as "Safe, Sane, and Consensual" (SSC) and "Risk Aware Consensual Kink" (RACK) in order to emphasize the importance of safety, mutual consent, and

---

40 Meg Barker et al., "Kinky Clients, Kinky Counselling? The Challenges and Potentials of BDSM," in *Feeling Queer or Queer Feelings: Radical Approaches to Counselling Sex, Sexualities and Genders*, ed. Lindsey Moon, 106–24 (London: Routledge, 2007), http://oro.open.ac.uk/17272/2/4AD665D2.pdf.

41 British Columbia Civil Liberties Association, "BCCLA Position Paper: Sexuality and Civil Rights: Freedom from Government Reprisal," n.d., 4, http://bccla.org/wp-content/uploads/2012/04/2006-BCCLA-Paper-BDSM.pdf; see also Nicklas Nordling et al., "Differences and Similarities Between Gay and Straight Individuals Involved in the Sadomasochistic Subculture," *Journal of Homosexuality* 50 (2006): 41–57.

42 S.S. Janus and C.L. Janus, *Janus Report on Sexual Behavior* (Hoboken, NJ: John Wiley & Sons, 1994); Barker et al., "Kinky Clients."

43 "BDSM in Advertising," n.d., http://www.bdsmattitude.com/en/art_photography/bdsm_in_advertising.html.

44 See the image at the following blog: The Gathering Party (n.d.), http://www.thegatheringparty.org/forum/viewtopic.php?f=4&t=1816.

45 A. Ritchie and M. Baker, "Feminist SM: A Contradiction in Terms or a Way of Challenging Traditional Gendered Dynamics Through Sexual Practice?" *Lesbian and Gay Psychology Review* 6, no. 3 (2005): 227–39; Barker et al., "Kinky Clients."

managed risk-taking. Advocates say the level of risk is similar to that associated with sports such as hockey or mountain climbing. And few people would argue for prohibiting the latter activities.

Despite these considerations, the legal status of BDSM is unclear. Although BDSM participants are rarely prosecuted under the law, they can be prosecuted for assault and other crimes. For example, the 1993 "Spanner case" in Great Britain involved a group of gay men who consensually participated in BDSM activities. Although none of them suffered lasting injuries and none of them complained to the police, their activities became known through a video recording they made. On the basis of this videotaped evidence, they were tried and convicted of assault. The trial judge claimed that the consent of the victims was not a legitimate defense, a position that was upheld on appeal, both in the UK and the European Union. While consent can be used as a defense for legal activities, such as surgery and sporting activities, it was successfully argued that it cannot be used for illegal ones, such as assault.[46]

Similar cases have occurred in Canada and the U.S. In Canada, the Ontario Court of Appeal maintained that

> [A] victim cannot consent to the infliction of bodily harm upon
> himself or herself, as defined by s. 267(2) of the *Code*, unless
> the accused is acting in the course of a generally approved
> social purpose when afflicting the harm. Specifically, … consent
> may be a defense to certain activities such as rough
> sporting activities, medical treatment, social interventions,
> and "daredevil activities" performed by stuntmen, "in
> creation of socially liable cultural product." Acts of sexual
> violence, however, were conspicuously not included among
> these exceptions.[47]

U.S. courts have issued similar rulings proscribing the use of consent as a legitimate line of defense in assault cases involving BDSM, which date back (at least) to the 1967 California case *People v. Samuels*.[48] The issue here isn't whether the "victim's" consent is genuine, but rather even when it is, this circumstance does not absolve the accused. The government's use of assault laws to prosecute consensual "rough" sex in private among adults might strike some as excessively paternalistic.

The moral status of BDSM is also debatable. Some Utilitarians might argue that so long as BDSM participants derive, on balance, more happiness or pleasure than misery or pain from their activities, then BDSM is morally permissible.

---

46 BCCLA, "BCCLA Position Paper," 5.

47 Ibid., 6

48 National Coalition for Sexual Freedom (NSCF), https://ncsfreedom.org/key-programs/
    consent-counts/consent-counts/item/580-consent-and-bdsm-the-state-of-the-law.html.

Some Kantian moral theorists might argue that, so long as the agents can consistently will that all others similarly placed could act the same, and if they are choosing autonomously, and no one is treated merely as means to the ends of others, then BDSM activities are permissible. Moral theorists who consider BDSM to be immoral and intolerable generally contend that BDSM activities are not truly consensual.

One line of argument against BDSM maintains that consent is lacking because people engaged in BDSM are suffering from some deep-seated psychological illness.[49] As a result, their behavior is determined by their pathology, and not by their autonomous choice. A second line of attack, taken by some feminist writers, is that defenders of BDSM conceive autonomy in individualistic and proceduralist terms—e.g., I consent if I say "I consent."[50] These critics argue that we need to recognize the larger contexts in which choices are made, and these contexts include inequalities of power that people bring to a BDSM transaction. For example, a BDSM relationship in which a woman is sexually submissive to a male dominant may involve forms of social coercion and subjugation that are harmful to women, even if she technically consents. Similarly, feminist writers have questioned whether women are acting autonomously when they participate in commercial pornography and prostitution that cater to men. We will look at these two lines of criticism more closely to see if the arguments hold up.

J. Roger Lee maintains that sadomasochism, and more generally BDSM, is indicative of mental illness. In particular, he writes that sadomasochists fail to develop a proper sense of their "own self as a functioning entity distinct from, first Mother, and then from other[s]."[51] As such, they develop "Narcissistic Personality Disorder," which typically has its origin in childhood abuse and/or neglect. Children suffer when they do not get the love, support, and nurturance they need. According to Lee, some become masochists and believe that they are responsible for their abuse or neglect, and that they therefore deserve the pain they receive in punishment. Others become sadists, who believe that the vast majority of people have a fundamentally incorrect vision of the world, which they—the sadist—must correct through the infliction of pain.

In sexual activities, Lee maintains, the sadist (the "top") and the masochist (the "bottom") replay the same theme over and over. He writes, "The top brings

---

49   J. Roger Lee, "Sadomasochism: An Ethical Analysis," in *Philosophical Perspectives on Sex and Love*, ed. Robert M. Stewart, 125–37 (New York and Oxford: Oxford University Press, 1995).

50   See, e.g., Claudia Card, *Lesbian Choices* (New York: Columbia University Press, 1995), http://www.feminist-reprise.org/docs/card.htm; Claudia Card, "Review Essay: Sadomasochism and Sexual Preference," *Journal of Social Philosophy* 15, no. 2 (1984): 42–52, http://onlinelibrary.wiley.com/doi/10.1111/j.1467-9833.1984.tb00575.x/abstract; Sonya Charles, "How Should Feminist Theorists Respond to the Problem of Internalized Oppression?" *Social Theory and Practice* 36, no. 3 (2010): 143–64; and Marina Oshana, "Personal Autonomy and Society," *Journal of Social Philosophy* 29 (1998): 81–102.

51   Lee, "Sadomasochism," 126.

the bottom to a supposedly elevated level by getting him to accept, endure, and relish pain. The bottom, by being pain receptive, improves himself and is elevated to a transcendence of the pain."[52] But the theme is based on a fundamentally skewed perception of reality as unavoidably painful, which stems from a sadomasochist's abusive childhood.

Lee claims that the proper aim of sex is "bonding with one's sexual partner, through shared passion, intimacy, and rewarded trust.... Good sexual activity offers felt support for one's most immediate feelings, unguardedly exhibited. Such support is strength generating."[53] BDSM can't achieve these ends—even in cases where it appears to be otherwise—because all experiences in a BDSM encounter get filtered through the distorting lens of Narcissistic Personality Disorder. Hence, the passion, intimacy, trust, and support are not genuinely there. Analogously, we do not describe people as courageous when they lack a proper perspective on dangerous situations due to, say, post-traumatic stress disorder. Engaging in BDSM sex, then, cannot be, according to Lee, "expressive of or a manifestation of living well and doing well."[54]

While Lee's ethical analysis of BDSM draws on Aristotelian ideas about human flourishing, it also resonates with Kantian and Utilitarian ethics. As we have noted, for Kant, a moral action must be autonomous. But those suffering from mental illness, such as Narcissistic Personality Disorder, act heteronomously, not autonomously. That is, their disease determines their actions, not their individual will. While Kantians distinguish genuine and apparent choices, Utilitarians distinguish pleasures that are real or genuine from those that are only apparent. A Utilitarian might argue that BDSM activities are not genuinely enjoyable but only appear to be so when someone suffers from Narcissistic Personality Disorder, just as an alcoholic stupor may repeatedly be experienced as enjoyable if one is an alcoholic. In both cases, people cannot experience real pleasure or happiness, or live well, unless they receive therapy and become well.

Lee's ethical analysis of BDSM is dependent on his empirical claims about the nature of BDSM, including that its practitioners typically suffer from Narcissistic Personality Disorder. As Lee himself acknowledges, however, not everyone who engages in sexual activities with BDSM elements—such as spanking, biting, the use of physical restraint or derogatory language, etc.—actually suffers from this condition. As a result, whatever pleasure mentally healthy people derive from BDSM is genuine, and they are living well and acting autonomously. After conceding this point, however, Lee warns that even "normal" people must use BDSM very occasionally lest they begin to lose sight of the proper function of sex and slip into mental illness.[55]

---

52 Ibid., 129.
53 Ibid., 131.
54 Ibid.
55 Ibid., 133.

How people slip into mental illness and how to determine which BDSM practitioners are mentally ill are both quite challenging and controversial issues. As we have noted in earlier chapters, classifications of mental disorders can and do change over time. Several activities once included as "paraphilias" in the DSM have been removed, including homosexuality. The DSM-5 now distinguishes between paraphilias and paraphilic disorders. The idea here is that an atypical sexual interest is not a problem unless it causes a person distress or interferes with their ability to function.[56] So if a person's interest in BDSM does not do this, then presumably they do not need to be treated for it in order to live well. The DSM-5 has essentially depathologized BDSM and other paraphilias, treating uncommon interests and activities themselves not as signs of illness, and thus Lee's diagnosis lacks scientific credibility.[57] Moreover, the current definition and description of "Narcissistic Personality Disorder" (extraordinary sense of self-importance and entitlement, lacking empathy, and so on) does not suggest that people with this disorder would likely be interested in kinky sex, and health professionals claim that they do not fully understand its causes.[58]

Let us now consider the second kind of criticism against BDSM. Like the first line of attack, this one also focuses on whether the choice to engage in BDSM is truly autonomous, but it does so on the basis of reconceptualizing autonomy. The second type of critic alleges that liberal notions of autonomy are inadequate because they do not sufficiently investigate the causes of our desires, and so they falsely assume that we make choices from an unencumbered position. Claudia Card writes,

> My own approach to sadomasochism initially … was the liberal, "sexual preference" approach. … My present approach perceives sexual sadomasochism as enacting … roles of dominance and subordinance that characterize … the norms of a patriarchal, misogynist society that is also riddled with homophobia, racism, anti-Semitism, and other forms of oppression. On this understanding, sadomasochistic desires have roots not simply in individual psychologies but in society at large; they are not mysterious givens but social constructions. The direction of my

---

56 Mark Moran, "*DSM to Distinguish Paraphilias From Paraphilic Disorders,*" *Psychiatric News*, May 3, 2013, http://psychnews.psychiatryonline.org/newsarticle.aspx?articleid=1685438.

57 The most recent *International Classification of Disorders*—the ICD-10, published by the WHO— continues to classify BDSM and homosexuality as "disorders of sexual preference." A number of scholars and health professionals are working to remove from the ICD disorders related to sexual orientation. See, for example, "Group Recommends Removing Sexual Orientation-Related Disorders from the International Classification of Diseases," *Science Daily*, June 24, 2014, http://www.sciencedaily.com/releases/2014/06/140624171852.htm.

58 "Narcissistic Personality Disorder Symptoms," PsychCentral, http://psychcentral.com/disorders/narcissistic-personality-disorder-symptoms/.

ethical concern has shifted, accordingly, more to the process of their construction than to that of enactment.[59]

The liberal notion of autonomy—in which human desires are relatively neutral and universal, and so when we choose to indulge or resist them, we are self-directed—has come under considerable attack in the past fifty years. Some feminists use the idea of "adaptive preferences," which suggests that our desires or preferences can change according to our circumstances or situation. For example, the preferences of people living under oppressive conditions may change in order to avoid the frustration of unmet needs. Feminists have questioned whether some women's apparent preference for jobs with lower levels of pay and power reflects an adaptation to discrimination.

If human desires are not neutral or innate and are "constructed" in social contexts and relationships, then we need to think about autonomy not in terms of the freedom from influence by others, but in terms of how empowered we are in our relationships with others. Marilyn Friedman describes this new idea of "relational autonomy" as follows:

> According to the relational approach, persons are fundamentally social beings who develop the capacity for autonomy through social interaction with other persons....
>
> Autonomy is no longer thought to require one to be a social atom, that is, radically socially unencumbered, defined merely by the capacity to choose or to be able to exercise reason prior to any of her contingent ends or social engagements. It is now well recognized that our reflective capacities and our very identities are always partly constituted by our communal traditions and norms that we cannot put entirely into question without at the same time voiding our very capacities to reflect.[60]

It is within this framework that Card and other feminist critics understand BDSM, especially when it involves women. Card is concerned about how women come to have sadomasochistic desires, and whether such desires stem from various forms of social oppression and disempowerment. For example, is a woman's desire for breast implants indicative of a social context in which women can obtain love or support only when they have breasts of a certain size? From a liberal, proceduralist understanding of autonomy and consent, a woman who chooses to get breast implants is acting autonomously, as long as she is reasonably informed and not subject to direct coercion. Whether her choice stems

---

59 Card, *Lesbian Choices*, 3.

60 Marilyn Friedman, "Autonomy, Social Disruption, and Women," in *Relational Autonomy: Feminist Perspectives on Autonomy, Agency, and the Social Self,* ed. C. MacKenzie and N. Stoljar, 35–53 (Oxford: Oxford University Press, 2000).

from being disempowered is irrelevant.[61] Some feminists, such as Sonya Charles, have argued that it is unclear whether a woman can genuinely and freely choose to be a sexual submissive (in a BDSM context) or give up control, because women typically lack power in sexual situations. BDSM "play" therefore can "undermine a person's sense of self-worth, and thereby makes her complicit in her own oppression."[62]

Card considers whether "sadomasochistic sexuality undermines resistance to oppression by eroticizing domination and subordinance." She continues: "If so, what sadomasochism eliminates are hostile impulses that might otherwise be used in politically productive ways to bring about social change."[63] In other words, by eroticizing a practice we eliminate hostility or resistance to it. Feminists such as Catharine MacKinnon have argued that pornography operates similarly, and by eroticizing women's social and sexual subordination it operates as a kind of patriarchal propaganda that aims to win acceptance for misogyny. In a sense, when a practice is depicted as erotic or sexy, viewers lose the capacity to think critically about it. But this view of pornography has been strongly challenged by others, including some feminists, and there is little evidence showing that viewers of pornography, or indeed BDSM participants, are unable to think critically about their sexual enjoyments.

A number of philosophers argue that, although our desires are shaped by our social contexts, we can act autonomously if we are capable of critical reflection about our desires.[64] Diana Meyers suggests that such reflection allows one to form "a self-chosen identity rooted in the individual's most abiding feelings... yet subject to [a] critical perspective."[65] Drawing on Meyers's view, Joanna Zaslow writes,

> Meyers' account of relational autonomy... provides the grounds
> for understanding how women would not only make this
> choice to be sexually submissive, but to do so while holding
> self-respect.... one must critically engage with their own self in
> order to ensure that one's actions and one's self understanding
> are in harmony. This allows for a women to ensure that she
> is not coerced into choosing to enter into a Master/slave
> BDSM relationship, for she would not be able to function as

---

61 Quoted in Joanna Zaslow, "Control, Power and Pleasure: Relational Autonomy and Female Submission in BDSM," in *Talk About Sex: A Multidisciplinary Discussion*, ed. R.S. Stewart, 249–59 (Sydney, NS: Cape Breton University Press, 2013).

62 Cited in ibid., 214.

63 Card, *Lesbian Choices*, 12–13.

64 Gerald Dworkin, *The Theory and Practice of Autonomy* (Cambridge: Cambridge University Press, 1998), 10; Harry Frankfurt, "Freedom of the Will and the Concept of a Person," *Journal of Philosophy* 68, no. 1 (1971): 5–20, http://www.unc.edu/~dfrost/classes/Frankfurt71_ Freedom%20of%20the%20Will%20and%20the%20Concept%20of%20a%20Person.pdf.

65 Diana Meyers, *Self, Society and Personal Choice* (New York: Columbia University Press, 1989), 61.

an autonomous being if her life path were chosen or forced upon her. This means that, for Meyers, the sexually submissive women acts autonomously so long as this role follows the life path best suited for herself. The happiness that she gains from assuming this role and following such a life path would suggest this could be the case. [66]

In a BDSM encounter, power roles are negotiated and not simply assumed. Moreover, power roles are not dependent on gender, and many men find enjoyment in being sexually submissive. Importantly, the norms of the BDSM community show that sexual submission is compatible with masculinity, and is not something that only female-bodied individuals do. Furthermore, BDSM emphasizes and teaches skills in sexual negotiation, which involve ensuring that there is ongoing consent for the activities in which participants engage. One might argue that both men and women who practice BDSM are more critically aware of how social and sexual interaction involves domination and submission than people who only enjoy "vanilla" or non-kinky sex, and therefore they do not merely follow the social and sexual scripts that are often uncritically accepted by the latter.

The depathologizing and mainstreaming of BDSM show that it is becoming more widely viewed as a legitimate practice or recreation. As with homosexuality, once this happens, our criminal justice systems might begin to accept "consent" as reasonable defense, and stop prosecuting people who engage in BDSM in ways that are "safe, sane, and consensual."

---

66 Zaslow, "Control, Power and Pleasure," 245.

Discussion Questions

1. Would you vote for someone who had committed adultery?
2. Should adulterers be criminally prosecuted?
3. Should a competent, adult woman living in Canada or the U.S. be allowed to get a clitoridectomy?
4. Should parents be allowed to have circumcisions performed on their sons when they are infants or young children?
5. How should human rights activists respond to female genital cutting practices in societies outside their own?
6. How can we ensure that our sexual identities, activities, and practices are chosen autonomously?
7. In some instances, BDSM has led to serious injury and even death, usually when the dominant has been negligent, is untrained, or for some reason has not taken proper safety precautions. Should dominants be prosecuted when such accidents happen?

Further Reading

Card, Claudia. *Lesbian Choices*. New York: Columbia University Press, 1995.

Dworkin, Gerald. *The Theory and Practice of Autonomy*. Cambridge: Cambridge University Press, 1988.

Nussbaum, Martha. *Sex and Social Justice*. Oxford: Oxford University Press, 1999.

MacKenzie, C., and N. Stoljar, eds. *Relational Autonomy: Feminist Perspectives of Autonomy, Agency, and the Social Self*. New York: Oxford University Press, 2010.

Index

from the publisher

A name never says it all, but the word "broadview" expresses a good deal of the philosophy behind our company. We are open to a broad range of academic approaches and political viewpoints. We pay attention to the broad impact book publishing and book printing has in the wider world; we began using recycled stock more than a decade ago, and for some years now we have used 100% recycled paper for most titles. As a Canadian-based company we naturally publish a number of titles with a Canadian emphasis, but our publishing program overall is internationally oriented and broad-ranging. Our individual titles often appeal to a broad readership too; many are of interest as much to general readers as to academics and students.

Founded in 1985, Broadview remains a fully independent company owned by its shareholders—not an imprint or subsidiary of a larger multinational.

If you would like to find out more about Broadview and about the books we publish, please visit us at **www.broadviewpress.com**. And if you'd like to place an order through the site, we'd like to show our appreciation by extending a special discount to you: by entering the code below you will receive a 20% discount on purchases made through the Broadview website.

Discount code: **broadview20%**

Thank you for choosing Broadview.

Please note: this offer applies only to sales of bound books within the United States or Canada.

The interior of this book is printed on 100% recycled paper.